CONTRACTS
FOR THE
FILM
&
TELEVISION
INDUSTRY

Other books by Mark Litwak

Reel Power
Courtroom Crusaders
Dealmaking in the Film and Television Industry

CONTRACTS
FOR THE
FILM
&
TELEVISION
INDUSTRY

BY MARK LITWAK

SILMAN-JAMES PRESS
LOS ANGELES

First Edition
10 9 8 7 6 5 4 3 2 1

Library of Congress Cataloging-in-Publication Data

Litwak, Mark.
Contracts for the film and television industry / by Mark Litwak
p.   cm.
Includes bibliographical references and index.
1. Motion pictures industry—Law and legislation—United States.
2. Television—Law and legislation—United States.
3. Artists' contracts—United States. I. Title.
KF4302.L58   1994   384'.83'0973—dc20   94-24029
[347.303787902]

ISBN: 1-879505-17-7

Cover design by Heidi Frieder

Printed and bound in the United States of America

SILMAN-JAMES PRESS
distributed by
Samuel French Trade
7623 Sunset Blvd.
Hollywood, CA 90046

For Glenn, Ellen and Denise.

DISCLAIMER

This book is designed to help non-lawyers understand legal issues frequently encountered in the entertainment industry. It will provide readers with an understanding of basic legal principles, enabling them to better communicate with their attorneys.

Nothing in this book should be construed as legal advice. The information provided is not a substitute for consulting with an experienced entertainment attorney and receiving counsel based on the facts and circumstances of a particular transaction. The sample contracts need to be tailored and modified to fit the circumstances. Moreover, the contracts are based on legal principles that are subject to change and that vary by state. Finally, exceptions and qualifications may not be noted in the text.

CONTENTS

PREFACE

In 1979, I moved from New York to Los Angeles to work in the entertainment industry. As a young New York lawyer with a background in public-interest law, the movie industry was an alien culture. I came across strange practices, confusing jargon and odd people.

After fifteen years in the industry, I no longer qualify as an outsider. However, I remember my frustration in trying to learn the ropes of the business. I didn't have a mentor and there was no guidebook available. I wrote my first book, *Reel Power* (William Morrow), in 1986 as an exploration into the practices and mores of the industry.

In 1993 I wrote *Dealmaking in the Motion Picture and Television Industry* (Silman-James Press), a non-lawyer's guide to entertainment law. This book is a companion volume. The contracts and commentary illustrate many of the principles discussed in *Dealmaking* and explain how they are used in the industry.

As with *Dealmaking*, I have attempted to explain complex legal concepts simply, avoid jargon and explain terms of art. The sample contracts are adapted from actual agreements used in the industry. In some instances, only the names of the parties have been deleted.

While there is no such thing as a standard contract, many contracts have similar provisions—so-called "boilerplate clauses." The contracts in this book contain many such provisions. However, readers should not mindlessly use such provisions unless they understand them and modify them to fit the circumstances.

I welcome comments and suggestions from readers. You can contact me at: Law Offices of Mark Litwak, P.O. Box 3226, Santa Monica, CA 90408, (310) 450-4500

I hope this book will prove useful to you.

Mark Litwak
November 1994

ACKNOWLEDGEMENTS

My special thanks to Robert L. Seigel, Gary Salt and Harris Tulchin for contributing sample contracts to this volume.

CHAPTER 1

INTRODUCTION

BASIC PRINCIPLES OF CONTRACT LAW

A contract is an agreement to do or not do a certain thing (Cal. Civil Code § 1549).[1] It gives rise to an obligation or legal duty, enforceable in an action at law (Cal. Civil Code § 1427, 1428).

In other words, a contract is a promise. If the promise is broken, the law provides a remedy. A contract may consist of a single promise or a series of promises that the parties regard as one contract.

ELEMENTS OF A CONTRACT

It is essential to the existence of a contract that there should be 1) parties capable of contracting, 2) mutual consent, 3) a lawful object, and 4) a sufficient cause or consideration (Cal. Civil Code § 1550).

1. Parties capable of contracting

Contracts made by minors, the insane and those who are intoxicated may not be enforceable. In California, minors are persons under age eighteen. Contracts entered into by minors may be either void or voidable (i.e., subject to disaffirmance). There are some exceptions. Contracts to pay for the reasonable value of necessities (i.e., food, shelter), and contracts approved by a court, can be enforced against minors (Cal. Civil Code § 36a).

Contracts made by persons of unsound mind may be completely void or voidable at the request of the person. Such people are not mentally competent to understand the nature and purpose of an agreement they may enter into. The burden of proof of insanity is on the party asserting it (Cal. Evidence Code §522).

---

[1] The California Code sections cited in the text can be found in the Appendix.

Likewise, a person who is drunk might not have the capacity to understand the consequences of his actions. Of course, the person must be so intoxicated that he does not understand what he is doing.

2. Mutual consent

Every contract requires mutual agreement or consent. Usually a party must intend to enter a contract in order to be bound by it. However, if a person outwardly appears to agree to a contract, but does not want to be bound, the other party may be able to enforce the agreement. The law protects the party who reasonably relies on a manifestation of consent, even if the other party doesn't consent. People cannot look into others' minds, so they must be able to rely on the outward manifestation of consent.

Mutual consent typically arises when one party makes an *offer* and the other party *accepts* it. The accepting party must accept the terms of the offer as it has been proposed. If the accepting party attempts to vary an essential (i.e, important) term, the accepting party is making a counter-offer. If the counter-offer is accepted, the parties have a contract.

Offers should be distinguished from "preliminary negotiations" that may lead to an agreement. Parties can discuss terms without being bound if that is their intent and they don't outwardly appear to enter an agreement. But if a party makes what appears to be an offer, and the other party accepts it, the offerer will be bound by the contract even if he doesn't want to make a contract.

Parties may engage in negotiations and reach an oral agreement with the understanding that a written contract will be signed later. If the parties intend that the contract be effective immediately, it may be enforceable before it is put in writing. On the other hand, the parties may intend that the "agreement" not be binding until it has been put in writing and signed by all parties.

What if the parties enter into an agreement but do not agree on all terms? If the essential terms are defined, then the contract will not be rendered unenforceable because of uncertainty as to some minor terms. However, if an essential element of the contract has not been agreed upon, a judge will not speculate what the parties might have agreed upon. The contract may be deemed fatally uncertain and unenforceable.

3. A lawful object

The object of a contract must be lawful (Cal. Civ. Code § 1550) and the consideration must be lawful (Cal. Civ. Code § 1607). A contract to hire another to commit murder, for instance, would be void.

California classifies illegal contracts as either 1) those contrary to express statutes, 2) those contrary to the policy of express statutes, and 3) those otherwise contrary to good morals. (Cal. Civ. Code § 1667).

4. Sufficient cause or consideration

Consideration is often money or something of value. It can also be an act, forbearance from acting or a promise. It may be a benefit agreed to be conferred on another, or a detriment agreed to be suffered. A contract is only binding with consideration. Consideration is what distinguishes a contract from a gift, which may be revocable.

Consideration must be something of value, although courts will not invalidate a contract simply because the value of what one party gives is not a fair exchange for what they receive. In other words, courts will not review the adequacy of consideration. Should you be foolish enough to sell your new Mercedes for $5,000, don't expect a judge to rescue you from the consequences of your poor judgment. Unless there was fraud or duress involved, the contract will be enforced, even if unfair. In extraordinary circumstances, courts may deem a contract unconscionable and refuse to enforce it.

The agreement should recite the consideration exchanged. This recital is evidence of consideration. To ensure that a contract is binding, agreements often state: "For ten dollars and other valuable consideration. . ." This establishes that there has been an exchange of value, even if it is nominal. Make sure that the consideration is actually paid. It is wise to pay by check so that you will have the canceled check as proof of payment.

Mutually exchanged promises can be adequate consideration. For example, a producer's efforts to develop a project could be deemed adequate consideration for an option. To be certain that their contracts are enforceable, however, producers often want to pay some money for an option.

Promises may be enforced without consideration if a party makes a promise upon which another party justifiably relies. Here the party making the promise will be stopped from denying its existence. This doctrine is referred to as "promissory estoppel." The person who makes the promise must reasonably expect to induce the other party to act or rely on the promise.

DEFENSES TO CONTRACT

If one or both parties consent to a contract induced by duress, undue influence, fraud or mistake, there may be a defense to formation of the contract. The innocent party may rescind the contract and/or sue for damages.

When one party uses physical force, threats of force or extortion to compel the other party to enter into an agreement, the contract may be invalidated on the grounds of DURESS. Similarly, if excessive pressure overcomes the will of a party, that party may raise UNDUE INFLUENCE as a defense. Usually courts require a confidential relationship between the parties for this defense.

If a person is tricked or defrauded into entering a contract, the party may have a defense of FRAUD or MISREPRESENTATION. When parties enter a contract under a MUTUAL MISTAKE about an important underlying fact, the contract may be invalidated. However, if one of the parties is merely mistaken as to the value of what he has bought or sold, mistake is usually not a defense.

If a contract is so one-sided and unfair that it is UNCONSCIONABLE, a court may refuse to enforce it. Often such an agreement is made between parties of unequal bargaining positions, and the weaker party is given an "adhesion" contract, the terms of which are not negotiable.

TYPES OF CONTRACTS

Contracts can be either WRITTEN or ORAL. Contrary to popular belief, oral contracts may be valid and binding. Most states have a law, known as the Statute of Frauds,[1] requiring that certain kinds of agreements be in writing to be valid. For example, you cannot transfer real estate orally. Other kinds of agreements may be made orally, but oral contracts may prove difficult to enforce.

Let's assume that you made an oral agreement with a buyer to sell your car for $3,000. You shake hands on the deal but don't put anything in writing. One month later there is a dispute and eventually you end up in small claims court.

The buyer informs the judge that you agreed to sell him your car for $3,000. You agree. The buyer then claims that you promised to fix a broken window before delivery. You disagree. There are no documents or witnesses or evidence to which the judge can look to determine the terms of the agreement. In this situation, whom should the judge believe? The judge may simply throw up her hands and refuse to enforce a contract for which she cannot ascertain its terms.

So while the law does not require that all contracts be in writing, it is usually advantageous to have a written agreement, if only for the sake of creating evidence. Otherwise, you risk having an unenforceable deal.

Another way to classify contracts is as EXPRESS or IMPLIED contracts. When parties make an express contract, it is explicit that they are making an agreement. Typically, they sign a piece of paper or shake hands. In other words, the parties to an express contract state its terms in words (Cal. Civ. Code § 1620).

An implied contract is a contract implied from conduct. It is implied wholly or partly from behavior of the parties. Let's suppose that you enter a store and pick up a candy bar. Without saying a word to anyone, you remove the wrapper and begin eating it. Then you head for the door. The proprietor says, "Hey, wait a minute, you didn't pay for the candy bar." You reply, "I never said I would pay for it." Under these circumstances, a court might imply that an agreement exists, based on your conduct. It is understood that when a person consumes merchandise in a store, he has agreed to buy it.

Sometimes implied contracts are not based on behavior but are implied by law in the name of equity and fairness, or to prevent the unjust enrichment of one party at the expense of another. These are called "Quasi-contracts." Unlike true contracts, they are not based on any intention of the parties to enter into an agreement. Their obligations arise from law.

---

[1] See e.g., California Civil Code § 1624.

The law of oral and implied contracts can provide the basis for a successful lawsuit for story theft. A basic tenet of copyright law is that ideas are not copyrightable because they are not considered an "expression of an author." As courts sometimes observe, "ideas are as free as the air." Similarly, concepts, themes and titles are not protected by copyright law.

A copyright does protect embellishments upon ideas, however. So while a single word cannot be copyrighted, the particular manner in which a writer organizes words—his craft, his approach—is protected. While other writers remain free to create work on the same topic, theme or idea, they cannot copy the particular expression of the writer.

Since one cannot protect an idea under copyright law, a writer who pitches a story idea to another is vulnerable to theft. Fortunately, there is another way to protect ideas. An idea can be the subject of a contract. A writer can protect himself by getting the recipient of an idea to agree to pay for it.

The best way for the writer to protect himself would be to use a written agreement. However, it may be awkward to begin a meeting by asking a producer to sign a contract, even a short one. Such a request might offend some producers or make them uncomfortable. They might worry about liability and might want to consult a lawyer. Since writers often have difficulty getting in the door to see powerful producers, asking for a written agreement may not be possible.

A less-threatening approach would be to make an oral agreement. The writer begins the meeting by simply saying: "Before I tell you my idea, I want to make sure you understand that I am telling you this idea with the understanding that if you decide to use it, I expect to receive reasonable compensation." The producer most likely will nod her head "Yes," or say "Of course," in which case you have a deal. If the producer indicates that she does not agree to these terms, don't pitch your story and leave.

Since this contract is oral, there might be a problem proving its existence and terms. That is why it's a good idea to have a witness or some documentation. You could bring a co-writer, agent or associate along to the meeting, and after the meeting you could send a letter to the producer reiterating your understanding. The letter should be cordial and non-threatening. You could write: "It was really a pleasure meeting with you to discuss my story about. . . . As we agreed, if you decide to exploit this material, I will receive reasonable compensation." If the terms set forth in your letter are not disavowed by the recipient, the letter could be used as evidence of your agreement.[1]

But what if the producer listening to your pitch doesn't steal your story but repeats it to another producer who uses it? You can protect yourself against this peril by saying: "I am telling you my idea with the understanding that you will keep it confidential and will not tell it to anyone else without my permission." If the producer nods her head okay or says yes, you have a deal, and you can sue if she breaches her promise.

---

[1] Since the letter has not been signed by the producer, his agreement is implied from the fact that he didn't object. Of course, if the producer confirms these terms in writing, that would be much better evidence.

INTERPRETATION OF CONTRACTS AND CHOICE OF LAW

Suppose a contract is made by a California producer who wants to buy movie rights to a novel written by a Maine author. The agreement is negotiated by the author's New York agent, and the movie is shot in Florida. Sometime after the agreement is made, a dispute arises concerning the rights of the parties under the contract. Which state's law applies to interpret the contract?

If the parties in their agreement have not specified which state's law applies, the contract will be governed by the law of the state that has the most significant relationship with the transaction and the parties. The following factors are important: 1) the place where the contract was made, 2) the place where the contract is to be performed, 3) the location of the subject matter of the contract and 4) the residence of the parties.

Applying these factors to a particular situation may not clearly indicate which state's law should apply. Therefore, parties may want to agree ahead of time which law will apply, to remove any ambiguity and potential litigation over the issue.

If the parties agree upon which state's law will govern their contract, courts will usually enforce that choice if there is some reasonable relationship between the law chosen and the parties/subject matter.

Many entertainment-industry disputes are resolved under New York or California law. Since there are many decisions applying the laws of those states to industry disputes, the law is more settled and certain than in other states. Therefore, it is often advantageous for the parties to choose to have their contracts interpreted according to New York or California law.

COMMON PROVISIONS OF ENTERTAINMENT CONTRACTS

Many industry contracts share certain "standard" or "boilerplate" provisions. Here are samples of such provisions and explanations of how they are used. These clauses have been taken from a variety of employment, literary-purchase and other agreements. Their form will vary depending on the type of agreement into which they are incorporated.

ASSIGNMENT

(a) Assignability: This Agreement is non-assignable by Writer. Production Company and any subsequent assignee may freely assign this Agreement and grant its rights hereunder, in whole or in part, to any person, firm, or corporation, if such party assumes and agrees in writing to keep and perform all of the executory obligations of Production Company hereunder. Upon such assumption, Production Company is hereby released from all further obligations to Writer hereunder, except that unless the assignee or borrower is a so-called major motion-klpicture company, or mini-major, Production Company shall remain secondarily liable under this agreement.

(b) Right to Lend to Others: Writer understands and acknowledges that the actual production entity of a motion picture to be made from the Product may be a party other than Production Company. In such event, Writer's services shall be rendered hereunder for the actual production entity but without releasing Production Company from its obligations hereunder.

An assignment clause permits a party to an agreement to assign certain rights or obligations in the agreement to another. It would, for example, allow a buyer of a literary property to assign those rights.

A producer will want the ability to assign rights because a distributor or financier may insist upon an assignment before financing a project. If the writer is concerned where the project may land, he may try to limit the assignment to major studios and networks. He could also ask that no assignments be permitted without his prior approval, which he might agree that he would not unreasonably withhold. The writer may want the assignment to say that any assignee will assume all obligations owed the writer, and perhaps the assignor will remain liable as well.

A producer will not want a writer to be able to assign his writing obligations to another. Producers hire writers because they admire their writing, and they don't want the writer to subcontract out the work to another. Producers usually don't mind, however, if the writer assigns money owed him.

RIGHT OF FIRST NEGOTIATION

Buyer shall have a right of first negotiation. The term "Right of First Nego-tiation" means that if, after the expiration of an applicable time limitation, Seller wants to dispose of or exercise a particular right reserved to Seller herein ("Re-served Right"), whether directly or indirectly, then Seller shall notify Buyer in writing and immediately negotiate with Buyer regarding such Reserved Right. If, after the expiration of _____ days following the receipt of such notice, no agreement has been reached, then Seller may negotiate with third parties regard-ing such Reserved Right, subject to Clause ___.

A Right of First Negotiation requires a party to negotiate a matter with a sec-ond party before negotiating with third parties. In a literary-purchase agreement, for example, a buyer (studio) may agree to let a writer retain certain rights, sub-ject to the writer giving the studio first shot at purchasing those rights should the writer later decide to sell them.

Suppose Writer A has sold the movie rights to his book to Paramount. The writer has retained all dramatic (play) rights. Paramount obtains a "Right of First Negotiation," giving it first opportunity to purchase the play rights if the Writer should choose to sell them. Paramount thinks that it is only fair for it to have such a right. It is investing millions of dollars in turning the writer's book into a movie, making the underlying property and all its derivative forms more valuable. The Right of First Negotiation only requires that the writer negotiate in good faith with Paramount first. If no agreement is reached within a set period (e.g., 30 days), the Writer can negotiate and sell the play rights to a third party.

RIGHT OF LAST REFUSAL

Buyer shall have a right of last refusal. The term "Right of Last Refusal" means that if Buyer and Seller fail to agree pursuant to Buyer's right of first negotiation, and Seller makes and/or receives any bona fide offer to license, lease and/or purchase the particular Reserved Right or any interest therein ("Third-Party Offer"), and if the proposed purchase price and other material terms of a Third-Party Of-fer are no more favorable to Seller than the terms that were acceptable to Buyer during the first negotiation period, Seller shall notify Buyer, by registered mail or telegram, if Seller proposes to accept such Third-Party Offer. Seller shall disclose the name of the offerer, the proposed purchase price and other terms of such Third Party Offer.

During the period of _____ days after Buyer's receipt of such notice, Buyer shall have the exclusive option to license, lease and/or purchase, as the case may be, the particular Reserved Right or interest referred to in such Third-Party Offer, at the same purchase price and upon the same terms and conditions as set forth in such notice. If Buyer elects to exercise his right of last refusal, he shall notify Seller by registered mail or telegram within such _____ day period, failing which Seller shall be free to accept such Third-Party Offer.

If any such proposed license, lease and/or sale is not consummated with a third party within _____ days following the expiration of this _____ day period, Buyer's Right of Last Refusal shall revive and shall apply to every further offer or offers received by Seller relating to the particular Reserved Right or any interest therein; provided, further, that Buyer's option shall continue in full force and effect, upon all of the terms and conditions of this paragraph, while Seller retains any rights, title or interests in or to the particular Reserved Right. Buyer's Right of Last Refusal shall inure to the benefit of Buyer, its successors and assigns, and shall bind Seller and Seller's heirs, successors and assigns.

The Right of Last Refusal may be combined with, or used as an alternative to, the Right of First Negotiation. With the Right of Last Refusal, the buyer has the right to acquire a reserved right under the same terms and conditions as any offer made by a third party. If Paramount had a Right of Last Refusal, then the Writer would be free to offer the right to another buyer. Before closing the deal, however, the writer would have to offer Paramount the right on the same terms as the best third-party offer.

As a practical matter, when a writer has given a studio a Right of Last Refusal, it can be difficult to interest third-party buyers. Why should Universal Pictures spend time negotiating the terms of a sale with the writer, only to have the deal supplanted at the last moment by Paramount? Thus, the Right of Last Refusal discourages third-party offers.

ADDITIONAL DOCUMENTATION

Seller agrees to obtain and execute any other and further instruments necessary to transfer, convey, assign and copyright all rights in the Property granted herein by Seller to Buyer in any country throughout the world. If it shall be necessary under the laws of any country that copyright registration be acquired in the name of Seller, Buyer is authorized by Seller to apply for said copyright registration; and, in such event, Seller shall and does hereby assign and transfer the same unto Buyer, subject to the rights in the Property reserved hereunder by Seller. Seller further agrees, upon request, to duly execute, acknowledge, obtain and deliver to Buyer such short-form assignments as may be requested by Buyer for the purpose of copyright recordation in any country, or otherwise. If Seller shall fail to so execute and deliver, or cause to be executed and delivered, the assignments or other instruments herein referred to, Buyer is hereby irrevocably granted the power coupled with an interest to execute such assignments and instruments in the name of Seller and as Seller's attorney-in-fact.

In the industry, short-form contracts and deal memos are often used by the parties to expedite matters. Sometimes the long-form agreement doesn't get signed until after the parties have fulfilled their contractual obligations. Sometimes the long-form contracts are never signed. This provision protects the parties to a deal memo by providing that if additional documentation is needed later, the other party will cooperate.

The provision also states that if a party refuses to provide the additional documentation needed, the other party has a power of attorney, which enables him to sign the documents on behalf of the defaulting party.

Any additional documentation requested must comply with and not contradict the terms of the deal memo. A party cannot force another to agree to unreasonable and different terms than originally agreed to. All that should be left for future documentation is to fill in the details of the prior agreement.

NOTICES

All notices to Buyer under this agreement shall be sent by United States registered mail, postage prepaid, or by telegram addressed to Buyer at _____ (address) with a courtesy copy to _____ (Buyer's attorney), and all notices to Seller under this agreement shall be sent by United States registered mail, postage prepaid, or by telegram addressed to _____ at _____(address) seller with a courtesy copy to _____ (Seller's attorney). The deposit of such notice in the United States mail or the delivery of the telegram message to the telegraph office shall constitute service of it, and the date of deposit shall be deemed to be the date of service of such notice.

A notice provision ensures that the parties know how and where to give notice to one another. Often, contracts require that one party notify the other of a default before an agreement can be terminated. To elimate confusion as to the manner of notice required, a notice clause is used.

FORCE MAJEURE

"Force majeure" means superior force and it refers to certain events beyond control of the production company that may force suspension of a contract. Such forces typically include fire, earthquake, acts of God and death or illness of a principal member of the cast or the director.

A force-majeure clause will set forth the parties' obligations to each other in case of suspension. While the production company may have the right to suspend the contract, and suspend compensation due the artist, this right is usually limited. At a certain point, the artist will have a right to terminate the agreement and go on to other projects. The production company may have the right to terminate the employment agreement if the suspension lasts more than a certain number of weeks.

Note that the clause here is written as a loan-out agreement. The "Lender" is the artist's loan-out company.[1] This company, which is usually owned by the artist, is lending out the artist's services. There may be certain tax advantages in structuring a deal as a loan-out agreement rather than a direct employment agreement.

---

[1] See Chapter 4 for a discussion of loan-out companies.

(a) Suspension:

If, (i) because of fire, earthquake, labor dispute or strike, act of God or public enemy, any municipal ordinance, any state or federal law, governmental order or regulation, or other cause beyond Production Company's control, Production Company is prevented from or hampered in the production of the Picture, or if,

(ii) because of the closing of substantially all the theaters in the United States for any of the aforesaid or other causes which would excuse Production Company's performance as a matter of law, Production Company's production of the Picture is postponed or suspended, or if,

(iii) because of any of the aforesaid contingencies or any other cause or occurrence not within Production Company's control, including but not limited to death, illness or incapacity of any principal member of the cast of the Picture or the director or individual producer, the preparation, commencement, production or completion of the Picture is hampered, interrupted or interfered with, and/or if,

(iv) Production Company's normal business operations are hampered or otherwise interfered with by virtue of any disruptive events which are beyond Production Company's control ("Production Company Disability"), then Production Company may postpone the commencement of or suspend the rendition of Writer's services and the running of time hereunder for such time as the Production Company Disability continues; and no compensation shall accrue or become payable to Lender hereunder during such suspension. Such suspension shall end upon the cessation of the cause of it.

(b) Termination:

(i) Production Company Termination Right: If a Production Company Disability continues for eight (8) weeks, Production Company may terminate this Agreement upon written notice to Lender.

(ii) Lender's Termination Right: If a Production Company Disability results in the payment of compensation being suspended hereunder for a period exceeding eight (8) weeks, Lender may terminate this Agreement upon written notice to Production Company.

(iii) Production Company Re-Establishment Right: Despite Lender's election to terminate this Agreement, within five (5) business days after Production Company's actual receipt of such written notice from Lender, Production Company may elect to re-establish the operation of this Agreement.

INCAPACITY

If, because of mental or physical disability, Writer shall be incapacitated from performing or complying with any of the terms or conditions hereof ("Writer's Incapacity") for a consecutive period exceeding fifteen days during the performance of Writer's services, then:

(a) Suspension: Production Company may suspend the rendition of services by Writer and the running of time hereunder while Writer's Incapacity continues.

(b) Termination: Production Company may terminate this Agreement and all of Production Company's obligations and liabilities hereunder upon written notice to Lender.

(c) Right of Examination: If any claim of mental or physical disability is made by or for Writer, the Production Company may have Writer examined by such physicians as Production Company may designate. Writer's physician may be present at such examination, and shall not interfere with it. Any tests performed on Writer shall be related to and be customary for the treatment, diagnosis or examination to be performed concerning Writer's claim.

An artist may become incapacitated due to an injury or illness. This clause sets forth the rights of the production company upon incapacity. The artist will want to make sure that the agreement does not allow the production company to terminate for a short illness or minor injury.

DEFAULT

If Lender or Writer fails or refuses to write, complete and deliver to Production Company the Product Form provided for herein within the respective periods specified, or if Lender or Writer otherwise fails or refuses to perform or comply with any of the terms or conditions hereof (other than because of Writer's Incapacity) ("Lender/Writer Default"), then:

(a) Suspension: Production Company may suspend the rendition of services by Writer and the running of time hereunder as long as the Lender/Writer Default shall continue.

(b) Termination: Production Company may terminate this Agreement and all of Production Company's obligations and liabilities hereunder upon written notice to Lender.

(c) Lender/Writer Default shall not include any failure or refusal of Writer to perform or comply with the material terms of this Agreement because of a breach or action by Production Company which makes the performance by Writer of his services impossible.

(d) Before termination of this Agreement by Production Company based upon Lender/Writer Default, Production Company shall notify Lender and Writer specifying the nature of the Lender/Writer Default, and Lender/Writer shall have a period of 72 hours after giving such notice to cure the Default. If the Lender/Writer Default is not cured within said period, Production Company may terminate this Agreement forthwith.

When one party fails to live up to his/her contractual obligations, they may be in default of the agreement. The innocent party may have a right to suspend performance of its obligations under the agreement and/or terminate the agreement. Often the innocent party is required, however, to first give notice of the default to the defaulting party.

EFFECT OF SUSPENSION

No compensation shall accrue to Lender during any suspension. During any period of suspension hereunder, Lender shall not permit Writer to render services for any party other than Production Company. However, Writer shall have the right to render services to third parties during any period of suspension based upon a Production Company Disability subject, however, to Production Company's right to require Writer to resume the rendition of services hereunder upon three (3) days' prior notice. Production Company shall have the right (exercisable at any time) to extend the period of services of Writer hereunder for a period equal to the period of such suspension. If Production Company shall have paid compensation to Lender during any period of Writer's Incapacity or Lender/ Writer Default, then Production Company shall have the right (exercisable at any time) to require Writer to render services hereunder without compensation for a period equal to that period of Writer's Incapacity or Lender/Writer Default.

This clause explains the effect suspension will have on the parties' rights and obligations.

EFFECT OF TERMINATION

Termination of this Agreement, whether by lapse of time, mutual consent, operation of law, exercise of right of termination or otherwise shall:

(a) Compensation: Terminate Production Company's obligation to pay Lender any further compensation. Nevertheless, if the termination is not for Lender/Writer Default, Production Company shall pay Lender any compensation due and unpaid prior to termination.

(b) Refund/Delivery: If termination occurs pursuant to Clauses _____, prior to Writer's delivery to Production Company of the Product Form on which Writer is then currently working, then Lender or Writer (or in the event of Writer's death, Writer's estate) shall, as Production Company requests, either forthwith refund to Production Company the compensation which may have been paid to Lender as of that time for such Product Form, or immediately deliver to Production Company all of the Product then completed or in progress, in whatever stage of completion it may be.

This clause explains the effect termination will have on the parties' rights and obligations.

RIGHT TO CURE

Any Writer's Incapacity or Lender/Writer Default shall be deemed to continue until Production Company's receipt of written notice from Lender specifying that Writer is ready, willing and able to perform the services required hereunder; provided that any such notice from Lender to Production Company shall not preclude Production Company from exercising any rights or remedies Production Company may have hereunder or at law or in equity by reason of Writer's Incapacity or Lender/Writer Default.

After default or incapacity, the artist may be required to give written notice that she is now able and willing to perform her obligations.

INDEMNIFICATION

Lender and Writer agree to indemnify Production Company, its successors, assigns, licensees, officers, directors and employees, and hold them harmless from and against any and all claims, liability, losses, damages, costs, expenses (including but not limited to attorneys' fees), judgments and penalties arising out of Lender's and Writer's breach of warranties under this Agreement. Production Company agrees to indemnify Lender, its successors, assigns, licensees, and employees, and hold them harmless from and against any and all claims, liability, losses, damages, costs, expenses (including but not limited to attorneys' fees), judgments and penalties arising out of any suit against Lender/Writer (arising from Lender's employment under this agreement) not based on Lender's/Writer's breach of her warranties under this Agreement.

The production company (buyer) of a literary property has no way of knowing for certain whether a literary property may infringe on another's rights. For example, a novelist may have plagiarized portions of his work from another. To protect the buyer, an indemnification clause will provide that the buyer has the right to be reimbursed any legal expenses and damages it may incur as a result of the seller (writer) breaching his warranties (promises).

NAME AND LIKENESS

Production Company shall always have the right to use and display Writer's name and likeness for advertising, publicizing and exploiting the Picture or the Product. However, such advertising may not include the direct endorsement of any product (other than the Picture) without Writer's prior written consent. Exhibition, advertising, publicizing or exploiting the Picture by any media, even though a part of or in connection with a product or a commercially-sponsored program, shall not be deemed an endorsement of any nature.

The employer will want the right to use the artist's name and likeness in promoting the film. This right is particularly valuable if the artist is a star or important director. Studios rarely use a writer's name and likeness to promote a movie.

While the employer has the right to use the name and likeness of the artist to promote a picture, the employer doesn't have the right to use their name and likeness to sell products such as celebrity coffee mugs or perfume.

PUBLICITY RESTRICTIONS

Lender or Writer shall not, individually or jointly, or by any means of press agents or publicity or advertising agencies or others, employed or paid by Lender or Writer or otherwise, circulate, publish or otherwise disseminate any news stories or articles, books or other publicity, containing Writer's name relating directly or indirectly to Lender's/Writer's employment by Production Company, the subject matter of this Agreement, the Picture, or the services to be rendered by Lender or Writer or others for the Picture, unless first approved by Production Company. Lender/Writer shall not transfer or attempt to transfer any right, privilege, title or interest in or to any of the aforestated things, nor shall Lender/Writer willingly permit any infringement upon the exclusive rights granted to Production Company. Lender and Writer authorizes Production Company, at Production Company's expense, in Lender's or Writer's name or otherwise, to institute any proper legal proceedings to prevent such infringement.

Studios want to carefully orchestrate and time their movie's publicity campaigns. This clause is meant to deter artists from going off on their own and giving interviews that may not be helpful to the promotion of the movie.

REMEDIES

(a) Remedies Cumulative: All remedies of Production Company or Lender shall be cumulative, and no one such remedy shall be exclusive of any other. Without waiving any rights or remedies under this Agreement or otherwise, Production Company may from time to time recover, by action, any damages arising out of any breach of this Agreement by Lender and/or Writer and may institute and maintain subsequent actions for additional damages which may arise from the same or other breaches. The commencement or maintaining of any such action or actions by Production Company shall not constitute or result in the termination of Lender's/Writer's engagement hereunder unless Production Company shall expressly so elect by written notice to Lender. The pursuit by Production Company or Lender of any remedy under this Agreement or otherwise shall not be deemed to waive any other or different remedy which may be available under this Agreement or otherwise.

(b) Services Unique: Lender and Writer acknowledge that Writer's services to be furnished hereunder and the rights herein granted are of a special, unique, unusual, extraordinary and intellectual character which gives them a peculiar value, the loss of which cannot be reasonably or adequately compensated in damages in an action at law, and that Lender's or Writer's Default will cause Production Company irreparable injury and damage. Lender and Writer agree that Production Company shall be entitled to injunctive and other equitable relief to prevent default by Lender or Writer. In addition to such equitable relief, Production Company shall be entitled to such other remedies as may be available at law, including damages.

Remedies are the means by which to enforce a right or obtain compensation. Remedies include money damages and injunctive relief (i.e., court orders). Subparagraph (a) above states that the election to use one remedy does not preclude other remedies.

Subparagraph (b) establishes the basis for injunctive relief. Courts usually won't grant injunctive relief if money damages can provide adequate relief. This clause acknowledges that the services of the artist are unique, loss of the services would cause irreparable harm, and money damages cannot adequately compensate the employer. Therefore, the employer might be able to obtain a court injunction ordering the artist not to work for another while the artist should be working for the employer. This could pressure the artist to return to work.

GUILDS AND UNIONS

(a) Membership: During Writer's engagement hereunder, as Production Company may lawfully require, Lender at Lender's sole cost and expense (and at Production Company's request) shall remain or become and remain a member in good standing of the then properly designated labor organization or organizations (as defined and determined under the then applicable law) representing persons performing services of the type and character required to be performed by Writer hereunder.

(b) Superseding Effect of Guild Arrangements: Nothing contained in this Agreement shall be construed so as to require the violation of the applicable WGA Agreement, which by its terms is controlling with respect to this Agreement; and whenever there is any conflict between any provision of this Agreement and any such WGA Agreement, the latter shall prevail. In such event, the provisions of this Agreement shall be curtailed and limited only to the extent necessary to permit compliance with such WGA Agreement.

If a studio was able to circumvent the terms of a collective-bargaining agreement by getting an employee to agree to less favorable terms, then the collective-bargaining agreement would be worthless. This clause makes it clear that if there is any conflict between the collective-bargaining agreement and the individual employment agreement, the terms of the collective-bargaining agreement prevail.

Of course, the collective-bargaining agreement only applies to companies that sign it (signatory companies) and artists who are members of the union. Provisions similar to the sample above are found in DGA and SAG employment agreements.

CREDITS

(a) Billing: Provided that Lender and Writer fully perform all of Lender's/ Writer's obligations hereunder and the Picture is completed and distributed, Production Company agrees that credits for authorship by Writer shall be determined and accorded pursuant to the provisions of the WGA Agreement in effect at the time of such determination.

(b) Inadvertent Non-Compliance: Subject to the foregoing provisions, Production Company shall determine, in Production Company's discretion, the manner of presenting such credits. No casual or inadvertent failure to comply with the provisions of this clause, nor any failure of any other person, firm or corporation to comply with its agreements with Production Company relating to such credits, shall constitute a breach by Production Company of Production Company's obligations under this clause. Lender and Writer hereby agree that if, through inadvertence, Production Company breaches its obligations pursuant to this Paragraph, the damages (if any) caused Lender or Writer by Production Company are not irreparable or sufficient to entitle Lender/Writer to injunctive or other equitable relief. Consequently, Lender's and/or Writer's rights and remedies in such event shall be limited to Lender's/Writer's rights, if any, to recover damages in an action at law, and Lender and Writer shall not be entitled to rescind this Agreement or any of the rights granted to Production Company hereunder, or to enjoin or restrain the distribution or exhibition of the Picture or any other rights granted to Production Company. Production Company agrees upon receipt of notice from Writer of Production Company's failure to comply with the provisions of this Paragraph, to take such steps as are reasonably practicable to cure such failure on future prints and advertisements.

The Writers Guild was formed as a result of writers' anger at studio moguls who assigned writing credit capriciously. Writers wanted to make sure that credit was given only to those who deserved it. The WGA's agreement with the studios provides that in the event of a credit dispute, the WGA will arbitrate and allocate credit among the writers involved.

While studios are willing to give up credit determination, they want to make sure that if they inadvertently drop a credit, the artist will not be able to go to court and get an injunction stopping distribution of the picture. Thus, the second paragraph of this clause limits the artist's remedies to money damages.

INSURANCE

Production Company may secure life, health, accident, cast or other insurance covering Writer, the cost of which shall be included as a direct charge of the Picture. Such insurance shall be for Production Company's sole benefit and Production Company shall be the beneficiary thereof, and Lender/Writer shall have no interest in the proceeds thereof. Lender and Writer shall assist in procuring such insurance by submitting to required examinations and tests and by preparing, signing and delivering such applications and other documents as may be reasonably required. Lender and Writer shall, to the best of their ability, observe all terms and conditions of such insurance which Production Company notifies Lender is necessary for continuing such insurance in effect.

Production companies may want to secure insurance to protect their interests and investment if an artist they contract with becomes incapacitated and unable to perform. This clause requires the artist to submit to a medical examination if needed to secure insurance and makes it clear that the insurance is for the benefit of the employer.

EMPLOYMENT OF OTHERS

Lender and Artist agree not to employ any person to serve in any capacity, nor contract for the purchase or renting of any article or material, nor make any agreement committing Production Company to pay any sum of money for any reason at all concerning the Picture or services to be rendered by Artist or provided by Lender hereunder, or otherwise, without written approval first being had and obtained from Production Company.

The employer doesn't want to be liable for persons hired by the artist, or any goods or services ordered by the artist. In some agreements, the studio may agree to hire members of a star's entourage, such as a favorite hairdresser, to work on the production.

GOVERNING LAW

This Agreement shall be construed according to the laws of the State of California applicable to agreements which are executed and fully performed within said State.

As explained on page 6, the parties may want to choose which law will apply to any dispute that may arise under the contract. This provision is particularly important when the parties reside in different states, or when the subject/performance of a contract will take place in a state other than one in which the parties reside. In those situations, it may be unclear which state's law applies.

CAPTIONS

The captions used concerning the clauses and subclauses of this Agreement are inserted only for reference. Such captions shall not be deemed to govern, limit, modify, or affect the scope, meaning or intent of the provisions of this Agreement or any part of it; nor shall such captions otherwise be given any legal effect.

This clause provides that the headlined paragraph captions are for ease of reading only and do not modify the detailed language of the agreement.

SERVICE OF PROCESS

In any action or proceeding commenced in any court in the State of California to enforce this Agreement or any right granted herein or growing out hereof, or any order or decree predicated thereon, any summons, order to show cause, writ, judgment, decree, or other process, issued by such court, may be delivered to Lender or Writer personally without the State of California; and when so delivered, Lender and Writer shall be subject to the jurisdiction of such court as though the same had been served within the State of California, but outside the county in which such action or proceeding is pending.

With this clause the parties consent to service of process outside the state of California as if the parties were within the state. This provision comes into play if a dispute arises and one of the parties is outside the state.

ILLEGALITY

Nothing contained herein shall require the commission of any act or the payment of any compensation which is contrary to an express provision of law or contrary to the policy of express law. If there shall exist any conflict between any provision contained herein and any such law or policy, the latter shall prevail; and the provision or provisions herein affected shall be curtailed, limited or eliminated to the extent (but only to the extent) necessary to remove such conflict; and as so modified the remaining provisions of this Agreement shall continue in full force and effect.

In the event a provision of the contract is found illegal, or requires the commission of an act that may be illegal, the question may arise whether the entire contract is nullified or just a part of it. The above clause says that if part of the contract is illegal, the parties want the remainder to be enforced.

EMPLOYMENT ELIGIBILITY

All of Production Company's obligations herein are expressly conditioned upon Writer's completion, to Production Company's satisfaction, of the I-9 form (Employee Eligibility Verification Form), and upon Writer's submission to Production Company of original documents satisfactory to demonstrate to Production Company Writer's employment eligibility.

Recent changes in the law impose penalties on employers who hire illegal aliens. This provision makes it clear that the employer can rescind the agreement if the employee cannot be employed legally.

ENTIRE AGREEMENT

This Agreement contains the entire agreement of the parties and all previous agreements, warranties and representations, if any, are merged herein.

Sometimes parties make several agreements concerning the same subject. For instance, the parties may make an oral agreement which is subsequently documented in a written one. If there is a dispute, a question may arise about which agreement should control. An "integration" clause provides that the earlier agreement(s) are merged and incorporated into the later agreement. The provisions of the later agreement will prevail over any inconsistent provisions in an earlier agreement.

ARBITRATION (short form)

Any controversy or claim arising out of or relating to this agreement or any breach of it shall be settled by arbitration according to the Rules of the American Arbitration Association; and judgment upon the award rendered by the arbitrators may be entered in any court having jurisdiction thereof. The prevailing party shall be entitled to reimbursement for costs and reasonable attorneys' fees.

OPTIONAL ARBITRATION PROVISIONS

The determination of the arbitrator in such proceeding shall be final, binding and non-appealable.

Nothing contained in this clause shall preclude any party from seeking and obtaining any injunctive relief or other provisional remedy available in a court of law.

ARBITRATION (long form)

Any controversy or claim arising out of or related to this agreement and to any part of it, including, but not limited to, this paragraph on arbitration, and to the performance, breach, interpretation or enforceability hereof, and all claims of fraud in the inducement of this agreement and all claims for rescission of this agreement, or any part of this agreement, shall be settled by arbitration. Such arbitration shall be held in the City of _____ unless otherwise agreed by the parties in writing, and heard and settled according to the rules of the American Arbitration Association. The arbitrator may make any order, decision, determination or award that he deems just and equitable and within the scope of the agreement of the parties, including, but not limited to, requiring any party to perform any of its obligations or undertakings. The arbitrator may also make any interim order, decision, determinations, or award he deems necessary to preserve the status quo until he can render a final order, decision, determination or award. Any final or interim order, decision, determination or award made by the arbitrator shall be conclusive and binding upon the parties and judgment upon any such order, decision, determination or award may be enforced and entered in any court having jurisdiction thereof.

Savvy filmmakers add arbitration clauses to their contracts. These provisions require that disputes be resolved through binding arbitration, not litigation. Arbitration is a much quicker, more informal and less expensive method of resolving disputes. Conflicts can be settled within a matter of months, rules of evidence don't apply and costs are much less.

It is particularly important to provide for arbitration if the party you are contracting with is wealthier than you. The wealthier party can finance a protracted court battle, which can impoverish the other party, forcing a settlement or dismissal. An arbitration clause levels the playing field.

The arbitration clause should provide that the prevailing party is entitled to reimbursement for costs and reasonable attorneys' fees. Without such a provision, the prevailing party in litigation or arbitration usually cannot recoup these expenses.

Binding arbitration awards are difficult to overturn. The grounds for appeal are quite limited. If the losing party does not voluntarily comply with the arbitration award, the prevailing party can go to court to seek confirmation of the award. Once confirmed, the award is no different from any court judgment. A Judgment Creditor can have the Sheriff seize the Judgment Debtor's assets to satisfy the award.

CHAPTER 2

DEPICTION RELEASES

When you buy the right to portray someone in a film or television program you buy a bundle of rights. These rights include protection from suits based on defamation, invasion of privacy and the right to publicity. You may also be buying the cooperation of the subject and his family or heirs. Perhaps you want access to a diary that is not otherwise available to you. The agreement used to purchase these rights is called a depiction release.

Before purchasing depiction rights, one should always consider the possibility of fictionalizing the story. If you change the names of the individuals involved, change the location and make other alterations so that real-life people are not recognizable to the public, you may forego the depiction release. However, if the story's appeal is based on the fact that it is a true story, and you want to be able to use the identities of real people, fictionalization is not a workable alternative.

In negotiating for life-story rights, there are a number of important issues that need to be resolved. At the outset, the parties must determine the extent of the rights granted. Does the grant include remakes, sequels, television series, merchandising, novelization, live-stage rights and radio rights? Are the rights worldwide? Buyers will usually want as broad a grant as possible. The seller may want to retain certain rights.

The buyer should also think about other releases that may be necessary. Are releases needed from the subject's spouse, children, friends, etc.? Will these people consent to be portrayed? Will the subject ask his friends and relatives to cooperate? Can some or all of these secondary characters be fictionalized? If the producer is planning to tell the story of the domestic life of a mother, it may not make any sense to purchase her rights without obtaining similar rights from her immediate family.

The purchase of life-story rights can be structured as either an option/purchase or an outright sale, perhaps with a reversion clause. A reversion clause provides that if the buyer does not exploit the rights within a certain number of years (i.e., the movie is not made), then all rights revert to the seller (subject). This provision protects the subject if he has sold rights to his life story to a producer who is unable to produce the project. With a reversion clause, the subject eventually regains these rights and can sell or option them to another.

Subjects are often paid a fixed fee for a depiction release. A producer could also give the subject points (percentage of net profits), consulting fees, and/or bonuses to be paid when the film is exploited in ancillary markets.

An important part of any depiction agreement is the "Warranties and Representations" clause. A warranty is a promise. The buyer will want the seller to promise never to sue for invasion of publicity, privacy or damage to reputation (defamation). The warranties must cover all 50 states and all conceivable situations. No one wants to buy a lawsuit.

Typically, the buyer has the right to embellish, fictionalize, dramatize and adapt the life story in any way he chooses. This is a frequent sticking point in negotiations. The subject is delighted to have her story told, but when presented with a depiction release, she becomes concerned. She may ask, "This document says you can change my story any way you like and I can't sue for defamation. How do I know you won't portray me as a criminal?" The subject may demand script approval.

Can a producer give script approval? No sane producer would. No producer is going to expend a lot of time and money developing a script only to find that the subject has changed his mind or is unreasonably withholding approval.

If the subject doesn't trust the producer, are any compromises possible? Yes. The subject could have approval over the treatment or selection of the writer. Perhaps the subject will figure that if he approves only a prestigious writer, his portrayal will be acceptable.

Alternatively, the producer could offer to make the subject a creative or technical consultant to the production. "You'll be right there by the side of the director," says the producer, "giving him advice and suggestions to ensure that everything is authentic." The producer may not mention that the director doesn't want the subject on the set and is not required to follow the subject's suggestions.

Another possible compromise could limit the subject matter and period portrayed. Perhaps the subject is concerned that an embarrassing incident in his life not be re-enacted in Panavision. The release could say that certain incidents, (e.g., a divorce), are not included in the release. Or the release could cover limited periods of the subject's life, (e.g., only those incidents that occurred before 1947).

Finally, the subject might have the right to decide screen notice. He could decide if the film will be billed as a true story or a dramatized account. Alternatively, he could decide whether real names will be given to the characters.

DEPICTION RELEASE (GRANT WITH REVERSION)

CONSENT AND RELEASE

To: Very Big Productions, Inc., a California Corporation

I understand that you desire to use all or parts of the events of my life in order to have one or more teleplays or screenplays written, and to produce, distribute, exhibit and exploit one or more television programs and/or motion pictures of any length in any media now known or hereafter devised and sound recordings in any media now known or hereafter devised. I have agreed to grant you certain rights in that connection. This Consent and Release confirms our agreement as follows:

1. CONSIDERATION; GRANT OF RIGHTS: In consideration of your efforts to produce my story, payment to me of $_____$, upon the beginning of principal photography of a full-length feature film, and/or $_____$ upon the beginning of production of a television movie, and/or $\_\_\_\_\_$upon the beginning of production of a pilot program and a royalty of $\_\_\_\_\_$ for each episode, and for other valuable consideration, with full knowledge I hereby grant you, perpetually and irrevocably, the unconditional and exclusive right throughout the world to use, simulate and portray my name, likeness, voice, personality, personal identification and personal experiences, incidents, situations and events which heretofore occurred or hereafter occur (in whole or in part) based upon or taken from my life or otherwise in and in connection with motion pictures, sound recordings, publications and any other media of any nature at all, whether now known or hereafter devised. Without limiting the generality of the foregoing, it is understood and agreed that said exclusive right includes theatrical, television, dramatic stage, radio, sound recording, music, publishing, commercial tie-up, merchandising, advertising and publicity rights in all media of every nature whatsoever, whether now known or hereafter devised. I reserve no rights with respect to such uses. (All said rights are after this called the "Granted Rights"). It is further understood and agreed that the Granted Rights may be used in any manner and by any means, whether now known or unknown, and either factually or with such fictionalization, portrayal, impersonation, simulation and/or imitation or other modification as you, your successors and assigns, determine in your sole discretion. I further acknowledge that I am to receive no further payment with respect to any matter referred to herein. Any and all of the Granted Rights shall be freely assignable by you.

2. PAYMENT OF CONSIDERATION; REVERSION OF RIGHTS: I understand that you shall make the payments mentioned in paragraph 1 only if you begin production of a feature film or television movie or television pilot. In the event that you do not begin such a production within three years of the date this agreement was executed, all rights granted by me under this agreement shall revert to me. I understand that if you do begin production within three years of the date this agreement was executed, all rights granted by me under this agreement shall be perpetual.

3. RELEASE: I agree hereby to release and discharge you, your employees, agents, licensees, successors and assigns from any and all claims, demands or causes of actions that I may now have or may hereafter have for libel, defamation, invasion of privacy or right of publicity, infringement of copyright or violation of any other right arising out of or relating to any utilization of the Granted Rights or based upon any failure or omission to make use thereof.

4. NAME - PSEUDONYM: You have informed me and I agree that in exercising the Granted Rights, you, if you so elect, may refrain from using my real name and may use a pseudonym which will be dissimilar to my real name. However, such agreement does not preclude you from the use of my real name should you in your sole discretion elect and in connection therewith I shall have no claim arising out of the so-called right of privacy and/or right of publicity.

5. FURTHER DOCUMENTS: I agree to execute such further documents and instruments as you may reasonably request to effectuate the terms and intentions of this Consent and Release, and in the event I fail or am unable to execute any such documents or instruments, I hereby appoint you as my irrevocable attorney-in- fact to execute any such documents and instruments, if said documents and instruments shall not be inconsistent with the terms and conditions of this Consent and Release. Your rights under this Clause 4 constitute a power coupled with an interest and are irrevocable.

6. REMEDIES: No breach of this Consent and Release shall entitle me to terminate or rescind the rights granted to you herein, and I hereby waive the right, in the event of any such breach, to equitable relief or to enjoin, restrain or interfere with the production, distribution, exploitation, exhibition or use of any of the Granted Rights granted, it being my understanding that my sole remedy shall be the right to recover damages with respect to any such breach.

7. PUBLIC DOMAIN MATERIAL: Nothing in this Consent and Release shall ever be construed to restrict, diminish or impair the rights of either you or me to use freely, in any work or media, any story, idea, pilot, theme, sequence, scene, episode, incident, name, characterization or dialogue which may be in the public domain from whatever source derived.

8. ENTIRE UNDERSTANDING: This Consent and Release expresses the entire understanding between you and me, and I agree that no oral understandings have been made with regard thereto. This Consent and Release may be amended only by written instrument signed by you and me. I acknowledge that in granting the Granted Rights I have not been induced to do so by any representations or assurances, whether written or oral, by you or your representatives concerning the manner in which the Granted Rights may be exercised and I agree that you are under no obligation to exercise any of the Granted Rights and agree I have not received any promises or inducements other than as herein set forth. The provisions hereof shall be binding upon me and my heirs, executors, administrators and successors. I acknowledge that you have explained to me that this Consent and Release has been prepared by your attorney and that you have recommended to me that I consult with my attorney concerning this Consent and Release. This Consent and Release shall be construed according to the laws of the State of California applicable to agreements which are fully signed and performed within the State of California and I hereby waive any rights I may have, known or unknown, pursuant to Section 1542 of the California Civil code which provides:

"A general release does not extend to claims which the creditor does not know or suspect to exist in his favor at the time of executing the release, which if known by him must have materially affected his settlement with the debtor."

In witness hereof and in full understanding of the foregoing, I have signed this Consent and Release on this   day of   , 19__.

_____
(Signature)

_____
(Name, please print)

_____
(Address)

AGREED: _____

DEPICTION RELEASE (OPTION, SHORT FORM)

_____

(date)

Mr. John Doe
242 Beverly Hills Lane
Beverly Hills, CA

Dear John:

It was a pleasure speaking to you recently. As I mentioned, I am interested in producing a television program or feature film about your life story.

This letter is intended to set forth the basic terms of our agreement regarding acquisition of the exclusive right and option to purchase all motion picture, television and allied rights concerning your life story. Please feel free to consult an entertainment attorney or an agent before signing this document.

Our agreement is as follows:

1) In consideration of the mutual promises contained herein, and other valuable consideration, you grant my company, Very Big Productions, Inc. ("Big"), the exclusive and irrevocable right to option the motion picture, television and all allied, ancillary and subsidiary rights for the period of one year from the date of the signing of this agreement. Big shall have the right to extend the initial option period for an additional year by sending notice to you before the expiration of the initial period, along with the payment of two thousand dollars ($2,000), which sum shall be applicable against the full purchase price.

2) Big promises to use its best efforts to produce a television program or feature film about your life story, and is acting in reliance upon your promises in this agreement.

3) If the option is exercised, Big shall compensate you as full and final consideration for all rights conveyed as follows:

   a) Television Movie-of-the-week or Mini-Series: A sum of ten thousand dollars ($10,000) for a motion picture made for television based on the material.

   b) Theatrical Motion Picture: A sum of fifteen thousand dollars ($15,000) for a theatrical motion picture based on the material.

   c) Television Series: A sum of three thousand five hundred dollars ($3,500) for the pilot episode and the sum of three hundred and fifty dollars ($350) for each episode after that.

All of the consideration described in this paragraph shall be payable upon completion of principal photography.

4) Consulting Services: You agree to serve as a creative consultant concerning any production made under this agreement. You shall receive one thousand dollars ($1,000) per week for each week your services are required, not to exceed four weeks unless both parties agree otherwise. If you are required to travel more than fifty miles from your home, Big shall furnish you with First Class

roundtrip transportation and accommodations. Before the time that the option is exercised, at Big's request you shall disclose, without compensation, any information in your possession or under your control relating to your life story, including newspaper and magazine clippings, photographs, transcripts and notes, and you will consult with any writer hired by Big, and share with him your observations, recollections, opinions and experiences concerning events and activities in your life story.

5) If the option is exercised, Big will obtain the perpetual, exclusive and irrevocable right to depict you, whether wholly or partially factual or fictional, and to use your name or likeness and voice, and biography concerning the material and any production and the advertising and exploitation of it in any and all media. While it is Big's intention to portray your story as factually as possible, Big shall have the right to include such actual or fictional events, scenes, situations and dialogue as it may consider desirable or necessary in its sole discretion.

6) You agree to use your best efforts to obtain for Big at no additional cost, those releases Big deems necessary from individuals who are a part of your life story or depicted in any information or materials you may supply Big. It is understood that you will not be expected to violate any confidences arising from any attorney-client relationship.

7) You understand that Big shall not be obligated under this agreement to exercise any of its rights or to initiate production. If Big does not commence principal photography within five (5) years of the date the option is exercised, all rights shall revert to you.

8) Big may sell, assign and/or license any of its rights under this agreement. You agree to execute any other assignments or other instruments necessary or expedient to carry out and effectuate the purposes and intent of this agreement. You agree to execute a complete long-form agreement with the customary language covering grants of biographical rights and a full release which will waive any claims or actions you may have against Big arising from the exercise of any of its rights under this agreement.

9) This agreement shall be governed and controlled by the laws of the State of California. This agreement constitutes the entire agreement between the parties and cannot be modified except in writing. Neither of the parties have made any promises or warranties other than those set forth herein.

Sincerely,

_____
on behalf of Very Big Prods.

AGREED TO AND ACCEPTED

_____
John Doe

DATE: _____

DEPICTION RELEASE (DOCUMENTARY, SHORT FORM)

MOTION PICTURE AND TELEVISION RELEASE

I hereby irrevocably agree and consent that you (Very Big Productions, Inc.), and your assigns, may use all or part of your videotaped or filmed interview of me for your documentary program about _____.

You have the right to use my picture, silhouette and other reproductions of my likeness and voice in connection with any motion picture or television program in which this interview may be incorporated, and in any advertising material promoting it.

You may edit my appearance as you see fit.

You shall have all right, title and interest in any and all results and proceeds from said use or appearance.

The rights granted you are perpetual and include the use of this interview in any medium all or part of the program may be shown, including broadcast and cable television, and videocassettes.

This consent is given as an inducement for you to interview me and I understand you will incur substantial expense in reliance thereof.

You are not obliged to make any use of this interview or exercise any of the rights granted you by this release.

I have read and understand the meaning of this release.

_____   _____
Signature   Date

_____   _____
Print Name   Phone

STILL PHOTO RELEASE

A photo release gives the buyer the right to incorporate a still photo in the buyer's production.

PHOTO RELEASE

_____ Corporation

Owner:_____

Fee: $____

Subject hereby grants to _____ Corporation ("Company") the exclusive right to use the photograph(s) depicting subject listed in Exhibit A, attached hereto, for all merchandising purposes. Subject acknowledges that the depiction of him in the Photo may be duplicated and distributed in any and all manner and media throughout the world in perpetuity.

Subject grants Company the exclusive right, license and privilege to utilize the names, characters, artist's portrayal of characters, likeness, and visual representations in the Photo in connection with the manufacture, advertising, distribution and sale of any articles or products. Such granted rights include the unconditional and exclusive right throughout the world to use, simulate and portray subject's likeness, voice, personality, personal identification and personal experiences, incidents, situations and events which heretofore occurred or hereafter occur (in whole or in part) in any and all other media of any nature whatsoever, whether now known or hereafter devised. Subject agrees that Company may elect to refrain from using subject's real name and may use a pseudonym.

Subject hereby releases and discharges Company, its employees, agents, licensees, successors and assigns from any and all claims, demands or causes of actions that it may have or may in the future have for libel, defamation, invasion of privacy or right of publicity, infringement of copyright or trademark, or violation of any other right arising out of or relating to any utilization of the rights granted under this agreement.

Subject warrants and represents that Subject possesses all rights necessary for the grant of this license, and will indemnify and hold Company, its licensees and assigns, harmless from and against any and all claims, damages, liabilities, costs and expenses arising out of a breach of the foregoing warranty.

Subject agrees that Company shall have the unlimited right to vary, change, alter, modify, add to and/or delete from his depiction in the Photo, and to rearrange and/or transpose his depiction, and to use a portion or portions of his depiction or character together with any other literary, dramatic or other material of any kind.

Subject has not committed or omitted to perform any act by which such rights could or will be encumbered, diminished or impaired; Subject further represents and warrants that no attempt shall be made from now on to encumber, diminish or impair any of the rights granted herein and that all appropriate protection of such rights will continue to be maintained by Subject.

All rights, licenses and privileges herein granted to Company are irrevocable and not subject to rescission, restraint or injunction under any circumstances.

Nothing herein shall be construed to obligate Company to produce, distribute or use any of the rights granted herein.

This agreement shall be construed according to the laws of the State of California applicable to agreements which are executed and fully performed within said State.

This agreement contains the entire understanding of the parties relating to the subject matter, and this agreement cannot be changed except by written agreement executed by the party to be bound.

IN WITNESS WHEREOF, the parties hereto have signed this Agreement as of _____, 199_.

_____
("Subject")

_____

For _____ Corporation ("Company")

STATE OF   )
) ss.:
COUNTY OF   )

On the   day of   , 199_, before me personally came_____to me known and known to be the individual described in and who executed the foregoing instrument, and he did duly acknowledge to me that he executed the same.

_____
Notary Public

CHAPTER 3

LITERARY SUBMISSION AND SALE

Rights to literary property, like personal property, can be bought and sold. The buyer will want to make sure that the seller owns what he purports to sell. The seller may want to limit the rights sold.

Nowadays, buyers may not be willing to read a property without a submission release. Such a release makes it more difficult for a writer to successfully pursue a frivolous lawsuit for story theft. A release is usually not requested for submissions from veteran writers and those who have agents or attorneys.

SUBMISSION RELEASE

Paul Producer
1219 LaVine Ave
Hollywood, CA 90088

Dear Mr. Producer:

I am submitting the enclosed material ("said material") to you:
_____, an original screenplay. WGA REGISTRATION
NO._____. Copyright Registration No._____.

The material is submitted on the following conditions:

1. I acknowledge that because of your position in the entertainment industry you receive numerous unsolicited submissions of ideas, formats, stories, suggestions and the like and that many such submissions received by you are similar to or identical to those developed by you or your employees or otherwise available to you. I agree that I will not be entitled to any compensation because of the use by you of any such similar or identical material.

2. I further understand that you would refuse to accept and evaluate said material in the absence of my acceptance of each and all of the provisions of this agreement. I shall retain all rights to submit this or similar material to persons other than you. I acknowledge that no fiduciary or confidential relationship now exists between you and me, and I further acknowledge that no such relationships are established between you and me by reason of this agreement or by reason of my submission to you of said material.

3. I request that you read and evaluate said material with a view to deciding whether you will undertake to acquire it.

4. I represent and warrant that I am the author of said material, having acquired said material as the employer-for-hire of all writers thereof; that I am the present and sole owner of all right, title and interest in and to said material; that I have the exclusive, unconditional right and authority to submit and/or convey said material to you upon the terms and conditions set forth herein; that no third party is entitled to any payment or other consideration as a condition of the exploitation of said material.

5. I agree to indemnify you from and against any and all claims, expenses, losses, or liabilities (including, without limitation, reasonable attorneys' fees and punitive damages) that may be asserted against you or incurred by you at any time in connection with said material, or any use thereof, including without limitation those arising from any breach of the warranties and promises given by me herein.

6. You may use without any obligation or payment to me any of said material which is not protectable as literary property under the laws of plagiarism, or which a third person would be free to use if the material had not been submitted to him or had not been the subject of any agreement with him, or which is in the public domain. Any of said material which, in accordance with the preceding sentence, you are entitled to use without obligation to me is hereinafter referred to as "unprotected material." If all or any part of said material does not fall in

the category of unprotected material it is hereinafter referred to as "protected material."

7. You agree that if you use or cause to be used any protected material provided it has not been obtained from, or independently created by, another source, you will pay or cause to be paid to me an amount which is comparable to the compensation customarily paid for similar material.

8. I agree to give you written notice by registered mail of any claim arising in connection with said material or arising in connection with this agreement, within sixty (60) calendar days after I acquire knowledge of such claim, or of your breach or failure to perform the provisions of this agreement, or if it be sooner, within sixty (60) calendar days after I acquire knowledge of facts sufficient to put me on notice of any such claim, or breach or failure to perform; my failure to so give you written notice will be deemed an irrevocable waiver of any rights I might otherwise have with respect to such claim, breach or failure to perform. You shall have sixty (60) calendar days after receipt of said notice to attempt to cure any alleged breach or failure to perform prior to the time that I may file a Demand for Arbitration.

9. In the event of any dispute concerning said material or concerning any claim of any kind or nature arising in connection with said material or arising in connection with this agreement, such dispute will be submitted to binding arbitration. Each party hereby waives any and all rights and benefits which he or it may otherwise have or be entitled to under the laws of the State of California to litigate any such dispute in court, it being the intention of the parties to arbitrate all such disputes. Either party may commence arbitration proceedings by giving the other party written notice thereof by registered mail and proceeding thereafter in accordance with the rules and procedures of the American Arbitration Association. The arbitration shall be conducted in the County of Los Angeles, State of California, and shall be governed by and subject to the laws of the State of California and the then prevailing rules of the American Arbitration Association. The arbitrators' award shall be final and binding and a judgment upon the award may be enforced by any court of competent jurisdiction.

10. I have retained at least one copy of said material, and I release you from any and all liability for loss or other damage to the copies of said material submitted to you hereunder.

11. Either party to this agreement may assign or license its or their rights hereunder, but such assignment or license shall not relieve such party of its or their obligations hereunder. This agreement shall inure to the benefit of the parties hereto and their heirs, successors, representatives, assigns and licensees, and any such heir, successor, representative, assign or licensee shall be deemed a third party beneficiary under this agreement.

12. I hereby acknowledge and agree that there are no prior or contemporaneous oral agreements in effect between you and me pertaining to said material, or pertaining to any material (including, but not limited to, agreements pertaining to the submission by me of any ideas, formats, plots, characters, or the like). I further agree that no other obligations exist or shall exist or be deemed to exist unless and until a formal written agreement has been prepared and entered into by both you and me, and then your and my rights and obligations shall be only such as are expressed in said formal written agreement.

13. I understand that whenever the word "you" or "your" is used above, it refers to (1) you, (2) any company affiliated with you by way of common stock ownership or otherwise, (3) your subsidiaries, (4) subsidiaries of such affiliated companies, (5) any firm, person or corporation to whom you are leasing production facilities, (6) clients of any subsidiary or affiliated company of yours, and (7) the officers, agents, servants, employees, stockholders, clients, successors and assigns of you, and of all such person, corporations referred to in (1) through (6) hereof. If said material is submitted by more than one person, the word "I" shall be deemed changed to "we," and this agreement will be binding jointly and severally upon all the persons so submitting said material.

14. Should any provision or part of any provision be void or unenforceable, such provision or part thereof shall be deemed omitted, and this agreement with such provision or part thereof omitted shall remain in full force and effect.

15. This agreement shall be governed by the laws of the state of California applicable to agreements executed and to be fully performed therein.

16. I have read and understand this agreement and no oral representations of any kind have been made to me and this agreement states our entire understanding with reference to the subject matter hereof. Any modification or waiver of any of the provisions of this agreement must be in writing and signed by both of us.

Sincerely,

_____

Signature

_____

Wally Writer

_____

Address

_____

Telephone Number

ACCEPTED AND AGREED TO:

_____

By Paul Producer

STATE OF   )

) ss.:

COUNTY OF   )

   On the   day of   , 19__, before me personally came_____to me known and known to be the individual described in and who executed the foregoing instrument, and he did duly acknowledge to me that he executed the same.

_____

Notary Public

NON-DISCLOSURE

A non-disclosure agreement serves the opposite purpose of a submission release. Here the discloser (e.g. the writer) wants protection. The agreement provides that the recipient will keep certain information (i.e. a story or script) confidential.

NON-DISCLOSURE AGREEMENT

This agreement made this _____ day of _____, 19__, by and between: _____, ("Writer"), and _____ ("Producer"), _____.

WHEREAS, Writer has written a script ("Submission") for a possible future theatrical or motion picture production.

WHEREAS, Writer wishes Producer to evaluate said "Submission" for the sole purpose of determining whether said Submission may be further developed into a motion picture ("Project").

NOW, THEREAFTER, in consideration of the premises and mutual covenants herein contained, the parties agree as follows:

1. All information disclosed by Writer to Producer, in writing, whether or not such information is also disclosed orally, that relates or refers, directly or indirectly, to the Submission, including the Submission itself, shall be deemed confidential and shall constitute Confidential Information, and shall include (i) all documents generated by Producer which contain, comment upon, or relate in any way to any Confidential Information received form Writer, and (ii) any written samples of the Submission received from Writer together with any information derived by Producer therefrom.

2. Confidential Information shall not include any information:

(i) That Producer can show by documentary evidence was known to Producer or prior to the date of its disclosure to Producer by Writer or

(ii) That becomes publicly known, by publication or otherwise, not due to any unauthorized act or omission of Producer or any other party having an obligation of confidentiality to Writer; or,

(iii) That is subsequently disclosed by Writer to any person, firm or corporation on a non-confidential basis; or

(iv) That Producer can conclusively show by documentary evidence that such information was developed independent of any access to the Confidential Information.

3. Writer will disclose the Confidential Information to Producer solely for the purpose of allowing Producer to evaluate the Submission to determine, in its sole discretion, whether the Submission may be further developed into a Project.

4. Producer agrees to accept disclosure of the Confidential Information and to exercise the same degree of care to maintain the Confidential Information secret

and confidential as is employed by Producer to preserve and safeguard its own materials and confidential information.

5. The Confidential Information shall remain the property of Writer and shall not be disclosed or revealed by Producer or to anyone else except employees of Producer who have a need to know the information in connection with Producer's evaluation of the Submission, and who have entered into a secrecy agreement with Producer under which such employees are required to keep confidential the Confidential Information of Writer, and such employees shall be advised by Producer of the confidential nature of the information and that the information shall be treated accordingly. Producer shall be liable for any improper disclosure of the Confidential Information by its employees.

6. (i) Producer shall notify Writer of any determination it may arrive at with respect to the further development of the Submission, provided, however, that, in doing so, Producer shall not directly or indirectly disclose any Confidential Information to any third party, without the consent of Writer.

    (ii) If Producer determines that the Submission cannot be further developed into a Project, within [...] months of the receipt of the Submission, Producer shall within five (5) business days after such determination return any and all Confidential Information to Writer, along with all copies or derivatives thereof and all writings generated by Producer in connection with Producer's evaluation of the Submission or the Confidential Information.

7. If Producer determines that the Submission is suitable for further development into a Project, Producer and Writer will attempt to agree on a schedule for development, and compensation to Writer for the Submission.

8. Other than as specifically provided herein, Producer will not use the Confidential Information for any purpose whatsoever other than for the sole purpose permitted in paragraph 3 hereof, unless and until a further executed agreement is first made between the parties setting forth the terms and conditions under which rights to the Submission and the Confidential Information are to be licensed to, or acquired by, Producer.

9. Writer agrees that it will not contact any party or parties other than Producer concerning the Confidential Information without prior written authorization from Producer during the term of this agreement.

10. Producer's obligations under paragraphs 3, 4, and 8 of this agreement shall extend from the date of this agreement and shall survive the expiration or termination of this agreement, provided, however, that Producer's obligations under paragraphs 3 and 4 of this agreement shall terminate immediately in the event that Writer shall purposefully disclose the Confidential Information to any other person, firm, or corporation on a non-confidential basis, during the term of this Agreement.

11. Writer hereby expressly warrants that it has the full right and authority to disclose the Confidential Information to Producer, and that no prior public non-confidential disclosure of the Confidential Information has been made by Writer nor, to the best of Writer's knowledge, by any other party.

12. Nothing in this agreement shall be deemed a sale or offer for sale of the Submission, and nothing contained herein shall in any way obligate Writer to grant to Producer a license or any other rights, directly or by implication, estoppel or

otherwise to the Confidential Information or the Submission.

13. Subject to paragraph 10 above, this agreement shall terminate _____ years from the date of this agreement, unless extended by mutual agreement of the parties. This agreement may be terminated prior to the expiration of _____ from the date of this agreement by either Writer or Producer upon thirty (30) days' written notice to the other parties of an intention to terminate.

14. This agreement sets forth the entire agreement between the parties and may not be amended or modified except by a writing signed by all of the parties.

15. This agreement shall be governed by the laws of the State of California without regard to the conflict of laws provisions thereof.

16. This agreement may be executed in counterparts.

IN WITNESS WHEREOF, the parties have executed this agreement as of the day and year first above written.

WRITER   PRODUCER

By: _____   By: _____

Name: Name:

                                                      Title:

Date: _____   Date:

QUITCLAIM

A quitclaim release is used to transfer whatever rights a party might have in a property. It is often used to clear claims of ownership or title to a property.

QUITCLAIM RELEASE

I_____, residing at _____, City of _____, State of_____, for good and valuable considerations received from _____, residing at _____,City of _____, State of _____,

Have remised, released and forever quitclaimed, and do by these presents, justly and absolutely remise, release and forever quitclaim unto_____any and all right, title or interest that I may have in or to the following:

[describe literary property]

To have and to hold the same unto _____ for his sole use and behoof, so that neither I nor any other person or persons in my name and behalf shall or will hereafter claim or demand any right, title or interest in or to the above-described property or any part thereof, but they and every one of them shall by these presents be excluded and forever barred therefrom.

[I am executing this quitclaim pursuant to the provisions of a certain agreement which I entered into with _____ under date of _____]

This quitclaim shall bind my heirs, executors, administrators and assigns, and shall enure to _____ heirs, executors, administrators and assigns.

IN WITNESS WHEREOF I have hereunto set my hand and seal this _____day of _____ 19___,

_____

Witnessed by:

_____

STATE OF   )
) ss.:
COUNTY OF   )

    On the   day of   , 199_, before me personally came_____to me known and known to be the individual described in and who executed the foregoing instrument, and he did duly acknowledge to me that he executed the same.

_____
Notary Public

LITERARY OPTION AND PURCHASE

A literary acquisition contract is an agreement to acquire all or some rights in a literary property such as a novel or a play. Producers typically use it to obtain screenplays or movie rights to literary works.

Buyers, (e.g., producers) will want owners, (e.g., writers), to warrant that they own all the rights they are selling, free and clear of any other obligations (encumbrances). Sellers will disclose their copyright registration number so that buyers can check the copyright records and review the chain of title to ensure they obtain all the rights they desire.

Each agreement needs to define the extent of the rights being sold. Sometimes, all rights, the entire copyright, is sold. Other times limited rights, on either an exclusive or non-exclusive basis, are licensed.

If movie rights are sold, the buyer typically will have the right to adapt the work into a motion picture and release it in ancillary markets such as home video. The buyer may also obtain sequel and remake rights, although an additional payment may be due if and when these rights are exploited. The buyer is routinely granted the right to excerpt up to 7,500 words from the book for advertising and promotion purposes.

Writers may want to reserve certain rights. A writer who allows adaptation of his novel into film might want to retain publication rights, stage rights, radio rights and the right to use his characters in a new novel (a sequel book). The latter right should be distinguished from sequel motion picture rights which provide the buyer with the right to use the characters in sequel motion pictures.

Another point important to the buyer will be the unlimited right to make changes to the work when adapting it. Paramount Pictures is not going to invest large sums of money to develop a screenplay only to find itself in a vulnerable position later, unable to change a line of dialogue without the author's permission. Suppose the movie is in the midst of production and the author cannot be located? What if the author unreasonably withholds consent? No studio is going to let a writer hold a gun to its head by withholding permission to make changes.

On the other hand, authors frequently complain that studios and directors ruin their work. They are embarrassed when a studio releases a movie inferior to the original work it is based on. Some countries, such as France, grant artists so-called moral rights ("Droit Moral") which may prevent buyers from desecrating or changing an artist's work without their permission. The United States does not expressly recognize the doctrine of moral rights. However, a variety of state and federal laws accomplish much the same result in a more roundabout manner. At any rate, the buyer is going to ask the seller to waive any moral rights the seller may have.

Buyers want sellers to make certain warranties, or promises. For example, the writer will often warrant that the work does not defame or invade anyone's privacy, or infringe on another's copyright. Buyers prefer that the warranties be absolute, while writers want the warranties based on the best of the writer's knowledge and belief. The difference is this: if the writer unknowingly defames another, he would be liable under an absolute warranty but not necessarily liable under one limited to the best of his knowledge and belief. Thus, if the writer in good faith believed he had not defamed anyone, he wouldn't be liable.

Buyers want writers to stand behind their warranties and indemnify them. When a writer indemnifies a buyer, the writer agrees to reimburse the buyer for any litigation costs and judgment that may be rendered as a result of the writer's breach of warranty.

Of course, an indemnity is only worth as much as the person standing behind it. It would be a waste of time for a studio to seek reimbursement from an impoverished writer.

To protect themselves from potential liability, producers and studios may purchase Errors and Omissions (E & O) insurance. Writers often ask that they be added as an additional named insured on the policy. This may add a few hundred dollars to the cost of the premium but will ensure that the insurance company defends the writer as well as the studio, and bears any litigation expense. A writer purchasing his own policy would pay much more.

Credit is another topic that needs to be addressed. The buyer wants the right to use the name and likeness of the author to promote the picture, although the writer is rarely featured in advertising. As for billing credit, the Writer's Guild agreement will usually determine who receives writing credits (assuming the Writer is in the guild and the production company is a guild signatory). The producer cannot arbitrarily assign credit. In case of a dispute over credits, the Writer's Guild will impanel a group of impartial writers to arbitrate. They will read all the drafts of the script and allocate credit.

The literary purchase agreement will also contain an explicit provision stating that the producer is under no obligation to actually produce a film. The producer wants the right to make a motion picture but not be obliged to do so. This prevents the writer from forcing the producer into production.

If the writer has a reversion clause, all rights to the script can revert to him if production is not commenced within a set time, (e.g., five years from the date the movie rights were bought). Thus the writer will regain rights to the property and has a chance to set it up elsewhere.

The acquisition of literary rights can be structured as an outright purchase or as an option/purchase agreement. Buyers typically prefer to take an option on a property to reduce their up-front risk. A party who buys an option on a literary property is obtaining the exclusive right to purchase the movie rights for a certain period into the future.

Suppose you are a producer and you read a wonderful novel written by Alice. You want to make a movie out of this book. You approach Alice and offer to buy the movie rights. She says "Fine, I would like $50,000." You cannot afford to pay $50,000 at this time. Even if you could afford it, an outright purchase would be risky. What if the screenwriter you hire doesn't produce a satisfactory screenplay? What if you cannot arrange production financing? There are many obstacles to getting a movie produced, and if you buy the movie rights and cannot get the movie produced, you have bought something you ultimately don't need.

Another way to structure the deal would be to option the rights instead of buying them. Let's say you offer Alice $5,000 for a one-year option. During that one-year period you have the exclusive right to exercise the option and buy the movie rights. Let's also suppose that the purchase price is $50,000. As a rule of thumb options are often 10% of the full purchase price, but the amount is negotiable. Sometimes sellers are willing to give a "free" option or an option for a nominal sum (e.g., "for ten dollars"). Of course, a seller is not required to give an option for movie rights, and if you are dealing with the author of a best seller, she may insist on an outright sale.

The option period can be any length of time but is often a year. The buyer may seek certain rights of renewal, which allow the buyer to extend the option upon payment of an additional sum. Let's suppose that you have taken a one-year option for $5,000, and have a right of renewal to extend the option for a second year for $6,000. The right of renewal must be exercised before the initial option period expires. If the parties agreed to give the buyer a second or third right of renewal, the buyer could extend the option further.

Renewals let the purchaser extend an option without exercising it. Assume Alice sells a producer a one-year option that is about to expire. The producer has commissioned a screenplay which she is pleased with, and she has the interest of an important director. But she doesn't have a star attached to the project and financing is not in place. At this time the producer doesn't want to buy the movie rights for $50,000, but she also doesn't want to lose the right to buy those rights in the future. If she has a right of renewal she can extend the option. Usually buyers don't want to purchase movie rights until the first day of principal photography, when they know for certain that a movie will be produced.

Note that an option gives the buyer the exclusive right to purchase movie rights within the option period. No one else can buy the movie rights during that time. The seller can do nothing that would interfere with the buyer purchasing those rights during the option period.

Once the option expires, however, the writer retains not only the option money but all movie rights as well. Some writers have sold options on the same property repeatedly because earlier options expired without being exercised. Of course, once an option is exercised, the buyer owns the movie rights outright, and the writer can't sell or option what he no longer owns.

The option payments, and any payments for rights of renewals, can be applicable or non-applicable. If the payments are applicable they count as an advance against the purchase price. If they are non-applicable, they do not apply against the purchase price. For example, if an option was for $5,000 applicable against a purchase price of $50,000, a buyer wanting to exercise the option would pay an additional $45,000. If the $5,000 option was non-applicable, the buyer would pay an additional $50,000 because the $5,000 option payment would not count against the purchase price.

The most important point to remember when taking (purchasing) an option is that you must simultaneously negotiate the terms of the purchase agreement. Usually the option contract is a two- or three-page document with a literary purchase agreement attached as an exhibit. When the option is exercised, the literary purchase agreement automatically kicks in. A buyer who enters an option agreement without negotiating the underlying literary purchase agreement has purchased a WORTHLESS OPTION. All you have bought is the right to haggle with the buyer in the future should you choose to buy the movie rights. The buyer is under no obligation to sell on the terms you propose.

For example, you purchase an option for $500 for one year but don't work out the terms of the literary purchase agreement. Nine months later you decide to exercise the option and buy the movie rights. You send the writer a check for $10,000. She objects, wanting $20,000. Since the parties have not agreed to this essential term of the sale, the contract is unenforceable. You have a worthless option, and the time and money you spent developing the project may be wasted. The writer now has you over the barrel, and can demand any amount she wants for the rights.

LITERARY OPTION AND PURCHASE AGREEMENT

THIS AGREEMENT, made and entered into as of _____(date), by and between _____(name and address of seller) ("Seller") and _____(name and address of buyer) ("Buyer").

1. SELLER'S REPRESENTATIONS AND WARRANTIES:

(a) Sole Proprietor: Seller represents and warrants to Buyer that Seller is the sole and exclusive proprietor, throughout the world of that certain original literary material written by _____ entitled _____ ("the Literary Material").

(b) Facts: Seller represents and warrants to Buyer that the following statements are true and correct in all respects with respect to said literary material:

(i) Seller is the sole author of the Literary Material.

(ii) The Literary Material was first published on (date) by _____, under the title _____, and was registered for copyright in the name of _____, under copyright registration number _____, in the Office of the United States Register of Copyrights, Washington, D.C.

No Motion Picture or dramatic version of the Literary Property, or any part of it, has been manufactured, produced, presented or authorized; no radio or television development, presentation or program based on the Literary Property, or any part of it, has been manufactured, produced, presented, broadcast or authorized; and no written or oral agreements or commitments at all with respect to the Literary Property or with respect to any right therein, have previously been made or entered into by or on behalf of Seller (except with respect to the publication of the Literary Material as set forth above).

(c) No Infringement or Violation of Third Party Rights: Seller represents and warrants to Buyer that Seller has not adapted the Literary Property from any other literary, dramatic or other material of any kind, nature or description, nor, excepting for material which is in the public domain, has Seller copied or used in the Literary Property the plot, scenes, sequence or story of any other literary, dramatic or other material; that the Literary Property does not infringe upon any common law or statutory rights in any other literary, dramatic, or other material; that to be best of Seller's knowledge, no material in the Literary Property is libelous or violative of the right of privacy of any person and the full use of the rights in the Literary Property which are covered by the within option would not violate any rights of any person, firm or corporation; and that the Literary Property is not in the public domain in any country in the world where copyright protection is available.

(d) No Impairment of Rights: Seller represents and warrants to Buyer that Seller is the exclusive proprietor, throughout the world, of the rights in the Literary Property which are covered by the within option; that Seller has not assigned, licensed nor in any manner encumbered, diminished or impaired these rights; that Seller has not committed nor omitted to perform any act by which these rights could or will be encumbered, diminished or impaired; and that there is no outstanding claim or litigation pending against or involving the title, ownership and/or copyright in the Literary Property, or in any part of it, or in the rights which are covered by the within option. Seller further represents and warrants that no attempt hereafter will be made to encumber, diminish or impair any of the rights herein granted and that all appropriate protections of such rights will continue to be maintained by Seller.

Without limiting any other rights Buyer may have in the premises, Seller agrees that if there is any claim and/or litigation involving any breach or alleged breach of any such representations and warranties of Seller, the option period granted hereunder and any periods within which Buyer may, pursuant to the provisions of Clause 3 hereof, extend the option, shall automatically be extended until no claim and/or litigation involving any breach or alleged breach of any such representation and warranties of seller is outstanding, but in any event for a period not more than one (1) additional year. Any time after the occurrence of such a claim and/or litigation until the expiration of the option period, as extended, Buyer may, besides any other rights and remedies Buyer may have in the premises, rescind this agreement and in such event, despite anything else to the contrary contained herein, Seller agrees to repay Buyer any monies paid by Buyer to Seller hereunder concerning the Property and any reasonable amounts expended by Buyer in developing or exploiting the Property. Without limiting the generality of the foregoing, Seller agrees that Seller will not, any time during the option period, exercise or authorize or permit the exercise by others of any of the rights covered by the option or any of the rights reserved by Seller under the provisions of Exhibit A which are not to be exercised or licensed to others during any period therein specified.

2. CONSIDERATION FOR OPTION: In consideration of the payment to Seller of the sum of $_____, receipt of which is hereby acknowledged, Seller agrees to and does hereby give and grant to Buyer the exclusive and irrevocable option to purchase from Seller the rights in the Property as described in Exhibit A for the total purchase price specified and payable as provided in Exhibit A, provided that any sums paid under this Clause 2 or any other provision of this agreement with respect to the option shall be credited against the first sums payable on account of such purchase price. If Buyer shall fail to exercise this option, then the sums paid to Seller hereunder with respect to the option shall be and remain the sole property of Seller.

3. OPTION PERIOD: The within option shall be effective during the period commencing on the date hereof and ending _____ ("the Initial Option Period"). The Initial Option Period may be extended for an additional _____ months by the payment of $_____ on or before the expiration date specified above ("the Second Option Period").

4. EXERCISE OF OPTION:

(a) Notice of Exercise: If Buyer elects to exercise the within option, Buyer (any time during the Option Period) shall serve upon Seller written notice of the exercise of it by addressing such notice to Seller at his address as specified in Exhibit A and by depositing such notice, so addressed by certified mail, return receipt requested with postage prepaid, in the United States mail. The deposit of such notice in the United States mail as herein specified shall constitute service of it, and the date of such deposit shall be deemed to be the date of service of such notice.

(b) The purchase price shall be paid to Seller according to Exhibit A.

(c) The option may be exercised only by notice in writing as aforesaid; no other action or oral statement by Buyer or his agents, representatives or employees shall constitute an exercise of the option.

(d) Additional Documents: If Buyer exercises the within option, Seller, without cost to Buyer (other than the consideration provided for herein or in Exhibit A) shall execute, acknowledge and deliver to Buyer, or shall cause the execution, acknowledgement and delivery to Buyer of, such further instruments as Buyer may reasonably require to confirm unto Buyer the rights, licenses, privileges and property which are the subject of the within option. If Seller shall fail to execute and deliver or to cause the execution and delivery to Buyer of any such instruments, Buyer is hereby irrevocably granted the power coupled with an interest to execute such instruments and to take such other steps and proceedings as may be necessary concerning it in the name and on behalf of Seller and as Seller's attorney-in-fact. Seller shall supply all supporting agreements and documentation requested by Buyer.

(e) Failure to Execute Documents: If Seller shall fail to execute, acknowledge or deliver to Buyer any agreements, assignments or other instruments to be executed, acknowledged and delivered by Seller hereunder, then Buyer is hereby irrevocably appointed Seller's attorney-in-fact with full right, power and authority to execute, acknowledge and deliver the same in the name of and on behalf of Seller, Seller acknowledging that the authority and agency given Buyer is a power coupled with an interest. If the property has not been published or registered for copyright in the United States Copyright Office, and as a result thereof Exhibits "A," "B" and "C," attached hereto, have not been completed with respect to the publication and copyright data and other data, then Buyer is authorized and instructed by Seller to insert the correct publication and copyright data in the appropriate blanks in Exhibits "A," "B" and "C" or after the property has been published and registered for copyright, and in this connection Seller agrees to notify Buyer promptly in writing of the publication and registration of the Property for copyright, specifying in such notice the name of the publisher, the date and place of publication, the name of the copyright proprietor and the date and entry number of the copyright registration in the United States Copyright Office, all of which information may be inserted by Buyer in the appropriate blanks in such documents.

5. EFFECTIVENESS OF EXHIBITS "A," "B" AND "C": Concurrently with the execution of this agreement Seller has executed Exhibits A (Literary Purchase Agreement), B (Short Form Option Agreement for Recordation) and C (Assignment of the Copyright), which are undated, and it is agreed that if Buyer shall exercise the option (but not otherwise) then the signature of Seller to Exhibits A, B and C shall be deemed to be effective and these Exhibits shall constitute valid and binding agreements and assignment effective as of the date of exercise of such option, and Buyer is hereby authorized and empowered to date such instruments accordingly. If Buyer shall fail to exercise the option, then the signature of Seller to Exhibits A, B and C shall be void and of no further force or effect whatever, and Buyer shall not be deemed to have acquired any rights in or to the Property other than the option hereinabove provided for. If Buyer exercises the option, Buyer will execute and deliver to Seller copies of Exhibit A, dated as of the date of the exercise of the option, and Seller will, if so requested by Buyer, execute and deliver to Buyer additional copies of Exhibits A, B and C. Notwithstanding the failure or omission of either party to execute and/or deliver such additional documents, it is agreed that upon the exercise of the option by Buyer all rights in and to the Property agreed to be transferred to Buyer pursuant to the provisions of Exhibit A shall be deemed vested in Buyer, effective as of the date of exercise of the option, which rights shall be irrevocable.

6. RIGHT TO ENGAGE IN PREPRODUCTION: Seller acknowledges that Buyer may, at its own expense, during the option period, undertake preproduction activities in connection with any of the rights to be acquired hereunder including, without limitation, the preparation and submission of treatments and/or screenplays based on the Property.

7. RESTRICTIONS: During the Option Period, Seller shall not exercise or otherwise use any of the rights herein granted to Buyer and as more particularly described in Exhibit A hereof nor the rights reserved to Seller pursuant to Clause 2 (Rights Reserved) of Exhibit A, nor shall Seller permit the use of nor shall Seller use any other right Seller has reserved in a way that would in any manner or for any purpose unfairly compete with, interfere with or conflict with the full and unrestricted use of the rights herein granted to Buyer and as described in Exhibit A.

8. ASSIGNMENT: This Option Agreement and the rights granted hereunder may be assigned by Buyer to any other person, firm or corporation.

9. OPTION REVERSION AND TURNAROUND RIGHT:

(a) If the Buyer does not timely exercise the option during its original or extended term and timely pay the purchase price, the option shall end and all rights in the Literary Property shall immediately revert to the seller. The seller shall retain all sums therefore paid. Buyer shall immediately execute and deliver to seller any assignments and documents required to effectuate the Reversion. If Buyer shall fail or be unable to do so, Buyer hereby grants seller a power coupled with an interest to execute and deliver such documents as Buyer's attorney-in-fact.

(b) If the option is timely exercised and the purchase price paid and if a motion picture company does not produce a motion picture based on the Literary Property within _____ years from purchase of the Literary Property, seller shall have a turnaround right to reacquire and set up the Literary Property elsewhere and upon obtaining such other commitment to reimburse the Buyer or Motion Picture company for its actual direct out-of-pocket development costs in connection with the Literary Property, such as fees to scriptwriters, but excluding payments to Seller and any payments to Buyer not directly related to scripting services.

(c) In addition, if Buyer decides not to exercise the option in Clause 1, above, any time before the expiration of the Option Period, or decides not to extend such option for _____ , Buyer agrees to notify Seller of such decision as soon as reasonably possible, but in no event later than the applicable option or extension deadline. When such notice is given, the option granted hereunder to Buyer shall automatically revert to Seller.

10. FORCE MAJEURE: "Force Majeure" means any fire, flood, earthquake, or public disaster; strike, labor dispute or unrest; embargo, riot, war, insurrection or civil unrest; any act of God, any act of legally constituted authority; or any other cause beyond the buyer's control which would excuse buyer's performance as a matter of law. If because of force majeure, buyer's performance hereunder is delayed or prevented then the option period provided herein and any performance by purchase shall be extended for the time of such delay or prevention.

11. SECTION HEADINGS: The headings of paragraphs, sections and other sub-divisions of this agreement are for convenient reference only. They shall not be used in any way to govern, limit, modify, construe this agreement or any part or provision of it.

12. ARBITRATION: Any controversy or claim arising out of or relating to this agreement or any breach thereof shall be settled by arbitration in accordance with the Rules of the American Arbitration Association; and judgment upon the award rendered by the arbitrators may be entered in any court having jurisdiction thereof. The prevailing party shall be entitled to reimbursement for costs and reasonable attorney's fees. The determination of the arbitrator in such proceeding shall be final, binding and non-appealable.

13. ENTIRE AGREEMENT: This agreement, including the Exhibits attached hereto, contains the complete understanding and agreement between the parties with respect to the within subject matter, and supersedes all other agreements between the parties whether written or oral relating thereto, and may not be modified or amended except by written instrument executed by both of the parties hereto. This agreement shall in all respects be subject to the laws of the State of _____ applicable to agreements executed and wholly performed within such State. All the rights, licenses, privileges and property herein granted to Buyer are irrevocable and not subject to rescission, restraint, or injunction under any or all circumstances.

IN WITNESS WHEREOF, the parties hereto have signed this Option Agreement as of the day and year first hereinabove written.

SELLER:

_____

BUYER:

_____

EXHIBIT A

This Agreement made on _____(date) by and between _____ ("Seller") and _____ ("Buyer").

WITNESSETH

WHEREAS, Seller is the sole and exclusive seller throughout the world of all rights in and to the literary work entitled: _____, written by _____, which work has been filed in the United States Copyright Office under Copyright Registration Number _____; this work including all adaptations and/or versions, the titles, characters, plots, themes and storyline is collectively called the "Property"; and

WHEREAS, Buyer wants to acquire certain rights of the Seller in consideration for the purchase price provided herein and in reliance upon the Seller's representations and warranties;

NOW, THEREFORE, the parties agree to as follows:

1. RIGHTS GRANTED: Seller hereby sells, grants, conveys and assigns to Buyer, its successors, licensees and assigns exclusively and forever, all motion picture rights (including all silent, sound dialogue and musical motion picture rights), all television motion picture and other television rights, with limited radio broadcasting rights and 7,500 word publication rights for advertisement, publicity and exploitation purposes, and certain incidental and allied rights, throughout the world, in and to the Property and in and to the copyright of it and all renewals and extensions of copyright. Included among the rights granted to Buyer hereunder (without in any way limiting the grant of rights hereinabove made) are the following sole and exclusive rights throughout the world:

(a) To make, produce, adapt and copyright one or more motion picture adaptations or versions, whether fixed on film, tape, disc, wire, audio-visual cartridge, cassette or through any other technical process whether now known or from now on devised, based in whole or in part on the Property, of every size, gauge, color or type, including, but not limited to, musical motion pictures and remakes of and sequels to any motion picture produced hereunder and motion pictures in series or serial form, and for such purposes to record and reproduce and license others to record and reproduce, in synchronization with such motion pictures, spoken words taken from or based upon the text or theme of the Property and any kinds of music, musical accompaniments and/or lyrics to be performed or sung by the performers in any such motion picture and any other kinds of sound and sound effects.

(b) To exhibit, perform, rent, lease and generally deal in and with any motion picture produced hereunder:

(i) by all means or technical processes whatsoever, whether now known or from now on devised including, by way of example only, film, tape, disc, wire, audio-visual cartridge, cassette or television (including commercially sponsored, sustaining and subscription or pay-per-view television, or any derivative of it); and

(ii) anywhere whatsoever, including homes, theaters and elsewhere, and whether a fee is charged, directly or indirectly, for viewing any such motion picture.

(c) To broadcast, transmit or reproduce the Property or any adaptation or version of it (including without limitations any motion picture produced hereunder and/or any script or other material based on or using the Property or any of the characters, themes or plots of it), by means of television or any process analogous thereto whether now known or from now on devised (including commercially sponsored, sustaining and subscription or pay-per-view television), by motion pictures produced on films or by means of magnetic tape, wire, disc, audio-visual cartridge or any other device now known or from now on devised and including such television productions presented in series or serial form, and the exclusive right generally to exercise for television purposes all the rights granted to Buyer hereunder for motion picture purposes.

(d) Without limiting any other rights granted Buyer, to broadcast and/or transmit by television or radio or any process analogous thereto whether now known or from now on devised, all or any part of the Property or any adaptation or version of it, including any motion picture or any other version or versions of it, and announcements about said motion picture or other version or versions, for advertising, publicizing or exploiting such motion picture or other version or versions, which broadcasts or transmissions may be accomplished with living actors performing simultaneously with such broadcast or transmission or by any other method or means including the use of motion pictures (including trailers) reproduced on film or by means of magnetic tape or wire or through other recordings or transcriptions.

(e) To publish and copyright or cause to be published and copyrighted in the name of Buyer or its nominee in any languages throughout the world, in any form or media, synopses, novelizations, serializations, dramatizations, abridged and/or revised versions of the Property, not exceeding 7,500 words each, adapted from the Property or from any motion picture and/or other version of the Property for advertising, publicizing and/or exploiting any such motion picture and/or other version.

(f) For the foregoing purposes to use all or any part of the Property and any of the characters, plots, themes and/or ideas contained therein, and the title of the Property and any title or subtitle of any component of the Property, and to use said titles or subtitles for any motion picture or other version of adaptation whether the same is based on or adapted from the Property and/or as the title of any musical composition contained in any such motion picture or other version or adaptation.

(g) To use and exploit commercial or merchandise tie-ups and recordings of any sort and nature arising out of or connected with the Property and/or its motion picture or other versions and/or the title or titles of it and/or the characters of it and/or their names or characteristics.

All rights, licenses, privileges and property herein granted Buyer shall be cumulative and Buyer may exercise or use any or all said rights, licenses, privileges or property simultaneously with or in connection with or separately and apart from the exercise of any other of said rights, licenses, privileges and property. If Seller from now on makes or publishes or permits to be made or published any revision, adaptation, translation or dramatization or other versions of the Property, then Buyer shall have and Seller hereby grants to Buyer without payment therefore all of the same rights therein as are herein granted Buyer. The terms "Picture" and "Pictures" as used herein shall be deemed to mean or include any present or future kind of motion picture production based upon the

Property, with or without sound recorded and reproduced synchronously with it, whether the same is produced on film or by any other method or means now or from now on used for the production, exhibition and/or transmission of any kind of motion picture productions.

2. RIGHTS RESERVED: The following rights are reserved to Seller for Seller's use and disposition, subject, however, to the provisions of this agreement:

(a) Publication Rights: The right to publish and distribute printed versions of the Property owned or controlled by Seller in book form, whether hardcover or softcover, and in magazine or other periodicals, whether in installments or otherwise subject to Buyer's rights as provided for in Clause 1 supra.

(b) Stage Rights: The right to perform the Property or adaptations of it on the spoken stage with actors appearing in person in the immediate presence of the audience, provided no broadcast, telecast, recording, photography or other reproduction of such performance is made. Seller agrees not to exercise, or permit any other person to exercise, said stage rights earlier than _____ years after the first general release or telecast, if earlier, of the first Picture produced hereunder, or _____ years after the date of exercise of the buyer's option to acquire the property, whichever is earlier.

(c) Radio Rights: The right to broadcast the Property by sound (as distinguished from visually) by radio, subject however to Buyer's right always to: (i) exercise its radio rights provided in Clause 1 supra for advertising and exploitation purposes by living actors or otherwise, by using excerpts from or condensations of the Property or any Picture produced hereunder; and (ii) in any event to broadcast any Picture produced hereunder by radio. Seller agrees not to exercise, or permit any other person to exercise, Seller's radio rights earlier than _____ years after the first general release or initial telecast, if earlier, of the first Picture produced hereunder or _____ years after the date of exercise of buyer's option to acquire the property, whichever is earlier.

(d) Author-Written Sequel: A literary property (story, novel, drama or otherwise), whether written before or after the Property and whether written by Seller or by a successor in interest of Seller, using one or more of the characters appearing in the Property, participating in different events from those found in the Property, and whose plot is substantially different from that of the Property. Seller shall have the right to exercise publication rights (i.e., in book or magazine form) any time. Seller agrees not to exercise, or permit any other person to exercise, any other rights (including but not limited to motion picture or allied rights) of any kind in or to any author-written sequel earlier than _____ years after the first general release of the first Picture produced hereunder, or _____ years after the date of exercise of buyer's option to acquire the property, whichever is earlier, provided such restriction on Seller's exercise of said author-written sequel rights shall be extended to any period during which there is in effect, in any particular country or territory, a network television broadcasting agreement for a television motion picture, (i) based upon the Property, or (ii) based upon any Picture produced in the exercise of rights assigned herein, or (iii) using a character or characters of the Property, plus one (1) year, which shall also be a restricted period in such country or territory, whether such period occurs wholly or partly during or entirely after the _____ year period first referred to in this clause. Any disposition of motion picture or allied rights in an author-written sequel made to any person or company other than Buyer shall be made subject to the following limitations and restrictions:

(e) Since the characters of the Property are included in the exclusive grant of motion picture rights to Buyer, no sequel rights or television series rights may be granted to such other person or company, but such characters from the Property which are contained in the author-written sequel may be used in a motion picture and remakes of it whose plot is based substantially on the plot of the respective author-written sequel.

It is expressly agreed that Seller's reserved rights under this subclause relate only to material written or authorized by Seller and not to any revision, adaptation, sequel, translation or dramatization written or authorized by Buyer, although the same may contain characters or other elements contained in the Property.

3. RIGHT TO MAKE CHANGES: Seller agrees that Buyer shall have the unlimited right to vary, change, alter, modify, add to and/or delete from the Property, and to rearrange and/or transpose the Property and change the sequence of it and the characters and descriptions of the characters contained in the Property, and to use a portion or portions of the property or the characters, plots, or theme of it with any other literary, dramatic or other material of any kind. Seller hereby waives the benefits of any provisions of law known as the "droit moral" or any similar law in any country of the world and agrees not to permit or prosecute any action or lawsuit on the ground that any Picture or other version of the Property produced or exhibited by Buyer, its assigns or licensees, in any way constitutes an infringement of any of the Seller's droit moral or is in any way a defamation or mutilation of the Property or any part of it or contains unauthorized variations, alterations, modifications, changes or translations.

4. DURATION AND EXTENT OF RIGHTS GRANTED: Buyer shall enjoy, solely and exclusively, all the rights, licenses, privileges and property granted hereunder throughout the world, in perpetuity, as long as any rights in the Property are recognized in law or equity, except as far as such period of perpetuity may be shortened due to any now existing or future copyright by Seller of the Property and/or any adaptations of it, in which case Buyer shall enjoy its sole and exclusive rights, licenses, privileges and property hereunder to the fullest extent permissible under and for the full duration of such copyright or copyrights, whether common law or statutory, and any renewals and/or extensions of it, and shall after that enjoy all such rights, licenses, privileges and property non-exclusively in perpetuity throughout the world. The rights granted herein are in addition to and shall not be construed in derogation of any rights which Buyer may have as a member of the public or pursuant to any other agreement. All rights, licenses, privileges and property granted herein to Buyer are irrevocable and not subject to rescission, restraint or injunction under any circumstances.

5. CONSIDERATION: As consideration for all rights granted and assigned to Buyer and for seller's representations and warranties, Buyer agrees to pay to Seller, and Seller agrees to accept:

(a) For a theatrical or television motion picture $_____ besides any sums paid in connection with the option periods so payable upon exercise of the option to acquire the Property.

(b) For any mini-series, $_____ per hour, pro-rated for part hours.

(c) For any sequel or remake of a theatrical or television motion picture based on the Property, one-half and one-third, respectively, of the amount paid for the initial motion picture, payable upon commencement of principal photography of the subsequent production.

(d) For any television series produced, based on the Property, Buyer will pay the following royalties per initial production upon completion of production of each program: up to 30 minutes $_____; over 30, but not more than 60, minutes $_____; over 60 minutes $_____; and in addition to the foregoing, as a buy-out of all royalty obligations, one hundred percent (100%) of the applicable initial royalty amount, in equal installments over five (5) reruns, payable within thirty (30) days after each such rerun.

As and for contingent compensation _____ percent of one hundred percent of the net profits (including allied and ancillary rights) of each motion picture and television program or series based on the Property, in whole or in part, with profits defined according to the same definition obtained by Buyer; provided, however, that Seller's percentage shall not be subject to any reductions or preconditions whatsoever.

6. REPRESENTATIONS AND WARRANTIES:

(a) Sole Proprietor: Seller represents and warrants to Buyer that Seller is the sole and exclusive proprietor, throughout the universe, of that certain original literary material written by Seller entitled "_____."

(b) Facts: Seller represents and warrants to Buyer as follows:

(i) Seller is the sole author and creator of the Property.

(ii) The Property was first published in 19__ by _____ (publisher) under the title _____, and was registered for copyright in the name of _____, under copyright registration number _____, in the Office of the United States Register of Copyrights, Washington, D.C.

(iii) No motion picture or dramatic version of the Property, or any part of it, has been manufactured, produced, presented or authorized; no radio or television development, presentation, or program based on the Property, or any part of it, has been manufactured, produced, presented, broadcast or authorized; and no written or oral agreements or commitments at all with respect to the Property, or with respect to any rights therein, have been made or entered by or on behalf of Seller (except with respect to the Publication of the Property as set forth above).

(iv) None of the rights herein granted and assigned to Buyer have been granted and/or assigned to any person, firm or corporation other than Buyer.

(c) No Infringement or Violation of Third Party Rights: Seller represents and warrants to Buyer that Seller has not adapted the Property from any other literary, dramatic or other material of any kind, nature or description, nor, except material which is in the public domain, has Seller copied or used in the Property the plot, scenes, sequence or story of any other literary, dramatic or other material; that the Property does not infringe upon any common law or statutory rights in any other literary, dramatic or other material; that no material contained in the Property is libelous or violative of the right of privacy of any person; that the full utilization of any and all rights in and to the Property granted by Seller pursuant to this Agreement will not violate the rights of any person, firm or corporation; and that the Property is not in the public domain in any country in the world where copyright protection is available.

(d) No Impairment of Rights: Seller represents and warrants to Buyer that Seller is the exclusive proprietor, throughout the universe, of all rights in and to the Property granted herein to Buyer; that Seller has not assigned, licensed or in any manner encumbered, diminished or impaired any such rights; that Seller has not committed or omitted to perform any act by which such rights could or will be encumbered, diminished or impaired; and that there is no outstanding claim or litigation pending against or involving the title, ownership and/or copyright in the Property, or in any part thereof, or in any rights granted herein to Buyer. Seller further represents and warrants that no attempt shall be made hereafter to encumber, diminish or impair any of the rights granted herein and that all appropriate protection of such rights will continue to be maintained by Seller.

7. INDEMNIFICATION:

(a) Seller agrees to indemnify Buyer against all judgments, liability, damages, penalties, losses and expense (including reasonable attorneys' fees) which may be suffered or assumed by or obtained against Buyer by reason of any breach or failure of any warranty or agreement herein made by Seller.

(b) Buyer shall not be liable to Seller for damages of any kind in connection with any Picture it may produce, distribute or exhibit, or for damages for any breach of this agreement (except failure to pay the money consideration herein specified) occurring or accruing before Buyer has had reasonable notice and opportunity to adjust or correct such matters.

(c) All rights, licenses and privileges herein granted to Buyer are irrevocable and not subject to rescission, restraint or injunction under any circumstances.

8. PROTECTION OF RIGHTS GRANTED: Seller hereby grants to Buyer the free and unrestricted right, but at Buyer's own cost and expense, to institute in the name and on behalf of Seller, or Seller and Buyer jointly, any and all suits and proceedings at law or in equity, to enjoin and restrain any infringements of the rights herein granted, and hereby assigns and sets over to Buyer any and all causes of action relative to or based upon any such infringement, as well as any and all recoveries obtained thereon. Seller will not compromise, settle or in any manner interfere with such litigation if brought; and Buyer agrees to indemnify and hold Seller harmless from any costs, expenses or damages which Seller may suffer as a result of any such suit or proceeding.

9. COPYRIGHT: Regarding the copyright in and to the Property, Seller agrees that:

(a) Seller will prevent the Property and any arrangements, revisions, translations, novelizations, dramatizations or new versions thereof whether published or unpublished and whether copyrighted or not copyrighted, from vesting in the public domain, and will take or cause to be taken any and all steps and proceedings required for copyright or similar protection in any and all countries in which the same may be published or offered for sale, insofar as such countries now or hereafter provide for copyright or similar protection. Any contract or agreement entered into by Seller authorizing or permitting the publication of the Property or any arrangements, revisions, translations, novelizations, dramatizations or new versions thereof in any country will contain appropriate provisions requiring such publisher to comply with all the provisions of this clause.

(b) Without limiting the generality of the foregoing, if the Property or any arrangement, revision, translation, novelization, dramatization or new version thereof is published in the United States or in any other country in which registration is required for copyright or similar protection in accordance with the laws and regulations of such country, Seller agrees to affix or cause to be affixed to each copy of the Property or any arrangement, revision, translation, novelization, dramatization or new version thereof which is published or offered for sale such notice or notices as may be required for copyright or similar protection in any country in which such publication or sale occurs.

(c) At least _____ months prior to the expiration of any copyright required by this provision for the protection of the Property, Seller will renew (or cause to be renewed) such copyright, as permitted by applicable law, and any and all rights granted Buyer hereunder shall be deemed granted to Buyer throughout the full period of such renewed copyright, without the payment of any additional consideration, it being agreed that the consideration payable to Seller under this agreement shall be deemed to include full consideration for the grant of such rights to Buyer throughout the period of such renewed copyright.

(d) If the Property, or any arrangement, revision, translation, novelization, dramatization or new version thereof, shall ever enter the public domain, then nothing contained in this agreement shall impair any rights or privileges that the Buyer might be entitled to as a member of the public; thus, the Buyer may exercise any and all such rights and privileges as though this agreement were not in existence. The rights granted herein by Seller to Buyer, and the representations, warranties, undertakings and agreements made hereunder by Seller shall endure in perpetuity and shall be in addition to any rights, licenses, privileges or property of Buyer referred to in this subclause (d).

10. CREDIT OBLIGATIONS: Buyer shall have the right to publish, advertise, announce and use, in any manner or medium, the name, biography and photographs or likenesses of Seller in connection with any exercise by Buyer of its rights hereunder, provided such use shall not constitute an endorsement of any product or service.

During the term of the Writer's Guild of America Minimum Basic Agreement ("WGA Agreement"), as it may be amended, the credit provisions of the WGA Agreement shall govern the determination of credits, if any, which the Buyer shall accord the Seller hereunder in connection with photoplays.

Subject to the foregoing, Seller shall be accorded the following credit on a single card on screen and in paid ads controlled by Buyer and in which any other writer is accorded credit, and in size of type (as to height, width, thickness and boldness) equal to the largest size of type in which any other writer is accorded credit:

(a) If the title of the Picture is the same as the title of the Property "_____"; or

(b) If the title of the Picture differs from the title of the Work, "_____".

Additionally, if Buyer shall exploit any other rights in and to the Property, then Buyer agrees to give appropriate source material credit to the Property, to the extent that such source material credits are customarily given in connection with the exploitation of such rights.

No casual or inadvertent failure to comply with any of the provisions of this clause shall be deemed a breach of this agreement by the Buyer. Seller hereby expressly acknowledges that in the event of a failure or omission constituting a breach of the provisions of this paragraph, the damage (if any) caused Seller thereby is not irreparable or sufficient to entitle Seller to injunctive or other equitable relief. Consequently, Seller's rights and remedies in the event of such breach shall be limited to the right to recover damages in an action at law. Buyer agrees to provide in its contracts with distributors of the Picture that such distributors shall honor Buyer's contractual credit commitments and agrees to inform such distributors of the credit provisions herein.

11. RIGHT OF FIRST NEGOTIATION: The term "Right of First Negotiation" means that if, after the expiration of an applicable time limitation, Seller desires to dispose of or exercise a particular right reserved to Seller herein ("Reserved Right"), whether directly or indirectly, then Seller shall notify Buyer in writing and immediately negotiate with Buyer regarding such Reserved Right. If, after the expiration of _____ days following the receipt of such notice, no agreement has been reached, then Seller may negotiate with third parties regarding such Reserved Right subject to Clause 12 infra.

12. RIGHT OF LAST REFUSAL: The term "Right of Last Refusal" means that if Buyer and Seller fail to reach an agreement pursuant to Buyer's right of first negotiation, and Seller makes and/or receives any bona fide offer to license, lease and/or purchase the particular Reserved Right or any interest therein ("Third Party Offer"), and if the proposed purchase price and other material terms of a Third Party Offer are no more favorable to Seller than the terms which were acceptable to Buyer during the first negotiation period, Seller shall notify Buyer, by registered mail or telegram, if Seller proposes to accept such Third Party Offer, the name of the offerer, the proposed purchase price, and other terms of such Third Party Offer. During the period of _____ days after Buyer's receipt of such notice, Buyer shall have the exclusive option to license, lease and/or purchase, as the case may be, the particular Reserved Right or interest referred to in such Third Party Offer, at the same purchase price and upon the same terms and conditions as set forth in such notice. If Buyer elects to exercise thereof by registered mail or telegram within such _____ day period, failing which Seller shall be free to accept such Third Party Offer; provided that if any such proposed license, lease and/or sale is not consummated with a third party within _____ days following the expiration of the aforesaid _____ day period, Buyer's Right of last refusal shall revive and shall apply to each and every further offer or offers at any time received by Seller relating to the particular Reserved Right or any interest therein; provided, further, that Buyer's option shall continue in full force and effect, upon all of the terms and conditions of this paragraph, so long as Seller retains any rights, title or interests in or to the particular Reserved Right. Buyer's Right of Last Refusal shall inure to the benefit of Buyer, its successors and assigns, and shall bind Seller and Seller's heirs, successors and assigns.

13. NO OBLIGATION TO PRODUCE: Nothing herein shall be construed to obligate Buyer to produce, distribute, release, perform or exhibit any motion picture, television, theatrical or other production based upon, adapted from or suggested by the Property, in whole or in part, or otherwise to exercise, exploit or make any use of any rights, licenses, privileges or property granted herein to Buyer.

14. ASSIGNMENT: Buyer may assign and transfer this agreement or all or any part of its rights hereunder to any person, firm or corporation without limitation, and this agreement shall be binding upon and inure to the benefit of the parties hereto and their successors, representatives and assigns forever.

15. NO PUBLICITY: Seller will not, without Buyer's prior written consent in each instance, issue or authorize the issuance or publication of any news story or publicity relating to (i) this Agreement, (ii) the subject matter or terms hereof.

16. AGENT COMMISSIONS: Buyer shall not be liable for any compensation or fee to any agent of Seller in connection with this Agreement.

17. ADDITIONAL DOCUMENTATION: Seller agrees to execute and procure any other and further instruments necessary to transfer, convey, assign and copyright all rights in the Property granted herein by Seller to Buyer in any country throughout the world. If it shall be necessary under the laws of any country that copyright registration be acquired in the name of Seller, Buyer is hereby authorized by Seller to apply for said copyright registration thereof; and, in such event, Seller shall and does hereby assign and transfer the same unto Buyer, subject to the rights in the Property reserved hereunder by Seller. Seller further agrees, upon request, to duly execute, acknowledge, procure and deliver to Buyer such short form assignments as may be requested by Buyer for the purpose of copyright recordation in any country, or otherwise. If Seller shall fail to so execute and deliver, or cause to be executed and delivered, the assignments or other instruments herein referred to, Buyer is hereby irrevocably granted the power coupled with an interest to execute such assignments and instruments in the name of Seller and as Seller's attorney-in-fact.

18. NOTICES: All notices to Buyer under this agreement shall be sent by United States registered mail, postage prepaid, or by telegram addressed to Buyer at _____(address) with a courtesy copy to _____(Buyer's attorney), and all notices to Seller under this agreement shall be sent by United States registered mail, postage prepaid, or by telegram addressed to at _____(address) seller with a courtesy copy to _____(Seller's attorney). The deposit of such notice in the United States mail or the delivery of the telegram message to the telegraph office shall constitute service thereof, and the date of such deposit shall be deemed to be the date of service of such notice.

19. ARBITRATION: Any controversy or claim arising out of or relating to this agreement or any breach thereof shall be settled by arbitration in accordance with the Rules of the American Arbitration Association; and judgment upon the award rendered by the arbitrator(s) may be entered in any court having jurisdiction thereof. The prevailing party shall be entitled to reimbursement for costs and reasonable attorney's fees. The determination of the arbitrator in such proceeding shall be final, binding and non-appealable.

20. MISCELLANEOUS:

(a) Relationship: This agreement between the parties does not constitute a joint venture or partnership of any kind.

(b) Cumulative Rights and Remedies: All rights, remedies, licenses, undertakings, obligations, covenants, privileges and other property granted herein shall be cumulative, and Buyer may exercise or use any of them separately or in conjunction with any one or more of the others.

(c) Waiver: A waiver by either party of any term or condition of this agreement in any instance shall not be deemed or construed to be a waiver of such term or condition for the future, or any subsequent breach thereof.

(d) Severability: If any provision of this agreement as applied to either party or any circumstances shall be adjudged by a court to be void and unenforceable, such shall in no way affect any other provision of this agreement, the application of such provision in any other circumstance, or the validity or enforceability of this agreement.

(e) Governing Law: This agreement shall be construed in accordance with the laws of the State of _____ applicable to agreements which are executed and fully performed within said State.

(f) Captions: Captions are inserted for reference and convenience only and in no way define, limit or describe the scope of this agreement or intent of any provision.

(g) Entire Understanding: This agreement contains the entire understanding of the parties relating to the subject matter, and this agreement cannot be changed except by written agreement executed by the party to be bound.

IN WITNESS WHEREOF, the parties hereto have signed this Agreement as of the day and year first above written.

_____

("Seller")

_____

("Buyer")

EXHIBIT B

OPTION AGREEMENT
(SHORT FORM FOR RECORDATION AT U.S. COPYRIGHT OFFICE)

For good and valuable consideration, receipt of which is hereby acknowledged, the undersigned hereby grants to _____ (the "BUYER"), its successors and assigns, the sole and exclusive option to purchase all motion picture and certain allied rights, in the original literary and/or dramatic work (the "Work") described as follows:

Title:
Author:
Publisher:
Date of Publication:
Copyright Registration:

The Work includes but is not limited to: (i) all contents; (ii) all present and future adaptations and versions; (iii) the title, characters and theme; and (iv) the copyright and all renewals and extensions of copyright.

This instrument is executed in accordance with and is subject to the agreement (the "Option Agreement") between the undersigned and the Buyer dated as of _____(date) relating to the option granted to the Buyer to purchase the above-mentioned rights in the Work, which rights are more fully described in the Purchase Agreement, attached to the Option Agreement.

Date: _____

Attest _____   _____
     (name of witness)   (name of seller)

EXHIBIT C
SHORT FORM COPYRIGHT ASSIGNMENT

KNOW ALL MEN BY THESE PRESENTS that, in consideration of One Dollar ($1.00) and other good and valuable consideration, receipt of which is hereby acknowledged, the undersigned _____ ("Assignor") do(es) hereby sell, grant, convey and assign unto _____ ("Assignee"), its successors, assigns and licensees forever, all right, title and interest including but not limited to the exclusive worldwide Motion Picture and allied rights of Assignor in and to that certain literary work to wit: that certain original screenplay written by _____ entitled _____ ("Literary Property"), and all drafts, revisions, arrangements, adaptations, dramatizations, translations, sequels and other versions of the Literary Property which may heretofore have been written or which may hereafter be written with the sanction of Assignor.

Dated this _____ day of _____, 19__.

_____
("Assignor")

AGREED TO:

_____
("Assignee")

Acknowledgment

STATE OF   )
) ss.:
COUNTY OF   )

On the   day of   , 199_, before me personally came_____to me known and known to be the individual described in and who executed the foregoing instrument, and he did duly acknowledge to me that he executed the same.

_____

Notary Public

CHAPTER 4

ARTIST EMPLOYMENT

A producer seeking to employ an artist can either hire that person directly or contract with his company for his services. Many writers, directors and actors have incorporated themselves by setting up "loan out" companies. At one time there were significant tax advantages to establishing such companies. Most of these benefits have now been abolished, although some pension and health plan benefits remain.

The company is called a "loan-out" company because it lends the talent's services first to studio A, then to studio B, and so on. All the money earned from the talent's services are paid to the company. The loan-out company pays the talent's business expenses and a salary.

Studios don't object to paying talent through their loan-out companies if the studio's interests are protected. The studio will want the talent to sign an "Inducement Agreement." This is a contract between the studio and the talent guaranteeing that the talent will abide by the terms of the loan-out agreement. Otherwise, the studio's only remedy for breach of contract is to sue the loan-out company which may not have any assets and which cannot perform the promised acts (i.e., corporations cannot act, write, direct, only people can).

When talent requests that the deal be structured as a loan-out deal, three agreements are needed. First is the employment contract between the studio and the loan-out company. Second is the agreement between the studio and the talent, the so-called inducement agreement. And third is an employment agreement between the loan-out company and the talent.

The terms of a loan-out agreement are not much different than a direct employment agreement. One can immediately recognize a loan-out deal because it refers to one party as the "Lender." The "Lender" is the loan-out company, not a bank.

WRITER EMPLOYMENT

Writers can create screenplays on their own and sell them to a studio (or a producer). Screenplays are a form of intellectual property and can be sold like personal property. As discussed in Chapter 3, option agreements and literary purchase agreements are contracts for the sale of a writer's rights in literary property.

Another method studios use to acquire screenplays entails hiring someone to write one for them. The idea for the screenplay may be suggested by the writer in a pitch meeting, or it may come from the studio.[1]

Writers often prefer to be hired to write rather than create scripts on their own. That is because the employer takes the risk of the project not turning out well. A writer who spends six months on his own creating a screenplay that he can't sell has no income to show for his work. The employed writer, on the other hand, receives a guaranteed payment for his labor, even if the script never gets produced. And if the script is produced, the writer may receive additional compensation in the form of a bonus or a percentage of profits.

Studios employ writers to create scripts because they may not be able to acquire enough finished scripts to maintain their desired level of production. Also, a hot "spec" script can be quite expensive to acquire because several studios may be competing for it.

An employment contract is used to hire a writer. As a "work for hire," the employer owns the copyright. The writer gets the money; the studio gets the script. Since the studio owns the work, it can shelve the project or hire someone else to rewrite it.

Many of the provisions found in a writer's employment agreement are also present in actor and director employment agreements. The methods of structuring compensation, force majeure conditions and credit provisions are quite similar.

A producer can hire a writer on a step deal or a flat deal. In a step deal the employer has the right to terminate the writer's services after each step. Step deals are often used when an employer is hiring a novice writer. The employer reduces his financial risk by proceeding in a series of steps instead of hiring the writer to write a finished script.

Suppose a producer wants to hire a writer to create a romantic comedy but the writer has never written in that genre. The producer doesn't want to risk $50,000 (approximately WGA scale for a feature) to hire him. So the producer hires the writer on a step deal. The steps could be:

a) treatment/outline

b) first draft screenplay

c) second draft

d) rewrite

e) polish

The writer receives a payment for each step. After each step the producer has the option of whether to proceed to the next step. After any step the producer

---

[1] The idea could be an original one or one based on another work, such as play, magazine article or book, that the studio wants to adapt as a movie.

can decide to shelve the project or bring in another writer. As the employer, the producer owns all the writer's work. The writer retains the money for the steps completed.

The Writer's Guild sets minimums for each step, and the total compensation paid for the steps will be no less than the minimum scale payment for a flat deal for a complete screenplay.

A step deal will provide for "reading periods." These are periods, usually a couple of weeks, in which the producer has the opportunity to decide whether he wants to go on to the next step. If the producer does not exercise his right to proceed within the reading period, he risks losing the writer. During the reading period the writer cannot accept outside assignments that might prevent her from completing the remaining steps.

The writer's employment agreement will also set out the time requirements when various items are due. Usually the writer gets one to three months to complete a first draft.

TYPES OF COMPENSATION

There are different ways to compensate writers. Fixed compensation is a guaranteed sum. Typically, producers pay half the fee up-front, and half when the work is delivered. If the writer doesn't produce a craftsman-like work, the producer doesn't have to pay. But the producer must pay if a craftsman-like work is turned in even if the producer doesn't like the script. The producer takes the risk of the script turning out poorly.

The Writer's Guild prohibits its members from working on speculation without a guarantee of fixed compensation. The amount of fixed compensation is often minimum WGA scale for a novice writer. For more experienced writers, the amount is usually a modest increase over their last deal. Of course, if the writer wins an Academy Award or his last movie was a blockbuster hit, his price will skyrocket.

Bonus compensation is another form of payment. Let's say you are a producer and a writer asks to be paid $90,000. You can't afford to pay that up front so you counter by offering $60,000 fixed compensation, and another $30,000 as bonus compensation. Bonus compensation is not guaranteed. Payment is contingent on a certain event, such as the script going into production. If the script isn't produced, the bonus need not be paid. Thus, bonus compensation is more iffy than fixed compensation.

Deferred compensation is more iffy than bonus compensation. Deferments are often used in low-budget films when the producer can't afford to pay his cast and crew their usual wages. Perhaps the producer offers to hire everyone for $250 a week, and to defer the rest of the salary that they would normally earn. Deferments are usually not payable unless the script gets produced, the movie is released and revenue is received. Deferments can be payable before or after investors recoup their investment. The agreement may give priority to some deferment holders over others or it may provide that everyone shares equally (in pari passu).

The most iffy kind of payment is contingent compensation, or net profits (points). Here the employee will receive payment only if the script is produced, released and it generates enough revenue to cover all expenses and deductions, including distribution fees and marketing costs. Net profit participants rarely see any money from their net points. Artists often complain that studios use creative accounting to deny them their share of profits.

Writers typically receive between 1 and 5 percent of 100 percent of net profits. Why do we state the writer's share in terms of a percent of one hundred percent? So that there won't be any confusion as to the size of the writer's slice of net profits. If we simply said that the writer gets 5% of net profits, it would be unclear whether she gets 5% of all the net profits or 5% of the producer's share of net profits.

Typically, the studio and the producer split net profits 50/50. The producer, however, often must give a writer, director and star a portion of his net profits. These profit participants take from the producer's half of net profits. Nevertheless, the custom in the industry is to express net profits in terms of the whole (all profits) to avoid ambiguity. Of course, rather than giving a writer 5% of 100% of the net profits, one could give her 10% of 50%. It would be the same amount.

Another form of payment is known as "additional" compensation. This fee is payable if the producer makes a sequel, remake or television spin-off series based on the original work (assuming he has the right to make those works). Writers often receive 50 percent of what they were paid for the original movie for a sequel, and 33 percent for a remake. For a television spin-off series the writer usually gets a royalty for every episode. If the series is a hit, the writers may earn more in royalties from the series than they received for writing the film.

The series royalty is a passive one. That means the writer is not obliged to work on the series. The payment is compensation for his work on the original. So the writer is entitled to the royalty even if he is not involved in the series. If the writer is hired to work on the series, he would receive additional compensation for his services.

CREDIT

A writer's employment agreement will have a credit clause. For a WGA writer and a signatory company, the WGA credit rules determine how credit is allocated. Consequently, the producer does not have the discretion to allocate writing credits as he may choose. After the "Notice of Tentative Credits" is given, every writer on the project has the opportunity to object and request credit arbitration.

Credit is important for reasons besides ego and professional stature. The determination of credit can have financial repercussions. Often the amount of points a writer receives will vary depending on whether he receives sole, shared or no credit.

Writers sometimes complain about directors who have their writer friends needlessly rewrite a script. The first writer is forced to share credit and profits with another writer. However, the Writer's Guild credit guidelines give a strong preference to the first writer. The second writer will only obtain credit if his contribution is 50% or more of the completed script. Unfortunately this may encourage the second writer to extensively revise the work and throw out good material.

Performance standards will also be addressed in the agreement. The writer will be required to perform diligently and efficiently, to follow the suggestions and instructions of the company, and to devote all time exclusively to the project during the term of the agreement.

WRITER EMPLOYMENT AGREEMENT
(THEATRICAL WGA AGREEMENT)

Agreement dated _____ between _____ ("Writer"), and _____ Films ("Production Company").

1. EMPLOYMENT: Production Company agrees to employ Writer to perform and Writer agrees to perform, upon the terms and conditions herein specified, writing services for the proposed Theatrical Motion Picture currently entitled _____ ("Picture"), based upon a screenplay of the same name supplied by Production Company ("Basic Property"). [Writer shall perform such writing services in collaboration with Writer _____ pursuant to the Employment Agreement dated _____ , between _____ and Production Company ("Agreement"). Writer and _____ are hereinafter collectively referred to as the "Doe/Roe Team".]

2. THE PRODUCT AGREEMENT WITH OPTIONS: The completed results of Writer's services hereunder shall be deemed collectively the "Product" and individually the "Product Form," and shall be created as follows:

First Draft screenplay with option for one Revision/Draft thereof and dependent option for one polish.

3. COMMENCEMENT OF SERVICES: Writer shall commence services in writing the first draft of the screenplay upon execution of this agreement and Production Company becoming a signatory of the Writers Guild of America. Writer shall commence writing each subsequent Product Form on a date to be designated by Production Company, which date may be earlier, but shall not be later than the first business day after expiration of the then current Reading Period or Option Period, as the case may be, described in Clause 4.

4. TIME REQUIREMENTS (Agreement with Options): Writer's services shall be rendered pursuant to the following time requirements:

(a) Delivery Periods: Writer shall deliver each Product Form within the period ("Delivery Period") which commences on the date Writer is obligated to commence writing each designated Product Form and which ends upon expiration of the applicable time period listed in Clause 4(e).

(b) Reading Periods: Each time Writer delivers any Product Form, if Writer's engagement herein requires additional writing services, Production Company shall have a period ("Reading Period"), which commences on the first business day following the delivery of such Product Form and which continues for the length of time listed in Clause 4(e) opposite the description of the Product Form delivered within which to read such Product Form and advise Writer to commence writing the next Product Form.

(c) Postponement of Services: If Production Company does not exercise its right to require Writer to commence writing either the first set of revisions or the polish within the applicable Reading Period, Production Company may nonetheless require Writer to render such services at any time within the one (1) year period commencing upon delivery of the immediately preceding Product Form, subject to Writer's availability and provided: 1) Writer's services are to be rendered during the one year period, and 2) Production Company shall furnish Writer with thirty (30) days' prior written notice of the date designated for the commencement of such services, and 3) that Production Company has paid Writer in a timely manner for the postponed product forms as those services were timely rendered.

(d) Option Periods: Each Option, if any, under Clause 4(e), shall be exercised, if at all, in writing within the period ("Option Period") which commences on the first business day following the delivery of the Product Form immediately preceding that for which an Option may be exercised, or upon the expiration of the Delivery Period applicable to such Product Form, whichever is later, and which continues for the length of time listed in Clause 4(e) opposite the description of the Product Form delivered.

(e) Length of Periods: Delivery, Reading and Option Periods shall be the following lengths:

Product Form	Delivery Period	Reading/Option Period
First Draft Screenplay	8 weeks	2 weeks
First Revision/ Second Draft Screenplay	4 weeks	2 weeks
Polish of Screenplay	2 weeks	2 weeks

5. DELIVERY: TIME OF THE ESSENCE:

(a) Effective Delivery: Delivery of Product Form to any person other than _____ shall not constitute delivery of such Product Form as required by this Agreement.

(b) Time of the Essence: Writer shall write and deliver each Product Form for which Writer is engaged as soon as reasonably possible after commencement of Writer's services thereon, but not later than the date upon which the applicable Delivery Period expires. Time of delivery is of the essence.

(c) Revisions: For each Product Form which is in the nature of a Revision, Writer's services shall include the writing and delivery of such changes as may be required by Production Company within a reasonable time prior to the expiration of the Delivery Period applicable to such Product Form.

6. COMPENSATION:

(a) Fixed Compensation: Production Company shall pay Writer as set forth below for Writer's services and all rights granted by Writer:

(i) For First Draft Screenplay: $_____ , payable half upon commencement, half upon delivery.

(ii) For First Revision/Second Draft Screenplay: $_____ , payable half upon commencement, half upon delivery.

(iii) For Polish of Screenplay: $_____ , payable half upon commencement, half upon delivery.

(b) Payment: Production Company shall have no obligation to pay Writer any compensation with respect to any Product Form for which Production Company has failed to exercise its Option under Clause 4.

(c) Bonus Compensation: Subject to the production and release of the Picture, and to the Writer not being in material default hereunder, in addition to the Fixed Compensation set forth above, Writer shall be entitled to be paid the following:

(i) If Writer receives sole or shared screenplay credit pursuant to final Writer's Guild of America ("WGA") credit determination with respect to the Picture, Writer shall be entitled to receive as Bonus Compensation the sum of $25,000 over the compensation provided by Clause 6(a), less the aggregate of all sums paid to Writer pursuant to Clause 6(a) above, and shall be payable upon commencement of principal photography.

(ii) If the production budget is above $700,000, the bonus payment shall escalate $2,500 per $100,000 increase. If the production budget exceeds $1 million dollars, the production bonus will be $50,000. The sums payable under this section, shall be less the aggregate of all sums (not already deducted) paid to Writer pursuant to Clause 6 (a) and 6 (c) above and shall be payable 60 days after completion of principal photography.

(iii) Repayment: If Bonus Compensation set forth in Clause 6(c) above is paid to Writer as set forth hereinabove, and if Writer receives neither sole screenplay credit nor shared screenplay credit pursuant to final WGA credit determination for the Picture, the Writer shall repay to Production Company such sum so paid to Writer within five (5) days of such determination.

(d) Contingent Compensation: Subject to the production and release of the Picture and subject to Writer not being in default of his obligations hereunder, in addition to the Fixed Compensation and Bonus Compensation set forth above, Writer shall be entitled to be paid the following:

(i) Sole Screenplay Credit: If the Doe/Roe writing Team receives sole screenplay credit pursuant to final WGA credit determination for the Picture, Writer shall be entitled to receive as Contingent Compensation an amount equal to two and one-half percent (2-1/2%) of one hundred percent (100%) of the Net Profits of the Picture.

(ii) Shared Screenplay Credit: If the Doe/Roe Writing Team receives shared screenplay credit pursuant to final WGA credit determination for the Picture, Writer shall be entitled to receive as Contingent Compensation an amount equal to one and one-quarter percent (1-1/4%)] of one hundred percent (100%) of the Net Profits of the Picture.

(e) For purposes of this Agreement, "Net Profits" shall be computed, determined and paid in accordance with definition of net profits defined in the production/distribution agreement between production company and the distributor of the Picture, provided that Writer's definition shall be as favorable as any other net profit participant.

(f) Additional payments to Writer for Sequel, Remake and Television Use of the Work; Right of First Negotiation: Subject to the provisions of Clauses 6(g) and 6(h) below, and subject to the production and release of the Picture and the performance of all obligations of Writer hereunder:

(i) Sequel Theatrical Motion Picture: If the Doe/Roe Writing Team receives sole/shared screenplay credit or is accorded separation of rights pursuant to applicable WGA determination with respect to the Picture, then for each Sequel Theatrical Motion Picture based on the Picture produced and released, Writer shall be entitled to be paid an amount equal to fifty percent (50%) of one hundred percent (100%) of the sum paid to Writer as Compensation pursuant to Clause 6(a) and 6(c) supra, and a percentage participation in the Net Profits of such Sequel Theatrical Motion Picture in an amount equal to fifty percent (50%) of one hundred percent (100%) of the rate of percentage participation in Net Profits of the Picture payable to Writer as Contingent Compensation pursuant to Clauses 6(d)(i) or 6(d)(ii) above, if any.

(ii) Theatrical Remakes: If the Doe/Roe Writing Team receives sole/shared screenplay credit or is accorded separation of rights pursuant to applicable WGA determination for the Picture, then for each Theatrical Remake of the Picture produced and released by, Writer shall be entitled to be paid an amount equal to thirty three percent (33%) of one hundred percent (100%) of the sum paid to Writer as Compensation pursuant to Clause 6(a) and 6(c) supra, and thirty three percent (33%) of one hundred percent (100%) of the percentage participation in Net Profits of the Picture payable to Writer as Contingent Compensation pursuant to Clauses 6(d)(i) or 6(d)(ii) above, if any.

(iii) Sequel Television Motion Pictures and Television Remakes:

(A) Pilot and Series: If Writer is accorded separation of rights pursuant to applicable WGA determination with respect to the Picture, then for each Studio Sequel Television Motion Picture based upon the Picture and/or Television Remake of the Picture which is produced and licensed for exhibition by Production Company and which is a Pilot or an episode of an episodic or anthology television series (collectively "TV Program"), Writer shall be entitled to receive the following royalties:

(1) $___ for each TV Program of not more than thirty (30) minutes in length.

(2) $____ for each TV Program in excess of thirty (30) minutes but not more than sixty (60) minutes in length.

(3) $_____ for each TV Program in excess of sixty (60) minutes in length.

(4) If any TV Program is rerun, Writer shall be paid twenty percent (20%) of the applicable sum initially paid Writer pursuant to Subclauses (1), (2) or (3) above for the second run, third run, fourth run, fifth run, and sixth run respectively. No further rerun payments shall be due or payable for any rerun after the sixth run.

(B) Movies of the Week and Mini-Series: If Writer is accorded separation of rights pursuant to applicable WGA determination for the Picture, then for each Sequel Television Motion Picture or Television Remake of the Picture which is produced and licensed for exhibition by Production Company and which is a so-called "Movie of the Week" or so-called "Mini-Series," Writer shall be entitled to receive the following royalties which sum shall constitute full payment for all rerun use and/or other exploitation thereof:

(1) _____ for the first two (2) hours of running time of each such Movie of the Week and/or each such Mini-Series.

(2) $_____ for every hour of running time, if any, exceeding the first two (2) hours of running time of such Movie of the Week and/or such Mini-Series up to a maximum of $40,000.

(vi) Definitions — The following terms as utilized in connection with this Agreement, shall be defined as set forth below:

(A) "Television Remake": A remake primarily intended to be initially distributed for free-television exhibition.

(B) "Television Studio Sequel Motion Picture": A studio sequel motion picture primarily intended to be initially distributed for free-television exhibition.

(C) "Theatrical Remake": A remake primarily intended to be initially distributed for theatrical exhibition.

(D) "Theatrical Studio Sequel Motion Picture": A studio sequel motion picture primarily intended to be initially distributed for theatrical exhibition.

(E) WGA Agreement: All sums payable to Writer pursuant to this Agreement shall be in lieu of, and not in addition to, any similar payment to which Writer may be entitled pursuant to the current Writers Guild of America Theatrical and Television Agreement ("WGA Agreement").

7. CONDITIONS AFFECTING OR RELATED TO COMPENSATION:

(a) Method of Payment: All compensation which shall become due to Writer hereunder shall be sent to Writer at the address provided in Clause 26. Such address may be changed to such other address as Writer may hereafter notify Production Company in accordance with Clause 26.

(b) Performance: Production Company's obligation to pay compensation or otherwise perform hereunder shall be conditioned upon Writer not being in default of his obligations under the Agreement. No compensation shall accrue to Writer during Writer's inability, failure or refusal to perform, according to the terms and conditions of this Agreement, the services contracted for herein, nor shall compensation accrue during any period of Force Majeure, Suspension or upon Termination except as otherwise herein provided.

(c) Governmental Limitation: No withholding, deduction, reduction or limitation of compensation by Production Company which is required or authorized by law ("Governmental Limitation") shall be a breach of this Agreement by Production Company or relieve Writer from Writer's obligations hereunder. Payment of compensation as permitted pursuant to the Governmental Limitation shall continue while such Governmental Limitation is in effect and shall be deemed to constitute full performance by Production Company of its obligation to pay compensation hereunder.

(d) Garnishment/Attachment: If Production Company is required, because of the service of any garnishment, writ of execution or lien, or by the terms of any contract or assignment executed by Writer to withhold, or to pay all or any portion of the compensation due Writer hereunder to any other person, firm or corporation, the withholding or payment of such compensation or portion thereof, pursuant to the requirements of any such garnishment, writ of execution, lien, contract or assignment shall not be construed as a breach by Production Company of this Agreement.

(e) Overpayment/Offset: If Production Company makes any overpayment to Writer hereunder for any reason or if Writer is indebted to Production Company for any reason, Writer shall pay Production Company such overpayment or indebtedness on demand, or at the election of Production Company may deduct and retain for its own account an amount equal to all or any part of such overpayment or indebtedness from any sums that may be due or become due or payable by Production Company to Writer or for the account of Writer and such deduction or retention shall not be deemed a breach of this Agreement.

(f) Pay or Play: Production Company shall not be obligated to use Writer's services for the Picture, nor shall Production Company be obligated to produce, release, distribute, advertise, exploit or otherwise make use of the results and proceeds of Writer's services if such services are used. Production Company may elect to terminate Writer's services at any time without legal justification or excuse provided that the Fixed Compensation provided in Clause 6(a), which shall have been earned and accrued prior to such termination shall be paid to Writer. In the event of such termination, all other rights of Writer herein shall be deemed void ab initio except such rights as may have accrued to Writer in accordance with the terms of Clauses 21 (relating to Guilds and Unions), 22 (relating to Credits) and 6(c) (relating to bonus compensation).

8. PERFORMANCE STANDARDS: Writer's services hereunder shall be rendered promptly [in collaboration with _____] in a diligent, conscientious, artistic and efficient manner to Writer's best ability. Writer shall devote all of Writer's time and shall render Writer's services exclusively (during writing periods only) to Production Company in performing the writing services contemplated hereunder, and shall not render services for any other party during the period of Writer's engagement. Writer's services shall be rendered in such manner as Production Company may direct pursuant to the instructions, suggestions and ideas of and under the control of and at the times and places required by Production Company's authorized representatives. Writer shall, as and when requested by Production Company, consult with Production Company's daily authorized representatives and shall be available for conferences in person or by telephone with such representatives for such purposes at such times during Writer's engagement as may be required by such representatives.

9. RESULTS AND PROCEEDS OF SERVICES:

(a) Ownership: Production Company shall solely and exclusively own the Product, each Product Form and all of the results and proceeds thereof, in whatever stage of completion as may exist from time to time (including but not limited to all rights of whatever kind and character, throughout the world, in perpetuity, in any and all languages of copyright, trademark, patent, production, manufacture, recordation, reproduction, transcription, performance, broadcast and exhibition by any art, method or device, not known or hereafter devised, including without limitation radio broadcast, theatrical and non-theatrical exhibition, and television exhibition or otherwise) whether such results and proceeds consist of literary, dramatic, musical, motion picture, mechanical or any other form or works, themes, ideas, compositions, creations or products. Production Company's acquisition hereunder shall also include all rights generally known in the field of literary and musical endeavor as the "moral rights of authors" in and/or to the Product, each Product Form, and any musical and literary proceeds of Writer's services. Production Company shall have the right but not the obligation, with respect to the Product, each Product Form, the results and proceeds thereof, to add to, subtract from, change, arrange, revise, adapt, rearrange, make variations, and to translate the same into any and all languages, change the sequence, change the characters and the descriptions thereof contained therein, change the title of the same, record and photograph the same with or without sound (including spoken words, dialogue and music synchronously recorded), use said title or any of its components in connection with works or motion pictures wholly or partially independent thereof, to sell, copy and publish the same as Production Company may desire and to use all or any part thereof in new versions, adaptations and sequels in any and all languages and to obtain copyright therein throughout the world. Writer hereby expressly waives any and all rights which Writer may have, either in law, in equity, or otherwise, which Writer may have or claim to have as a result of any alleged infringements of Writer's so-called "moral rights of authors." Writer acknowledges that the results and proceeds of Writer's services are works specially ordered by Production Company for use as part of a motion picture and the results and proceeds of Writer's services shall be considered to be works made for hire for Production Company, and, therefore, Production Company shall be the author and copyright owner of the results and proceeds of Writer's services.

(b) Assignment and Vesting of Rights: All rights granted or agreed to be granted to Production Company hereunder shall vest in Production Company immediately and shall remain vested whether this Agreement expires in normal course or is terminated for any cause or reason, or whether Writer executes the Certificate of Authorship required infra. All material created, composed, submitted, added or interpolated by Writer hereunder shall automatically become Production Company's property, and Production Company, for this purpose, shall be deemed author thereof with Writer acting entirely as Production Company's employee. Writer does hereby assign and transfer to Production Company all of the foregoing without reservation, condition or limitation, and no right of any kind, nature or description is reserved by Writer. The said assignment and transfer to Production Company by Writer are subject to the limitations contained in the current Writer's Guild of America Theatrical and Television Film Basic Agreement ("WGA Agreement").

(c) Execution of Other Documents:

(i) Certificate of Authorship: Writer further agrees, if Production Company requests Writer to do so, to execute and deliver to Production Company, in connection with all material written by writer hereunder, a Certificate of Authorship in substantially the following form:

I hereby certify that I wrote the manuscript hereto attached, entitled
_____ [based upon a screenplay of the same name written by
_____,] as an employee of _____ Films which furnished my
services pursuant to an employment Agreement between _____ and
_____ Films dated _____, in performance of my duties
thereunder an in the regular course of my employment, and that Production Company is the author thereof and entitled to the copyright therein
and thereto, with the right to make such changes therein and such uses
thereof as it may from time to time determine as such author.

IN WITNESS WHEREOF, I have hereto set my hand this
_____ (date).

If Production Company desires to secure separate assignments or Certificates of Authorship of or for any of the foregoing, Writer agrees to
execute such certificate upon Production Company's request therefor.
Writer irrevocably grant(s) Production Company the power coupled with
an interest to execute such separate assignments or Certificates of Authorship in Writer's name and as Writer's attorney-in-fact.

(ii) Writer recognizes that the provisions in Clause 9(c)(iii) dealing with
any other documents to be signed by Writer are not to be construed in
derogation of Production Company's rights arising from the employer-employee relationship but are included because in certain jurisdictions
and in special circumstances the rights in and to the material which flow
from the employer-employee relationship may not be sufficient in and
of themselves to vest ownership in Production Company.

(iii) If Production Company desires to secure further documents covering, quitclaiming or assigning all or any of the results and proceeds of
Writer's services, or all or any rights in and to the same, then Writer agrees
to execute and deliver to Production Company any such documents at
any time and from time to time upon Production Company's request, and
in such form as may be prescribed by Production Company; without limiting the generality of the foregoing, Writer agrees to execute and deliver
to Production Company upon Production Company's request therefor an
assignment of all rights, it being agreed that all of the representations,
warranties and agreements made and to be made by Writer under this
Exhibit shall be deemed made by Writer as part of this agreement. If
Writer shall fail or refuse to execute and deliver the certificate above
described and/or any such documents within ten business days of a
written request, the Writer hereby irrevocably grants Production Company
the power coupled with an interest to execute this certificate and/or
documents in Writer's name and as Writer's attorney-in-fact. Writer's failure to execute this certificate and/or documents shall not affect or limit
any of Production Company's rights in and to the results and proceeds
of Writer's services.

(iv) Separation of Rights: Since Writer has been assigned material, he
is not expected to be entitled to separation of rights under the WGA
Agreement. Notwithstanding anything to the contrary contained herein,
Production Company shall have the right to publish and copyright, or

cause to be published and copyrighted, screenplays, teleplays and scripts adapted from or based upon the Product and the novelization of screenplays, teleplays and scripts adapted from or based upon the Product or any Product Form created hereunder.

10. WRITER'S WARRANTIES:

Subject to Article 28 of the WGA basic agreement Writer warrants:

(a) that, except as provided in the next sentence hereof, all material composed and/or submitted by Writer for or to Production Company shall be wholly original with Writer and shall not infringe upon or violate the right of privacy of, nor constitute a libel or slander against, nor violate any common law rights or any other rights of any person, firm or corporation. The same agreements and warranties are made by Writer regarding any and all material, incidents, treatments, characters and action which Writer may add to or interpolate in any material assigned by Production Company to Writer for preparation, but are not made regarding violations or infringements contained in the material so assigned by Production Company to Writer. The said agreements and warranties on Writer's part are subject to the limitations contained in the WGA Agreement.

(b) Further Warranties: Writer hereby warrants that Writer is under no obligation or disability, created by law or otherwise, which would in any manner or to any extent prevent or restrict Writer from entering into and fully performing this Agreement, and Writer hereby accepts the obligations hereunder. Writer warrants that Writer has not entered into any agreement or commitment that would prevent his fulfilling Writer's commitments with Production Company hereunder and that Writer will not enter into any such agreement or commitment without Production Company's specific approval. Writer hereby agrees that Writer shall devote his entire time and attention and best talents and ability exclusively to Production Company as specified herein and observe and be governed by the rules of conduct established by Production Company for the conduct of its employees.

(c) Indemnification: Writer agrees to indemnify Production Company, its successors, assigns, licensees, officers, directors and employees, and hold them harmless from and against any and all claims, liability, losses, damages, costs, expenses (including but not limited to attorneys' fees), judgments and penalties arising out of Writer's breach of warranties under this Agreement. Production Company agrees to indemnify Writer, its successors, assigns, licensees, and employees, and hold them harmless from and against any and all claims, liability, losses, damages, costs, expenses (including but not limited to attorneys' fees), judgments and penalties arising out of any suit against Writer (arising from Writer's employment under this agreement) not based on Writer's breach of his warranties under this Agreement.

11. NAME AND LIKENESS: Production Company shall always have the right to use and display Writer's name and likeness for advertising, publicizing and exploiting the Picture or the Product. However, such advertising may not include the direct endorsement of any product (other than the Picture) without Writer's prior written consent. Exhibition, advertising, publicizing or exploiting the Picture by any media, even through a part of or in connection with a product or a commercially-sponsored program, shall not be deemed an endorsement of any nature.

12. PUBLICITY RESTRICTIONS: Writer shall not, individually or jointly, or by any means of press agents or publicity or advertising agencies or others, employed or paid by Writer or otherwise, circulate, publish or otherwise disseminate any news stories or articles, books or other publicity, containing Writer's name relating directly or indirectly to Writer's employment by Production Company, the subject matter of this Agreement, the Picture, or the services to be rendered by Writer or others for the Picture, unless first approved by Production Company. Writer shall not transfer or attempt to transfer any right, privilege, title or interest in or to any of the aforestated things, nor shall Writer willingly permit any infringement upon the exclusive rights granted to Production Company. Writer authorizes Production Company, at Production Company's expense, in Writer's name or otherwise, to institute any proper legal proceedings to prevent such infringement.

13. REMEDIES:

(a) Remedies Cumulative: All remedies of Production Company or Writer shall be cumulative, and no one such remedy shall be exclusive of any other. Without waiving any rights or remedies under this Agreement or otherwise, Production Company may from time to time recover, by action, any damages arising out of any breach of this Agreement by Writer and may institute and maintain subsequent actions for additional damages which may arise from the same or other breaches. The commencement or maintaining of any such action or actions by Production Company shall not constitute or result in the termination of Writer's engagement hereunder unless Production Company shall expressly so elect by written notice to Writer. The pursuit by Production Company or Writer of any remedy under this Agreement or otherwise shall not be deemed to waive any other or different remedy which may be available under this Agreement or otherwise.

(b) Services Unique: Writer acknowledges that Writer's services to be furnished hereunder and the rights herein granted are of a special, unique, unusual, extraordinary and intellectual character which gives them a peculiar value, the loss of which cannot be reasonably or adequately compensated in damages in an action at law, and that Writer's Default will cause Production Company irreparable injury and damage. Writer agrees that Production Company shall be entitled to injunctive and other equitable relief to prevent default by Writer. In addition to such equitable relief, Production Company shall be entitled to such other remedies as may be available at law, including damages.

14. FORCE MAJEURE:

(a) Suspension: If, (i) by reason of fire, earthquake, labor dispute or strike, act of God or public enemy, any municipal ordinance, any state or federal law, governmental order or regulation, or other cause beyond Production Company's control, Production Company is prevented from or hampered in the production of the Picture, or if, (ii) by reason of the closing of substantially all the theatres in the United States for any of the aforesaid or other causes which would excuse Production Company's performance as a matter of law, Production Company's production of the Picture is postponed or suspended, or if, (iii) by reason of any of the aforesaid contingencies or any other cause or occurrence not within Production Company's control, including but not limited to the death, illness or incapacity of any principal member of the cast of the Picture or the director or individual producer, the preparation, commencement, production or completion of the Picture is hampered, interrupted or interfered with, and/or if, (iv) Production Company's normal business operations are hampered or otherwise interfered with by virtue of any disruptive events which are beyond

Production Company's control ("Production Company Disability"), then Production Company may postpone the commencement of or suspend the rendition of Writer's services and the running of time hereunder for such time as the Production Company Disability continues; and no compensation shall accrue or become payable to Writer hereunder during such suspension. Such suspension shall end upon the cessation of the cause thereof.

(b) Termination:

(i) Production Company Termination Right: If a Production Company Disability continues for a period of eight (8) weeks, Production Company may terminate this Agreement upon written notice to Writer.

(ii) Writer's Termination Right: If a Production Company Disability results in the payment of compensation being suspended hereunder for a period exceeding eight (8) weeks, Writer may terminate this Agreement upon written notice to Production Company.

(iii) Production Company Re-Establishment Right: Despite Writer's election to terminate this Agreement, within five (5) business days after Production Company's actual receipt of such written notice from Writer, Production Company may elect to re-establish the operation of this Agreement.

15. WRITER'S INCAPACITY: If, by reason of mental or physical disability, Writer shall be incapacitated from performing or complying with any of the terms or conditions hereof ("Writer's Incapacity") for a consecutive period exceeding fifteen days or thirty days cumulatively, during the performance of Writer's services, then:

(a) Suspension: Production Company may suspend the rendition of services by Writer and the running of time hereunder so long as Writer's Incapacity shall continue.

(b) Termination: Production Company may terminate this Agreement and all of Production Company's obligations and liabilities hereunder upon written notice to Writer.

(c) Right of Examination: If any claim of mental or physical disability is made by Writer or on Writer's behalf, the Production Company may have Writer examined by such physicians as Production Company may designate at Production Company's expense. Writer's physician may be present at such examination, but shall not interfere therewith. Any tests performed on Writer shall be related to and be customary for the treatment, diagnosis or examination to be performed in connection with Writer's claim.

16. WRITER DEFAULT: If Writer fails or refuses to write, complete and deliver to Production Company the Product Form provided for herein within the respective periods specified or if Writer otherwise fails or refuses to perform or comply with any of the terms or conditions hereof (other than by reason of Writer's Incapacity) ("Writer's Default"), then:

(a) Suspension: Production Company may suspend the rendition of services by Writer and the running of time hereunder as long as the Writer Default shall continue.

(b) Termination: Production Company may terminate this Agreement and all of Production Company's obligations and liabilities hereunder upon written notice to Writer.

(c) Writer Default shall not include any failure or refusal of Writer to perform or comply with the material terms of this Agreement by reason of a breach or action by Production Company which makes the performance by Writer of his services impossible.

(d) Prior to termination of this Agreement by Production Company based upon Writer Default, Production Company shall notify Writer specifying the nature of the Writer Default and Writer shall have a period of 72 hours after giving of such notice to cure the Writer Default. If the Writer Default is not cured within said period, Production Company may terminate this Agreement forthwith.

17. EFFECT OF TERMINATION: Termination of this Agreement, whether by lapse of time, mutual consent, operation of law, exercise of right of termination or otherwise shall:

(a) Compensation: Terminate Production Company's obligation to pay Writer any further compensation. Nevertheless, if the termination is not for Writer Default, Production Company shall pay Writer any compensation due and unpaid prior to termination;

(b) Refund/Delivery: If termination occurs pursuant to Clauses 14, 15, or 16, prior to Writer's delivery to Production Company of the Product Form on which Writer is then currently working, then Writer (or in the event of Writer's death, Writer's estate) shall, as Production Company requests, either forthwith refund to Production Company the compensation which may have been paid to Writer as of that time for such Product Form, or immediately deliver to Production Company all of the Product then completed or in progress, in whatever stage of completion it may be.

18. EFFECT OF SUSPENSION: No compensation shall accrue to Writer during any suspension. During any period of suspension hereunder, Writer shall not render services for any party other than Production Company. However, Writer shall have the right to render services to third parties during any period of suspension based upon a Production Company Disability subject, however, to Production Company's right to require Writer to resume the rendition of services hereunder upon three (3) days prior notice. Production Company shall have the right (exercisable at any time) to extend the period of services of Writer hereunder for a period equal to the period of such suspension. If Production Company shall have paid compensation to Writer during any period of Writer's Incapacity or Writer Default, then Production Company shall have the right (exercisable at any time) to require Writer to render services hereunder without compensation for a period equal to that period of Writer's Incapacity or Default.

19. WRITER'S RIGHT TO CURE: Any Writer's Incapacity or Writer Default shall be deemed to continue until Production Company's receipt of written notice from Writer specifying that Writer is ready, willing and able to perform the services required hereunder; provided that any such notice from Writer to Production Company shall not preclude Production Company from exercising any rights or remedies Production Company may have hereunder or at law or in equity by reason of Writer's Incapacity or Writer Default.

20. TEAM OF WRITERS: The obligations of the Doe/Roe Team of Writers under this Agreement shall be joint and several, and references in this Agreement to Writer shall be deemed to refer to the Team of Writers jointly and severally. Should any right of termination arise as a result of the Incapacity or Default of any one of the Team of Writers, the remedies of the Production Company may be exercised either as to such Writer or as to the Team of Writers, at Production Company's election. Should Production Company elect to exercise its remedies only as to the Writer affected, the engagement of the other Writer or Writers shall continue and such remaining Writer shall receive only his share of the compensation provided herein.

21. GUILDS AND UNIONS:

(a) Membership: During Writer's engagement hereunder, as Production Company may lawfully require, Writer at Writer's sole cost and expense (and at Production Company's request) shall remain or become and remain a member in good standing of the then properly designated labor organization or organizations (as defined and determined under the then applicable law) representing persons performing services of the type and character required to be performed by Writer hereunder.

(b) Superseding Effect of Guild Arrangements: Nothing contained in this Agreement shall be construed so as to require the violation of the applicable WGA Agreement, which by its terms is controlling with respect to this Agreement; and whenever there is any conflict between any provision of this Agreement and any such WGA Agreement, the latter shall prevail. In such event the provisions of this Agreement shall be curtailed and limited only to the extent necessary to permit compliance with such WGA Agreement.

22. CREDITS:

(a) Billing: Provided that Writer fully performs all of Writer's obligations hereunder and the Picture is completed and distributed, Production Company agrees that credits for authorship by Writer shall be determined and accorded pursuant to the provisions of the WGA Agreement in effect at the time of such determination.

(b) Inadvertent Non-Compliance: Subject to the foregoing provisions, Production Company shall determine, in Production Company's discretion, the manner of presenting such credits. No casual or inadvertent failure to comply with the provisions of this clause, nor any failure of any other person, firm or corporation to comply with its agreements with Production Company relating to such credits, shall constitute a breach by Production Company of Production Company's obligations under this clause. Writer hereby agrees that if through inadvertence Production Company breaches its obligations pursuant to this Paragraph, the damages (if any) caused Writer by Production Company are not irreparable or sufficient to entitle Writer to injunctive or other equitable relief. Consequently, Writer's rights and remedies in such event, shall be limited to Writer's rights, if any, to recover damages in an action at law, and Writer shall not be entitled to rescind this Agreement or any of the rights granted to Production Company hereunder, or to enjoin or restrain the distribution or exhibition of the Picture or any other rights granted to Production Company. Production Company agrees upon receipt of notice from Writer of Production Company's failure to comply with the provisions of this Paragraph, to take such steps as are reasonably practicable to cure such failure on future prints and advertisements.

23. INSURANCE: Production Company may secure life, health, accident, cast or other insurance covering Writer, the cost of which shall be included as a direct charge of the Picture. Such insurance shall be for Production Company's sole benefit and Production Company shall be the beneficiary thereof, and Writer shall have no interest in the proceeds thereof. Writer shall assist in procuring such in-

surance by submitting to required examinations and tests and by preparing, signing and delivering such applications and other documents as may be reasonably required. Writer shall, to the best of Writer's ability, observe all terms and conditions of such insurance of which Production Company notifies Writer as necessary for continuing such insurance in effect.

24. EMPLOYMENT OF OTHERS: Writer agrees not to employ any person to serve in any capacity, nor contract for the purchase or renting of any article or material, nor make any agreement committing Production Company to pay any sum of money for any reason whatsoever in connection with the Picture or services to be rendered by Writer hereunder, or otherwise, without written approval first being obtained from Production Company.

25. ASSIGNMENT AND LENDING:

(a) Assignability: This Agreement is non-assignable by Writer. Production Company and any subsequent assignee may freely assign this Agreement and grant its rights hereunder, in whole or in part to any person, firm, or corporation provided that such party assumes and agrees in writing to keep and perform all of the executory obligations of Production Company hereunder. Upon such assumption, Production Company is hereby released from all further obligations to Writer hereunder, except that unless the assignee or borrower is a so-called major motion picture company, or mini-major, Production Company shall remain secondarily liable under this agreement.

(b) Right to Lend to Others: Writer understands and acknowledges that the actual production entity of a motion picture to be made from the Product may be a party other than Production Company. In such event, Writer's services shall be rendered hereunder for the actual production entity but without releasing Production Company from its obligations hereunder.

26. NOTICES:

(a) Writer's Address: All notices from Production Company to Writer, in connection with this Agreement, may be given in writing by addressing the same to Writer c/o _____. Production Company may deliver such notice to Writer personally, either orally or in writing. A courtesy copy shall be given to _____ at the address above. If such notice is sent by mail, the date of mailing shall be deemed to be the date of service of such notice.

(b) Writing Requirement: Any oral notice given in respect to any right of termination, suspension or extension under this Agreement shall be confirmed in writing. If any notice is delivered to Writer personally, a copy of such notice shall be sent to Writer at the above address.

(c) Producer's Address: All notices from Writer to Production Company hereunder shall be given in writing addressed to Production Company as follows: _____ and by depositing the same, so addressed, postage prepaid, in the mail. A courtesy copy shall be given to _____, Attorney at Law, _____. Unless otherwise expressly provided, the date of mailing shall be deemed to be the date of service of such notice.

27. TRANSPORTATION AND EXPENSES: When Writer's services are required by Production Company to be rendered hereunder at a place more than fifty (50) miles from Writer's domicile, Production Company shall furnish Writer transportation to and from such places and meals and lodging accommodations while Writer is on location to render Writer's services.

28. GOVERNING LAW: This Agreement shall be construed in accordance with the laws of the State of California applicable to agreements which are executed and fully performed within said State.

29. CAPTIONS: The captions used in connection with the clauses and subclauses of this Agreement are inserted only for the purpose of reference. Such captions shall not be deemed to govern, limit, modify, or in any other manner affect the scope, meaning or intent of the provisions of this Agreement or any part thereof; nor shall such captions otherwise be given any legal effect.

30. SERVICE OF PROCESS: In any action or proceeding commenced in any court in the State of California for the purpose of enforcing this Agreement or any right granted herein or growing out hereof, or any order or decree predicated thereon, any summons, order to show cause, writ, judgment, decree, or other process, issued by such court, may be delivered to Writer personally without the State of California; and when so delivered, Writer shall be subject to the jurisdiction of such court as though the same had been served within the State of California, but outside the county in which such action or proceeding is pending.

31. ILLEGALITY: Nothing contained herein shall require the commission of any act or the payment of any compensation which is contrary to an express provision of law or contrary to the policy of express law. If there shall exist any conflict between any provision contained herein and any such law or policy, the latter shall prevail; and the provision or provisions herein affected shall be curtailed, limited or eliminated to the extent (but only to the extent) necessary to remove such conflict; and as so modified the remaining provisions of this Agreement shall continue in full force and effect.

32. EMPLOYMENT ELIGIBILITY: All of Production Company's obligations herein are expressly conditioned upon Writer's completion, to Production Company's satisfaction, of the I-9 form (Employee Eligibility Verification Form), and upon Writer's submission to Production Company of original documents satisfactory to demonstrate to Production Company Writer's employment eligibility.

36. ENTIRE AGREEMENT: This Agreement contains the entire agreement of the parties and all previous agreements, warranties and representations, if any, are merged herein.

By signing in the spaces provided below, Writer and Production Company accept and agree to all of the terms and conditions of this Agreement.

_____
("Writer")   Date:

_____Films
("Production Company")

By: _____   Date:
    Its President.

WRITER EMPLOYMENT AGREEMENT
(LOW-BUDGET, NON-UNION)

WRITER EMPLOYMENT AGREEMENT

Agreement effective _____ , 19__, between _____ Productions, a California Corporation ("Producer"), and _____ ("Writer").

1. EMPLOYMENT: Producer employs Writer to perform and Writer agrees to perform writing services for Producer's proposed motion picture currently entitled _____ ("The Picture"), based on an original story by Producer. All of Producer's obligations under this Agreement are expressly conditioned upon Writer's completion, to Producer's satisfaction, of Form I-9 (Employment Eligibility Verification Form) and Writer's submission to Producer of original documents satisfactory to Producer to prove Writer's employment eligibility.

2. SERVICES/FORM OF WORK: The completed results and product of Writer's services (including all material created, added, interpolated and submitted by Writer) shall be deemed the "Work" which shall be created in each of the applicable forms listed below ("Form of Work"):

FORMS OF WORK: Screenplay

                                  One rewrite

(a) Use of Work: In Producer's sole, absolute and unfettered discretion, Producer may use or not use the Work and may make any changes in, deletions from or additions to the Work.

(b) Underlying Property: If the Work is based on an original idea or material ("Property") created by Writer, Writer hereby grants Producer the same rights in the Property as Producer is acquiring hereunder in the Work. The compensation payable to Writer pursuant to Paragraph 5 includes payment for said rights in the Property and for the writing services of Writer hereunder.

[(c) Option to direct: In the event the Picture is produced for a production budget of less than three hundred thousand dollar ($300,00), financed by _____ Productions, Writer shall have the option to direct the picture. Compensation and terms for directing services shall be pursuant to the director's employment agreement attached hereto as "Exhibit A."]

3. DELIVERY: Writer agrees to complete and deliver each Form of Work and the Work, including any changes and revisions required by Producer as follows: Screenplay due: _____. Rewrite due:_____.

4. PERFORMANCE STANDARDS: All of Writer's services shall be rendered promptly in a diligent, conscientious, artistic and efficient manner and Writer shall devote Writer's entire time and attention and best talents and abilities to the services to be rendered, either alone or in collaboration with others. Writer's services shall be rendered in such manner as Producer may reasonably direct pursuant to the instructions, suggestions and ideas of, and under the control of, and at the times and places reasonably required by, Producer's duly authorized representatives. Writer, as and when reasonably requested by Producer, shall consult with Producer's duly authorized representatives and shall be available for conferences with such representatives for such purposes at such times and places during Writer's employment as may be required by such representatives.

5. COMPENSATION: Conditioned upon Writer's full performance of all of Writer's obligations hereunder, Producer will pay Writer as full compensation for all services rendered and rights granted as follows:

(a) Fixed compensation: _____ thousand dollars which shall be paid one half upon execution of this agreement, and one-half upon delivery of the last Form of Work due Producer. Plus:

(b) Bonus compensation as follows:

(i) If a motion picture is produced based on the Work with a final production budget of three hundred thousand dollars ($300,000) or less, and if Writer receives sole or shared screenplay credit, a bonus of $_____ thousand dollars ($), shall be paid to Writer, payable on the first day of principal photography, or

(ii) If a motion picture is produced based on the Work with a final production budget more than three hundred thousand dollars ($300,000) but less than five hundred thousand dollars ($500,000), and if Writer receives sole or shared screenplay credit, a bonus of $_____ thousand dollars ($), shall be paid to Writer, payable on the first day of principal photography, or

(iii) If a motion picture is produced based on the Work with a final production budget of five hundred thousand dollars ($500,000) or more, but less than one million dollars ($1,000,000), and if Writer receives sole or shared screenplay credit, a bonus of $_____ thousand dollars ($), shall be paid to Writer, payable on the first day of principal photography, or

(iv) If a motion picture is produced based on the Work with a final production budget of one million dollars or more, but less than one and one-half million dollars ($1,500,000), and if Writer receives sole or shared screenplay credit, a bonus of $_____ thousand dollars ($), shall be paid to Writer, payable on the first day of principal photography, or

(v) If a motion picture is produced based on the Work with a final production budget of one and one-half million dollars ($1,500,000) or more, but less than two million dollars ($2,000,000) and if Writer receives sole or shared screenplay credit, an additional _____ thousand dollars ($), shall be paid to Writer, payable on the first day of principal photography, or

(vi) If a motion picture is produced based on the Work with a final production budget of two million dollars ($2,000,000) or more, and if Writer receives sole or shared screenplay credit, an additional _____ thousand dollars ($), shall be paid to Writer, payable on the first day of principal photography.

(c) Contingent Compensation: In addition to the Fixed Compensation payable under Clause 5(a), and any Bonus Compensation payable under Clause 5(b), subject to the production and release of the Picture and subject to the performance of Writer's obligations hereunder Writer shall be entitled to receive as Contingent Compensation an amount equal to _____ percent of one nundred percent (100%) of the Net Profits of the Picture, if any.

(d) Net Profits Definition: Net Profits shall be computed, determined and paid in accordance with the distribution agreements entered into by Producer and any distributor.

(e) Sequels and Remakes: If Writer pursuant to final credit determination, receives sole or shared screenplay credit, and Producer produces a sequel of a theatrical motion picture based on the Property, Producer shall pay Writer an additional payment equal to one half (1/2) of the total fixed and bonus compensation paid to Writer for the Original work. If Writer pursuant to final credit determination receives sole or shared screenplay credit, and Producer produces a remake of a theatrical motion picture based on the Property, an additional payment equal to one third (1/3) of the total fixed and bonus compensation paid to Writer for the Original Work. Said payments are payable on the first day of principal photography for said sequel or remake, and are payable only for the first sequel or remake.

(f) Series spin-off: If Producer produces and licenses a Series based on the Work and Writer, pursuant to final credit determination, receives sole or shared screenplay credit, Producer will pay Writer the applicable royalties as follows:

(i) Pilot program: _____ thousand dollars.

(ii) Additional episodes of any length: _____ dollars per episode.

(iii) Reruns payments: twenty percent (20%) of the payment for original broadcast for each rerun, up to five runs. Thereafter no payments.

These payments under (i) and (ii) shall be made within thirty (30) days of completion of principal photography of any pilot or episode.

6. WARRANTIES, REPRESENTATIONS, INDEMNITIES:

(a) Writer Warranties and Representations: Writer warrants and represents that each Form of Work and the Work shall be wholly original with Writer, except as to matters within the public domain and except as to material inserted by Writer pursuant to specific instructions of Producer, and shall not infringe upon or violate the rights of privacy or publicity of, or constitute a libel or slander against, or violate any common law or any other rights of, any person, firm or corporation.

(b) Writer's Indemnities: Writer shall indemnify Producer and Producer's licensees and assigns and its or their officers, agents and employees, from all liabilities, actions, suits or other claims arising out of any breach by Writer of Writer's warranties and representations and/or out of the use by Producer of the Work and from reasonable attorneys' fees and costs in defending against the same. The foregoing shall apply only to material created or furnished by Writer, and shall not extend to changes or additions made therein by Producer, or to claims for defamation or invasion of the privacy of any person unless Writer knowingly uses the name or personality of such person or should have known, in the exercise of reasonable prudence, that such person would or might claim that such person's personality was used in the Work.

(c) Producer's Indemnities: Producer shall indemnify Writer to the same extent that Writer indemnifies Producer hereunder, as to any material supplied by Producer to Writer for incorporation into the Work.

(d) Notice and Pendency of Claims: The party receiving notice of any claim or action subject to indemnity hereunder shall promptly notify the other party.

7. OWNERSHIP: As Writer's employer, Producer shall solely and exclusively own throughout the world in perpetuity all rights of every kind and nature in the Work, and all of the results and proceeds thereof in whatever stage of completion as may exist from time to time, together with the rights generally known as the "moral rights of authors." Writer acknowledges that the Work is being written by Writer for use as a Motion Picture and that each Form of Work is being written by Writer as a "work made for hire" within the scope of Writer's employment by Producer, and, therefore, Producer shall be the author and copyright owner of the Work.

8. FCC: Writer understands that, as to any Television Program based on the Work, it is a Federal offense, unless disclosed prior to broadcast to Producer or to the station or licensee which broadcasts the Program, to:

(a) Give or agree to give any member of the production staff, anyone associated in any manner with the Program or any representative of the Producer, the station or network, any portion of compensation payable to Writer or anything else of value for arranging Writer's employment in connection with the Program.

(b) Accept or agree to accept anything of value, other than compensation payable to Writer under this Agreement, to promote any product, service or venture on the air, or to incorporate any material containing such a promotion in the Program.

Writer is aware that Producer prohibits such conduct with or without disclosure to Producer, and any such conduct or failure to disclose shall be a material breach of this Agreement.

9. NOTICES/PAYMENT:

(a) To Writer: All notices from Producer to Writer may be given in writing by mailing the notice to Writer, postage prepaid, or at Producer's option, Producer may deliver such notice to Writer personally, either orally or in writing. The date of mailing or of personal delivery shall be deemed to be the date of service. Payments and written notice to Writer shall be sent to Writer at _____.

(b) To Producer: All notices from Writer to Producer shall be given in writing by mail, messenger, cable, telex or telecopier addressed as indicated below. The date of mailing, messengering, cabling, telexing or telecopying shall be deemed to be the date of service.

Mail:

FAX:

(c) Change of Address: The address of Writer and of Producer set forth herein may be changed to such other address as Writer or Producer may hereafter specify by written notice given to the other Party.

10. ASSIGNMENT: This Agreement is non-assignable by Writer. This Agreement shall inure to the benefit of Producer's successors, assigns, licensees and grantees and associated, affiliated and subsidiary companies. Producer and any subsequent assign may freely assign this Agreement, in whole or in part, to any party provided that such party assumes and agrees in writing to keep and perform all of the executory obligations of Producer hereunder.

11. NAME AND LIKENESS: Producer shall have the right to use and permit others (including any exhibitor or sponsor of the Program or Series) to use Writer's name and likeness for the purpose of advertising and publicizing the Work, any Program based on the Work, and any of exhibitor's or sponsor's products and services, but not as an endorsement or testimonial.

12. PAY OR PLAY: The rights in this Paragraph shall be in addition to, and shall not in any way diminish or detract from, Producer's rights as otherwise set forth. Producer shall not be obligated to use Writer's services, nor use the results and product of Writers services, nor produce, release, distribute, exhibit, advertise, exploit or otherwise make use of the Program. Producer may at any time, without legal justification or excuse, elect not to use Writer's services. If Producer elects not to use Writer's services pursuant to this Paragraph, Writer shall be paid the Compensation set forth in Paragraph 5 (a) if Writer performs those services.

13. CREDIT:

(a) The writing credits shall read: "Story by _____," and "Written by _____," (or another name chosen by Writer), if a substantial amount of Writer's work is incorporated in the Picture. In determining whether Writer is awarded sole, shared or no writing credit, reference shall be made to the principles of the WGA credit arbitration rules. Although Producer is not a WGA signatory, to the extent possible, the principles of the WGA credit arbitration rules shall be followed by the parties. In the event of a credit dispute, the arbitrator of such a dispute shall follow the WGA credit rules to the extent they do not conflict with the rules of the American Arbitration Association.

(b) In the event that writer also directs the picture, writer shall receive an appropriate directing credit in accordance with the rules of the DGA. Although Producer is not a DGA signatory, and writer is not a DGA member, to the extent possible, the principles of the DGA credit rules shall be followed by the parties. In the event of a credit dispute, the arbitrator of such a dispute shall follow the DGA credit rules to the extent they do not conflict with the rules of the American Arbitration Association.

14. CONDITIONS AFFECTING OR RELATED TO COMPENSATION :

(a) Method of Payment: All compensation which shall become due to Writer shall be paid by Producer by check and sent to Writer at the address provided in the Notices and Payments provision of this Agreement.

(b) Governmental Limitation: No withholding, deduction, reduction or limitation of compensation by Producer which is required or authorized by law ("Governmental Limitation") shall be a breach by Producer or relieve Writer from Writer's obligations. Payment of compensation as permitted pursuant to the Governmental Limitation shall continue while such Governmental Limitation is in effect and shall be deemed to constitute full performance by Producer of its obligations respecting the payment of compensation. The foregoing notwithstanding, if at such time as the Governmental Limitation is no longer in effect there is compensation remaining unpaid to Writer, Producer shall cooperate with Writer in connection with the processing of any applications relative to the payment of such unpaid compensation and Producer shall pay such compensation to Writer at such time as Producer is legally permitted to do so.

(c) Garnishment/Attachment: If Producer shall be required, because of the service of any garnishment, attachment, writ of execution, or lien, or by the terms of any contract or assignment executed by Writer, to withhold, or to pay to any other Party all or any portion of the compensation due Writer, the withholding or payment of such compensation or any portion thereof in accordance with the requirements of any such attachment, garnishment, writ of execution, lien, contract or assignment shall not be construed as a breach by Producer.

(d) Overpayment/Offset: If Producer makes any overpayment to Writer for any reason or if Writer is indebted to Producer for any reason, Writer shall pay Producer such overpayment or indebtedness on demand, or at the election of Producer, Producer may deduct and retain for its own account an amount equal to all or any part of such overpayment or indebtedness from any sums that may be due or become due or payable by Producer to Writer or for the account of Writer and such deduction or retention shall not be construed as a breach by Producer.

15. ARBITRATION: Any controversy or claim arising out of or relating to this agreement or any breach thereof shall be settled by arbitration in accordance with the Rules of the American Arbitration Association; and judgment upon the award rendered by the arbitrators may be entered in any court having jurisdiction thereof. The prevailing party shall be entitled to reimbursement for costs and reasonable attorneys' fees.

Signed and agreed to by the undersigned as of _____.

_____

_____ on behalf of

_____ Productions
("Producer")

_____

("Writer")

Social Security #

DIRECTOR EMPLOYMENT

Director employment agreements share many provisions of writer employment agreements. Once again, the deal may be structured as direct employment or through a loan-out arrangement.

Directors are hired for the period of principal photography as well as the time needed beforehand to prepare for filming (pre-production) and time afterwards to supervise editing (post-production). The director may also work with the writer during development.

Often the director is hired on a flat fee basis that covers all these phases. Payments are made in installments with most of the fee paid during principal photography. A director is typically hired on an exclusive basis, preventing her from accepting outside employment and working on more than one film at a time.

The agreement is frequently a "pay or play" deal which means that if the studio does not use the director's services, or replaces her, the director is still entitled to fixed compensation. The director may also receive bonus, deferred, contingent and additional compensation, although these payments may not vest until and unless the person is entitled to a director credit.

Usually the director does not have the right of "final cut," which is the power to determine the composition of the final edited version of the picture. Studios may insist on reserving this right to protect their investment and make sure that the director does not create an artistic masterpiece that is a commercial flop. The agreement will also specify that the film be a certain length (e.g., within 90-120 minutes). Directors may be required to produce two versions of the film: one for theatrical release and another for television broadcast.

The director may have the right to select key personnel such as the Director of Photography, Production Manager and Editor. A veteran director with clout will have the power to hire certain cast and crew members without studio approval.

DIRECTOR EMPLOYMENT AGREEMENT

AGREEMENT

Agreement dated _____ between _____("Director") and _____ ("Production Company").

1. EMPLOYMENT: Production Company agrees to employ Director to perform and Director agrees to perform, upon the terms and conditions herein specified, directing services in connection with the Theatrical Motion Picture currently entitled _____ ("Picture").

2. TERM: The Term of this agreement shall commence on _____ and shall continue until the completion of all of Director's required services on the Picture.

3. SERVICES:

(a) Pre-Production: Director shall be available and undertake a location search on or about _____.

(b) Photography: Director's exclusive services for the Picture shall commence _____ weeks prior to the start of principal photography and shall be rendered exclusively after that until completion of all photography. The start date of principal photography shall be mutually approved by Production Company and Director. The scheduled start date of principal photography is _____.

(c) Post-Production: Director's post-production services shall be rendered on a non-exclusive but first-call basis, if Production Company so requires, in order to work during the post-production period with the editor until completion of the final corrected answer print. Director's other undertakings shall not interfere with director's post-production services hereunder.

(i) Cooperation with Editor: Director hereby warrants and agrees that Director will do nothing to hinder or delay the assemblage of film by the editor during the photography of the Picture so that the assembled sequences will be completed immediately following the completion of principal photography.

(ii) Post-Production Schedule: Attached hereto marked Exhibit "S" and by this reference incorporated herein is a schedule for the post-production work on the Picture which has been agreed to by Director and Production Company. Director agrees that this schedule will be followed by Director.

(iii) Final Cutting Authority: _____ is designated as the Production Company Executive with final cutting authority over the Picture. The foregoing shall be subject to applicable guild and union requirements, if any.

(d) Dailies: Production Company shall have the right to view the dailies during the production of the Picture, the rough cut and all subsequent cuts of the Picture.

(e) Television Cover Shots: Director shall furnish Production Company with protective cover shots necessary for the release of the Picture on television, based on network continuity standards in existence at the time of commencement of principal photography.

(f) Additional Post-Production Services: If, after the completion of principal photography, Production Company requires retakes, changes, dubbing, transparencies, added scenes, further photography, trailers, sound track, process shots or other language versions (herein collectively called "retakes, etc.") for the Picture, Director shall report to Production Company for such retakes, etc., at such place or places and on such consecutive or non-consecutive days as Production Company may designate, Subject to Director's professional availability. Director shall cooperate to make such services available to Production Company at the earliest possible date.

4. COMPENSATION: As full and complete consideration for Director's services and Director's undertakings hereunder and for all rights granted to Production Company hereunder, and subject to Director's full compliance with the terms and conditions of this Agreement, Production Company agrees to pay Director as follows:

(a) Fixed Compensation:

(i) The total sum of _____ payable:

(A) $_____ upon approval of the Budgeted Negative Cost for production of the Picture.

(B) $_____ prorated commencing ____ weeks prior to the start of principal photography of the Picture.

(C) $_____ payable in equal weekly installments over the scheduled period of principal photography.

(D) $_____ upon delivery of the director's cut.

(E) $_____ upon the completion of the final answer print of the Picture.

(ii) Flat Fee Basis: Production Company and Director hereby mutually acknowledge that the Fixed Compensation as hereinabove specified is a "flat fee" and Director shall not be entitled to any additional and/or so-called "overage" compensation for any services rendered by Director during the development, pre-production, production or post-production phases, or for additional post-production services rendered by Director. Without limiting the generality of the foregoing, no additional compensation shall be payable to Director under Clause 4(a)(i)(C) above if the actual principal photography period for the Picture exceeds the scheduled principal photography period, nor for any services rendered pursuant to Clause 3(f).

(b) Deferred Compensation: In addition to the Fixed Compensation payable under Clause 4(a), subject to the production and release of the Picture and subject to the performance of all obligations of Director hereunder, Director shall be entitled to receive the sum of _____ which shall be deferred and paid pro rata with all similar deferments of compensation payable _____ at the point just preceding the payment of percentage participations in the Net Profits of the Picture.

(c) Contingent Compensation: In addition to the Fixed Compensation payable under Clause 4(a), and any Deferred Compensation payable under Clause

4(b), subject to the production and release of the Picture and subject to the performance of Director's obligations hereunder Director shall be entitled to receive as Contingent Compensation an amount equal to _____ percent of the Net Profits of the Picture, if any.

(d) Net Profits Definition: Net Profits shall be computed, determined and paid in accordance with Exhibit ___ attached hereto and by this reference incorporated herein.

(e) Conditions Related to Compensation: Notwithstanding anything to the contrary contained in any of the above compensation provisions:

(i) Performance: No compensation shall accrue or become payable to Director during Director's inability, failure or refusal to perform the services contracted for herein according to the terms and conditions of this Agreement.

(ii) Pay or Play: Production Company shall not be obligated to use Director's services on the Picture, nor shall Production Company be obligated to produce, release, distribute, advertise, exploit or otherwise make use of the Picture; provided, however, that the full amount of the Fixed Compensation hereinabove specified shall be paid to Director should Production Company without legal justification or excuse (as provided elsewhere in this Agreement or by operation of law), elect not to utilize Director's services.

(f) Vesting: The Fixed Compensation and Contingent Compensation hereinabove specified shall be deemed fully vested if, notwithstanding the termination of Director's services due to Producer Disability or Director's incapacity or Director default, Director shall be entitled to receive "Directed by" credit pursuant to the Director's Guild of America Basic Agreement of 1973, as same may be amended from time to time ("Basic Agreement").

If the services of Director are terminated by Production Company due to Production Disability or Director's Incapacity or Director Default, as defined below, and Director is not entitled to receive credit pursuant to the Basic Agreement, then the Fixed Compensation shall vest and accrue in the same manner as set forth herein and the Contingent Compensation shall accrue and vest in the same ratio that the number of linear feet in the completed Picture as released, which was directed by Director, bears to the total number of linear feet in the completed Picture as released. Notwithstanding the foregoing, if principal photography has not commenced on the scheduled start date as set forth in Clause 3(b) hereof, then the total Fixed Compensation shall vest and accrue on the aforesaid scheduled start date and production of the Picture is thereafter terminated prior to completion of principal photography and/or delivery of the final answer print to Production Company, then that portion of the Fixed Compensation not theretofore accrued shall fully vest and accrue on the date of such termination. If Production Company terminates this Agreement by reason of a Director Default, notwithstanding any vesting of Fixed Compensation and/or Contingent Compensation as set forth above, such vesting shall be subject to any and all the rights accorded to Production Company at law and in equity.

(g) Mitigation: If Production Company elects to exercise its pay or play right as set forth above and/or fails to produce the Picture, Director shall have no obligation to mitigate damages.

5. CREDITS:

(a) Credit: Subject to the production and release of the Picture and provided Director performs his material obligations hereunder, then Production Company shall accord Director credit in connection with the Picture in accordance with the requirements of the Directors Guild of America, Inc. Basic Agreement of 1973 immediately after the main title which shall be fifty percent (50%) of the size of the title, on a separate card.

(b) Artwork Title Exception: If both a regular (or repeat) title and an artwork title are used, the position and percentage requirements above, as they relate to the title of the Picture, shall relate to the regular (or repeat) title. If only an artwork title is used, the percentage requirements above, as they relate to the title, shall be not less than 15 percent (15%) of the average size of the letters used in the artwork title.

(c) Credit Limitation: Production Company agrees that no other individual and/or entity (other than members of the cast receiving "starring" billing before or after the title of the Picture or the company distributing and/or financing the Picture) shall receive credit larger than that used to display the credit accorded to Director.

(d) Inadvertent Non-Compliance: No casual or inadvertent failure to comply with the provisions of this Paragraph shall be deemed to be a breach of this Agreement by Production Company. Director hereby recognizes and confirms that in the event of a failure or omission by Production Company constituting a breach of Production Company obligations under this Paragraph, the damages, if any, caused Director by Production Company are not irreparable or sufficient to entitle Director to injunctive or other equitable relief. Consequently, Director's rights and remedies hereunder shall be limited to the right, if any, to obtain damages at law and Director shall have no right in such event to rescind this Agreement or any of the rights assigned to Production Company hereunder or to enjoin or restrain the distribution or exhibition of the Picture. Production Company agrees to advise its assignees and licensees of the credit requirements herein. If Production Company shall learn of such failure of a third party to give such credit, Production Company shall notify such party of s;such failure and Production Company may, but shall not be obligated to, 'take action to cause such party to prospectively cure such failure.

6. TRANSPORTATION AND EXPENSES: If, at Production Company's request, Director's services are required to be rendered on location more than (e.g., fifty) miles from the City of Los Angeles, Production Company shall furnish Director first-class round trip transportation for (e.g., one) and Production Company shall reimburse Director for Director's living expenses in the amount of $_____ per week. If Director can demonstrate to Production Company's satisfaction that said living expense allowance is insufficient for any particular location, Production Company shall, at such time, give good faith consideration to an increase. For any period week which is less than one (1) week, said reimbursement shall be upon the pro rata basis that one (1) day is equal to one-seventh (1/7) of one (1) week. Director shall furnish Production Company with itemized detailed accountings of such living expenses, including vouchers, bills, receipts and statements satisfactory to meet the requirements and regulations of the Internal Revenue Service.

7. PERFORMANCE STANDARDS: Except as specifically provided to the contrary herein, during the Term of this Agreement, Director shall render his directing

services exclusively to Production Company and, to such extent as Production Company may require, in otherwise assisting in the production of the Picture. Said services shall be rendered either alone or in collaboration with another or other artists in such manner as Production Company may direct, pursuant to the instructions, controls and schedules established by Production Company, and at the times, places and in the manner required by Production Company. Such manners, instructions, directions, and controls shall be exercised by Production Company in accordance with standards of reasonableness and also with what is customary practice in the Motion Picture industry. Such services shall be rendered in an artistic, conscientious, efficient and punctual manner, to the best of Director's ability and with full regard to the careful, efficient, economical and expeditious production of the Picture within the budget and shooting schedule established by Production Company immediately prior to the commencement of principal photography, it being further understood that the production of motion pictures by Production Company involves matters of discretion to be exercised by Production Company with respect to art and taste, and Director's services and the manner of rendition thereof is to be governed entirely by Production Company.

8. UNIQUE SERVICES: Except as specifically provided to the contrary hereinabove, Director's services shall be rendered exclusively to Production Company until expiration of the Term of this Agreement, it being mutually understood that said services are extraordinary, unique and not replaceable, and that there is no adequate remedy at law for breach of this contract by Director, and that Production Company, in the event of such breach by Director, shall be entitled to equitable relief by way of injunction or otherwise to prevent default by Director.

9. RESULTS AND PROCEEDS OF SERVICES: Production Company shall be entitled to and shall solely and exclusively own, in addition to Director's services hereunder, all results and proceeds thereof (including but not limited to all rights, throughout the world, of copyright, trademark, patent, production, manufacture, recordation, reproduction, transcription, performance, broadcast and exhibition of any art or method now known or hereafter devised, including radio broadcasting, theatrical and nontheatrical exhibition, and exhibition by the medium of television or otherwise), whether such results and proceeds consist of literary, dramatic, musical, motion picture, mechanical or any other forms of works, themes, ideas, compositions, creations or production, together with the rights generally known in the field of literary and musical endeavor as the "moral rights of authors" in and/or to any musical and/or literary proceeds of Director's services, including but not limited to the right to add to, subtract from, arrange, revise, adapt, rearrange, make variations of the property, and to translate the same into any and all languages, change the sequence, change the characters and the descriptions thereof contained in the property, change the title of the same, [record and photocopy the same with or without sound (including spoken words, dialogue and music synchronously recorded), use this title or any of its components in connection with works or motion pictures wholly or partially independent of said property, and to use all or any part of the property in new versions, adaptations and sequels in any and all languages, and to obtain copyright therein throughout the world, and Director does assign and transfer to Production Company all the foregoing without reservation, condition, or limitations, and no right of any kind, nature, or description is reserved by Director. If Production Company shall desire separate assignments or other documents to implement the foregoing, Director shall execute the same upon Production Company's request, and if Director fails or refuses to execute and deliver any such separate assignments or other documents, Production Company shall have and is granted the right and authority to execute the same in Director's name and as Director's attorney-in-fact. Production Company shall supply Director with a copy of any document so executed.

10. WARRANTIES RELATED TO CREATED MATERIAL: Director hereby warrants and agrees that all material, works, writings, idea, "gags" or dialogue written, composed, prepared, submitted or interpolated by; Director in connection with the Picture or its preparation or production, shall be wholly original with Director and shall not be copied in whole or in part from any other work, except that submitted to Director by Production Company as a basis for such material. Director further warrants that neither the said material nor any part thereof will, to the best of Director's knowledge, violate the rights of privacy or constitute a libel or slander against any person, firm, or corporation, and that the material will not infringe upon the copyright, literary, dramatic or photoplay rights of any person. Director further warrants and agrees to hold Production Company and its successors, licensees, and assigns harmless against all liability or loss which they or any of them may suffer by reason of the breach of any of the terms or warranties of this Clause.

11. VESTING OF PRODUCTION COMPANY'S RIGHTS: All rights granted or agreed to be granted to Production Company hereunder shall vest in Production Company immediately and shall remain so vested whether this Agreement expires in normal course or is terminated for any cause or reason.

12. NAME AND LIKENESS: Production Company shall always have the right to use and display Director's name and likeness for advertising, publicizing, and exploiting the picture. However, such advertising may not include the direct endorsement of any product (other than the Picture) without Directors's consent. Exhibition, advertising, publicizing or exploiting the Picture by any media, even though a part of or in connection with a product or a commercially sponsored program, shall not be deemed an endorsement of any nature.d

13. PUBLICITY RESTRICTIONS: Director shall not, individually or by means of press agents or publicity or advertising agencies or others employed or paid by Director or otherwise, circulate, publish or otherwise disseminate any news stories or articles, books or other publicity containing Director's name relating to Director's employment by Production Company, the subject matter of this contract, the Picture or the services to be rendered by Director or others in connection with the Picture unless first approved by Production Company. Director shall not transfer any right, privilege, title, or interest in or to any of the things above specified, nor shall Director authorize or willingly permit infringement upon the exclusive rights granted to Production Company, and Director authorizes Production Company, at Production Company's expense, in Director's name or otherwise, to institute any proper legal proceedings to prevent any infringement.

14. FORCE MAJEURE:

(a) Suspension: If, by reason of fire, earthquake, labor dispute or strike, act of God or public enemy, any municipal ordinance, any state or federal law, governmental order or regulation, or other cause beyond Production Company's control which would excuse Production Company's performance as a matter of law, Production Company is prevented from or hampered in the production of the Picture, or if, by reason of the closing of substantially all theaters in the

United States, which would excuse Production Company's performance as a matter of law Production Company's production of the Picture is postponed or suspended, or if, by reason of any of the aforesaid contingencies or any other cause or occurrence not within Production Company's control, including but not limited to the death, illness or incapability of any principal member of the cast of the Picture, the preparation or production of the Picture is interrupted or delayed and/or, if Production Company's normal business operations are interrupted or otherwise interfered with by virtue of any disruptive events which are beyond Production Company's control ("Production Company Disability"), then Production Company may postpone the commencement of or suspend the rendition of services by Director and the running of time hereunder for such time as the Production Company Disability shall continue; and no compensation shall accrue or become payable to Director hereunder during the period of such suspension. Such suspension shall end upon the cessation of the cause thereof.

(b) Termination:

(i) Production Company Termination Right: If a Production Company Disability continues for a period in excess of six (6) weeks, Production Company shall have the right to terminate this Agreement upon written notice to Director.

(ii) Director's Termination Right: If a Production Company Disability results in compensation being suspended hereunder for a period in excess of six (6) weeks, Director shall have the right to terminate this Agreement upon written notice to Production Company.

(iii) Production Company Re-Establishment Right: Despite Director's election to terminate this Agreement, within _____ days after Production Company's actual receipt of such written notice from Director, Production Company shall have the right to elect to re-establish the operation of this Agreement by giving Director written notice and resuming payment of compensation.

15. DIRECTOR'S INCAPACITY:

(a) Effect of Director's Incapacity: If, by reason of mental or physical disability, Director is incapacitated from performing or complying with any of the terms of conditions hereof ("Director's Incapacity") for a consecutive period in excess of seven (7) days or aggregate period in excess of ten (10) days, then Production Company shall have the right to terminate this Agreement upon written notice to Director.

(b) Right of Examination: If any claim of mental or physical disability is made by Director or on Director's behalf, Production Company shall have the right to have Director examined by such physicians as Production Company may designate. Director's physician may be present at such examination but shall not interfere therewith. Any tests performed on Director shall be related to and customary for the treatment, diagnosis or examination to be performed in connection with Director's claim.

16. DIRECTOR'S DEFAULT: If Director fails or refuses to perform or comply with any of the material terms or conditions hereof (other than by reason of Director's Incapacity) ("Director's Default"), then Production Company may terminate this Agreement upon written notice to Director. Director's Default shall not include any failure or refusal of Director to perform or comply with the material terms of this Agreement due to a breach or action by Production Company which makes the performance by Director of his services impossible. Prior to termination of this Agreement by Production Company based upon Director's Default, Production Company shall notify Director specifying the nature of the Director's Default and Director shall have a period of 48 hours to cure the Director Default. If the Director Default is not cured within said 48 hour period, Production Company may terminate this Agreement forthwith.

17. EFFECT OF TERMINATION: Termination of this Agreement, whether by lapse of time, mutual consent, operation of law, exercise of a right of termination or otherwise, shall:

(a) Terminate Production Company's obligation to pay Director any further compensation. Nevertheless, if the termination is not for Director's Default, Production Company shall pay Director any compensation due and unpaid prior to the termination, and;

(b) Production Company shall not be deemed to have waived any other rights it may have or alter Production Company's rights or any of Director's agreements or warranties relating to the rendition of Director's services prior to termination.

18. PRODUCTION COMPANY RIGHT TO SUSPEND: In the event of Director's Incapacity or Director's Default, Production Company may upon written notice postpone the commencement of or suspend the rendition of services by Director and the running of time hereunder so long as any Director's Disability or Director's Default shall continue; and no compensation shall accrue or become payable to Director during the period of such suspension.

(a) Director's Right to Cure: Any Director's Incapacity or Director's Default shall be deemed to continue until Production Company's receipt of written notice from Director specifying that Director is ready, willing and able to perform the services required hereunder; provided that any such notice from Director to Production Company shall not preclude Production Company from exercising any rights or remedies Production Company may have hereunder or at law or in equity by reason of Director's Incapacity or Director's Default.

(b) Alternative Services Restricted: During any period of suspension hereunder, Director shall not render services for any person, firm or corporation other than Production Company. However, Director shall have the right to render services to third parties during any period of suspension based upon a Production Company Disability, subject, however, to Production Company's right to require Director to resume the rendition of services hereunder upon 24 hours prior notice.

(c) Production Company Right to Extend: If Production Company elects to suspend the rendition of services by Director as herein specified, then Production Company shall have the right (exercisable at any time) to extend the period of services of Director hereunder for a period equal to the period of such suspension.

(d) Additional Services: If Production Company shall have paid compensation to Director during any period of Director's Incapacity or Director's Default, then Production Company shall have the right (exercisable at any time) to require Director to render services hereunder without compensation for a period equal to the period for which Production Company shall have paid compensation to Director during such Director's Incapacity or Director's Default.

19. FURTHER WARRANTIES: Director hereby warrants that Director is not under any obligation or disability, created by law or otherwise, which would in any manner or to any extent prevent or restrict Director from entering into and fully performing this Agreement; Director warrants that Director has not entered into any agreement or commitment that would prevent Director's fulfilling Director's commitments with Production Company hereunder and that Director will not enter into any such agreement or commitment without Production Company's specific approval and Director hereby accepts the obligation hereunder and agrees to devote Director's entire time and attention and best talents and abilities exclusively to Production Company as specified herein, and to observe and to be governed by the rules of conduct established by Production Company for the conduct of its employees.

(a) Indemnity: Director shall at all times indemnify Production Company, its successors, assigns and licensees, from and against any and all costs, expenses, losses, damages, judgments and attorneys' fees arising out of or connected with or resulting from any claims, demands or causes of action by any person or entity which is inconsistent with any of Director's representations, warranties or agreements hereunder. Director will reimburse Production Company on demand for any payment made by Production Company at any time after the date hereof in respect of any liability, loss, damage, cost or expense to which the foregoing indemnity relates.

20. REMEDIES: All remedies accorded herein or otherwise available to either Production Company or Director shall be cumulative, and no one such remedy shall be exclusive of any other. Without waiving any rights or remedies under this Agreement or otherwise, Production Company may from time to time recover, by action, any damages arising out of any breach of this Agreement by Director, and may institute and maintain subsequent actions for additional damages which may arise from the same or other breaches. The commencement or maintenance of any such action or actions by Production Company shall not constitute an election on Production Company's part to terminate this Agreement nor constitute or result in termination of Director's services hereunder unless Production Company shall expressly so elect by written notice to Director. The pursuit by either Production Company or Director of any remedy under this Agreement or otherwise shall not be deemed to waive any other or different remedy which may be available under this Agreement or otherwise, either at law or in equity.

21. INSURANCE:

(a) Production Company may secure life, health, accident, cast, or other insurance covering Director, the cost of which shall be included as a Direct Charge of the Picture. Such insurance shall be for Production Company's sole benefit and Production Company shall be the beneficiary thereof, and Director shall have no interest in the proceeds thereof. Director shall assist in procuring such insurance by submitting to required examinations and tests and by preparing, signing, and delivering such applications and other documents as may be reasonably required. Director shall, to the best of Director's ability, observe all terms and conditions of such insurance of which Production Company notifies Director as necessary for continuing such insurance in effect.

(b) If Production Company is unable to obtain pre-production or cast insurance covering Director at prevailing standard rates and without any exclusions, restrictions, conditions, or exceptions of any kind, Director shall have the right to pay any premium in excess of the prevailing standard rate in order for Production Company to obtain such insurance. If Director fails, refuses to pay such excess premium, or if, Production Company having obtained such insurance, Director fails to observe all terms and conditions necessary to maintain such insurance in effect, Production Company shall have the right to terminate this Agreement without any obligation to Director by giving Director written notice of termination.

22. EMPLOYMENT OF OTHERS: Director agrees not to employ any person to serve in any capacity, nor contract for the purchase or renting of any article or material, nor make any agreement committing Production Company to pay any sum of money for any reason whatsoever in connection with the Picture or services to be rendered by Director hereunder or otherwise, without written approval first being asked and obtained from Production Company.

23. ASSIGNMENT: This Agreement, at the election of Production Company, shall inure to the benefit of Production Company's administrators, successors, assigns, licensees, grantees, and associated, affiliated and subsidiary companies, and Director agrees that Production Company and any subsequent assignee may freely assign this Agreement and grant its rights hereunder, in whole or in part, to any person, firm or corporation, provided that such person, firm or corporation assumes and agrees in writing to keep and perform all of the executory obligations of Production Company hereunder.

24. ARBITRATION: Any controversy or claim arising out of or relating to this agreement or any breach thereof shall be settled by arbitration in accordance with the Rules of the American Arbitration Association; and judgment upon the award rendered by the arbitrators may be entered in any court having jurisdiction thereof. The prevailing party shall be entitled to reimbursement for costs and reasonable attorneys' fees.

Signed and agreed to by the undersigned as of _____199_.

_____
John Doe on behalf of
Big Productions Inc.
("Production Company")

_____
Henry Smith
("Director")

ACTOR EMPLOYMENT

Actor employment agreements contain many provisions found in writer and director agreements. Agreements often refer to the employer as the "Producer" and the employee as the "Player."

The actor's employment agreement will grant the producer the right to use the name and likeness of the actor in the film. The producer may obtain the right to use the actor's name and likeness for merchandising, in which case the actor will be entitled to a percentage participation of the revenues received by the producer.

Typically the producer will supply any costumes required for a role. If a contemporary story is being filmed, the producer may ask the player to provide his own clothing. In this case, the actor should receive a cleaning allowance.

Employment of child actors raises special concerns because minors can repudiate contracts.[1] A producer cannot enforce a disaffirmed contract. However, the law provides that when a minor is employed as an entertainer, he cannot disaffirm a contract if that contract has been approved by the Superior Court beforehand. The minor or the employer must petition the Superior Court to determine if the contract is fair to the minor. The court may require that part of the minor's earnings be set aside in a trust fund for him.

In hiring a minor, the employer must also comply with provisions of the California Labor Code and regulations of the Labor Commission. For example, an employer must obtain a work permit from the Division of Labor Standards Enforcement.[2] Minors cannot perform work that is hazardous or detrimental to their health, safety, morals or education.[3]

Actor employment agreements may contain a "morals" clause which requires the actor to conduct himself so as not to violate public conventions or subject himself to public hatred, contempt or ridicule. If the actor violates this clause, the employer has the right to terminate the agreement.

The employer may want to purchase life, accident or health insurance covering the actor. The actor is typically required to submit to a medical examination to obtain this coverage. If the employer is unable to obtain insurance at standard rates, the employer may have the right to terminate the agreement. If the actor fails the medical exam or insurance coverage is denied, the employer may be required to give prompt notice to the actor.

Negotiators sometimes try to resolve issues by agreeing to a "favored nations" clause. Such a provision guarantees that no other actor on the picture will obtain more advantageous terms. If another actor negotiates a better deal, there is an automatic upgrade for actors who have a favored nations clause in their contracts. Such a clause makes sense for a fledgling actor. If an actor with more clout gets a better deal, the fledgling actor will benefit.

A producer who hires an actor for a television series will want to have an

---

[1] See California Civil Code § 35.

[2] California Administrative Code Title 8, §11753.

[3] California Administrative Code, Title 8, §11751.

option on that actor's services for five to seven years. The actor may have to turn down attractive offers that conflict with this commitment. Before an actor enters an exclusive agreement he needs to consider whether it will restrict him from performing in such related fields as theatrical motion pictures, the legitimate stage and commercials.

When a novice signs a series deal he has little bargaining power. The agreement will set the amount of compensation due in subsequent years. If the series becomes a hit, and the actor becomes a star, he may chafe under the terms of an agreement that he now considers unfair. With his newfound clout he may try to renegotiate the deal. Sometimes he will refuse to work or become uncooperative or "sick" to pressure the employer to sweeten the deal. The employer may threaten to sue. Often a compromise is reached as neither party wants to kill the goose that lays the golden eggs.

What can the employer do if the actor refuses to perform under the contract? Certainly the employer can sue for money damages to compensate the employer for any loss incurred as a result of a wrongful breach. However, the actor may not have enough assets to satisfy any damages awarded the employer.

The employer cannot get a court order forcing the employee to perform because that would be form of involuntary servitude prohibited by the Constitution. However, if the services are of a special, unique, extraordinary or intellectual character so that the loss of these services cannot be reasonably or adequately compensated by money, a court may enjoin the employee from working for others during the term of the agreement. This is often referred to as a "negative injunction."

Note that under California Labor Code personal service contracts cannot exceed seven years (Cal. Labor Code § 2855) and injunctions will not be granted to enforce contracts unless the agreement is in writing and the minimum compensation is not less than six thousand dollars a year [Cal. Civil Code 3423, Cal. Code of Civil Procedure 526(5).] In New York personal services contracts have been enforced with court orders when the performer's services are special, unique or extraordinary and the terms are sufficiently definite.

CONTRACTS
FOR THE
FILM AND
TELEVISION
INDUSTRY

100

ACTOR EMPLOYMENT AGREEMENT
(SAG WEEKLY THEATRICAL)

Continuous Employment
Weekly Basis
Weekly Salary

One WeekMinimum Employment

THIS AGREEMENT is made this _____ day of_____, 199___, between _____, hereafter called "Producer", and _____, hereafter called "Player."

1. PHOTOPLAY, ROLE, SALARY AND GUARANTEE: Producer hereby engages Player to render services as such in the role of _____, in a photoplay, the working title of which is now_____, at the salary of $_____ Dollars per "studio week" (Schedule B Players must receive an additional overtime payment of four (4) hours at straight time rate for each overnight location Saturday.) Player accepts such engagement upon the terms herein specified. Producer guarantees that it will furnish Player not less than _____ weeks employment (if this blank is not filled in, the guarantee shall be one week). Player shall be paid pro rata for each additional day beyond guarantee until dismissal.

2. TERM: The term of employment hereunder shall begin on or about _____, and shall continue thereafter until the completion of the photography and recordation of said role.

3. BASIC CONTRACT: All provisions of the collective bargaining agreement between Screen Actors Guild, Inc. and Producer, relating to theatrical motion pictures, which are applicable to the employment of the Player hereunder, shall be deemed incorporated herein.

4. PLAYER'S ADDRESS: All notices which the Producer is required or may desire to give to the Player may be given either by mailing the same addressed to the Player at _____, or such notice may be given to the Player personally, either orally or in writing.

5. PLAYER'S TELEPHONE: The Player must keep the Producer's casting office or the assistant director of said photoplay advised as to where the Player may be reached by telephone without unreasonable delay. The current telephone number of the Player is _____.

6. MOTION PICTURE RELIEF FUND: The Player does not hereby authorize the Producer to deduct from the compensation hereinabove specified an amount equal to _____ per cent of each installment of compensation due the Player hereunder, and to pay the amount so deducted to the Motion Picture and Television Relief Fund of America, Inc.

7. FURNISHING OF WARDROBE: The Player agrees to furnish all modern wardrobe and wearing apparel reasonably necessary for the portrayal of said role; it being agreed, however, that should so-called "character" or "period" costumes be required, the Producer shall supply the same. When Player furnishes any wardrobe, Player shall receive the cleaning allowance and reimbursement, if any, specified in the basic contract.

Number of outfits furnished by Player:

_____ @ $_____

(formal)   _____ @ $_____

8. ARBITRATION OF DISPUTES: Should any dispute or controversy arise between the parties hereto with reference to this contract, or the employment herein provided for, such dispute or controversy shall be settled and determined by conciliation and arbitration in accordance with the conciliation and arbitration provisions of the collective bargaining agreement between the Producer and Screen Actors Guild relating to theatrical motion pictures, and such provisions are hereby referred to and by such reference incorporated herein and made a part of this Agreement with the same effect as though the same were set forth herein in detail.

9. NEXT STARTING DATE: The starting date of Player's next engagement is:_____.

10. The Player may not waive any provision of this contract without the written consent of the Screen Actors Guild, Inc.

11. Producer makes the material representation that either it is presently a signatory to the Screen Actors Guild collective bargaining agreement covering the employment contracted for herein, or, that the above-referred-to photoplay is covered by such collective bargaining agreement under the Independent Production provisions of the General Provisions of the Producer-Screen Actors Guild Codified Basic Agreement of 1983 as the same may be supplemented and/or amended.

12. Producer shall have the exclusive right to make one or more promotional films of thirty (30) minutes or less and to utilize the results and proceeds of Player's services therein upon all of the terms and provisions set forth in the SAG Agreement. Player agrees to render such services for said promotional films during the term of his employment hereunder as Producer may request and Player further agrees to use by Producer of film clips and behind-the-scenes shots in which Player appears in such promotional films. Provided Player appears therein, Producer shall pay to Player the sum specified by the SAG Agreement of _____ within ten (10) days after the first use of each such promotional film on television or before a paying audience.

13. Producer shall have the exclusive right to use and to license the use of Player's name, sobriquet, photograph, likeness, voice and/or caricature and shall have the right to simulate Player's voice, signature and appearance by any means in and in connection with the film and the advertising, publicizing, exhibition, and/or other exploitation thereof in any manner and by any means and in connection with commercial advertising and publicity tie-ups.

14. Producer is also granted the further exclusive right and license, but only in connection with the role portrayed by Player in the film to use and to license the use of Player's name, sobriquet, photograph, likeness, caricature and/or signature (collectively referred to herein as "name and likeness") in and in connection with any merchandising and/or publishing undertakings. In consideration therefore, Producer shall pay Player a pro rata share (payable among all players whose name, etc. is used) of two-and-a-half percent (2$\frac{1}{2}$%) of the gross monies actually derived by Producer after deducting therefrom a distribution fee

CONTRACTS
FOR THE
FILM AND
TELEVISION
INDUSTRY

102

of fifty percent (50%) and a sum equal to all Producer's actual out-of-pocket expenses in connection therewith, for the use of such name or likeness on merchandising and publishing items which utilize Player's name and likeness, other than in a listing of cast credits.

15. Producer is also granted the further and exclusive right to use and to license the use of and to advertise and publicize the use of Player's voice from the soundtrack of the film on commercial phonograph records and albums and the exclusive right to use Player's name and likeness on jackets and labels of such commercial phonograph records and albums. If Producer issues or authorizes the issuance of such record or album using Player's voice, Producer shall pay to Player a sum equal to applicable AFTRA scale.

16. EMPLOYMENT ELIGIBILITY: All of Production Company's obligation herein are expressly conditioned upon Performer's completion, to Production Company's satisfaction, of the I-9 form (Employee Eligibility Verification Form), and upon Performer's submission to Production Company of original documents satisfactory to demonstrate to Production Company Performer's employment eligibility.

IN WITNESS WHEREOF, the parties have executed this agreement on the day and year first above written.

Producer_____

By_____

Player_____

Social Security No._____

ACTOR EMPLOYMENT AGREEMENT
(LOW-BUDGET, NON-UNION DAY PLAYER)[1]

THIS AGREEMENT is made and entered into as of the _____ day of_____, 1993, by and between Big Deal Entertainment, Inc., a California corporation, (hereinafter "Producer"), and _____ (hereinafter "Player").

    A. Producer intends to produce a theatrical motion picture (hereinafter the "Picture") based upon that certain screenplay tentatively entitled "_____" (hereinafter the "Screenplay") which Picture is intended for initial theatrical exhibition.

    B. Producer wishes to utilize the services of Player in connection with the Picture upon the terms and conditions herein contained.

    ACCORDINGLY, IT IS AGREED AS FOLLOWS:

1. PHOTOPLAY, ROLE, SALARY AND GUARANTEE: Producer hereby engages Player to render services as such in the role of _____, in the screenplay, at the salary of $_____ dollars per day. Player accepts such engagement upon the terms herein specified. Producer guarantees that it will furnish Player not less than _____ day's employment.

2. TERM: The term of employment hereunder shall begin on or about _____, 199_ (the "Start Date") and continue until _____, 199_, or until the completion of the photography and recordation of said role.

3. PLAYER'S ADDRESS: All notices which the Producer is required or may desire to give to the Player may be given either by mailing the same addressed to the Player at the address listed at the end of this agreement, or such notice may be given to the Player personally, either orally or in writing.

4. PLAYER'S TELEPHONE: The Player must keep the Producer's casting office or the assistant director of said photoplay advised as to where the Player may be reached by telephone without unreasonable delay. The current telephone number of the Player is listed at the end of this agreement.

5. FURNISHING OF WARDROBE: The Player agrees to furnish all modern wardrobe and wearing apparel reasonably necessary for the portrayal of said role; it being agreed, however, that should so-called "character" or "period" costumes be required, the Producer shall supply the same. When Player furnishes any wardrobe, Player shall receive a reasonable cleaning allowance and reimbursement for any soiled or damaged clothes.

Number of outfits furnished by Player:

_____ @ $_____

_____ @ $_____

6. NEXT STARTING DATE: The starting date of Player's next engagement is:_____.

---

[1] This contract is less favorable to the Actor then the preceding SAG contract.

CONTRACTS
FOR THE
FILM AND
TELEVISION
INDUSTRY

104

7. NON-UNION PICTURE: Producer makes the material representation that it is not a signatory to the Screen Actors Guild collective bargaining agreement or any other union or guild agreement. Player warrants that Player is not a member of any union or guild, memberships in which would prevent Player from working in this picture.

8. PROMOTIONAL FILM: Producer shall have the exclusive right to make one or more promotional films of thirty (30) minutes or less and to utilize the results and proceeds of Player's services therein. Player agrees to render such services for said promotional films during the term of his employment hereunder as Producer may request and Player further agrees to use by Producer of film clips and behind-the-scenes shots in which Player appears in such promotional films. Provided Player appears therein, Producer shall pay to Player the sum of one hundred dollars ($100) within ten (10) days after the first use of each such promotional film on television or before a paying audience.

9. NAME AND LIKENESS: Producer shall have the exclusive right to use and to license the use of Player's name, sobriquet, photograph, likeness, voice and/ or caricature and shall have the right to simulate Player's voice, signature and appearance by any means in and in connection with the film and the advertising, publicizing, exhibition, and/or other exploitation thereof in any manner and by any means and in connection with commercial advertising and publicity tie-ups.

10. MERCHANDISING: Producer is also granted the further exclusive right and license, but only in connection with the role portrayed by Player in the film to use and to license the use of Player's name, sobriquet, photograph, likeness, caricature and/or signature (collectively referred to herein as "name and likeness") in and in connection with any merchandising and/or publishing undertakings. In consideration therefore, Producer shall pay Player a pro rata share (payable among all players whose name, etc. is used) of two-and-a-half percent (2½%) of the gross monies actually derived by Producer after deducting therefrom a distribution fee of fifty percent (50%) thereof and a sum equal to all Producer's actual out-of-pocket expenses in connection therewith, for the use of such name or likeness on merchandising and publishing items which utilize Player's name and likeness, other than in a listing of cast credits.

11. TRAVEL EXPENSES: Any right of Player to transportation and expenses pursuant to this Agreement shall be effective when and only when Player is required by Producer to render services more than seventy-five (75) miles from Player's principal place of residence. Any weekly expense allowance provided Employee under this Agreement shall be prorated at one-seventh (1/7th) thereof per day. Player shall be reimbursed at the rate of _____ per mile for use of Player's car to travel to distant locations.

12. INCLUSIVE PAYMENTS: All payments to Player hereunder shall be deemed to be equitable and inclusive remuneration for all services rendered by Player in connection with the Picture and to be paid by way of a complete buy-out of all rights granted to Producer hereunder and no further sums shall be payable to Player by Producer by reason of the exploitation of the Picture and all results and proceeds of Player's services hereunder in any and all media throughout the universe pursuant to any collective bargaining agreement, if any, or otherwise, by way of residuals, repeat fees, pension contributions, or any other monies whatsoever.

13. ARBITRATION: Any controversy or claim arising out of or relating to this agreement or any breach thereof shall be settled by arbitration in accordance with the Rules of the American Arbitration Association; and judgment upon the award rendered by the arbitrators may be entered in any court having jurisdiction thereof. The prevailing party shall be entitled to reimbursement for costs and reasonable attorney's fees. The determination of the arbitrator in such proceeding shall be final, binding and non-appealable.

14. EMPLOYMENT ELIGIBILITY: All of Production Producer's obligation herein are expressly conditioned upon Performer's completion, to Production Producer's satisfaction, of the I-9 form (Employee Eligibility Verification Form), and upon Performer's submission to Production Producer of original documents satisfactory to demonstrate to Production Producer Performer's employment eligibility.

IN WITNESS WHEREOF, the parties have executed this agreement on the day and year first above written.

AGREED TO AND ACCEPTED:

_____ (signature)

_____ (print name),
"Player"

Player address: _____

Player Phone number: _____

Player Social Security #_____

AGREED TO AND ACCEPTED:

Big Deal Entertainment, Inc.,

By:_____
   Pat Producer, its President

CONTRACTS
FOR THE
FILM AND
TELEVISION
INDUSTRY

106

RIDER TO DAY PLAYER AGREEMENT

1. SERVICES/TERM: Producer engages Player as an actor in the Role set forth in the Principal Agreement and shall cause Player to render all services customarily rendered by actors in feature-length motion pictures at such times and places designated by Producer and in full compliance with Producer's instructions in all matters. Without limiting the foregoing, Player's services shall be in accordance with the following:

(a) Start Date: Principal Photography of the Picture shall commence on or about _____, 1993 but no later than _____, 1993. The Start Date shall be automatically extended without notice for a period equal to the duration of any default, disability and/or force majeure (as such terms are defined below and regardless of whether Player's services are suspended therefore), or due to any location requirements, director and/or cast availability, weather conditions, and/or other similar contingencies.

(b) Exclusivity: Player's services hereunder shall be non-exclusive first priority during the Pre-Production, exclusive during Production Periods, non-exclusive, but on a first-priority basis, during the Post-Production Period.

(c) Retakes and Other Additional Services: During and after the Term, Player shall render such services as Producer may desire in making retakes, added scenes, transparencies, closeups, sound track (including dubbing and looping), process shots, trick shots and trailers for changes in and foreign versions of the Picture. Compensation for such additional services shall be payable pursuant to Paragraph 1 of the principal agreement; provided, however, that no compensation shall be payable for such additional services to the extent they are rendered during any period for which Producer is otherwise obligated to pay or has paid Player compensation, or its entitled to Player's services without compensation.

(d) Nights, Weekends, Holidays, Work Time: No increased or additional compensation shall accrue or be payable to Player for services rendered by Player at night or on weekends or holidays, or after the expiration of any number of hours of service in any period.

2. CREDIT: There shall be no obligation to accord Player credit in paid advertising and/or publicity, although Producer may from time to time elect, in its sole discretion, to accord Player such credit. Producer shall accord Player customary shared screen credit.

3. RIGHTS: Player grants, and Producer shall have, the perpetual and universal right to photograph and re-photograph Player (still and moving) and to record and re-record, double and dub Player's voice and performances, by any present or future methods or means and to use and authorize others to use Player's name, voice and likeness for and in connection with the Picture, the soundtrack (including a soundtrack album), trailers, and documentary and/or "making of" pictures, and all advertising (including Player's name and likeness on sleeves, jackets and other packaging for soundtrack albums, video cassettes, videodiscs, written publications and the like), merchandising, commercial tie-ups, publicity, and other means of exploitation of any and all rights pertaining to the Picture and any element thereof. Producer shall own all results and proceeds of Player's services hereunder, including the copyrights thereof, and as such owner shall have the right (among all other rights of ownership): (i) to include such results and proceeds in the Picture and in advertising and publicity relating to the Picture, (ii) to reproduce such results and proceeds by any present or future means, (iii) to combine such results and proceeds with photographs and recordings made by others for use in the Picture, (iv) to exhibit and perform such results and proceeds in theaters, on the radio and television, and in or by any other present or future media, for profit and otherwise, and for commercial or non-commercial purposes and purposes of trade, and (v) to license and assign its rights to any other person or producer. Without in any way limiting the foregoing, the results and proceeds of Player's services hereunder include any and all material, words, writings, ideas, "gags," dialogue, melody and lyrics composed, submitted or interpolated by Player in connection with the preparation or production of the Picture (hereinafter referred to as "material"). All said material, the copyright therein, and all renewals, extensions or reversions of copyright now or hereafter provided, shall automatically become the property of Producer, which shall be deemed the author thereof, it being agreed and acknowledged that all of the results and proceeds of Player's services hereunder are a specially ordered and commissioned "work made for hire" within the meaning of the 1976 Copyright Act for the compensation provided in the Principal Agreement. Player hereby expressly waives and relinquishes any moral rights or "droit morale" in and to any material created by or contributed to the Picture by Player including all of Player's performance.

4. FORCE MAJEURE: As used herein the term "force majeure" means epidemic, act of God, strike, lockout, labor condition, unavailability of materials, transportation, power or other commodity, delay of common carrier, civil disturbance, riot, war or armed conflict (whether or not there has been an official declaration of war), the enactment of any law, the issuance of any executive or judicial order or decree, breach of contract by, or disability of, the Producer, Director, other principal cast member, breach of contract by a financier or completion guarantor, or other similar occurrence beyond the control of Producer, which causes an interruption of or materially hampers or materially interferes with the production of the Picture.

5. INSURANCE: Player warrants that to the best of Player's knowledge Player is in good health and has no condition which would prevent Producer from obtaining life, health, accident, cast or other insurance covering Player at premium rates normal to Player's age and sex, without any unusual exclusion or limitation of liability on the part of the insurer.

6. WITHHOLDING: Producer may deduct and withhold from any monies otherwise payable under this Agreement such amounts as Producer may reasonably believe it is legally required to deduct and withhold.

7. ASSIGNMENT: Producer shall have the right to assign this Agreement and any of the rights granted herein, in whole or in part, to any person, firm, corporation or entity, and nothing contained herein shall imply anything to the contrary. Upon the assign's assumption of the obligations of Producer with respect to the rights so assigned, Producer shall be relieved of all such obligations. Producer shall also have the right to lend the services of Player to any person, firm or corporation which is a subsidiary, parent or affiliate of Producer or the successor to Producer by a merger or by a transfer of substantially all of Producer's assets hereunder. In the event of any such lending, Player agrees to render his services to the best of his ability to the person, firm, or corporation to whom his services are loaned hereunder.

AGREED TO AND ACCEPTED:

_____

Player

CONTRACTS
FOR THE
FILM AND
TELEVISION
INDUSTRY

108

EXTRA AGREEMENT

Producer:

MOTION PICTURE:

EMPLOYEE EMPLOYMENT DATE(S): _____

ROLE: _____

EMPLOYEE NAME: _____

ADDRESS: _____

PHONE: Home: _____ Work: _____

SOCIAL SECURITY # _____

RATE: $_____

OTHER TERMS: _____

TERMS AND CONDITIONS OF EMPLOYMENT

1. Payment of Wages: Wages shall be paid to all employees no later than Friday following the week in which services were performed. Pay date may be delayed by reason of an intervening federal or state holiday. Employee is responsible for submitting her/his time card at the end of the work week to insure timely payment. No employee will be paid without fully completing these forms.

2. Employee shall not be beneficiary of additional overtime, turnaround or other hourly payments except as expressly provided in this deal memo.

3. Nights, Weekends, Holidays, Work Time: Unless expressly provided elsewhere in this deal memo, no increased or additional compensation shall accrue or be payable to employee for the rendering of services at night or on weekends or holidays, or after the expiration of any particular number of hours of service in any period.

4. The Producer will provide meal breaks and/or food service at approximately six (6) hour intervals.

5. Immigration Reform and Control Act of 1986 (IRCA): Employment (or the engagement of services) hereunder is subject to employee providing the requisite documents required by IRCA and completing and signing the required Form I-9 pursuant to IRCA Section 274a.2. Employee shall comply with the immigration verification employment eligibility provisions required by law.

7. Use of alcohol or drugs during hours of employment will result in employee's immediate termination.

8. Employee's services are on an exclusive basis to the production of the motion picture (the "Picture") referred to in this deal memo for such period of time as required unless otherwise specified in this deal memo.

9. Screen credit is at Producer's discretion subject to employee's performing all services required through completion of term.

10. Unless expressly provided elsewhere in this agreement, employee's employment hereunder shall not be for a "run of the show" or for any guaranteed period of employment. Production reserves the right to discharge employee at any time, subject only to the obligation to pay the balance of any guaranteed compensation due. Producer will attempt to notify employees a minimum of twenty-four (24) hours in advance of layoff. This agreement is subject to immediate suspension and/or termination (at Production's election) without further obligation on the part of Production in the event of any incapacity or default of employee or in the case of any suspension, postponement or interference with the production by reason of labor controversy, strike, earthquake, act of God, governmental action, regulation, or decree or for any other customary force majeure reason.

11. The terms and conditions of this deal memo are binding on Producer and employee and shall not be waived or altered by any method.

12. Producer shall be the owner of all of the results and proceeds of employee's services and shall have the right to use employee's name, voice, picture and likeness in connection with the Picture, the advertising and publicizing thereof, and any promotional films or clips respecting the Picture without additional compensation therefore.

13. Any controversy or claim arising out of or relating to this agreement or any breach thereof shall be settled by arbitration in accordance with the Rules of the American Arbitration Association; and judgment upon the award rendered by the arbitrators may be entered in any court having jurisdiction thereof. The prevailing party shall be entitled to reimbursement for costs and reasonable attorney's fees.

EMPLOYEE ACCEPTS ALL CONDITIONS OF EMPLOYMENT AS DESCRIBED ABOVE.

AGREED TO AND ACCEPTED:

EMPLOYEE SIGNATURE: _____DATE: _____

PRODUCER SIGNATURE: _____DATE: _____

CONTRACTS
FOR THE
FILM AND
TELEVISION
INDUSTRY

110

EXTRA RELEASE

FOR GOOD AND VALUABLE CONSIDERATION, I hereby grant to Big Deal Entertainment, Inc. ("Producer") and to its licensees, assigns, and other successors-in-interest all rights of every kind and character whatsoever in perpetuity in and to my performance, appearance, name and/or voice and the results and proceeds thereof ("the Performance") in connection with the motion picture currently entitled _____ ("The Picture"), and I hereby authorize Producer to photograph and record (on film, tape, or otherwise), the Performance; to edit same at its discretion and to include it with the performance of others and with sound effects, special effects and music; to incorporate same into Picture or other program or not; to use and to license others to use such recordings and photographs in any manner or media whatsoever, including without limitation unrestricted use for purposes of publicity, advertising and sales promotion; and to use my name, likeness, voice, biographic or other information concerning me in connection with the Picture, commercial tie-ups, merchandising, and for any other purpose. I agree that Producer owns all rights and proceeds of my services rendered in connection herewith.

AGREED TO AND ACCEPTED:

_____DATE: _____
Extra Player

CHAPTER 5

COLLABORATION

WRITER COLLABORATION

Many writers begin a collaboration with great promise only to discover later that the partnership is not working. Not only has time been wasted, but difficult questions may arise as to ownership of work that has been created. The breakup may engender animosity, making it difficult to resolve these issues. If ownership of the embryonic story is unclear, neither party may safely use it. Thus, writers are well advised to enter a written collaboration agreement beforehand.

Negotiating a collaboration agreement is also useful because it forces the parties to resolve important issues before they invest a lot of time and effort in the partnership. If the relationship is not going to work it is best to know as early as possible.

CONTRACTS
FOR THE
FILM AND
TELEVISION
INDUSTRY

112

WRITER COLLABORATION AGREEMENT

This Agreement between _____ , residing at _____, (herein called Writer A), and _____ , residing at_____ ,
(herein called Writer B).

WITNESSETH

The parties desire to collaborate in the writing of a screenplay, on the terms hereinafter set forth.

NOW THEREFORE, in consideration of the premises, and of the mutual undertakings herein contained, and for other good and valuable considerations, the parties agree as follows:

1. The parties hereby undertake to collaborate in the writing of a certain original feature-length screenplay (herein called the Screenplay or Work) dealing with a _____ , and provisionally entitled _____.

2. The parties shall collaborate in the writing of the work and upon completion thereof shall be the joint owners of the work sharing all rights equally.

3. The parties contemplate that they will complete the manuscript of the Screenplay by _____. However, failure to complete the screenplay by such date shall not be construed as a breach of this Agreement on the part of either party.

4. If, prior to the completion of the work, either party shall voluntarily withdraw from the collaboration, then the other party shall have the right to complete the work alone or in conjunction with another collaborator or collaborators, and in such event the percentage of ownership, as hereinbefore provided in paragraph 2, shall be revised by mutual agreement in writing or, failing such agreement, by arbitration in accordance with the procedures hereinafter prescribed.

5. If, prior to the completion of the Work, there shall be a dispute of any kind with respect to the Work, then either party may terminate this Collaboration Agreement by written notice to the other party, and should they fail to agree upon the terms of such termination agreement, they shall submit the dispute for arbitration in accordance with the procedures hereinafter prescribed.

6. Any contract for the sale or other disposition of the Work, where the Work has been completed by the Parties in accordance herewith, shall require that the story and writing credits shall be equally shared by the parties, unless the parties agree otherwise.

7. Neither party shall sell, or otherwise voluntarily dispose of the Work, or his share therein, without the written consent of the other, which consent, however, shall not be unreasonably withheld.

8. Both parties agree that each shall be responsible for its own expenses incurred in the preparation of the Work.

9. The parties agree that all income received from the world-wide sale of motion picture and/or television (all markets and media) rights (including but not limited to all sequel, remake and television spin-off rights, novelization, merchandising, play, radio and audio rights) to the screenplay shall be shared equally.

10. Should the Work be sold or otherwise disposed of and, as an incident thereto, the Parties be employed to revise the Work, the total compensation provided for in such employment agreement shall be shared equally by the parties.

11. If either party shall be unavailable for the purposes of collaborating on such revision, then the Party who is available shall be permitted to do such revision and shall be entitled to the full amount of compensation in connection therewith.

12. If either party hereto shall desire to use the Work, or any right therein or with respect thereto, in any venture in which such Party shall have a financial interest, whether direct or indirect, the Party desiring so to do shall notify the other Party of that fact and shall afford such other Party the opportunity to participate in the venture in the proportion of such other Party's interest in the Work. If such other Party shall be unwilling to participate in such venture, the Party shall desiring to proceed therein shall be required to pay such other Party an amount equal to that which such other Party would have received if the Work or right, as the case may be, intended to be so used had been sold to a disinterested person at the price at which the same shall last have been offered, or if it shall not have been offered, at its fair market value which, in the absence of mutual agreement of the Parties, shall be determined by arbitration.

13. The copyright in the Work shall be obtained in the names of both parties, and shall be held jointly by them.

14. If either party (herein called the First Party) desires to transfer his rights to a third person, he shall give written notice by registered mail to the other party (herein called the Second Party) of his intention to do so.

(a) In such case the Second Party shall have an option for a period of 30 days to purchase the First Party's share at a price and upon such terms indicated in the written notice.

(b) If the Second Party fails to exercise his option in writing within the aforesaid period of 30 days, or if, having exercised it, fails to complete the purchase upon the terms stated in the notice, the First Party may transfer his rights to the third person at the price and upon the identical terms stated in the notice; and he shall forthwith send to the Second Party a copy of the contract of sale of such rights, with a statement that the transfer has been made.

(c) If the First Party fails for any reason to make such transfer to the third person, and if he desires to make a subsequent transfer to someone else, the Second Party's option shall apply to such proposed subsequent transfer.

15. Nothing herein contained shall be construed to create a partnership between the parties. Their relation shall be one of collaboration on a single work.

16. This agreement shall continue for the life of the copyright therein.

17. If either party dies before the completion of the screenplay, the survivor shall have the right to complete the same, to make changes in the text previously prepared, to negotiate and contract for sale or production and for the disposition of any of the subsidiary rights, and generally to act with regard thereto as though he were the sole author, except that (a) the name of the decedent shall always receive credit as agreed herein; and (b) the survivor shall cause the decedent's share of the proceeds to be paid to his estate, and shall furnish to the estate true copies of all contracts made by the survivor pertaining to the Work.

CONTRACTS
FOR THE
FILM AND
TELEVISION
INDUSTRY

114

18. If either party dies after the completion of the screenplay, the survivor shall have the right to negotiate and contract for sale and/or production (if not theretofore arranged) and for the disposition of any of the subsidiary rights, to make revisions in any subsequent drafts, and generally to act with regard thereto as if he were the sole author, subject only to the conditions set forth in subdivisions (a) and (b) of clause 14.

19. Any controversy or claim arising out of or relating to this agreement or any breach thereof shall be settled by arbitration in accordance with the Rules of the American Arbitration Association; and judgment upon the award rendered by the arbitrators may be entered in any court having jurisdiction thereof. The prevailing party shall be entitled to reimbursement for costs and reasonable attorneys' fees.

20. This agreement shall inure to the benefit of, and shall be binding upon, the executors, administrators and assigns of the parties.

21. This agreement constitutes the entire understanding of the parties.

22. This agreement is governed by and construed in accordance with the laws of the State of California.

23. If any provision of this Agreement or the application thereof to any Person or circumstance shall be invalid or unenforceable to any extent, the remainder of this Agreement and the application of such provisions to other persons or circumstances shall not be affected thereby and shall be enforced to the greatest extent permitted by law.

IN WITNESS WHEREOF, the parties hereunto set their respective hand and seal this _____ day of _____, 19__.

_____
Writer A

_____
Writer B

A joint venture is a type of partnership. You should choose your partners carefully as you may be liable for their acts that are within the scope of the partnership.

General partnerships should be distinguished from limited partnerships. In a general partnership the parties share control over the enterprise. In a limited partnership, one or more limited partners (i.e. investors) provide financing but do not exercise control over the management of the enterprise. Limited partners have limited liability as well. Limited partnership agreements are discussed in greater detail in Chapter 7.

The following joint venture agreement is between two individuals to develop and produce projects for television. Since they jointly manage the enterprise they are general partners.

JOINT VENTURE AGREEMENT

THIS JOINT VENTURE AGREEMENT is made as of _____ by and between _____, ("Martin") and _____ ("Betty") (individually or collectively referred to hereinafter as "Partner" or "Partners" respectively).

NOW, THEREFORE, it is mutually agreed by and between the parties hereto as follows:

1. PURPOSE: Martin and Betty hereby enter into a joint venture (the "Venture") for the term hereinafter set forth for the purpose of creating, developing, producing and exploiting a story currently entitled _____ as a television motion picture (the "Picture"), and any other properties listed in Exhibit A to which both parties have affixed their signatures. Each idea, story, and/or Picture and all ancillary rights therein are hereinafter referred to as the "Property."

2. TERM: The term of the Venture shall commence as of the effective date of this Agreement and, unless sooner terminated in accordance with the provisions hereof, shall continue for the longer of: (a) the duration of any and all copyrights owned by the Venture in connection with the Property, or (b) the aggregate term of any and all agreements relating to the Property (the "Term").

3. NAME AND STATUTORY COMPLIANCE: The name of the Venture shall be "_____." Upon execution of this Agreement, the Partners shall sign and cause to be filed and published in Los Angeles the appropriate notice indicating that the Venture will be conducting business under said name.

4. TITLE: Any and all property and asset of the Venture as well as all intangible rights, including, without limitation, all copyrights, trade names and trademarks, in and to the Screenplay, the Picture and all other forms of exploitation of the Property, and all ancillary, merchandising, music and book publishing rights, shall be owned by and title held in the name of the Venture.

5. PRINCIPAL OFFICE: The location of the principal office of the Venture shall be _____, or shall be at such other place or places in California as the Partners shall from time to time determine.

CONTRACTS
FOR THE
FILM AND
TELEVISION
INDUSTRY

116

6. NAME AND RESIDENCE OF EACH PARTNER:

(a)

(b)

7. CONTRACTS AND AGREEMENTS:

(a) All contracts or agreements to be entered into by, on behalf of, or for the benefit of the Venture must be signed by Betty on behalf of the partnership. It is understood that Martin shall not have the right to bind the Venture with respect to the Property without the express written consent of Betty. 1. Many joint venture agreements require the signature and/or consent of both partners.

(b) The proceeds of any contracts entered into by any Partner hereto for personal services of such Partner as a writer, producer, director, actor/actress or otherwise with any third party motion picture company after such motion picture company has acquired the Property hereunder, shall belong solely to such Partner; provided, however, that it is specifically agreed that any such agreement with a motion picture company must agree to employ both Partners hereunder as producers of any motion picture based on the Property with fixed, contingent and deferred compensation, and participations and credit to both Partners equal in all respects to one another and must embody the credit provisions of Clause 12.

8. CAPITAL CONTRIBUTIONS:

(a) The Partners shall not be obligated to make any additional contributions to the capital of the Venture. If a need for additional capital arises, each Partner may contribute whatever portion of the total sum required that each elects to contribute, in its sole discretion.

(b) In furtherance of Subclause 8(a) above, Martin and Betty hereby assign, transfer and convey to the Venture all their respective rights, titles and interests including copyrights and copyright rights and all extensions and renewals thereof, in and to the property.

9. ALLOCATION OF PROFITS AND LOSSES; TAX CREDITS AND DEDUCTIONS:

(a) The net profits or net losses of the Venture shall be allocated, credited or charged as the case may be, to the Partners in equal shares of fifty percent (50%) each. The terms "net profits" and "net losses" as used herein shall be defined as gross receipts received by the Venture from any and all sources in connection with the Screenplay, the Picture, the Property and all uses thereof and ancillary rights thereto (including, without limitation, merchandising, music and publishing), less the aggregate of all costs, charges, fees and expenses of the Venture including, without limitation, third party gross or net profit participations.

(b) Any and all tax credits and/or deductions to which the Venture shall become entitled shall be allocated (equally between the Partners in shares of fifty percent (50%) each).

10. BOOKS, RECORDS, BANK ACCOUNTS, CHECKING:

(a) At all times during the term hereof, the Venture shall keep or cause to be kept, at the principal place of business of the Venture or at such other place as the Venture may determine, books and accounting records for the business and operations of the Venture. Such books shall be open to inspection by the Partners, or their authorized representatives, during reasonable working hours. The accounting for Venture purposes, including the determination of "net profits" and "net losses" shall be in accordance with generally accepted accounting principles consistently applied. The Venture shall engage the services of an accountant who shall be selected with the mutual approval of both parties.

(b) There shall be maintained for each Partner a capital account and an income account. Each Partner's distributive share of profits and losses, and monthly and end-of-the-year withdrawals not previously posted shall be credited or debited to the respective Partner's income account as of the close of the calendar year. Thereafter, any debit or credit balance remaining in the income account of a Partner shall be debited, or credited, as the case may be, to his respective capital account.

(c) The Venture shall be on a calendar year basis for accounting purposes (the "fiscal year"). As soon after the close of each fiscal year as is reasonably practical, a full and accurate accounting shall be made of the affairs of the Venture as of the close of each fiscal year. On such accounting being made, the net profit or the net loss sustained by the Venture during such fiscal year shall be ascertained and credited or charged, as the case may be, in the books of account of the Venture in the proportions hereinabove specified.

(d) From time to time, but no less than annually, the Venture shall make distributions from the capital of the Venture which shall be in excess of the reasonable needs of the Venture for working capital and reserves as mutually determined by the Partners in accordance with Clause 16(a); provided, however, that so long as any Partner has any indebtedness or other outstanding obligations to the Venture, any distribution that would otherwise be made shall first be applied toward any such indebtedness or other obligations.

(e) All funds of the Venture shall be deposited in an account or accounts in the name of the Venture at such bank or banks as may from time to time be selected by the Venture. All withdrawals from any such account or accounts shall be made by check or other written instrument which shall require the signature of a representative of Martin and the signature of a representative of Betty.

11. MANAGEMENT AND RESPONSIBILITIES OF THE PARTIES: The Partners shall have equal power, authority and control over all creative, business, financial and legal matters in connection with the Venture and the development, production and exploitation of the Property, and all subsidiary and ancillary rights thereto and all exploitation thereof including, without limitation, decisions regarding the budget, the motion picture studio and/or distributor, the name of the Screenplay and the Picture, and director, cast, producer, music, writers, and the consideration for any rights granted or services rendered hereunder by Partners and others, and all decisions regarding the foregoing shall be made only by the unanimous agreement of the Partners. The foregoing provisions are not intended to prevent or prohibit Betty from engaging in discussions with third party motion picture studios with respect to the Screenplay, provided Betty fully discloses such discussions and the parties thereto to Martin and consults with Martin regarding same.

12. CREDITS:

(a) The partners shall receive equal producer credit on any property they develop or produce.

CONTRACTS
FOR THE
FILM AND
TELEVISION
INDUSTRY

118

(b) No casual or inadvertent failure of the Venture to comply with the provisions of this Section, and no failure of others to comply with their obligations to the Venture shall constitute a breach of this Agreement by the Venture. The rights and remedies of (names of persons and parties) in the event of a breach of this clause by the Venture shall be limited to their rights, if any, to recover damages in an action at law and in no event shall they be entitled by reason of any such breach to terminate this Agreement or to enjoin or restrain the production, distribution or exhibition of any production (motion picture, television, or otherwise) produced pursuant to this Agreement.

13. WARRANTIES, INDEMNIFICATION:

(a) Each Partner hereby warrants and represents to the other(s) that he, she or it:

(i) Has the right and capacity to enter into this agreement;

(ii) Shall not encumber or sell any property, assets or intangible rights of the Venture without the written consent of the other Partner(s);

(iii) Shall not assign, mortgage, hypothecate or encumber his, her or its interest in the Venture without the written consent of the other Partner(s);

(iv) Shall not loan any funds or extend the credit of the Venture to any person or entity without the written consent of the other Partner(s);

(v) Shall not incur any cost, expense, liability or obligation in the name or on the credit of the Venture without the written consent of the other Partner(s);

(vi) Each Partner hereby indemnifies and holds harmless the other Partners from and against any and all claims, liabilities, damages and costs (including but not limited to reasonable attorneys' fees and court costs) arising from any breach by such Partner of any representation, warranty or agreement made by such Partner hereunder.

14. EXCLUSIVITY: Neither of the Partners shall be exclusive to the Venture and each Partner may develop other properties and engage in other activities in the motion picture and television industries separate and apart from the Venture and the other Partners. However, it is agreed by the Partners that each Partner shall devote as much time as shall be reasonably necessary to fulfill his, her or its duties and obligations in connection with the Venture and the Screenplay, Picture or Property, subject, however, to their availability.

15. DISSOLUTION AND TERMINATION OF THE VENTURE:

(a) The Venture shall be dissolved and terminated and its business wound up upon the first to occur of the following:

(i) The expiration of the term referred to in Clause 2, above;

(ii) Mutual agreement of the Partners;

(iii) Operation of law;

(iv) Material breach of this Agreement by any Partner(s), which breach is not cured within fifteen (15) days) after written notice thereof from the non-defaulting Partner; provided, however, it is understood that only the non-defaulting Partner(s) shall have the right to terminate the Venture pursuant to this Clause (a)(4). Such termination shall not release the defaulting Partner(s) from any obligations or liabilities to the other Partner(s), whether pursuant to the provisions of this Agreement or at law or in equity.

(b) Upon termination of the Venture, the business of the Venture shall be wound up and assets and properties of the Venture shall be liquidated. Upon the happening of any one of the events mentioned in Clause 15(a) hereof, the Venture shall engage in no further business, other than that necessary to protect the assets of the Venture, wind-up its business and distribute its assets as provided herein.

16. DISTRIBUTIONS:

(a) Distributions Other than Upon Liquidation: Distributions of available cash shall be made at such times and in such amounts as, in the discretion of the Partners, the business, the affairs and the financial circumstances of the Venture permit.

(b) Distribution of Assets on Dissolution and Liquidation: Upon any dissolution and liquidation of the Venture, the assets of the Venture shall be liquidated in an orderly manner (subject, however, to the terms of Clause 16(c) hereof), with a view toward maximizing the proceeds from such liquidation, and the proceeds thereof shall be distributed in the following order of priority:

(i) The expenses of liquidation and the debts of the Venture, other than debts owing to the Partners, shall be paid;

(ii) Debts owing to the Partners, if any, shall be paid;

(iii) Distribution shall be made to the Partners of amounts equal to their respective capital account balances, if any, which shall be made in the ratio of their respective capital account balances;

(iv) Any funds remaining after the amounts described in the foregoing Clauses (1), (2) and (3) have been paid shall be distributed to the Partners in the proportion in which the Partners share the net profits of the Venture at the time of such distribution.

If the Partners have not sold the assets of the Venture, except as otherwise provided in Clause 16(c) hereof, within two (2) years following dissolution, then there shall be distributed to the Partners as tenants in common, subject to the foregoing Subclauses (i), (ii), (iii) and (iv) of this Clause 16(b), undivided interests in the assets of the Venture, as valued and constituted on that date.

(c) However, it is understood and agreed that upon dissolution of the Venture if all the rights in the Property have not been disposed of by the Venture prior to such dissolution then any and all copyrights and copyright rights ancillary thereto of the Venture in and to the Screenplay and the Picture shall be promptly transferred to and belong in shares of fifty percent (50%) to Martin and fifty percent (50%) to Betty, respectively, as tenants in common, and in furtherance thereof the Partners hereto agree to promptly execute all necessary and proper assignments and/or other documents to effectuate said transfer.

17. GAIN OR LOSS DURING DISSOLUTION: Any gain or loss arising out of the disposition of assets of the Venture during the course of dissolution shall be borne by the Partners in the same proportions as such gain or loss was shared by the Partners hereunder immediately prior to the dissolution.

CONTRACTS
FOR THE
FILM AND
TELEVISION
INDUSTRY

120

18. OPPORTUNITIES AND CONFLICTS OF INTEREST:

(a) Any of the Partners may engage or possess an interest in any other business venture of every kind, nature and description, including ventures or enterprises which may be competitive in nature with the Venture, and neither the Venture nor any of the Partners shall have any rights in and to said business ventures, or to the income or profits derived therefrom.

(b) No Partner shall be obligated to offer any investment or business opportunities to the other Partners or to the Venture. Any Partner may invest or otherwise participate in such opportunities without notice to the Venture or to the other Partners, without affording the Venture or the other Partners an opportunity of participating in same and without any liability whatsoever to the Venture or to any other Partner. Each Partner hereby waives any right he may have against the other Partner(s) for capitalizing on information learned as a consequence of his connection with the affairs of the Venture.

19. DEATH, INCAPACITY, DISABILITY OF A PARTNER:

(a) Upon the death, legal incapacity or total disability of a Partner leaving the other Partner(s) surviving, this joint venture shall not dissolve but shall continue as a limited partnership with the successor(s) in interest of such deceased, incapacitated or disabled Partner(s) as a limited partner thereof, which limited partner shall not be entitled to vote on partnership matters or participate in the management of the partnership business except that such limited partner's written approval and signature shall be required for any sale or other disposition of the Property.

(b) If in the opinion of legal counsel for the deceased Partner(s), the joint venture interest of such deceased, incapacitated or disabled Partner cannot be converted to a limited partnership interest without adverse tax consequences, then upon the death, incapacity or disability of such Partner, this joint venture shall not dissolve but shall continue with the remaining Partner and the legal representative or successor in interest of such deceased, incapacitated or disabled Partner, which legal representative or successor in interest shall thereafter be deemed a Class B Partner in the Venture. Such Class B Partner shall be entitled to the same economic rights, preferences as to distribution, capital and profits interest in the Venture as was the deceased, incapacitated or disabled Partner, including the right to approve all withdrawals; provided, however, that such Class B Partner shall not be entitled to vote on Venture matters or to participate in the management of the Venture business, except that such Class B Partner's written approval and signature shall be required for any sale or other disposition of the Property.

20. MISCELLANEOUS:

(a) Notices: All such notices which any party is required or may desire to serve hereunder shall be in writing and shall be served by personal delivery to the other parties or by prepaid registered or certified mail addressed to the parties at their respective addresses as set forth in Clause 6 hereof, or at such other address as the parties may from time to time designate in writing upon the books of the Venture.

(b) Arbitration: Any controversy or dispute arising out of or relating to the Venture or the breach or alleged breach of any provision of this Agreement shall be settled by arbitration in Los Angeles, in accordance with the rules of the American Arbitration Association and judgment upon the award rendered by the arbitrator may be entered in any court having jurisdiction thereof. The prevailing party in any such arbitration shall be entitled to recover from the other party reasonable attorneys' fees and costs incurred in connection therewith. The determination of the arbitrator in such proceeding shall be final, binding and non-appealable.

(c) This Agreement shall be construed, interpreted and enforced in accordance with the laws of the State of California applicable to agreements executed and to be wholly performed within such state.

(d) Nothing contained in this Agreement shall be construed so as to require the commission of any act or the payment of any compensation which is contrary to law or to require the violation of any guild or union agreement applicable hereto which may, from time to time, be in effect and by its terms controlling of this Agreement. If there is any conflict between any provision of this Agreement and any such applicable law or guild or union agreement and the latter shall prevail, then the provisions of this Agreement affected shall be modified to the extent (but only to the extent) necessary to remove such conflict and permit such compliance with law or guild or union agreement.

(e) No waiver by any party hereof of any failure by any other party to keep or perform any covenant or condition hereof shall be deemed a waiver of any preceding or succeeding breach of the same or any other covenant or condition.

(f) This Agreement may not be amended or changed except by a written instrument duly executed by each of the Partners.

(g) Each Partner shall execute and deliver any and all additional papers, documents and other instruments and shall do any and all further acts and things reasonably necessary in connection with the performance of his, her or its obligations hereunder to carry out the intent of the Venture.

(h) The remedies accorded herein or otherwise available to the Partners shall be cumulative and no one such remedy shall be exclusive of any other and the exercise of any one shall not preclude the exercise or be deemed a waiver of any other remedy nor shall the specification of any remedy exclude or be deemed to be a waiver of any right or remedy at law or in equity which may be available to a partner including any rights to damages or injunctive relief.

(i) Any and all consents and agreements provided for or permitted by this Agreement shall be in writing and a signed copy thereof shall be filed and kept with the books of the Venture.

(j) This Agreement contains the sole and only agreement of the Partners relating to the Venture and correctly sets forth the rights, duties and obligations of each to the other as of its date. Any prior agreements, promises, amendments, negotiations or representations not expressly set forth in this Agreement are of no force and effect.

(k) No Partner shall sell, assign, mortgage, hypothecate or encumber his or her interest, or any portion thereof, in the Venture without the prior written consent of the other Partner.

IN WITNESS WHEREOF, this Agreement is effective as of the date and year first above written.

_____

"Martin"   Date:

_____

"Betty"   Date:

CONTRACTS
FOR THE
FILM AND
TELEVISION
INDUSTRY

122

EXHIBIT A

Additional projects of the joint venture:

1. _____

Agreed and Accepted: _____ _____
                          Martin   Betty

Date: _____

2. _____

Agreed and Accepted: _____ _____
                          Martin   Betty

Date: _____

3. _____

Agreed and Accepted: _____ _____
                          Martin   Betty

Date: _____

4. _____

Agreed and Accepted: _____ _____
                          Martin   Betty

Date: _____

When partners decide to dissolve a partnership they may need to resolve outstanding issues, including the division of partnership property.

If the partners have a written partnership agreement, that agreement should be looked to for the terms by which the partnership should be dissolved. However, parties may not have a written agreement, or the agreement may not address dissolution. In this case the partners will have to negotiate an agreement to dissolve the partnership.

AGREEMENT TO DISSOLVE JOINT VENTURE

This Agreement between _____ , residing at _____ (herein called "John Doe"), and _____ , Inc., at _____ (herein called "TTT") is for the dissolution of the joint venture entered into between the parties on _____ 19__, pursuant to a two page agreement signed by the parties on that date. The joint venture has produced a completed video program _____ (herein "Program") comprised of a collection of four titles as set forth in Schedule "A".

1. The parties hereby dissolve their joint venture.

2. Any and all remaining assets of the joint venture including future income from the sale or licensing of the Program (with the exception of the copyright to the program and the raw footage), shall be liquidated, and the proceeds realized from the liquidation shall be distributed according to the following order of priority:

First, to payments of all outstanding joint venture expenses, if any, including obligations, royalties, debts, salaries, and taxes, and expenses necessary to wind up the joint venture.

Second, to the parties according to the following formula:

(a) revenues up to the first $_____, shall be split equally (50/50) between the parties, then

(b) revenues shall be divided 75% to TTT and 25% to John Doe until the cost of production has been recouped, then

(c) after the cost of production has been recouped, all additional revenues shall be split 50/50 between the parties.

3. Upon the request of either party, a complete and final audit of the books, records, and accounts of the joint venture shall be conducted, and all final adjustments between the parties shall be made on the basis of such audit.

4. If, after the termination of the joint venture, any claim, liability, or expense shall be asserted against the joint venture which was not used in computing the profits and losses of the joint venture and which is a proper item of computation, the parties shall bear any such claim, liability, or expense equally.

5. The copyright in the Program and all raw footage shot for the program shall

CONTRACTS
FOR THE
FILM AND
TELEVISION
INDUSTRY

124

be owned by the parties as tenants in common and held in the names of both parties jointly.

6. Neither party shall sell, or otherwise voluntarily dispose of their copyright to the Program, or his share therein, without the written consent of the other, which consent, however, shall not be unreasonably withheld.

7. The parties agree that all income received from the world-wide exploitation of the program (all markets and media including but not limited to all sequel, remake and television spin-off rights, novelization, merchandising, play, radio and audio rights) shall be shared equally.

8. Should the Program be sold, licensed or otherwise disposed of and, as an incident thereto, the parties be employed to revise the Work, the total compensation provided for in such employment agreement shall be shared equally by the parties.

9. If either party shall be unavailable for the purposes of collaborating on such revision, then the party who is available shall be permitted to do such revision and shall be entitled to the full amount of compensation in connection therewith.

10. If either party hereto shall desire to use the Program, or any right therein or with respect thereto, in any venture in which such party shall have a financial interest, whether direct or indirect, the party desiring so to do shall notify the other party of that fact and shall afford such other party the opportunity to participate in the venture in the proportion of such other party's interest in the program. If such other party shall be unwilling to participate in such venture, the party desiring to proceed therein shall be required to pay such other party an amount equal to that which such other Party would have received if the program or right, as the case may be, intended to be so used had been sold to a disinterested person at the price at which the same shall last have been offered, or if it shall not have been offered, at its fair market value which, in the absence of mutual agreement of the parties, shall be determined by arbitration.

11. If either party (herein called the First Party) desires to transfer his copyright to a third person, he shall give written notice by registered mail to the other party (herein called the Second Party) of his intention to do so.

(a) In such case the Second Party shall have an option for a period of thirty (30) days to purchase the First Party's share at a price and upon such terms indicated in the written notice.

(b) If the Second Party fails to exercise his option in writing within the aforesaid period of thirty (30) days, or if, having exercised it, he fails to complete the purchase upon the terms stated in the notice, the First Party may transfer his rights to the third person at the price and upon the identical terms stated in the notice; and he shall forthwith send to the Second Party a copy of the contract of sale of such rights, with a statement that the transfer has been made.

(c) If the First Party fails for any reason to make such transfer to the third person, and if he desires to make a subsequent transfer to someone else, the Second Party's option shall apply to such proposed subsequent transfer.

12. Nothing herein contained shall be construed to create a partnership between the parties.

13. Any controversy or claim arising out of or relating to this agreement or any breach thereof shall be settled by arbitration in accordance with the Rules of the American Arbitration Association; and judgment upon the award rendered by the arbitrators may be entered in any court having jurisdiction thereof. The prevailing party shall be entitled to reimbursement for costs and reasonable attorney's fees.

14. This agreement shall inure to the benefit of, and shall be binding upon, the executors, administrators and assigns of the parties.

15. This agreement constitutes the entire understanding of the parties.

16. This agreement is governed by and construed in accordance with the laws of the State of California.

17. If any provision of this Agreement or the application thereof to any Person or circumstance shall be invalid or unenforceable to any extent, the remainder of this Agreement and the application of such provisions to other persons or circumstances shall not be affected thereby and shall be enforced to the greatest extent permitted by law.

18. The parties agree to execute such further documents and instruments as you may reasonably request in order to effectuate the terms and intentions of this agreement, and in the event either party is unable to execute any such documents or instruments, each appoints the other as their irrevocable attorney in fact to execute any such documents and instruments, provided that said documents and instruments shall not be inconsistent with the terms and conditions of this agreement. The rights under this Clause constitute a power coupled with an interest and are irrevocable.

19. This agreement expresses the entire understanding between the parties and both agree that no oral understandings have been made with regard thereto. This agreement may be amended only by written instrument signed by both parties. Each party acknowledges that it has not been induced to enter this agreement by any representations or assurances, whether written or oral, and agree that each has not received any promises or inducements other than as herein set forth. The provisions hereof shall be binding upon each party's heirs, assigns, executors, administrators and successors.

AGREED TO AND ACCEPTED

_____   Date:

John Doe

_____

By:

_____

President
TTT, Inc.   Date:

CONTRACTS
FOR THE
FILM AND
TELEVISION
INDUSTRY

126

CO-PRODUCTION

In a co-production agreement, one or more partners agree to co-produce a project. Here is a fairly simple agreement for the production of a cable television show.

CO-PRODUCTION AGREEMENT

This letter confirms the understanding between _____("Doe"), residing at _____, and _____ dba Big Film Productions ("Big") whose office is at _____, with respect to co-production of a television program in a series about _____, tentatively titled _____ (The "Series"). The program is tentatively titled _____.

1. FINANCING: Big will use its best efforts to obtain financing for the program and shall exercise sole and exclusive control over the disbursement of monies for all production, marketing and distribution expenses. Big shall arrange for the facilities, equipment and personnel needed for the production of the program, within the limits of the budget as set forth in Exhibit A, attached hereto. Nothing in this agreement shall obligate Big to produce the series.

2. **SERVICES PROVIDED**: Doe shall provide consultative and administrative services and shall serve as liaison with artists, museums and galleries and enlist their support and participation in the Series. Doe shall:

a) Procure historical data, photographs, audio tapes and literature from artists and organizations participating in the series,

b) Procure a signed depiction and location release at no expense to Big on forms supplied by Big for each museum and any persons appearing in the series.

c) Use his best efforts to arrange for the sale of the broadcast, cable, home video and ancillary rights to the series in the United States and foreign territories, and

d) Use his best efforts to recruit advertising sponsors for the series.

3. COMPENSATION: As full and complete consideration for his services, Doe shall be entitled to receive twenty-five percent (25%) of all net profits derived from the programs in which he serves as co-producer and in which he performs that function. Net profits shall be that amount of revenue remaining after all production, marketing and distribution expenses (and a reasonable reserve) have been recouped and accounted for in accordance with industry custom and practice.

At Doe's option, he may invest any amounts due him under this agreement for the production of future episodes of the series. In the event he does contribute such amounts, he will be entitled to a greater share of net profits from the episodes to which he contributes financing in accordance with the following formula:

> For every one percent of the entire budget Doe
> contributes, he shall be entitled to one-quarter
> percent (1/4%) increment in his share of net profits, but
> in no event shall Doe's share of profits exceed
> a total of forty percent (40%).

By way of example, if Doe contributes four thousand dollars ($4,000) to the production of a future episode produced on a budget of ten thousand dollars ($10,000), then Doe would have contributed forty percent (40%) of the entire budget and would be entitled to an additional ten percent (10%) of net profits as well as his customary twenty-five percent (25%) of net profits for a total of thirty-five percent (35%) of net profits.

In calculating Doe's share according to the abovementioned formula, contributions shall be rounded to the nearest percentile.

Profits shall be payable annually.

4. CREDIT: For each program which Doe co-produces, on a single card following the introduction of the program, the credit shall read: "Produced by _____ and _____ ."

5. COPYRIGHT: Big shall be the sole copyright holder for the series. Doe shall be considered an employee-for-hire for all work done for the series.

6. ACCOUNTING: Doe shall have the right to inspect and copy the books and records maintained by Big at all times upon reasonable notice. At Doe's request, Big shall retain a Certified Public Accountant to prepare an annual financial report for all expenditures and revenues from the program. Big shall provide Doe with quarterly accounting statements from the time the series begins to produce revenue.

7. ASSIGNMENT: Neither party may assign its rights and obligations pursuant to this Agreement without the prior written consent of the other.

8. AGENCY: The parties are entering into this Agreement as independent contractors, and neither party shall have the right to bind the other without the express written consent of the party to be bound.

9. WARRANTIES: Doe warrants and represents that he is free to enter into this agreement; and that to the best of his knowledge and belief all the rights and releases necessary for production of the series have been or will be secured; and that the production of this series will not violate or infringe the rights of any person, company or corporation. Both parties agree that they shall not accept any promotional consideration unless disclosed and approved by the other party. Both parties agree to hold each other harmless and indemnify each other for any breach of the warranties in this paragraph, including claims, damages and reasonable attorneys' fees.

10. BREACH: In the event Doe breaches his obligations under this agreement, Big shall have the right to terminate this agreement after Big gives written notice to Doe of his breach and Doe does not cure the breach within 30 days of his receipt of said notice. In the event of an uncured breach, Doe shall continue to be entitled to receive compensation for programs previously produced but shall not receive any compensation from future programs produced. In the event Big breaches its obligations under this agreement, Doe shall be entitled to monetary damages but no injunctive relief.

11. ARBITRATION: Any controversy or claim arising of or relating to this Agreement, shall be settled by binding arbitration in accordance with the arbitration service of California Lawyers for the Arts, and judgment upon the award may be entered into in any court of law. The prevailing party shall be entitled to reimbursement of all costs and reasonable attorneys' fees.

12. ENTIRE UNDERSTANDING: This Agreement contains the entire understanding of the parties with respect to the subject matter hereof; it may not be
changed or amended except in writing signed by the parties; and it shall be construed and governed in accordance with the laws of the State of California. This
Agreement shall inure to the benefit of, and shall be binding upon, the successors, heirs, executors and administrators of the parties.

AGREED TO AND ACCEPTED:

_____

dba Big Productions   Date:

_____

Doe   Date:

CHAPTER 6

SOUNDTRACKS

A producer can create a soundtrack either by obtaining the right to use existing music (e.g., a popular song), or by commissioning an original musical score (i.e., hire a composer to create something new for the movie), or a combination of both.

BUYING EXISTING MUSIC

Music is a work of authorship protected under copyright law. Determining ownership in music can be complex since several persons may share a copyright. For example, the composer may own the copyright to the composition, the lyricist may own the copyright to the lyrics, the musicians may own the copyright to their performances and the record label may own the copyright to the recording. A film producer must determine which parties have ownership interests in each song and then license the appropriate rights.

Low-budget independent producers often run out of money by the time they reach post-production. They can economize by using songs by unknown songwriters that are available for little or no money. Fledgling songwriters often want to gain visibility and stature by having their music in a movie. The producer should keep in mind that a song performed in a movie that is broadcast can generate royalties for the songwriter (through ASCAP or BMI). Thus songwriters have a financial incentive to have their music on a soundtrack even if they do not receive a fee from the producer.

Another way for a producer to reduce music costs is to use music in the public domain. One must make sure that *all* rights are in the public domain. Let's say

CONTRACTS
FOR THE
FILM AND
TELEVISION
INDUSTRY

130

a low-budget filmmaker decides to put Beethoven's Fifth Symphony on his soundtrack. He purchases a copy of the Boston Symphony Pops recording of Beethoven's Fifth. While the composition is in the public domain, this particular recording may not be. The filmmaker is free to use Beethoven's composition, but he will have to find a recording in the public domain, or hire musicians to make his own recording.

To produce a new recording, a producer will have to strike a deal with a recording studio, musicians and/or vocalists. AF of M, AFTRA and SAG collective bargaining agreements will apply to films made by Guild signatories. A star artist may receive $20,000 or more as a fee, as well as royalties based on the retail price of the soundtrack album. If the artist is exclusive to a record label, its permission will be needed.

If a producer wants to put recorded pre-existing music (not in the public domain) on a soundtrack, a Master Use License will be needed from the record company that owns the recording.[1] Fees range from several hundred dollars for use of a short excerpt to tens of thousands of dollars for the work of a superstar. The artist may have approval rights over licensing his music to another, in which case the artist's permission must also be obtained. Re-use payments to musicians and performers will be required if the recording was made by union members.

To use an existing musical composition on television, a Television Music Rights License will be needed. This license is often obtained from The Harry Fox Agency which represents many music publishers.

COMMISSIONING AN ORIGINAL SCORE

The producer must take care in hiring a composer/lyricist or songwriter. The agreement between the parties will determine whether the artist is deemed an employee-for-hire or an independent contractor, which in turn will determine who is the author for copyright purposes. There can be joint ownership of a musical score (a participation agreement). Permission may also be needed from a record company if you use an artist under contract to them.

The producer will usually want the work to be considered one that is "made-for-hire," so that he automatically owns the copyright. The composer will be entitled to a fee for his work and royalties from non-movie uses of his music.[2] A top songwriter may demand to share the copyright under a co-publishing agreement. The expenses of recording the soundtrack are borne by the producer.

For low-budget movies a composer may wear several hats.[3] He may write,

---

[1] A producer who has obtained synchronization and performance licenses from the artist's publisher could make its own sound-alike recording if the artist's record label refuses to grant a license to use its recording. That is, the producer could create his own recording that sounds exactly like the original as long as it was not copied from the original. See, Soundtrack Music by Lionel S. Sobel, Chapter 184A, Entertainment Industry Contracts, Volume 4, Mathew Bender.

[2] Composer's royalties from soundtrack albums are typically 50% of the mechanical license fees paid the studio by the record company that releases the album. Also, the composer will receive 50% of the public performance fees collected by the agencies ASCAP or BMI, which is paid directly to the composer by his agency. Additionally, the composer will receive a royalty from the sale of sheet music and in some circumstances may receive a royalty for conducting and/or producing the soundtrack album.

[3] Composers are not unionized. However, the American Federation of Musicians represents orchestrators and conductors, a role often performed by composers in delivering soundtracks.

arrange, orchestrate, conduct and perform the music. A composer may even agree to produce and deliver a finished master recording at his own expense. Some producers minimize costs by using non-union musicians or electronic synthesizers.

Occasionally an artist anxious to break into movie composing will compose a soundtrack or song on speculation. Here the producer is not obliged to pay for the work unless he uses it.

A producer could also proceed under a step deal. The songwriter[1] is paid a modest upfront payment for composing the song and then the producer decides if he wants to use it. If the producer uses the song, he will pay an additional fee. If he doesn't use the song, the writer will retain all rights to it. In that event, the producer may seek reimbursement of the upfront payment if the song ever generates income.

When a popular artist is commissioned to provide a song, the studio will pay him a creative fee for his services. The deal can be structured by providing the artist with a fund that includes payment for all writing and recording expenses. Thus the artist is paid a flat fee and is responsible for delivering the song and master and paying all recording expenses. Such a deal limits the studio's liability for recording costs, and can provide greater compensation to the artist if expenses can be kept low.

Complications arise with popular songwriters because many have entered agreements granting a publisher the exclusive right to the songwriter's services. Both the publisher and the studio, which may have its own music publishing arm, will want copyright ownership and management of a song written for a movie. The parties will need to reach an agreement unless the artist has already fulfilled his songwriting contract.

Similarly, a soundtrack artist may be exclusive to a record label for recordings over a term of years or for several albums. The recording company may demand a royalty from the film studio in return for granting permission to use the artist on the soundtrack. Often the label and the artist share royalties.

Assuming all necessary permissions have been obtained from the artist's record label, a soundtrack recording agreement will be used to employ an artist. The agreement will give the studio both the right to use the song on the soundtrack and the right to include it on a soundtrack album.

Since several artists may contribute material to a soundtrack, each will want to ensure that they receive a fair deal compared to the others. An artist will often ask for a "Most Favored Nations" clause, which guarantees the artist as favorable terms as those given any other artist.

An artist may also seek to limit a studio's recoupment of recording costs and advances to those expenses directly incurred by that artist. Thus, the artist's royalty will not be reduced by expenses attributable to others. If the studio agrees to such a provision, it must maintain a separate accounting for each artist.

---

[1] The songwriter creates a song for the soundtrack while the composer creates an entire score. The employment agreements are similar.

CONTRACTS
FOR THE
FILM AND
TELEVISION
INDUSTRY

132

TV MUSIC RIGHTS LICENSE

1. In consideration of the payment of _____, and upon the payment of it to the undersigned, the undersigned does hereby grant to Licensee the non-exclusive, irrevocable right and license to record the following copyrighted musical composition(s) (the "Compositions") in synchronization or timed-relation with a picture produced by Licensee (the "Picture") for television broadcast and exhibition only, and known as:

Title:
Composer:
Publisher:
Length of Composition & Manner of Use:

2. This is a license to record only, and the exercise of the recording rights herein granted is conditioned upon performance of the Composition(s) over television stations having valid licenses from the copyright owner ("the Owner"), or from the person, firm, corporation or other entity having the legal right to issue performance rights licenses for the Owner in the respective territories in which the Composition(s) shall be performed. The Composition(s) shall not be used in any manner and media or be recorded for any other purpose, except those specifically set forth herein, without the express written consent of the Owner. No sound recordings produced pursuant to this license are to be manufactured, sold and/or used separately from the Picture; and the Picture shall not be exhibited in or televised into theaters or other public places of amusement where motion pictures are customarily exhibited.

3. This license is granted for the following territory: The United States, its territories and possessions.

4. This license shall end on _____. Upon such date rights herein granted shall immediately cease and end, and the right derived from this license to make or authorize any further use or distribution of the Picture with the licensed music shall also cease and end upon such date.

5. This license cannot be assigned or transferred without the express written consent of the undersigned.

6. The undersigned warrants, on behalf of the principal for whom the undersigned is acting, that it is the owner of the recording rights herein licensed, and this license is given without other warranty or recourse, except to repay the consideration paid for this license if said warranty shall be breached. The undersigned's warranty is limited to the amount of consideration paid for this license; and the undersigned further reserves all rights and uses in and to the Composition(s) not herein specifically granted.

_____
Publisher

AGREED AND ACCEPTED:

_____
Producer

COMPOSER AGREEMENT
(LOW-BUDGET FEATURE)

_____ 19__

Mr. John Doe
Melody Lane
Los Angeles, CA

Dear Mr. Doe:

This letter, when signed by you (the "Composer"), will confirm our mutual agreement whereby Very Independent Productions, Inc., (the "Producer") has engaged you as an employee for hire to render certain services and to furnish a complete and original musical score (the "Work") for the documentary feature _____ (the "Picture").

Producer agrees to pay composer as full compensation for all services required of him in connection with the Picture and for all the rights granted by the Composer, upon condition that the Composer shall fully and faithfully perform all the services required of him hereunder, the sum of ten dollars ($10) and other valuable consideration including one VHS copy of the Picture with musical score and a credit in the picture.

Producer employs Composer to write, compose, orchestrate, perform, record and submit to Producer music suitable for use as the complete background score for the Picture. Composer shall bear the full cost of any musicians, studio or equipment rental, guild or union fees or any other costs incurred in preparing the work except for tape stock costs.

The Composer grants the Producer the perpetual nonexclusive right to use and license others to use his name and likeness in any advertising or exploitation of the Picture.

The Composer agrees that Producer may perpetually use or authorize others to use any of the rights herein granted for commercial advertising or publicity in connection with any product, commodity or service manufactured, distributed or offered by the Producer or others, provided such advertising refers to the Picture, or to the Composer's employment by the Producer.

Composer warrants that all material written, composed, prepared or submitted by him during the term hereof or any extension of it shall be wholly original with him and shall not be copied in whole or in part from any other work, except that submitted to the Composer by the Producer as a basis for such material. The Composer further warrants that said material will not infringe upon the copyright, literary, dramatic or photoplay rights of any person. Composer warrants and agrees to indemnify and hold Producer and Producer's officers, shareholders, employees, successors and assigns, harmless from and against any claim, demand, damage, debt, liability, account, reckoning, obligation, cost, expense, lien, action and cause of action (including the payment of attorneys' fees and costs incurred) arising out of any breach or failure of any of Composer's warranties, representations or covenants herein contained.

CONTRACTS
FOR THE
FILM AND
TELEVISION
INDUSTRY

134

The Composer further agrees that all the material which he may write, compose, prepare or submit under this agreement shall be the sole property of the Producer. All of the material shall be written, composed, prepared and submitted by him as the employee of the Producer, and not otherwise. The Producer shall be the author and first proprietor of the copyright, and the Composer shall have no right, title or interest in the material. Producer shall have the right to obtain copyrights, patents and/or other protection therefore. The Composer further agrees to execute, verify, acknowledge, and deliver any documents which the Producer shall deem necessary or advisable to evidence, establish, maintain, protect, enforce or defend its rights and/or title in or to the said material or any part of it. Producer shall have the right, but not the duty, to use, adapt, edit, add to, subtract from, arrange, rearrange, revise and change said material or any part of it, and to vend, copy, publish, reproduce, record, transmit, broadcast by radio and/or television, perform, photograph with or without sound, including spoken works, dialogue and/or music synchronously recorded, and to communicate the same by any means now known or from now on devised, either publicly and for profit, or otherwise.

Producer, its successors and assigns, shall in addition to the Composer's services be entitled to and own in perpetuity, solely and exclusively, all of the results and proceeds of said services and material, including all rights throughout the world of production, manufacture, recordation and reproduction by any art or method, whether now known or from now on devised, and whether such results and proceeds consist of literary, dramatic, musical, motion picture, mechanical, or any other form of work, theme, idea, composition, creation or product.

The Composer will at the request of the Producer execute such assignments or other instruments as the Producer may deem necessary or desirable to evidence, establish or defend his right or title in the Work. The Composer hereby appoints the Producer the true and lawful attorney-in-fact of the Composer irrevocably to execute, verify, acknowledge and deliver any such instruments or documents which the Composer shall fail or refuse to execute.

Producer shall have and is hereby granted the complete control of the publication of all or any of the musical material written by the Composer hereunder. Producer agrees, however, that in the event it publishes the musical material or causes the musical material to be published by a third party, Producer shall pay to the composer the following fees:

(a) five cents (.05) per copy for each piano copy of the Composition and for each dance orchestration of the Composition printed, published and sold in the United States and Canada by Publisher or its licensees for which payments have been received by Publisher, after deduction of returns.

(b) Ten percent (10%) of the wholesale selling price of each printed copy of each other arrangement and edition of the Composition printed, published and sold in the United States and Canada by Publisher or its licensees for which payment has been received, after deduction of returns, except that in the event the Composition shall be used or caused to be used, in whole or in part, with one or more other compositions in a folio, album or other publication, Composer shall be entitled to receive that proportion of said royalty which the Composition shall bear to the total number of compositions contained in such folio, album or other publication for which royalties are payable.

(c) Fifty percent (50%) of any and all net sums actually received (less any costs for collection) by Publisher in the United States from the exploitation in the United States and Canada by licensees of Publisher of mechanical rights, electrical transcription and reproducing rights, motion picture and television synchronization rights and all other rights (except printing and public performance rights) in the Composition, whether such licensees are affiliated with, owned in whole or in part by, or controlled by Publisher.

(d) Composer shall receive his public performance royalties throughout the world directly from his own affiliated performing rights society and shall have no claims at all against Publisher for any royalties received by Publisher from any performing rights society which makes payment directly (or indirectly other than through Publisher) to writers, authors and composers.

(e) Fifty percent (50%) of any and all net sums, after deduction of foreign taxes, actually received (less any costs of collection) by Publisher in the United States from sales, licenses and other uses of the Composition in countries outside of the United States and Canada (other than the public performance royalties as hereinabove mentioned in paragraph (d)) from collection agents, licensees, subpublishers or others, whether same are affiliated with, owned in whole or in part by, or controlled by Publisher.

(f) Publisher shall not be required to pay any royalties on professional or complimentary printed copies of the Composition which are distributed gratuitously to performing artists, orchestra leaders and disc jockeys or for advertising, promotional or exploitation purposes. Furthermore, no royalties shall be payable to Composer on consigned copies of the Composition unless paid for, and not until an accounting therefore can properly be made.

Notwithstanding anything to the contrary contained in this Agreement, Producer, its lessees, licensees and all other persons permitted by Producer to distribute, exhibit or exploit any picture in connection with which any material written, prepared or composed by Composer hereunder is used, shall have the free and unrestricted right to use any such material and to make mechanical reproductions of it without the payment of any sums at all, and in no event shall Composer be permitted or entitled to participate in any rentals or other forms of royalty received by Producer, its licensees or any other persons permitted by Producer to use any such material or mechanical reproductions of it in connection with the exhibition, distribution, exploitation or advertising of any present or future kind of motion picture, nor shall Producer be obligated to account to Composer for any sums received by Producer from any other persons from the sale or licensing or other disposition of any material written, created, or composed by Composer hereunder in connection with the exhibition, distribution, exploitation or advertising of any motion picture. Without limiting the foregoing, Composer shall not be entitled to any portion of any synchronization fee due to the use of the material or any portion of it in motion pictures produced by Producer or by any of its subsidiaries, affiliates or related companies.

Provided Composer fully and satisfactorily renders his services pursuant to the terms and conditions of this Agreement, and that all of the original music contained in the Picture as released is the product of Composer's services, Producer shall accord Composer billing on a separate card by the phrase, "MUSIC BY JOHN DOE" or a phrase substantially similar thereto on the positive prints of said Picture. Except as set forth in the preceding sentence, all other matters about billing shall be decided in Producer's sole discretion.

CONTRACTS
FOR THE
FILM AND
TELEVISION
INDUSTRY

136

If Producer, its successors or assigns shall exercise their right hereunder to make, distribute and sell, or authorize others to make, distribute and sell, commercial phonograph records (including, without limitation, discs of any speed or size, tape and wire demos and any and all other demos, whether now known or unknown, for the recording of sound) embodying the material for the Picture and if said records contain Composer's performance as a conductor, they shall pay or cause to be paid to Composer in connection with it a reasonable royalty as is customarily paid in the industry.

Composer's sole remedy for any breach hereof shall be an action at law for damages, if any. In no event shall Composer have the right to rescind this Agreement or any of the rights granted hereunder nor to seek or obtain injunctions or other equitable relief restraining or enjoining the production, exhibition or exploitation of any motion pictures based upon or using any portion of the Work.

Nothing contained in this Agreement shall be deemed to require Producer or its assigns to publish, record, reproduce or otherwise use the Work or any part of it, whether in connection with the Picture or otherwise.

This instrument is the entire Agreement between the parties and cannot be modified except by a written instrument signed by the Composer and an authorized officer of the Producer.

This agreement shall be deemed to have been made in the State of California and its validity, construction and effect shall be governed by and construed under the laws and judicial decisions of the State of California applicable to agreements wholly performed therein.

Very truly yours,

By: John Smith
President
Very Independent Prods.

ACCEPTED AND AGREED TO:

_____

John Doe
Composer

I hereby certify that I wrote the material hereto attached as an employee of Very Independent Productions, Inc, pursuant to an agreement dated the ____ day of _____, 19___, in performance of my duties thereunder and in the regular course of employment, and that said Very Independent Productions, Inc., is the author of it and entitled to the copyright therein and thereto, with the right to make such changes therein and such uses of it as it may determine as such author.

IN WITNESS WHEREOF, I have hereto set my hand this _____day of 19__.

_____

John Doe

A motion picture studio will negotiate an agreement with a record label for the production and distribution of the soundtrack album. Record companies can earn significant revenue from such releases and will pay the studio a royalty and often an advance as well. Record companies prefer soundtracks with major artists and pop songs rather than orchestral performances.

The royalty will range from 10 to 19 percent of the retail price, although the studio will pay a portion to musical artists. The record company may ask the studio to put up matching funds for promotion. The studio will want the album's release to coincide with the film's release.

SOUNDTRACK RECORDING AGREEMENT

THIS AGREEMENT, is made as of the __ day of   ., 1993 by and between _____ ("Company") and _____ f/s/o _____ and _____ f/s/o _____ in connection with a master sound recording (the "Master") embodying the musical composition entitled _____ (the "Composition "), for possible inclusion in the theatrical motion picture presently entitled _____ (the "Picture"), and in a soundtrack album (the "Album") and any other phonograph records to be derived therefrom. _____ and _____ are hereafter referred to jointly and severally as "Lender", and _____ and _____ are hereafter jointly and severally referred to as "Artist." In consideration of the mutual covenants made herein, Company and Artist hereby agree as follows:

1. SERVICES TO BE PROVIDED: Company hereby employs Lender to cause Artist to render Artist's vocal and/or musical services to record the Master for possible inclusion in the Picture. Artist shall comply with all of Company's instructions and requests in connection with Artist's services hereunder. Artist shall render such services upon the terms and conditions set forth herein and in accordance with a production schedule to be designated by Company in its sole discretion.

2. TERM: The tear of this Agreement shall commence as of the date hereof and shall continue thereafter until such time as Artist has fully rendered all of Artist's services required hereunder.

3. OWNERSHIP:

(a) All results and proceeds of Artist's services hereunder shall constitute or contribute to a work specially ordered or commissioned by Company for use as part of a motion picture or other audio-visual work and accordingly all such results and proceeds shall constitute a "work-made-for-hire" (as such term is defined in the United States Copyright Act of 1976). Company shall own the Master, together with the performances embodied thereon and all copyrights therein and thereto, and all the results and proceeds of Artist's services hereunder throughout the universe in perpetuity, free of any and all claims by Lender, Artist or any person, corporation or other entity deriving any rights from Lender or Artist.

CONTRACTS
FOR THE
FILM AND
TELEVISION
INDUSTRY

138

(b) Without limiting the generality of clause 3(a) hereof, Company shall have the exclusive, perpetual and worldwide right, but not the obligation, to use and perform the Master, and the results and proceeds of Artist's services hereunder:

(i) in synchronization with the Picture and any other audio-visual works for exploitation in any and all media now known or hereafter devised (including, but not limited to, audio-visual devices), and in advertisements, trailers, "music videos" and other promotional and ancillary uses of the Picture or such other audio-visual work; and

(ii) to manufacture, sell, distribute and advertise the Album and any other phonograph records embodying the Master by any methods and in any configurations now known or hereafter devised; for the release of same under any trademarks, tradenames or label; to perform the Album and any other phonograph records derived therefrom publicly; and to commit to public performance thereof by radio and/or television, or by any other media now known or hereafter devised, all upon such terms and conditions as Company may approve, and to permit any other person, corporation or other entity to do any or all of the foregoing.

4. NAME AND LIKENESS: Lender hereby grants to Company the irrevocable worldwide right, in perpetuity, to use and permit others to use Lender's or Artist's name, voice, approved photograph, likeness and biographical material concerning Artist in connection with the Picture, Master, Album and any other phonograph records derived therefrom and any promotions and advertisements thereof. Any photograph, likenesses or biographical material submitted or furnished by Lender or Artist to Company shall be deemed approved, and, promptly following the execution of this Agreement, Lender shall submit to Company a reasonable assortment of approved photographs, likenesses and biographical materials for use by Company in connection herewith. All such materials submitted by Company to Lender for approval (which approval shall not be unreasonably withheld) shall be deemed given in the event Lender fails to submit written objections thereto within five (5) days after the applicable photographs, likenesses and/or biographical materials have been submitted to Lender for approval.

5. PRE-RECORDING: Company shall have the right to re-record, edit, mix and re-mix, dub and re-dub the Master in Company's sole discretion, and nothing contained herein shall be construed to obligate Company to employ Artist in connection with same.

6. COMPENSATION:

(a) Provided Lender and Artist fully perform all their material obligations under Clause 1 above, and in full consideration of all rights granted herein, Company shall pay or cause to be paid to Lender, upon the later to occur of the date of the full completion of all of Lender's or Artist's services hereunder, or the date of Lender's and Artist's execution hereof, an amount equal to the minimum scale amount specified for Artist's recording services hereunder in any applicable union collective bargaining agreements. The provisions of any applicable union collective bargaining contract between Company and any labor organization which are required by the terms of such contract to be included in this Agreement shall be deemed incorporated herein.

(b) It is specifically understood and agreed that the sums set forth in this Clause 6 and the record royalties set forth in Clause 7 below shall constitute payment in full to Lender and Artist, and to all persons or entities deriving or claiming rights through either Lender and/or Artist.

7. ROYALTIES:

(a) With respect to the exploitation of the Master if embodied on the Album or other phonograph records derived therefrom, Company shall pay or cause any phonograph record distributor ("Distributor") of the Album, Single or phonograph records derived therefrom, to pay to Lender a basic royalty at the rate of five (5%) percent (the "Basic Album Rate") of the applicable suggested retail list price ("SRLP") in respect of net sales of Albums sold through normal retail channels in the United States in the form of black vinyl discs and cassettes, pro-rated by multiplying the applicable royalty rate by a fraction, the numerator of which is the number one (1), and the denominator of which is the total number of master recordings, including the Master, contained on the Album (the "Lender Fraction").

(b) The royalty payable to Lender hereunder for singles, budget records, compact discs, foreign record sales and other sales of records or exploitations of the Master shall be reduced and pro-rated in the same proportion that the basic United States Album rate payable to Company in respect of the Album (the "Basic Distributor Rate") is reduced or pro-rated pursuant to Company's agreement with the applicable Distributor, provided that with respect to such sales of records or exploitations of the Master for which Company receives a royalty which is computed as a flat fee or as a percentage of the Distributor's net receipts from such use, Lender's royalty hereunder in respect of such sale or use shall be equal to the amount of Company's flat fee or net receipts, multiplied by the product of the following:

$$\frac{\text{Basic Album Rate}}{\text{Basic Distributor Rate}} \quad X \quad \text{Lender Fraction}$$

(c) Except as otherwise provided in this Agreement, Lender's royalties hereunder shall be computed, determined, calculated and paid to Lender on the same basis (e.g., packaging deductions, free goods, reserves, definition of suggested retail list price, percentage of sales, discounts, returns policy, taxes, etc.) and at the same times as royalties are paid to Company by the applicable Distributor.

(d) Notwithstanding anything to the contrary contained in this Agreement, (i) Lender shall not be entitled to receive any record royalties at all with respect to records sold prior to the recoupment of all Recording Costs and Conversion Costs from the royalties otherwise payable to Lender hereunder; and (ii) following such recoupment Lender's royalties shall be credited to Lender's account hereunder solely in respect of records thereafter sold which embody the Master. The term "Recording Costs" shall mean all direct costs incurred in the course of producing and recording the Master hereunder including, without limitation, the cost of studio time, musician fees, union payments, instrument rentals, producer's fees and advances and the costs of tape, editing, mixing, re-mixing and mastering and other similar costs customarily regarded as recording costs in the phonograph record industry. The term "Conversion Costs" shall mean all direct costs incurred in connection with the conversion of the Master from use in the Picture to use in the Album and other phonograph records derived therefrom including, without limitation, new-use, re-use, re-mixing, and re-editing costs and all other costs which are now or hereafter recognized as conversion costs in the phonograph record and motion picture industries.

CONTRACTS
FOR THE
FILM AND
TELEVISION
INDUSTRY

140

(e) Lender shall be deemed to have consented to all royalty statements and all other accounts rendered by Company, unless specific objection in writing, stating the basis thereof, is given by Leader to Company within one (1) year from the date such statement is rendered. During this one (1) year period, Lender may, at its expense, but not more than once annually, audit the books and records of Company, solely in connection with royalties payable to Lender pursuant to this Agreement, provided such audit is conducted by a reputable certified public accountant during business hours and upon reasonable written notice. Lender shall be foreclosed from maintaining any action, claim or proceeding against Company in any forum or tribunal with respect to any statement or accounting rendered hereunder unless such action, claim or proceeding is commenced against Company in a court of competent jurisdiction within one (1) year after the date on which Company receives Lender's written objection.

8. CREDITS:

(a) If the Master is contained in the Picture, Company shall accord Artist a credit in substantially the following form in the end titles of release prints of the Picture approximately adjacent to the titles of the Composition:

"WRITTEN BY (name of writer) AND
(name of other, writer)"

"PERFORMED BY (name of performer) AND
(name of other performer)"

The type, size, shape, color, placement, duration and all other characteristics of the credit shall be at Company's sole and absolute discretion. Without limiting the generality of the foregoing, such credit may be shared with and/or adjacent to credits relating to other contributors to the Master and/or the Composition.

(b) No casual or inadvertent failure by Company or any failure by a third party to comply with the provisions of this Clause 8 shall constitute a breach of this Agreement.

9. WARRANTIES: Lender, on its own and on Artist's behalf, hereby warrants and represents that:

(a) it has the full right, power and authority to enter into this Agreement and to grant all rights granted herein, that it is not under nor will it be under, any disability, restriction or prohibition with respect to its rights to fully perform in accordance with the terms and conditions of this Agreement and that there shall be no liens, claims or other interests which may interfere with, impair or be in derogation of the fights granted herein;

(b) the Master shall be freely available for use by Company in the Album, the Single(s) and other phonograph records and in the Picture in all media (whether now known or hereafter devised) in which the Picture is to be distributed (and in any and all advertising therefor), throughout the world including, without limitation, in theaters, free and pay television, in home video devices, and in radio, television and theatrical trailers, without further payment by Company, except as set forth herein;

(c) any party who may be entitled to Artist's exclusive recording services shall have given a written waiver of such rights in connection with Company's exploitation of the Master as herein provided;

(d) Company shall not be required to make any payments of any nature for, or in connection with, the acquisition, exercise or exploitation of rights by Company pursuant to this Agreement except as specifically provided in this Agreement;

(e) neither Lender nor Artist shall, prior to the date five (5) years after the delivery of the Master, produce or re-record or authorize the production or re-recording of the Composition for any third party; and

(f) neither the Master, nor the Composition nor any other material supplied by Artist will violate or infringe upon any common law or statutory right of any person, firm or corporation including, without limitation, contractual rights, copyrights, and rights of privacy.

10. INDEMNITY: Lender hereby agrees to indemnify Company, Company's successors, licensees, distributors, sub-distributors and assigns, and the respective officers, directors, agents and employees of each of the foregoing, from and against any damages, liabilities, costs and expenses, including reasonable attorneys' fees actually incurred, arising out of or in any way connected with any claim, demand or action inconsistent with this Agreement or any warranty, representation or agreement made by Lender and/or Artist herein.

11. UNIQUE SERVICE: Lender acknowledges that the services performed by Artist hereunder and the rights hereunder granted are of a special, unique, extraordinary and unusual character which gives them a peculiar value, the loss of which cannot be reasonably or adequately compensated in damages in an action of law, and that any default by Lender and/or Artist will cause Company irreparable harm and injury. Lender agrees that Company shall be entitled to seek injunctive and other equitable relief in addition to Company's remedies at law, in the event of any default by Artist.

12. REMEDIES FOR BREACH: Lender's rights and remedies in the event of a breach or alleged breach of this Agreement by Company shall be limited to Lender's right to recover damages in an action of law and in no event shall Lender be entitled by reason of any such breach or alleged breach to enjoin, restrain, or to seek to enjoin or restrain, the distribution or other exploitation of the Picture, Album, Single, or other work which may embody the Master. This Agreement shall not be deemed to give any right or remedy to any third party whatsoever unless the right or remedy is specifically granted by the parties hereto in writing to the third party. Lender shall execute any further documents necessary to fully effectuate the intent and purposes of this Agreement.

13. ASSIGNMENT: Company shall have the right, at Company's election, to assign any of Company's rights hereunder, in whole or in part, to any person, firm or corporation including, without limitation, any distributor or subdistributor of the Picture, Album or other phonograph records derived therefrom, or other work which may embody the Master. Lender shall not assign rights without Company's prior written consent and any attempted assignment without such consent shall be void and shall transfer no rights to the purported assignee.

14. ENTIRE AGREEMENT: This Agreement sets forth the entire understanding of the parties thereto relating to the subject matter hereof and supersedes all prior agreements, whether oral or written, pertaining thereto. No modification, amendment, or waiver of this Agreement or any of the terms or provisions hereof shall be binding upon Lender or Company unless confirmed by a written instrument signed by authorized officers of both Lender and Company. No waiver by Artist

CONTRACTS
FOR THE
FILM AND
TELEVISION
INDUSTRY

142

or Company of any terms or provisions of this Agreement or of any default hereunder shall affect their respective rights thereafter to enforce such term or provision or to exercise any right or remedy upon any other default, whether or not similar.

15. RIGHT TO CURE: No failure by Company to perform any of Company's obligations hereunder shall be deemed a breach hereof, unless Lender gives Company written notice of such failure and Company fails to cure such nonperformance within thirty (30) days after Company's receipt of such notice.

16.NOTICES: All notices hereunder shall be sent certified mail, return receipt requested, or delivered by hand to the applicable address set forth below; unless and until written notice of a change of address, sent via registered mail is received by the other party.

If to Company: _____ . Courtesy copies to: _____.

If to Lender: _____ .

Notwithstanding the foregoing, all accounting statements and payments may be sent by regular mail. Except as required by law, the date of mailing of such notice shall be deemed the date upon which such notice was given or sent.

17. APPLICABLE LAW: This Agreement has been entered into in the State of California, and its validity, construction, interpretation and legal effect shall be governed by the laws of the State of California applicable to contracts entered into and performed entirely within the State of California. The California Courts will have jurisdiction in any controversies regarding this Agreement; and, any action or other proceeding which involves such a controversy will be brought in the courts located within the State of California and not elsewhere. Any process in any action or proceeding commenced in the courts of the State of California arising out of any such claim, dispute or disagreement, may, among other methods, be served upon Lender by delivering or mailing the same, via registered or certified mail, addressed to Lender at the address first above written or such other address as Lender may designate at the address first above written or such other address as Lender may designate pursuant to clause 16 hereof. Any such delivery or mail service shall be deemed to have the same force and effect as personal service with the State of California. This Agreement shall not become effective until signed by a duly authorized officer of Lender and countersigned by a duly authorized officer of Company.

IN WITNESS WHEREOF, the parties hereto have executed this Agreement as of the year and date first above written.

COMPANY

By: _____

Accepted And Agreed To:

LENDER

By _____

INDUCEMENT AGREEMENT

In order to induce _____ ("Company") to enter into the foregoing agreement ("Agreement") with (name of first artist's loan-out company) and (name of second artist's loan-out company), the undersigned hereby:

(a) acknowledges that he has read and is familiar with all the terms and conditions of the Agreement;

(b) assents to the execution of the Agreement and agrees to be bound by those provisions of the Agreement that relate to the undersigned in any way, including the services to be rendered thereunder by the undersigned and restrictions imposed upon the undersigned in accordance with the provisions of the Agreement;

(c) acknowledges and agrees that Company shall be under no obligation to make any payments to the undersigned or otherwise, for or in connection with this inducement and for or in connection with the services rendered by the undersigned or in connection with the rights granted to Company thereunder and the fulfillment of the undersigned's obligations pursuant to the Agreement, and that the undersigned shall look solely to (name of artist's loan-out company) for payment of any sums due him in connection with his services under the Agreement.

_____

Artist

CHAPTER 7

FINANCING

Independent films are often financed through pre-sale agreements and/or limited partnership agreements. In a pre-sale agreement, a buyer pre-buys movie distribution rights for a territory(s) before the film has been completed. In a limited partnership agreement, investors (limited partners) put up the money needed to produce a film.

PRESALE AGREEMENTS

If the buyer's commitment to purchase is sufficiently firm, and the buyer financially solid, a bank may be willing to lend the producer money to make a film on the strength of the paper (i.e., contract). However, a contract that merely says a buyer will consider purchasing a film upon completion is not strong enough to borrow against. Banks want to be assured that the buyer will purchase the film as long as it meets minimum technical standards for a feature film, even if artistically the film is a disappointment. The bank will likely insist on a completion bond to insure that there are sufficient funds to complete production. The terms of a pre-sale agreement are similar to the terms of a Negative Pick-Up agreement discussed in Chapter 9.

LIMITED PARTNERSHIPS

Another way to fund production is with investors. Investors usually want limited liability. That is, they don't want to be financially responsible for any cost overruns or liability that might arise if a stunt person is injured. They want their potential loss limited to the extent of their investment.

CONTRACTS
FOR THE
FILM AND
TELEVISION
INDUSTRY

146

In a limited partnership agreement the limited partners (i.e., the investors) have limited liability and limited control over the enterprise. If they begin to manage the enterprise they will lose their limited liability.

The enterprise is managed by one or more general partners. General partners (i.e., the producers) are fully liable. Sometimes, general partners will set up a corporation that will become the general partner in an attempt to protect their personal assets from liability. The courts will not consider the corporation a separate legal entity, however, if the transaction is deemed a sham designed only to insulate the owners from liability.

The courts will consider a corporation a separate legal entity if it operates like one. The company must be adequately capitalized and corporate formalities need to be observed. There should be no commingling of corporate and personal funds. The company must maintain separate books, records and bank accounts, and periodic board of director meetings need to be held. Furthermore, all contracts for the making of the movie should be entered into on behalf of the corporation, and not by the producers personally.

Because limited partnership interests are considered securities (investments), they are subject to state and federal securities laws. These laws are complex and have strict requirements. A single technical violation can subject general partners to liability. Therefore, it is important that filmmakers retain an attorney with experience in both securities and entertainment. This is an area where filmmakers should never attempt to do it themselves.

The law requires that securities be registered with state and/or federal governments. Registration is too time-consuming and expensive for most low-budget filmmakers. Filmmakers can avoid the cost and expense of securities registration, however, if they qualify for one or more exemptions.

There is a federal exemption, for example, for offerings limited to $500,000 or less raised during a twelve month period. Another federal exemption is for an intrastate offering limited to investors all of whom reside in one state. However, relying solely on this exemption can be risky. If an offer is made to a single non-resident the exemption may be lost.

State registration can be avoided by complying with the requirements for limited offering exemptions under state law. These laws are often referred to as "Blue Sky" laws. They were enacted after the stock market crash that occurred during the Great Depression. They are designed to protect buyers from being duped into buying securities that are worthless—backed by nothing more than blue sky.

The above mentioned federal and state exemptions restrict general partners in several important respects. For example, sales may be limited to thirty-five purchasers, the purchasers may need to have a pre-existing relationship with the issuer (or investment sophistication adequate to understand the transactions), the purchasers cannot purchase for resale, and no advertising or general solicitation is permitted.

A "pre-existing relationship" is defined as any relationship consisting of personal or business contacts of a nature and duration such as would enable a reasonably prudent purchaser to be aware of the character, business acumen and general business and financial circumstances of the person with whom the relationship exists.

The "offering" is usually comprised of several documents. There is a prospectus or limited offering memorandum, a proposed limited partnership agreement, which becomes effective upon funding, and an investor questionnaire used to determine if the investor is qualified to invest.

Other documents may need to be filed with the federal and state government. For example, a Certificate of Limited Partnership may need to be filed with the Secretary of State to establish the partnership. In California, a notice of the transaction and Consent to Service of Process is filed with the Department of Corporations. If a fictitious name is used for the enterprise, a DBA (Doing Business As) notice may need to be published and filed. If the transaction is subject to federal law, a Reg. D form will need to be filed with the Securities and Exchange Commission (SEC) soon after the first and last sales.

Once a limited partnership is formed the partners need to abide by all the laws regulating limited partnerships as well as the terms of the limited partnership agreement. The partnership is a separate legal entity from the individual partners. The partnership should establish a separate partnership bank account and not commingle the partnership's funds with personal assets.

The partnership should retain an accountant and seek advice as to the tax consequences of participating in the partnership. A separate informational return will need to be filed for the partnership, even though the partnership's profits and losses are passed onto the partners.

State law may require that the partnership keep the following documents at its office:

a) Current list of the full name and last-known business or residence address of each partner set forth in alphabetical order, together with the contribution and the share of profits and losses of each partner.

b) A copy of the certificate of limited partnership and all certificates of amendment thereto, together with executed copies of any powers of attorney pursuant to which any certificate has been executed.

c) Copies of the limited partnership's federal, state and local income tax or information returns and reports, if any, for the most recent taxable years.

d) Copies of the partnership agreement and all amendments.

e) Financial statements of the limited partnership for the most recent fiscal years.

f) The partnership's books and records.

Finally, the partnership may be required to file a Certificate of Dissolution when the partnership dissolves.

CONTRACTS
FOR THE
FILM AND
TELEVISION
INDUSTRY

148

FINDERS

Producers sometime use intermediaries, or finders, to help them raise funds. Finders are subject to the same state and federal restrictions as the offerer. Here is a sample finder agreement where the finder may also license foreign distribution rights.

FINDER AGREEMENT

THIS AGREEMENT, made and entered into as of _____ , by and between _____ , Inc. (Finder) and _____ Productions (Producer) with respect to the following facts:

A. Producer owns, controls or otherwise has the right to produce a screenplay tentatively entitled _____ ("Picture") written by _____ as an employee for hire of _____ Productions.

B. Finder is a company engaged in financing and distribution activities in the motion picture business.

C. The parties want to enter an agreement whereby Finder would be encouraged to introduce Producer to third parties (herein collectively referred to as the "Financier" or "Financiers"), who may be interested in lending for, investing in, or in any other way financing all or a portion of development, production and/or distribution of the Picture.

WHEREFORE, for good and valuable consideration, the parties agree as follows:

1. SERVICES; TERM: Commencing on the date hereof, and continuing until the earlier of (a) termination by either party of this Agreement, or (b) the concluding of an agreement between Producer (or any designee, assignee, transferee, or other successor-in-interest of Producer in or to the Screenplay and/or Picture, collectively referred to hereinafter as "Producer") and a Financier, Finder shall use its best efforts to introduce Producer to parties who may be interested in financing, investing or lending money with respect to the production of the Picture or otherwise in becoming a Financier. The foregoing period of time is hereinafter referred to as the "Term."

2. COMPENSATION: If at any time during the Term or any time thereafter, Producer enters into any agreement with any Financier to invest in, lend for, or finance production and/or distribution of the Picture, then Finder shall receive an amount equal to five percent of the amount of any funds, credits or other consideration paid or lent by Financiers to Producer and used by Producer in the development and Production of the Picture, provided, that the amounts paid to Finder shall not exceed a total of forty-fuve thousand dollars ($45,000). [Moreover, if Finder obtains ninety percent (90%) or more of the total financing needed to produce the Picture, _____ and_____ shall receive "Executive Producer" credits] Finder shall receive the Commission when Producer has the right to use the amounts.

3. NO OBLIGATION: Nothing in this agreement shall obligate Producer to enter into an agreement with any Financiers.

4. NO SALE OF SECURITIES: Finder agrees not to sell or offer to sell securities related to investing in the development and/or production of the Picture. Finder agrees to indemnify and hold Producer harmless from all damage and expense (including reasonable attorneys' fees) upon a breach or claim of breach of this provision.

5. RELATIONSHIP OF THE PARTIES: Finder is an independent contractor and shall not act as an employee, agent or broker of Producer.

6. FINDER'S REPRESENTATIONS AND WARRANTIES: Finder represents and warrants to Producer that the following statements are true and correct in all respects:

(a) Finder is in the business of arranging financing and international distribution of motion pictures, has substantial experience in said business, is not insolvent or in any danger of insolvency or bankruptcy, and is not in dissolution proceedings.

(b) Finder represents and warrants to Producer that he has the full and complete authority to enter into this agreement, and that there are no outstanding claims or litigation pending against Finder.

If Finder breaches any of its warranties and representations, or otherwise breaches this agreement, Producer, in addition to its other equitable and legal remedies, may rescind this agreement and recover any reasonable amounts expended by Producer in developing or exploiting this property with Finder, and reasonable attorney' fees. Finder shall at all times indemnify and hold Producer, its licensees, assigns, officers, employees and agents harmless against and from any and all claims, damages, liabilities cost and expenses, including reasonable attorneys' fees arising out of any breach or alleged breach by Finder of any of representation, warranty or other provision hereof.

7. DISTRIBUTION RIGHTS: If Producer licenses foreign theatrical distribution rights to Finder pursuant to paragraph 2 above, the following provisions shall be included in any agreement between Producer ("Licensor") and Finder ("Licensee"):

(a) "Security Interest: As security for the payment to Licensor of fees due under this agreement, Licensee does hereby grant, assign and convey a continuing security interest in all Licensee's right, title and interest in all properties and revenues relating to the Picture, including but not limited to the following: the Picture, all distribution, sub-distribution and exhibition contracts, rentals, rights and revenues, whether now existing or owned or hereafter entered into, or acquired by Licensee and all sums due or to become due from the foregoing in any form and from any source (all of which are hereinafter referred to as "Collateral"). Licensor's security interest in collateral shall be prior to the rights of all other parties in such collateral."

(b) "Licensor agrees to commit and spend a minimum of one million dollars ($1,000,000) to advertise and publicize the Picture."

(c) "Licensee shall pay late charges of one and one-half (1 1/2%) per month on any amounts due Licensor that are more than ten days delinquent."

(d) "The occurrence of any of the following events shall constitute a default:

(i) Any material misrepresentation or breach of warranty in this agreement.

CONTRACTS
FOR THE
FILM AND
TELEVISION
INDUSTRY

150

(ii) Nonpayment, when due, of any amount payable hereunder or failure of Licensee to perform any obligation contained herein.

(iii) Insolvency of Licensee, assignment for the benefit of creditors by Licensee, or institution of any proceeding by or against Licensee alleging that Licensee is insolvent.

(iv) Dissolution, merger or consolidation of Licensee or transfer of a substantial part of its property.

On any default hereunder, Licensor shall have the option of making all remaining installments on the note immediately due and payable.

No delay by Licensor in the exercise of any right under this agreement shall operate as a waiver thereof and no partial exercise by Licensor of any right or remedy hereunder shall preclude further exercise of any other right or remedy.

If suit is commenced by Licensor to collect any payment, Licensee shall pay to Licensor a reasonable attorneys' fee. Licensee shall pay a reasonable collection charge should collection by referred to a collection agency. Licensee hereby waives (1) presentment, demand, protest, notice of dishonor and/or protest and notice of non-payment."

(e) Distribution fee: Licensee shall receive 30% of receipts as a distribution fee. Any sub-distributors, sales agents or other distributors engaged by Licensee shall be compensated by Licensee entirely from its 30% distribution fee.

8. ADDITIONAL DOCUMENTS: Finder agrees to execute, acknowledge and deliver to Producer and to procure the execution, acknowledgement and delivery to Producer of any additional documents or instruments which Producer may reasonably require to fully effectuate and carry out the intent and purposes of this agreement.

9. ARBITRATION: Any controversy or claim arising out of or relating to this Agreement or the validity, construction or performance of this Agreement or the breach thereof, shall be resolved by arbitration according to the rules and procedures of the American Arbitration Association, as they may be amended. Such rules and procedures are incorporated herein and made a part of this Agreement by reference. The parties agree that they will abide by and perform any award rendered in any such arbitration and that any court having jurisdiction may issue a judgment based upon the award. Moreover, the prevailing party shall be entitled to reimbursement of reasonable attorneys' fees and costs.

10. ASSIGNMENT: Finder shall not have the right to assign this agreement or any part hereof.

11. SECTION HEADINGS: The headings of paragraphs, sections and other subdivisions of this agreement are for convenient reference only. They shall not be used in any way to govern, limit, modify, construe this agreement or any part or provision thereof or otherwise be given any legal effect.

12. ENTIRE AGREEMENT: This agreement contains the full and complete understanding and agreement between the parties with respect to the within subject matter, and supersedes all other agreements between the parties whether written or oral relating thereto, and may not be modified or amended except by written instrument executed by both of the parties hereto. This agreement shall in all respects be subject to the laws of the State of California applicable to agreements executed and wholly performed within such State.

AGREED TO AND ACCEPTED:

_____

"Finder"

_____

"Producer"

CONTRACTS
FOR THE
FILM AND
TELEVISION
INDUSTRY

152

THE PROSPECTUS

The Prospectus (aka Limited Offering Memorandum or Private Placement Memorandum), is similar to a business plan in that it discloses the essential facts an investor needs to determine whether they want to invest in the project. The offerer of the partnership interests will be liable if there are any misrepresentations in the prospectus or any omissions of material facts.

The following sample documents were used to raise financing for a low-budget equity-waiver play. This is a fairly simple prospectus. Many of the terms are similar to those used for low-budget films, although the risk factors and background information will differ.

PRIVATE PLACEMENT MEMORANDUM

<u>Jane Doe PRODUCTIONS</u>
a California limited partnership to be formed

Dated:

THESE SECURITIES INVOLVE A HIGH DEGREE OF RISK
AND SHOULD NOT BE PURCHASED BY PERSONS WHO
CANNOT AFFORD THE LOSS OF THEIR ENTIRE INVESTMENT

Jane Doe and JOHN DOE
General Partners

offer $24,500

of limited partnership interests

of $500.00 each

to finance the equity-waiver production of

"_____"
_____

By _____

By Jane Doe Productions,
a California limited partnership to be formed

THESE SECURITIES ARE BEING OFFERED UNDER AN EXEMPTION FROM REGISTRATION PURSUANT TO SECURITIES AND EXCHANGE COMMISSION RULE 504 AND CALIFORNIA CORPORATIONS CODE SECTION 25102(f). WHETHER THESE SECURITIES ARE EXEMPT FROM REGISTRATION PURSUANT TO RULE 504 OR OTHERWISE HAS NOT BEEN PASSED UPON BY THE SECURITIES AND EXCHANGE COMMISSION, THE DEPARTMENT OF CORPO-

TABLE OF CONTENTS

Page

CONTRACTS
FOR THE
FILM AND
TELEVISION
INDUSTRY

154

A. THE OFFERING

Jane Doe and John Doe (the "Producers") intend to present "_____" (the "Play") in a limited nine-week engagement in the _____ Theatre 99-seat equity-waiver theatre in Los Angeles starting _____.

The Producers have obtained from the author of the play an option for the exclusive right and license to produce the play in Los Angeles to open on or before _____. After presenting the play for an initial run in Los Angeles, the Producers have the option to present the play as a First-Class production or as an off-Broadway or off-off-Broadway or regional theatre presentation in the United States and Canada. The Producers will obtain a five percent (5%) interest in the subsidiary rights to the play if the play is presented by producers for 49 or more performances in accordance with the terms of the Literary Option Agreement (Attached as Exhibit A to the Limited Partnership Agreement).

Jane Doe and John Doe intend to form a limited partnership (the "Partnership") under the name of "JANE DOE PRODUCTIONS, A CALIFORNIA LIMITED PARTNERSHIP." The net profits (as defined in the Partnership Agreement) will be distributed as follows:

1. Jane Doe shall receive twenty-five percent (25%) of the net profits as General Partner and Producer of the Partnership;

2. John Doe shall receive twenty-five percent (25%) of the net profits as General Partner and Producer of the Partnership;

3. The remaining fifty percent (50%) of the net profits will be distributed to the Limited Partners in proportion to their respective contributions. If there are no net profits, the Limited Partners will bear the risk of loss to the entire extent of their respective contributions. Any loss in excess of that amount will be borne by the General Partners. The General Partners may elect to purchase Limited Partnership interests in the Partnership and as such will be entitled to their pro rata share of Limited Partnership profits and losses. Any other profits derived by the Partnership will be distributed in the same manner.

The minimum fixed amount that each individual Limited Partner must contribute is $500.00. A contribution of $500.00 entitles a Limited Partner to one and two hundreth's percent (1.02%) of the net profits. There shall be no call for additional contributions from the Limited Partners.

The rights and obligations of the General and Limited Partners are set forth in the Limited Partnership Agreement. This must be signed by all the Limited Partners with the investor questionnaire. All forms may be obtained from Jane Doe at _____.

B. RISK TO INVESTORS

1. The sole business of the Partnership will be the equity waiver production of the Play. In such a venture, the risk of loss is especially high in comparison with the prospect for any profits. The Partnership interests should not be purchased unless the investor is prepared for the possibility of total loss of the investment.

2. On the basis of a nine-week run and 37 performances, and on the basis of the estimated expenses as of the date of this Offering, capital recoupment of the investment will occur at 73% of theatre capacity.

3. The General Partners, at their absolute discretion, may abandon the production of the Play at any time, for any reason whatsoever.

4. If the General Partners arrange for loans or themselves loan money to the Partnership or arrange for a letter of credit which is called, those monies must be repaid before the repayment of any Limited Partner's contributions or the distribution of net profits.

5. If the production start date is extended beyond March 10, the Limited Partners' contributions may be held without interest until as late as December 31, 1988 when, if the full $24,500, has not been raised or the difference loaned to the Partnership, such contributions will be returned without interest to the Limited Partners, except to the extent that such return has been individually waived by any Limited Partners.

6. The success or failure of a play depends heavily upon reviews.

7. The potential gross ticket sales presented in this Offering Memorandum are based upon a $10.00 and $15.00 ticket price. This is a typical ticket price for equity-waiver theatre in Los Angeles in 1988.

8. As this is an equity-waiver production, the cast may not be under contract. Therefore, any cast member may abandon the production at any time.

C. SUBSCRIPTIONS:

1. Offers to purchase Limited Partnership interests are subject to acceptance by the General Partners. A questionnaire in the form attached hereto as Exhibit A must be completed by each proposed Limited Partner. Contributions by the prospective Limited Partner are to be made in cash or by check at the time of the signing of the Limited Partnership Agreement. All contributions will be kept in a special bank account until applied towards Partnership expenses.

2. The securities represented by the Limited Partnership interests are being offered pursuant to an exemption from registration under the Federal Securities Act of 1933, as amended, and under Section 25102(f) of the California Corporations Code. As such, such interests may not be resold or transferred without registration under federal and state securities laws, or an exemption from the provisions thereof.

D. MONIES ADVANCED BY THE GENERAL PARTNERS:

To the extent that the General Partners advance funds for production expenses, they will be reimbursed upon the formation of the Partnership (unless such expenditures are for the purchase of contributions to the Limited Partnership interests). As of the date of this Offering Memorandum, expenses paid to date total approximately $3,000.00.

E. THE PRODUCERS:

(producer bios)

CONTRACTS
FOR THE
FILM AND
TELEVISION
INDUSTRY

156

F. THE PLAY

   1. General Background:

   THE AUTHOR

(author bio)

   2. Present Production. The equity waiver production to be mounted by the Partnership marks the world premiere of the Play. The production will be mounted on or about _____19__ for a nine-week period in a 99-seat theatre. The Producers may extend the production beyond the nine (9) weeks, move it to another theatre or mount a first class production in a mid-sized house in Los Angeles or elsewhere.

   3. Story and Talent". Although _____ has not been performed before (other than the workshop presentation previously mentioned), it has already achieved some critical notoriety. The Actors Theatre of _____ awarded _____ finalist honors in its ____ contest.

(play synopsis)

(director bio)

(composer bio)

(actor bios)

   4.. The Theatre and Production Schedule: The Producers are under contract to produce _____ at the _____ Theatre in Los Angeles. The theatre has 99 seats. A nine-week lease was signed with an option to extend. Rental is estimated at $750.00 for the Preview week, $1,750.00 for the opening and closing weeks, and $750.00 plus a percentage of the boxoffice receipts for the remaining middle weeks. The full rental must be paid prior to production occupancy.

   The Partnership intends to produce the Play by _____ , 19__. There will be 4 performances per week. Week #1 will be at preview prices of $10.00. On week #2 there will be five performances: the Wednesday performance of that week will be at the preview price. There will be a total of 37 performances. This schedule is subject to change and will depend upon audience demand and the cooperation of the 13-member cast who are working without pay under special arrangements with Actor's Equity.

   If the production is successful, the Producers intend to extend the run, to move to another theatre or to mount a first class production.

5. <u>Estimated Production Expenses</u>: The proceeds of this Offering will be used for the payment of certain production expenses. The following are estimated expenses of production. There is no assurance that these estimates will meet actual costs:

Estimated Production Expenses

Business expenses	$125.00
Office supplies	150.00
Scripts	20.00
Casting expenses	165.00
Rehearsal space	40.00
Stage Manager	450.00
Set Designer	500.00
Lighting Designer	100.00
Costume Designer	200.00
Publicity Fee	1,200.00
Advertising	1,700.00
Printing (flyers, programs, etc.)	1,250.00
Photography	500.00
Sets	2,000.00
Props	250.00
Sound	250.00
Lighting	400.00
Costumes	500.00
Mailing	1,000.00
Construction Crew	200.00
Opening Weekend	750.00
Legal and Accounting	1,500.00
Subtotal	13,250.00
Theatre rental	11,250.00 + % of the boxoffice receipts
TOTAL	$24,500.00 +

6. <u>Running Expenses</u>: The running expenses of the show over a nine-week period will vary depending upon personnel costs. An average budget is presented:

Nine-Week Running Expenses

Stage Manager	550.00
Lighting Board Operator	800.00
Author's Royalties	150.00
Advertising	2,000.00
TOTAL	$3,500.00

7. <u>Author's Royalty</u>: As his royalty, the author will receive for equity-waiver performances $_____ for the first regular performance and $____ for every other performance thereafter, but no royalty for preview performances. If the play is subsequently presented as a First Class production or Off-Broadway production, the author shall receive a royalty of five percent (5%) of the gross weekly box office receipts. The author has informally agreed to waive 90% of his royalty for the initial nine-week equity-waiver run in Los Angeles.

CONTRACTS
FOR THE
FILM AND
TELEVISION
INDUSTRY

158

8. <u>Potential Weekly Gross</u>: The potential weekly gross of the Play at 100% capacity for four performances per week is as follows:

99   x $15 = $1,485 x   4 = $5,940   -$1,782.00 = $4,158.00

Seats x Price = Total x   # Performances = Total - 20%   = Total
                Per Week   Theatre Earnings Rental

At four performances per week the potential weekly gross at 100% capacity is $4,158.00 for weeks #3 through #8. On week #2 and week #9 of the run there will be no theatre percentage out of the boxoffice for the theatre. The total gross per week for weeks #2 and #9 would be $5,940.00. There will be four preview performances in week #1 and one preview performance in week #2 at the reduced ticket price of $10.00 for a gross of $2,970.00. This total includes percentage to the theatre rental.

<u>Potential Weekly Gross for 100% Capacity</u>

Week #1	Previews	$2,970.00	$ 2,970.00
Weeks 2/9	Opening, Closing	5,940.00 x2	11,880.00
Weeks #3-8	Run	4,158.00 x6	24,948.00

TOTAL FOR NINE-WEEK RUN 100% CAPACITY: $39,798.00

9. <u>Potential Profits</u>: Assuming 100% capacity for 37 performances, including five previews, gross revenues would amount to $39,798.00. At 75% capacity, the production would gross $30,150.00, thereby generating $1,850.00 to the Partnership after nine weeks.

In order to meet the production expenses and return the initial capital of $24,500.00, the production must reach 73% of capacity for 37 performances.

G. <u>EXTENSION OF THE RUN OR RELOCATION</u>:

In the event that there is sufficient audience demand, the Producers have an option to extend at the _____ Theatre or mount a first-class production in a theatre of 300 seats or more.

H. <u>FIRST CLASS PRODUCTION AND THE PARTNERSHIP'S FUTURE INTEREST</u>:

If the Play is well received, the General Partners may mount a first-class production in a theatre of 300 seats or greater. A new limited partnership will be formed to finance the first class production which will cost roughly $180,000. Limited partners in this Limited Partnership will have the first right to participate in the first-class production and will have an interest in the first-class production, regardless of whether or not they elect to participate in the first-class production. That future interest will be a percentage of the General Partners' net profit participation in the first class production. The details of this future participation are defined in the Limited Partnership Agreement.

I. <u>SALE OF OPTION ON THEATRICAL RIGHTS TO THE PLAY</u>:

In the event that another producer wishes to produce the Play in California within the period in which the Partnership holds the rights to the production, the Producers may elect to sell those rights. The proceeds of such sale will be assigned to the Partnership and distributed in the same manner as other revenues of the Partnership.

J. SUBSIDIARY RIGHTS

The General Partners may become entitled to subsidiary rights in the Play pursuant to the terms and conditions of the Literary Option Agreement (Exhibit A to Limited Partnership Agreement). The General Partners are entitled to receive five percent of net receipts (regardless of when paid) if the Play has been produced for 49 performances before the expiration of five years from the date of the last paid performance of the Play in Los Angeles. Such rights include worldwide motion picture rights, and Continental United States and Canadian rights to radio, television, touring performances, stock performances, Broadway performances, Off-Broadway performances, amateur performances, foreign language performances, condensed tabloid versions, so-called concert tour versions, commercial and merchandising uses, and audio and video cassettes and discs as follows.

In the event the General Partners acquire such subsidiary rights and receive monies from the Author's exploitation of such rights, such monies shall be an asset of the partnership and shall be divided between the General and Limited Partners like other partnership revenue.

K. FINANCIAL STATEMENTS:

The issuer of the securities represented hereby will be the Partnership which is yet to be formed. Accordingly, no financial statements are presently available. After the formation of the Partnership, all financial statements will be prepared and distributed by the General Partners in accordance with the requirements of California law.

L. LIABILITY OF THE PARTNERSHIP GENERAL PARTNERS:

The General Partners will not be liable to the Partnership or to the Limited Partners for any omissions or acts performed by them in good faith on behalf of the Partnership or in the furtherance of the Partnership interest. The General Partners will be liable only for fraud, bad faith or gross negligence.

M. ADDITIONAL INFORMATION:

This Offering is intended to summarize the significant aspects of the various documents, including the Limited Partnership Agreement. Statements contained herein regarding the documents are not necessarily complete and whatever reference is made to any document shall be deemed to be qualified and implied by the provisions of the document itself. All of the documents will be on file in the offices of the Partnership c/o Jane Doe, _____.

Acting on Behalf of the Partnership:

_____

CONTRACTS
FOR THE
FILM AND
TELEVISION
INDUSTRY

160

JANE DOE PRODUCTIONS

PURCHASER QUESTIONNAIRE

(All information will be treated confidentially)

1. Name:_____ Age:_____

    Marital Status:_____

2. Home Address:_____

    Telephone Number: (_____)_____

3. Occupation:_____ Title:_____

    Firm Name:_____

    Business Address:_____

    Telephone Number: (_____)_____

    Describe the nature of your current employment and
    position(s) held (include firm name and your title(s)).

    _____

    _____

    _____

    _____ How long?_____

4. List all business or professional education, indicating
    degrees received, if any.

    _____

    _____

    _____

5. Please indicate your preferred mailing address.

    ( ) Residential   ( ) Business

6. I represent that my net worth at the present time is in
    excess of $_____.

7. Have you or will you use the services of one or more purchaser representatives (lawyer, accountant, investment advisor) in connection with this investment to assist you in evaluating the merits and risks of this investment?

( ) Yes   ( ) No

If yes, please list name, address and telephone number of each person.

Name_____

Address_____

Telephone Number_____

Name_____

Address_____

Telephone Number_____

In addition, please describe the knowledge and experience in financial and investment matters of each such person.

_____

_____

_____

If there is any family relationship between you and any such of these persons, please describe:

_____

_____

_____

Do you customarily rely on any of these persons for investment recommendations or decisions?

( ) Yes   ( ) No

If yes, please give details:

_____

_____

_____

CONTRACTS
FOR THE
FILM AND
TELEVISION
INDUSTRY

162

Do you compensate any of these persons for providing investment recommendations or decisions?

( ) Yes ( ) No

If yes, please give details:

_____

_____

_____

8. Bank References (please include name and address of Bank and name of an officer):

_____

_____

9. Have you had a pre-existing personal or business relationship with either Jane Doe or John Doe?

( ) Yes ( ) No

If yes, please identify the person, describe the relationship and indicate the time period of the relationship.

_____

_____

_____

10. I understand that the information herein is being relied upon in connection with the offer and sale of securities pursuant to an exemption from registration under Regulation D of the United States Securities and Exchange Commission and under Section 25102(f) of the California Corporations code, and I represent that all such information is true, correct and complete as of the date hereof. I agree to notify the Limited Partnership immediately of any material change in the status of any of the information set forth herein.

_____

Signature of Purchaser

_____

Print or type name of Purchaser

_____

Date this Questionnaire Signed

LIMITED PARTNERSHIP AGREEMENT

THIS AGREEMENT is made in Los Angeles, California, as of _____, 19__, by and among Jane Doe and John Doe (the "General Partners") and such other persons as shall become signatories hereto (the "Limited Partners").

1. FORMATION OF THE PARTNERSHIP: The parties hereto hereby form a limited partnership (the "Partnership") pursuant to the provisions of Sections 15611 through 15723 of the California Corporations Code (the "California Revised Limited Partnership Act"), for the purpose of presenting an equity-waiver production of _____ (the "Play") written by _____.

The General Partners have acquired the rights to produce and perform the Play in Los Angeles from its Author, pursuant to the attached "Literary Option Agreement, attached as "Exhibit A." The General Partners also have the option to present the play as a First Class production, Off-Broadway production, Off-Off Broadway Production, or regional theatre presentation, anywhere in the United States or Canada, in addition to an initial four week run in Los Angeles, as provided by said agreement.

2. PARTNERSHIP NAME AND PRINCIPAL OFFICE: The Partnership shall be conducted under the name "Jane Doe Productions, A California limited partnership." The principal office of the Partnership shall be in care of Jane Doe, _____. The General Partners shall notify the Limited Partners in writing of any change in location of the office of the Partnership.

3. PARTNERSHIP CERTIFICATES: Upon the formation of the Partnership, a Certificate of Limited Partnership shall be signed and acknowledged by each of the Partners, or through an attorney-in-fact as provided in Paragraph 18, and recorded by the General Partners pursuant to the California Revised Limited Partnership Act.

4. BUSINESS OF THE PARTNERSHIP: The Partnership business and activities shall be limited to the presentation of the Play. Producer credit shall be given to the General Partners and/or such other persons or entities as the General Partners may determine in their sole discretion. The General Partners may enter into agreements with other persons as co-producers and/or associate producers whose sole purpose is the raising of capital for the production.

5. TERM: The Partnership shall commence upon the filing of a Certificate of Limited Partnership and shall continue until the General Partners shall have terminated all Partnership activities, at which time they shall so notify each of the Limited Partners, and the Partnership shall be terminated on such date as the General Partners may designate. As of the date so fixed, the term of the Partnership shall end and the General Partners shall liquidate the affairs thereof as provided in this Agreement.

Regardless of the foregoing, the term of the Partnership shall come to an end on the disability or bankruptcy of the General Partners or ten (10) years

CONTRACTS
FOR THE
FILM AND
TELEVISION
INDUSTRY

164

from the date hereof, whichever shall first occur. If a Limited Partner shall die, his executors or administrators, or, if he shall become insane, his conservators or other representatives, shall have the same rights that the Limited Partner would have had if he or she had not died or become insane and the share of such Limited Partner in the assets of the Partnership shall be subject to all the terms and conditions of this Agreement as if such Limited Partner had not died or become insane. The Limited Partners are prohibited from assigning or otherwise transferring their interest in the Partnership unless the General Partners consent thereto. The General Partners will not be obligated to give such consent and if they do give such consent in one instance, that shall not operate to prevent the General Partners from withholding consent to any other such assignment.

6. CAPITAL CONTRIBUTIONS: The General Partners shall make no capital contribution to the Partnership, except that, to the extent they may deem desirable, the General Partners may make contribution(s) as a Limited Partner(s), and with respect to such contribution, they shall be treated in all respects as a Limited Partner. Each of the parties signatory hereto as a Limited Partner shall contribute to the capital of the Partnership at the commencement thereof the respective sum set forth next to said party's name. Said contribution shall be payable in full to the General Partners at the time of execution of this Agreement by the General Partners. Offers to subscribe to Limited Partnership interests are subject to acceptance by the General Partners.

Except as otherwise provided herein, the original capital of the Limited Partnership shall be in the total sum of _____ dollars.

7. LOANS BY GENERAL PARTNERS: If the General Partners believe that additional funds are necessary for the carrying on of the Partnership affairs, they shall have the right, in their sole discretion, to advance or to cause to be advanced or to borrow in the Partnership's name, the amount which they deem necessary on such terms (including interest) as they shall deem fit, except that there shall be no interest charged by the General Partners for any loans to the Partnership which they make. In such event, the money so advanced or caused to be advanced, or borrowed, shall be repaid before any of the contributions are repaid to any of the Limited Partners

8. DEFINITIONS: For the purposes of this Agreement, the following terms shall have the following meanings:

(a) The term "Net Profits" shall be deemed to mean the excess of Gross Receipts over all Production Expenses, Running Expenses and Other Expenses of the business of the Limited Partnership in connection with the Play.

(b) The term "Gross Receipts" shall be deemed to mean all sums derived by the Partnership from the presentation of the Play and from physical assets acquired with the funds of the Partnership.

(c) The term "Production Expenses" shall be deemed to mean the total expenses, charges and disbursements of whatsoever kind incurred by the Partnership in connection with the production of the Play preliminary to its first public performance including, without limitation, audition expenses (including casting assistant, audition staff), fees of the director, set director, sound designer, costume designer and other persons performing creative or administrative services, script printing, publicity and promotion, scenery, set design, design, construction of sets, sound equipment, properties, rehearsal expenses (including assistant stage manager, crew, rehearsal hall and miscellaneous), theatre rental security deposit, props, legal and auditing expenses, taxes of whatsoever kind or nature, expenses for replacement or substitution of any of the foregoing items and any and all other expenses usually included in the term "Production Expenses" and moving expenses for the purpose of continuing the waiver production.

(d) The term "Running Expenses" shall be deemed to mean expenses, charges, disbursements of whatsoever kind, including, without limitation, salaries of lighting technicians, house manager, general manager, stage manager and assistant stage manager, ongoing expenses of advertising, publicity and promotion, box office personnel and services, legal and auditing expenses, miscellaneous supplies, taxes of whatsoever kind and nature and any and all other expenses usually included in the term "Running Expenses."

(e) The term "Other Expenses" shall be deemed to mean all expenses of whatsoever kind or nature, other than those referred to in c) and d) above (and whether or not similar thereto) incurred in connection with or by reason of the operation of the business of the Partnership, including closing expenses, monies paid or payable in connection with claims for plagiarism, libel or negligence and other claims of a similar or dissimilar nature.

9. ALLOCATION OF NET PROFITS:

(a) Each Limited Partner shall receive that proportion of fifty (50) percent of the Net Profit as the amount of his or her contribution bears to the aggregate Limited Partnership contributions to the Partnership. The General Partners shall be entitled to receive the remaining fifty (50%) percent of the Net Profits. The General Partners reserve the right for any reason whatsoever to pay to individual investors or parties rendering services to the Partnership or others, a participation in Net Profits, which such participation shall be paid solely out of such General Partners' share of Net Profits.

(b) Such part of the Net Profits of the Partnership as can be paid in cash and still leave the Partnership with sufficient cash reserves for the payment of debts, liabilities and ongoing Partnership expenses shall, in the sole discretion of the General Partners, be paid not less frequently than quarterly to the General Partners and the Limited Partners.

10. ALLOCATION OF LOSSES: Until Net Profits shall have been earned, losses suffered and incurred by the Partnership up to but not exceeding the aggregate contributions of the Limited Partners shall be borne entirely by the Limited Partners in proportion to their respective contributions. After Net Profits shall have been earned, then to the extent of such Net Profits, the General Partners and Limited Partners shall share such losses pro rata in the same percentages as they are entitled to share in Net Profits pursuant to the provisions of Paragraph 9 hereof. No Limited Partner (other than a Partner who is both a Limited Partner and a General Partner) shall be personally liable for any debts, obligations or losses of the Partnership in any event, except to the extent of the capital contributed by said Limited Partner hereunder. The provisions of this Paragraph 10 shall not affect the obligations of the Limited Partners to return capital contributions or Net Profits theretofore paid to them, together with interest therein, actually received by them as provided in Paragraph 11 b) of this Agreement.

11. CASH DISTRIBUTION. RETURN OF CAPITAL AND NET PROFITS: Unless agreed in writing, the capital contributions of the Limited Partners shall be returned as follows:

CONTRACTS
FOR THE
FILM AND
TELEVISION
INDUSTRY

166

a) Upon the closing of the production and the abandonment of further intention of producing same, the assets of the Partnership shall (subject to the provisions of the following subparagraphs hereof) be liquidated as promptly as possible and the cash proceeds shall be applied as follows:

(i) to the payment of all debts, taxes, obligations and liabilities of the Partnership and the necessary expenses of liquidation. Where there is a contingent debt, obligation or liability, a reserve shall be set up to meet same.

(ii) to the repayment of the capital contributed by the Limited Partners (if any shall then remain unpaid) or such portion thereof as can be paid out of liquidation of the assets of the Partnership then remaining; said Limited Partners' payments to be in proportion to their respective cash contributions if the said assets shall not be sufficient to pay such contributions in full.

(iii) the surplus, if any, of the said assets then remaining shall be divided among the General and Limited Partners in the proportion that they share in Net Profits.

(b) If any repayment of contributions or distribution of Net Profits shall have been made prior to or subsequent to the termination date of the Partnership, and, if at anytime subsequent thereto, there shall be any unpaid debts, taxes, liabilities or obligations of the Partnership and the Partnership shall not have sufficient assets to meet them, then each Limited Partner and the General Partners shall be obligated to repay to the Partnership such an amount, not in excess of the capital so returned to him or her and Net Profits so distributed to him or her, as the General Partners deem necessary for such purposes. In such event, the Limited Partners and the General Partners shall first repay any Net Profits theretofore distributed to them, such repayment by them to be made in proportion to the amounts of such Net Profits theretofore distributed to them, respectively. If such distributed Net Profits shall be insufficient, the Limited Partners shall return contributions of capital which may have been repaid to them, such return by the Limited Partners to be made in proportion to the amounts of the contributions that may have been repaid, respectively. All such returns shall be made promptly after receipt by each Limited Partner from the General Partners of a written notice requesting such repayment.

(c) In liquidating assets, all physical assets which have a saleable value shall be sold at such price and upon such terms as the General Partners, in good faith, deem fair and equitable.

(d) The Limited Partners shall have no right to receive property other than cash.

12. BANK ACCOUNTS: The General Partners will, in the name of the Partnership, open and maintain a bank account or accounts in which shall be deposited all of the capital of the Partnership and all of the Gross Receipts (and no other funds). Any interest earned on such funds shall be an asset of the Partnership. All monies received from the offer and sale of Limited Partnership interests pursuant to this Agreement will be held in said bank account until actually employed for pre-production or production purposes (unless otherwise authorized by any Limited Partner) or returned to the Limited Partners, unless such return is waived by a Limited Partner. Withdrawals from any such bank account or accounts shall be made upon such signature or signatures as the General Partners may designate. In any event, the funds held in such account shall be used solely for the business of the Partnership.

13. BOOKS, RECORDS, ACCOUNTS: At all times during the continuance of the Partnership, the General Partners shall keep or cause to be kept full and faithful books of account in which shall be entered fully and accurately each transaction of the Partnership. All of the said books of account and all boxoffice statements received by any theatres shall at any reasonable times be open to the inspection and examination of the Limited Partners, or their representatives. The General Partners agree to deliver to the Limited Partners, not later than ninety (90) days after the opening of the Play, a complete statement of Production Expenses. The General Partners further agree that as long as the Play is being presented by the Partnership, an annual statement of operations prepared by a certified public accountant and such other financial statements as may be required by law will be delivered to the Limited Partners. The General Partners shall deliver to each Limited Partner all information necessary for preparation of federal and state income tax returns, including copies of Partnership tax returns.

14. RIGHTS AND POWERS OF THE GENERAL PARTNER: The Limited Partners may take no part in the conduct of or control of the business or creative affairs of the Partnership, such conduct and control being vested exclusively in the General Partners. In this connection, the General Partners agree to render, and shall be the sole parties rendering, the services customarily and usually rendered by theatrical producers in connection with a theatrical production and shall have full authority in connection therewith. Without in any way limiting the foregoing, the General Partners shall have the right to abandon the production of the Play at anytime, including prior to its first public showing in Los Angeles. The General Partners will devote as much time to the business of the Partnership as may be necessary, it being understood, of course, that the Partnership may employ such assistants as may be necessary. It is agreed that the General Partner shall not be responsible to the Partnership or to the Limited Partners for any action they may take in good faith within the scope of their authority as General Partners or for their inability to render services as General Partners for causes beyond their control.

The General Partners and each Limited Partner shall have the right, prior to, during and subsequent to the term of this Agreement to be engaged or interested in other enterprises, including, without limitation, theatrical enterprises, whether or not such other theatrical enterprises shall be in competition with the Play and each of them also has the right to render his or her services to other persons or entities.

15. ASSIGNMENT OF CONTRACTS: It is recognized and agreed that the General Partners will assign to the Partnership all contracts made by the General Partners to the Partnership, including the agreement with the Play's Author. The Partnership will reimburse the General Partners for any monies advanced in connection with such contracts.

16. AMENDMENT OR MODIFICATION: If at anytime during the continuance of the Partnership, the parties shall deem it necessary or expedient to make any alteration, amendment or addition hereto, for the more advantageous or satisfactory management of the Partnership business, such alteration, amendment or addition may be done by any writing supplementary to this Agreement; and all of such alterations, amendments and additions shall be adhered to and unless oth-

CONTRACTS
FOR THE
FILM AND
TELEVISION
INDUSTRY

168

erwise therein provided shall have the same effect as if the same had been origi-nally embodied in and formed a part of this Agreement. This Agreement may not be changed orally.

17. FIRST CLASS RIGHTS: The General Partners have the right to mount a First Class production of _____as provided in the Literary Option Agreement (Exhibit A). The General Partners have the sole discretionary power to exercise such rights or to assign such rights.

In the event that the General Partners elect to mount a First Class production, alone or in association with others, they intend to form a separate limited part-nership for that purpose ("First Class Partnership") and further intend to raise monies therefor. Such monies will be obtained by admitting "Class B Limited Partners" to the First Class Partnership, some or all of whom may be the Lim-ited Partners of this Partnership (referred to as "Class A Limited Partners"). Each Class A Limited Partner shall have the right, but not the obligation, prior to the admission of any Class B Limited Partners, to become a Class B Limited Part-ner by contributing to the First Class Partnership an amount which bears the same ratio to the total capital determined to be contributed by the Class B Lim-ited Partners as such Class A Limited Partner's contribution to this Partnership bears to the total capital contributions of all Class A Limited Partners. Unless oth-erwise specified in the First Class Partnership Agreement, such contributions by the Class A Limited Partners must be made within thirty (30) days of receipt of written notice from the General Partners of their intent to form a First Class Limited Partnership.

(a) ALLOCATION OF PROFITS, FIRST CLASS PRODUCTION. In consider-ation for the capital contribution by the Class A Limited Partners in the equity-waiver production, such Class A Limited Partners will have an ongoing share in the Net Profits of the First Class Partnership, regardless of whether or not they choose to make a capital contribution to the First Class Partnership.

(i) Net Profits of the First Class Partnership shall, subject to the fol-lowing terms and conditions, be allocated thirty-five (35%) percent to the General Partners, fifteen (15%) percent to the Class A Limited Partners and fifty (50%) percent to the Class B Limited Partners.

(ii) If the Class A Limited Partners have theretofore received distribu-tions from this Partnership sufficient to repay their initial contributions (or such other sum as determined hereunder), then their share of the Net Profits from the First Class Partnership shall be reduced from fifteen (15%) percent to seven-and-one-half (7.5%) percent. If the Class A Limited Partners have received distributions from this Partnership to repay part, but not all of their initial contributions, their share of the Net Profits from the First Class Partnership as set forth in subparagraph i), above, shall be reduced proportionately to the amounts repaid.

(iii) Notwithstanding anything herein to the contrary, if the General Partners admit additional general partners to the First Class Partnership and such additional general partners shall be entitled to share in Net Profits of the First Class Partnership, then the Class A Limited Partners' share of such Net Profits as set forth in this paragraph shall be further reduced to the extent of such additional general partners' share; provided, however, in no event shall the Class A Limited Partners' share be reduced more than the proportionate reduction of the original General Partners' share of net profits.

18. SALE OF PRODUCTION RIGHTS: In the event that the General Partners elect to sell their rights to the Play, the proceeds of such sale will be distributed to the Partnership.

19. SUBSIDIARY RIGHTS: The General Partners may become entitled to subsidiary rights to the Play pursuant to certain terms and conditions of the Literary Option Agreement (Exhibit A). The General Partners are entitled to receive five percent of net receipts (regardless of when paid) specified below if the Play has been produced for 49 performances before the expiration of five years subsequent to the date of the last paid performance of the Play in Los Angeles. Such rights include worldwide motion picture rights, and Continental United States and Canadian rights to radio, television, touring performances, stock performances, Broadway performances, Off-Broadway performances, amateur performances, foreign language performances, condensed tabloid versions, so-called concert tour versions, commercial and merchandising uses, and audio and video cassettes and discs as follows.

In the event the General Partners acquire such rights, and receive monies from the Author's exploitation of such rights, such monies shall be an asset of the partnership and shall be divided between the General and Limited Partners like any other partnership revenue.

20. FILING OF CERTIFICATES: Each undersigned Limited Partner makes, constitutes and appoints the General Partners his or her true and lawful attorneys-in-fact in his or her name, place and stead, to make, execute, sign, acknowledge and file:

   (a) A Certificate of Limited Partnership, as required under the laws of the State of California;

   (b) A Certificate of Dissolution of the Partnership; and

   (c) Such other instruments as may be necessary or deemed desirable by said attorney-in-fact, upon the termination of the Partnership.

21. EXECUTION OF COUNTERPARTS: This Agreement may be executed in counterpart originals, all of which taken together shall be deemed one original. The General Partners and each of the Limited Partners agree that one original of this Agreement (or set of original counterparts) shall be held at the office of the Partnership; that a Certificate of Limited Partnership shall be filed in the office of the Secretary of State of California and a duplicate original of said Certificate shall be held at the office of the Partnership and that there shall be distributed to each Partner a conformed copy of this Agreement.

22. ENTIRE AGREEMENT: This instrument incorporates the entire agreement between the parties hereto, regardless of anything to the contrary contained in the Certificate of Limited Partnership to be filed pursuant to this Agreement.

23. NOTICES: Unless otherwise notified in writing, the address of each party hereto for all purposes shall be that set forth next to his signature at the bottom hereof, and all notices hereunder shall be sent to each party, postage prepaid, at the address so indicated.

24. TERMINATION PRIOR TO OPENING: If _____ Thousand Dollars has not been contributed to the capital of the Partnership by December 31, 19__, the Partnership will not be formed and all contributions will be returned in full, unless the General Partners shall decide, in their sole discretion, to make loans or oth-

CONTRACTS
FOR THE
FILM AND
TELEVISION
INDUSTRY

170

erwise borrow funds, in the name of the Partnership, in an amount equal to the difference between the sums theretofore contributed and _____ Thousand Dollars, which such loans shall be in all respect subject to Paragraphs 7 and 12 or unless each Limited Partner, on an individual basis, shall waive his or her right thereunder, in which case such Limited Partner's proceeds will be used for such purposes related to the production as the General Partners shall deem necessary. In this event, all references herein to _____ Thousand Dollars shall be deemed to mean instead the actual limited contributions.

25. WARRANTIES OF LIMITED PARTNERS: Each Limited Partner represents and warrants that he is over twenty-one (21) years of age and a resident of the U.S.A. and has no present intention of transferring or assigning his Limited Partnership interest and is acquiring such interest for investment purposes only and not with a view to the resale or other distribution thereof. Each Limited Partner further represents: (a) that he has read and understands this Agreement and has sufficient knowledge and experience to evaluate the risks and merits of any investment made herein, or that he has consulted with an attorney, C.P.A. or certified investment adviser in connection herewith; (b) that he understands that the transaction represented hereby has not been registered with state or federal securities agencies; and (c) that he has sufficient net worth and/or annual income so that if he lost his entire investment, he will not suffer any material adverse change in financial condition.

26. SUCCESSORS AND ASSIGNS: This Agreement shall be binding upon and shall inure to the benefit of the parties hereto and their respective heirs, administrators, executors, distributees, successors and assigns.

IN WITNESS WHEREOF, the parties hereto have hereunto set their hands and seals as of the day and year first above written.

<u>GENERAL PARTNERS</u>

<u>Signature</u>   <u>Address</u>

_____

Jane Doe

_____

John Doe

<u>LIMITED PARTNERS</u>

_____   _____

Name   Date

_____   _____

Signature   Amount Contributed

_____   _____

Address   % of Profits

_____   _____

Telephone   Social Security No.

CHAPTER 8

PRODUCTION

PRODUCER EMPLOYMENT

The producer's job is often divided into "Executive Producer" and "Line Producer." The "Executive Producer" is the dealmaker, the financier. She may be producing a variety of projects at once. She will often hire a "Line Producer" to work for her. The line producer is in charge of logistics for the shoot. He will hire crew, order supplies and equipment and make sure the director has everything he needs to make the film. During production a line producer will work on one film at a time.

Some producers call themselves "independent producers." While they may not be tied to one studio, most are not entirely independent either. They may have to rely on studios to finance and distribute their pictures.

Producer deals can be structured different ways. When a studio funds development and production, the studio will pay the producer a fee from the production budget and give her a percentage of net profits. Often "Net profits" are defined in such a way that the producer is unlikely to see any revenue unless the picture is a smash hit.

On the other hand, if a producer funds development herself and/or production (i.e., using presale agreements or investor money), and the producer has a desirable film, she may be able to negotiate a much better deal. This so-called Negative Pick-up Deal, discussed in the Chapter 9, is more likely to return profits to the producer. However, the producer may have to share this revenue with investors.

Producer credits can be misleading. Sometimes people who don't produce receive a producing credit. That is because the Producers's Guild is not recog-

CONTRACTS
FOR THE
FILM AND
TELEVISION
INDUSTRY

172

nized as a union or a guild by the studios. The studios consider producers part of management and have refused to enter into a collective bargaining agreement with them.

The collective bargaining agreements with the DGA and WGA, on the other hand, severely restrict the studio's ability to allocate credit. Since studios can assign producer credits as they please, they can give such credits as perks to those who have not earned them.

Producer deals vary a great deal in their compensation and terms. Here is a sample line producer contract for a low-budget feature film.

LINE PRODUCER EMPLOYMENT AGREEMENT

THIS AGREEMENT is made and entered into as of the _____ day of_____, 19__, by and between _____ Entertainment, Inc., A California corporation, (hereinafter "Production Company"), and _____ (hereinafter "Employee").

This Agreement is entered into with reference to the following facts:

A. Production company intends to produce a theatrical motion picture (hereinafter the "Picture") based upon that certain screenplay tentatively entitled "_____" (hereinafter the "Screenplay") which Picture is intended for initial theatrical exhibition.

B. Production company wishes to utilize the services of Employee as line producer in connection with the production and delivery of the Picture upon the terms and conditions herein contained.

ACCORDINGLY, IT IS AGREED AS FOLLOWS:

1. ENGAGEMENT: Subject to events of force majeure, default, or the disability or death of Employee, Production company hereby engages the services of Employee on a "pay or "play" basis, and Employee agrees to render exclusive services as line producer, in connection with the production of the Picture upon the terms and conditions herein contained. Subject to Production Company's final approval, Employee shall supervise and be responsible for the preparation of the budget and the production schedule of the Picture, the testing of persons proposed for the cast, scouting for shooting locations, assembling the crew, the supervision of the photography of the Picture, the supervision of the editing and sound mixing, assisting in the selection of music, the supervision of the final dubbing and scoring, the supervision of all other post-production requirements of the Picture, the delivery of the final answer print and all other customary delivery items to Production company and its principal distributors, foreign and domestic, and perform such other services as are reasonably required by Production Company and are usually and customarily performed by producers in the motion picture industry. Employee will report to such place(s) as are reasonably designated by Production company, and will be available at all times and for such periods of time as are reasonably designated by Production Company. Employee will advise Production Company of Employee 's whereabouts so that Employee may be reached at any reasonable hour of the night or day. During the term of employment, Employee will render his services at all places and at all times reasonably required by Production Company, including nights, Saturdays, Sundays, and holidays.

In addition, Employee shall assist in the preparation and delivery to Production Company of a fully detailed and comprehensive preliminary and final below-the-line budget ("Budget") for the Picture, which Budget shall not exceed the sum of _____ , exclusive of contingency, completion bond fee, insurance, and any "above the line costs." Employee shall also consult with and assist Production Company, as and when requested by Production Company, in connection with Production Company's negotiations for the services of the production personnel and cast for the Picture.

2. TERM: Employee shall render the services required of him as set forth in paragraph 1 hereof during the period commencing on _____ 19__, and continuing thereafter for such time as required for pre-production, principal photography, and customary post-production and delivery of the Picture as required by Production Company. It is contemplated that principal photography of the Picture will commence approximately on _____ , 19__, and subject to extension for events beyond Production company's control and other events of force majeure, Employee 's exclusive services shall not be required beyond _____ 19__, but he shall nevertheless supervise the delivery of the Picture hereunder.

3. COMPENSATION: In consideration for all of the services to be rendered by Employee hereunder and for all of the rights granted by Employee to Production Company, and on condition that Employee is not in default hereunder, and subject to the terms and conditions specified herein, Production Company agrees to pay Employee, and Employee agrees to accept: $ _____ , contingent compensation as described in subparagraph (a) below and other valuable consideration. Payment of the _____ shall be within ten days of execution of this agreement.

(a) Contingent Compensation: If employee is entitled to a line producer credit in accordance with paragraph 9 of this agreement, Production company shall pay employee five percent of one hundred percent (5% of 100%) of the "net profit" in accordance with Production Company's agreement with the Domestic Distributor of the Picture. Notwithstanding the foregoing, "Net Profit" shall be the monies remaining, if any, after all customary deductions, including but not limited to all production expenses, interest, overhead, debts, deferred expenses and the cost of prints, advertising and marketing are deducted in accordance with Production Company's distribution agreement. Production Company shall only be obliged to pay Producer his share of "net profits" upon receipt of same from the distributor. Disbursements of contingent compensation shall be on a semi-annual basis, on a pro rata basis, beginning no later than six months after completion of the picture.

4. SERVICES: At all times during the term of Employee 's services hereunder, Employee will promptly and faithfully comply with all of Production company's reasonable instructions, directions, requests, rules and regulations. Employee will perform his services conscientiously and to the full limit of his talents and capabilities when and wherever reasonably required or desired by Production company and in accordance with Production company's reasonable instructions and directions in all matters, including those involving artistic taste and judgment. Employee will perform such service as Production Company may reasonably require of him, and as customarily and usually rendered by and required of producers employed to produce low-budget theatrical motion pictures in the motion picture industry.

CONTRACTS
FOR THE
FILM AND
TELEVISION
INDUSTRY

174

5. INSURANCE: Employee agrees that Production Company may at any time or times, either in Production Company's name or otherwise, but at Production company's expense and for Production Company's own benefit, apply for, and take out life, health, accident, and other insurance covering Employee, whether independently or together with others in, any reasonable amount which Production Company may deem necessary to protect Production Company's interests hereunder. Production Company shall own all rights in and to such insurance and in the cash values and proceeds thereof and Employee shall not have any right, title, or interest therein. Employee agrees to the customary examinations and correctly prepare, sign and deliver such applications and other documents as may be reasonably required.

6. CONTROL: Production Company shall have complete control of the production of the Picture including, but not limited to, all artistic controls and the right to cut, edit, add to, subtract from, arrange, rearrange, and revise the Picture in any manner. Production Company shall not be obligated to make any actual use of Employee's services or to produce or to release or to continue the distribution or release of the Picture once released.

7. RIGHTS: In addition to Employee's services as a line producer, Production Company shall be entitled to and shall own all of the results and proceeds thereof throughout the world in perpetuity (including, but not limited to, all rights throughout the world of production, public performance, manufacture, television, recordation, and reproduction by any art or method, whether now known or hereafter devised, copyright, trademark and patent) whether such results and proceeds consist of literary, dramatic, musical, motion picture, mechanical or any other form of works, ideas, themes, compositions, creations, or products and without obligation to pay any fees, royalties or other amounts except those expressly provided for in this Agreement. Specifically, but without in any way limiting the generality of the foregoing, Production Company shall own all rights of every kind and character in and to any and all acts, poses, plays and appearances of any and all kinds which Employee may write, suggest, direct or produce during the term hereof. In the event that Production Company shall desire to secure separate assignments of any of the foregoing, Employee agrees to execute them upon Production Company's request therefore. All rights granted or agreed to be granted to Production Company hereunder shall vest in Production Company immediately and shall remain vested in Production Company and Production Company's successors and assigns whether this Agreement expires in normal course or whether Employee's engagement hereunder is sooner terminated for any cause or reason. Production Company shall have the right to use and authorize others to use the name, voice and likeness of Employee, and any results and proceeds of his services hereunder, to advertise and publicize the Picture, including, but not limited to, the right to use the same in the credits of the Picture, in trailers, in commercial tie-ups, and in all other forms and media of advertising and publicity including merchandising, publications, records and commercial advertising and publicity tie-ups derived from or relating to the Picture.

8. REPRESENTATIONS, WARRANTIES AND INDEMNITY:

(a) Employee represents and warrants that all material of every kind authored, written, prepared, composed, and/or submitted by Employee hereunder for or to Production Company shall be wholly original with him, and shall not infringe or violate the right of privacy of, or constitute libel against, or violate any copyright, common law right or any other right of any person, firm or corporation. The foregoing warranties shall not apply to any material not authored, written, prepared, composed or submitted by Employee , but shall apply to all material, incidents and characterizations which Employee may add to or incorporate in or cause to be added to or incorporated in such material. Employee further represents and warrants that Employee is free to enter into this Agreement and to render the required services hereunder and that Employee is not subject to any obligations or disability which will or might interfere with Employee 's fully complying with this Agreement; that Employee has not made, and will not make any grant or assignment which might interfere with the complete enjoyment of the rights granted to Production Company hereunder; and that Employee will not at any time render any services or do any acts which shall derogate from the value of Employee 's services rendered pursuant to this Agreement or which shall interfere with the performance of any of Employee's covenants or obligations pursuant to this Agreement. Employee hereby indemnifies Production Company, its successors, assigns, licensees, officers and employees, and holds it harmless from and against any and all liability losses, damages and expenses (including attorneys' fees) arising out of (i) the use of any materials furnished by Employee for the Picture, or (ii) any breach by Employee of any warranty or agreement made by Employee hereunder.

(b) Production Company represents and warrants that Production Company has the right to enter into this Agreement, and to render the required obligations hereunder, and that Production Company is not subject to any other obligations or disabilities which will or might interfere with Production Company's fully complying with this Agreement; that Production Company has not made, and will not make, any grant or assignment which might interfere with the complete enjoyment of the compensation granted to Employee hereunder; that Production Company has secured all necessary financing to make all payments hereunder, and complete the Picture as budgeted; and that Production Company will not at any time render any services or do any acts which shall derogate from the value of Production Company's obligations pursuant to this Agreement, or which shall interfere with the performance of any of Production Company's covenants or obligations pursuant to this Agreement. Production Company hereby indemnifies Employee and his successors and assigns, and holds them harmless from and against any and all liability, losses, damages, and expenses (including reasonable attorneys' fees) arising out of any breach by Production Company of any warranty or agreement made by Production Company hereunder.

9. CREDIT: Provided that Employee shall fully and completely keep and perform all of his obligations and agreements hereunder, and if the Picture has been produced substantially with the use of Employee 's services hereunder, Employee shall receive a line producing credit on the positive prints and/or tape for the Picture in the main titles thereof, and in all paid advertisements (subject to customary distributor exclusions). Production Company shall determine in its sole discretion the manner of presenting and the size of such credits. No casual or inadvertent failure to comply with the provisions of this paragraph or failure of any third party to comply with same shall be deemed to be a breach of this Agreement by Production Company. In the event of a failure or omission by Production Company constituting a breach of its credit obligations under this Agreement, Employee's rights shall be limited to the right, if any, to seek damages at law, and Employee shall not have any right in such event to rescind this Agreement or any of the rights granted to Production Company hereunder, or to enjoin the distribution, exhibition, or other exploitation of the Picture or the advertising or pub-

CONTRACTS
FOR THE
FILM AND
TELEVISION
INDUSTRY

176

licizing thereof. Production Company shall, however, upon receipt of written notice of any such breach of its credit obligations, cure such breach on a prospective basis on materials to be created in the future.

10. CONTINGENCIES: If Employee shall become incapacitated or prevented from fully performing his services hereunder by reason of illness, accident, or mental and physical disability and/or if the production of the Picture is hampered or interrupted or interfered with for any event or reason beyond the control of Production Company or any other event of force majeure (hereinafter collectively referred to as "incapacity"), Production Company shall have the right to suspend Employee's services and the compensation payable to Employee during the continuance of any such incapacity. In the event any such incapacity continues for a period of seven (7) consecutive days or for an aggregate period of twenty-one (21) days, Production Company shall have the right to terminate Employee 's engagement hereunder. In the event that Employee should fail, refuse or neglect, other than because of incapacity, to perform any of his required services hereunder, Production Company shall have the right at any time to suspend Employee's services and the compensation payable to Employee during the continuance of such default, and Production Company shall have the right at any time to terminate Employee's engagement hereunder by reason of such default.

11. NO RIGHT TO CONTRACT: Employee acknowledges and agrees that he has no right or authority to and will not employ any person to serve in any capacity, nor contract for the purchase or rental of any article or material, nor make any commitment or agreement whereby Production Company shall be required to pay any monies or other consideration or which shall otherwise obligate Production Company, without Production Company's express prior written consent.

12. TRAVEL AND EXPENSES: If Production Company shall require Employee to render his services on location at any place(s) more than fifty (50) miles from his residence, Production Company shall furnish Employee with transportation from his residence to such place(s) and return, or reimburse employee 25 cents per mile if employee uses his own means of transportation. Production Company shall also furnish Employee with or reimburse Employee for actual reasonable expenses for each day Production Company requires Employee to render services away from Employee's residence on a no-less favorable basis than the expense allowance accorded the director. All transportation expenditures shall require the prior approval in writing by Production Company or its designee. Any miscellaneous expenses that employee incurs relating to his employment, shall be reimbursed by Production Company within seven days after receipts are submitted to Production Company.

13. ASSIGNMENT: Production Company may transfer and assign this Agreement or all or any of its rights hereunder to any person, firm or corporation, but no such assignment or transfer shall relieve Production Company of its executory obligations hereunder. This Agreement shall inure to the benefit of Production Company's successors, licensees and assigns. Employee shall not assign or transfer this Agreement, or any of his rights or obligations hereunder, it being understood that the obligations and duties of Employee are personal to Employee, and any purported assignment shall be void. Employee may, however, assign his right to receive any monies hereunder.

14. LIMITATION OF REMEDY: All rights assigned by this Agreement shall be irrevocable under all or any circumstances and shall not be subject to reversion, rescission, termination or injunction. Employee agrees that he shall not have the right to enjoin the exhibition, distribution or exploitation of any motion picture produced hereunder or to enjoin, rescind or terminate any rights granted to Production Company hereunder. Employee further agrees that Employee's sole remedy in the event of any default by Production Company hereunder, including the failure by Production Company to pay Employee any consideration payable to Employee pursuant hereto, or to accord Employee credit (to the extent that Production Company is obligated to accord Employee such credit) pursuant hereto, shall be an action at law for damages and/or for an accounting (if applicable). At all times, the Production Company shall have all rights and remedies which it has at law or in equity, pursuant hereto or otherwise.

15. PRODUCTION BUDGET AND SCHEDULE: Employee represents and warrants that Employee has read the Screenplay for the Picture, and based upon Employee's substantial experience in the production of motion pictures, Employee has advised Production Company that based upon the current Screenplay, and an anticipated _____ week schedule for principal photography the Picture can be produced for a below-the-line cost of $_____, excluding any contingencies, completion bond fees, insurance, events of force majeure and all "above the line" costs. It is of the essence of this Agreement that Employee produce the Picture in accordance with the approved production schedule and for a below-the-line cost not exceeding _____ thousand dollars ($_____). Employee agrees to timely notify Production Company of any potential over-budget situations and further agrees not to proceed with any production cost overages without the prior written consent of Production Company. If, after such notification, the below-the-line cost of the Picture exceeds the _____ dollars ($_____), or the approved production schedule through no fault of Employee, then Production Company shall be solely responsible for said cost overruns. If, however, Employee fails to give such timely notification, and/or proceeds with production cost overages without the written consent of Production Company, and as a result it reasonably appears, based upon Production Company's good faith judgment, that the below-the-line cost of the Picture will exceed the _____ dollars, or the approved production schedule by Five Percent (5%), then Production Company may, in addition to any other rights or remedies which Production Company may have at law or in equity, terminate this Agreement, and any further payments or other obligations due Employee hereunder. Under no circumstances will the Employee be personally liable for any cost overruns.

16. FURTHER DOCUMENTS: Employee agrees to execute any and all additional and further documents and instruments required by Production Company to further the intents and purposes of this Agreement and to vest in Production Company all right, title, and interest in and to the Picture. In the event Employee failsor refuses to execute such document or instrument, Employee hereby irrevocably appoints Production Company his attorney-in-fact (such appointment being coupled with an interest) to execute such documents or instruments on behalf of Employee.

17. NOTICES: All notices or payments which Production company may be required to give or make to Employee hereunder may be delivered personally or sent by certified or registered mail or telegraph, or by fax, to Employee at _____.

All notices which Employee may wish to give to Production company here-

CONTRACTS
FOR THE
FILM AND
TELEVISION
INDUSTRY

178

under may be delivered personally or sent by certified or registered mail or telegraph, or fax, to Production company at: _____.

The date of delivery, or attempted delivery, as the case may be, of any notice or payment hereunder shall be deemed to be the date of service of such notice or payment.

18. SECTION HEADINGS: The headings of paragraphs, sections or other subdivisions of this Agreement are for convenience of reference only. They will not be used in any way to govern, limit, modify, construe or otherwise be given any legal effect.

19. ARBITRATION: Any controversy or claim arising out of or relating to this agreement or any breach thereof shall be settled by arbitration in accordance with the Rules of the American Arbitration Association; and judgment upon the award rendered by the arbitrators may be entered in any court having jurisdiction thereof. The prevailing party shall be entitled to reimbursement for costs and reasonable attorneys' fees. The determination of the arbitrator in such proceeding shall be final, binding and non-appealable.

20. ENTIRE AGREEMENT: This Agreement represents the entire understanding between the parties hereto with respect to the subject matter hereof, and this Agreement supersedes all previous representations, understandings or agreements, oral or written, between the parties with respect to the subject matter hereof, and cannot be modified except by written instrument signed by the parties hereto. This Agreement shall be governed by and construed in accordance with the laws of the State of California, and the exclusive venue for resolution of any dispute arising out of, or in connection with this Agreement shall be in Los Angeles, California.

AGREED TO AND ACCEPTED:

_____
Employee

AGREED TO AND ACCEPTED:

_____ Entertainment, Inc.,

By:_____
   President

This agreement is in the form of a loan-out agreement where the casting company lends out the services of its employees (called here Smith and Jones) to the producer.

CASTING DIRECTOR EMPLOYMENT AGREEMENT

(DATE)

(ADDRESS OF CASTING COMPANY)

Re: (Name of Picture)

Dear:

This letter will confirm the terms of the agreement between _____ Casting ("Company") for the services of _____ ("Smith") and _____ Jones ("Jones") (collectively "Smith & Jones"), and Producer Pictures, Inc. ("Producer"), regarding Smith & Jones's services as Casting Director for the above-referenced theatrical motion picture (the "Picture") to be produced by Producer. Company understands and agrees that Smith and Jones will be the primary persons rendering the casting services hereunder.

1. EMPLOYMENT:

(a) Producer hereby engages Smith & Jones, commencing on a date in _____ , 199_ to be mutually agreed upon for a period of ten (10) weeks plus two (2) free weeks (which may include hiatus periods to be mutually agreed upon) to render all necessary casting services as Casting Director for the Picture. Such services will be those customarily provided in the motion picture industry by first class casting directors and shall include all re-casting an/or replacement casting, if necessary. Said services shall be rendered primarily in Los Angeles but may include travel to _____ (location). As full compensation for Smith & Jones's services Producer shall pay Company on a pay or play basis (subject only to default, disability, or events of force majeure) the sum of thirty thousand dollars ($30,000.). Such compensation shall be payable fifteen thousand dollars ($15,000.) on commencement of services, seven thousand, five hundred dollars ($7,500.) on Producer's regular pay day during the fifth (5th) week of casting; three thousand,seven hundred fifty dollars ($3,750.) on Producer's regular pay day during the tenth (10th) week of casting, and three thousand,seven hundred fifty dollars ($3,750.) upon completion of casting or commencement of principal photography, whichever is earlier. If the free weeks are required, Producer shall also reimburse Company for a casting assistant at the rate of five hundred ollars ($500.) per week.

(b) Smith & Jones's services hereunder shall be on a non-exclusive but first priority basis. Company agrees to make Smith & Jones available after the casting for the Picture is completed for all re-casting or replacement casting reasonably required by Producer. In the event that Casting Director's services are required substantially beyond the employment term referred to above, Company and Producer shall negotiate in good faith reasonable overages for the additional time required to cast the Picture.

CONTRACTS
FOR THE
FILM AND
TELEVISION
INDUSTRY

180

2. CONTINGENT DEFERMENT: Provided Smith & Jones fully performs all services required hereunder and is not in material breach of this Agreement, Company shall be entitled to a contingent deferment of twenty thousand dollars ($20,000.) payable pari passu and pro rata with all other contingent deferments respecting the Picture payable after Producer recoups 1.5 times the actual negative cost of the Picture, plus accrued interest thereon at the prime rate of interest plus four percent.

3. CREDIT: Provided Smith & Jones actually renders services as Casting Director on the Picture, and provided Smith & Jones is not in default hereof, Company will receive the following credit on a single in the main titles of the Picture, substantially as follows:

Casting by _____

Producer shall provide an "associate"/"assistant" casting credit in the end titles of the Picture to the casting associate/assistant.

No casual or inadvertent failure to accord such credits shall be deemed a breach of this Agreement.

4. BUSINESS CONTROLS: Company, Smith & Jones and Producer acknowledge that Smith & Jones does not have and shall not have hereunder any authority to enter into oral or written agreements or commitments on behalf of Producer without Producer's prior approval.

5. AFFIRMATIVE ACTION POLICY: Company and Smith & Jones are aware of and shall comply with Producer's policy not to discriminate against any prospective or actual cast member because of race, color, religion, sex, national origin, age, medical condition, sexual orientation, veteran's status or handicap and which policy includes a prohibition against sexual harassment. This nondiscrimination policy applies to all terms and conditions of the employment relationship, including, but not limited to, hiring, wages and benefits.

6. REIMBURSEMENT OF EXPENSES; OFFICE SPACE: During the period of Company's engagement hereunder, Producer shall reimburse Company for reasonable actual out-of-pocket casting expenses, i.e. messengers, photocopying, long distance calls, etc. Company and Smith & Jones acknowledge that the budget for the Picture is modest and shall conserve expenses as much as possible. Company shall furnish its own office space in Los Angeles for the casting services required hereunder.

7. TRAVEL: In the event Smith & Jones is required to travel to _____ for casting services, they will be furnished with first class (if available) air transportation, airport transfers, hotel accommodations, and per diem of $75.00 per day each.

8. CONTINGENCIES: If both Smith & Jones shall become incapacitated or prevented from fully performing their services hereunder by reason of illness, death, accident, or mental and physical disability and/or if the production of the Picture is hampered or interrupted or interfered with by reason of force majeure (as that term is understood in the entertainment industry), Producer shall have the right to suspend Smith & Jones's services and the compensation payable to Company during the continuance of any such incapacity. In the event any such incapacity continues for a period of seven (7) consecutive days, or for an aggregate period of twenty-one (21) days, Producer shall have the right to terminate Smith & Jones's engagement and any unpaid compensation hereunder. In the event that Smith & Jones should fail, refuse or neglect other than because of incapacity to perform any of Smith & Jones's required services hereunder, Producer shall have the right at any time to suspend Smith & Jones's services and the compensation payable to Company during the continuance of such default, and Producer shall also have the right at any time to terminate Company's engagement hereunder and any unpaid compensation due hereunder by reason of such default.

9. VIDEO CASSETTE: Producer shall furnish Company with a video cassette of the Picture when it is commercially available.

10. ARBITRATION: Any controversy or claim arising out of or relating to this agreement or any breach thereof shall be settled by arbitration in accordance with the Rules of the American Arbitration Association; and judgment upon the award rendered by the arbitrators may be entered in any court having jurisdiction thereof. The prevailing party shall be entitled to reimbursement for costs and reasonable attorneys fees.

This memorandum of agreement shall be deemed a binding agreement between the parties and any modification or amendment shall require the written consent of the parties hereto.

Please have Company and Smith & Jones indicate acceptance of these terms by signing the original and two (2) copies of this letter of agreement and returning them to me for counter-signature. I will thereafter send you a fully executed copy for your files.

Sincerely,

_____

Attorney for
Producer Pictures, Inc.

AGREED TO AND ACCEPTED:

_____Casting   Producer Pictures, Inc.

By:_____

By:_____

I have read this agreement and agree as an express inducement to the parties entering into the agreement to render all services and observe all requirements of Producer under this agreement. If I fail to do so, Producer will have the same rights vis-a-vis me personally as if I had entered into the agreement directly with Producer. I agree to look solely to Company as my employer for payment of compensation for my services and the discharge of all other obligations.

Smith: _____

Jones: _____

CONTRACTS
FOR THE
FILM AND
TELEVISION
INDUSTRY

182

CREW EMPLOYMENT

Below-the-line employees (i.e. the crew) are typically hired on a short form employment agreement.

CREW DEAL MEMO
SALARIED ON-CALL
EXEMPT EMPLOYEES

Producer:

MOTION PICTURE:

START DATE: _____ POSITION: _____

EMPLOYEE NAME: _____

ADDRESS: _____

PHONE: Home: _____ Work: _____

SOCIAL SECURITY # _____ FED I.D. #_____

****

(items below to be completed by production company only)

WEEKLY RATE: $_____ PRO-RATED DAILY RATE: $_____

RENTALS: _____
EMPLOYEE BOX AND EQUIPMENT IS SOLE RESPONSIBILITY
OF EMPLOYEE. PRODUCTION ASSUMES NO RESPONSIBILITY FOR SAME.

OTHER TERMS: _____

_____

_____

SALARIED/ON CALL
EXEMPT EMPLOYEES
TERMS AND CONDITIONS OF EMPLOYMENT

1. PAYMENT OF WAGES: Wages shall be paid to all employees no later than Friday following the week in which services were performed. Pay date may be delayed by reason of an intervening federal or state holiday. Employee is responsible for submitting her/his time card at the end of the work week to insure timely payment. No employee will be paid without fully completing these forms. Weekly rates are payment for a 6-day work week.

2. EXEMPT EMPLOYEES: Exempt employees shall not be beneficiary of additional overtime, turnaround or other hourly payments except as expressly provided in this deal memo.

3. NIGHTS, WEEKENDS, HOLIDAYS, WORK TIME: Unless expressly provided elsewhere in this deal memo, no increased or additional compensation shall accrue or be payable to employee for the rendering of services at night or on weekends or holidays, or after the expiration of any particular number of hours of service in any period.

4. The Producer will provide meal breaks and/or food service at approximately six (6) hour intervals.

5. IMMIGRATION REFORM AND CONTROL ACT OF 1986 (IRCA): Employment (or the engagement of services) hereunder is subject to employee providing the requisite documents required by IRCA and completing and signing the required Form I-9 pursuant to IRCA Section 274a.2. Employee shall comply with the immigration verification employment eligibility provisions required by law.

6. Kit Rentals are subject to W2 or 1099 reporting. No mileage payments or car allowances will be paid. Kit rentals will be prorated for partial weeks. Invoices for rentals should be attached to employees timecard and completed in accordance with instructions from Accounting department. Employee is responsible for liability and collision insurance and deductibles on her/his personal vehicle used in conjunction with their employment.

7. Use of alcohol or drugs during hours of employment will result in employee's immediate termination.

8. Employee will be held personally responsible for purchases, rentals and expenses not approved in advance by production.

9. Employee's services are on an exclusive basis to the production of the motion picture (the "Picture") referred to in this deal memo for such period of time as required unless otherwise specified in this deal memo.

10. Unless otherwise specified in this deal memo, screen credit is at Producer's discretion subject to employee's performing all services required through completion of term.

11. Unless expressly provided elsewhere in this agreement, employee's employment hereunder shall not be for a "run of the show" or for any guaranteed period of employment. Producer reserves the right to discharge employee at any time, subject only to the obligation to pay the balance of any guaranteed compensation due. Producer will attempt to notify employees a minimum of twenty-four (24) hours in advance of layoff. This agreement is subject to immediate suspension and/or termination (at Producer's election) without further obligation on the part of Producer in the event of any incapacity or default of employee or in the case of any suspension, postponement or interference with the production by reason of labor controversy, strike, earthquake, act of God, governmental action, regulation, or decree or for any other customary force majeure reason.

12. The terms and conditions of this deal memo are binding on Producer and employee and shall not be waived or altered by any method. Any added conditions on the front of this deal memo inconsistent with these conditions of employment shall be null and void.

CONTRACTS
FOR THE
FILM AND
TELEVISION
INDUSTRY

184

13. Producer shall be the owner of all of the results and proceeds of employee's services and shall have the right to use employee's name, voice, picture and likeness in connection with the Picture, the advertising and publicizing thereof, and any promotional films or clips respecting the Picture without additional compensation therefore.

14. Employee shall not directly or indirectly circulate, publish or otherwise disseminate any news story, article, book or other publicity concerning the Picture, or employee's or others' services without Producer's prior written consent, provided that employee may issue personal publicity mentioning the Picture so long as such references are not derogatory. Employee has permission to show a videotape of Picture in connection with seeking future employment.

15. Employee will receive one VHS tape of the Picture within 90 days of completion of post-production.

16. Arbitration: Any controversy or claim arising out of or relating to this agreement or any breach thereof shall be settled by arbitration in accordance with the Rules of the American Arbitration Association; and judgment upon the award rendered by the arbitrators may be entered in any court having jurisdiction thereof. The prevailing party shall be entitled to reimbursement for costs and reasonable attorneys' fees.

EMPLOYEE ACCEPTS ALL CONDITIONS OF EMPLOYMENT AS DESCRIBED ABOVE

AGREED TO AND ACCEPTED:

EMPLOYEE SIGNATURE: _____DATE: _____

PRODUCER SIGNATURE: _____DATE: _____

PRODUCTION SERVICES

Sometimes a financier desires to contract with a company to provide most or all of the production services necessary to produce a film. Here is an agreement used by a British company which provided financing and an American company which supervised the logistics of production.

PRODUCTION SERVICES AGREEMENT

THIS PRODUCTION SERVICES AGREEMENT is entered into as of   , 19__, between _____., a United Kingdom corporation ("Financier") and _____ PRODUCTIONS, Inc., a California corporation, ("Service Company"), and is made with reference to the following facts.

WHEREAS, Financier owns the right to produce and exploit a theatrical motion picture (the "Picture") based on the original screenplay entitled "_____" ("Screenplay") written by _____; and

WHEREAS, Financier has requested Service Company to supervise the production of the Screenplay in the State of California; and

WHEREAS, to that end, Service Company has arranged for the directing services of _____, and the producing services of _____ and _____ , all in accordance with a mutually approved budget and a production schedule which have been previously approved by Financier and Service Company; and

WHEREAS, Financier desires to finance and arrange for the production of the Picture, and Service Company desires to furnish the services set forth herein on the terms and conditions hereinafter set forth.

NOW, THEREFORE, in consideration of the promises and for other good and valuable consideration, receipt of which is hereby acknowledged, the parties hereto agree as follows:

1. PRODUCTION OF THE PICTURE:

(a) Subject to the terms and conditions hereinafter set forth, Financier agrees to furnish or cause a third party to furnish to Service Company on a mutually approved cash flow schedule ("Cash Flow Schedule"), the amount of financing which Service Company represents will be required to finance the production of the Picture, and Service Company shall use all sums advanced hereunder for the sole purpose of furnishing the production services for the Picture in accordance with the approved screenplay, budget and production schedule, subject only to deviations therefrom caused by the exigencies of production and approved in writing by Financier. All obligations of Financier shall be subject to Financier first obtaining a completion bond from a reputable company, which in form and substance shall be subject to Financier's approval. All sums advanced hereunder shall be deposited in a production account that has been designated, approved and controlled by Financier, and until such funds have been expended in the production of the Picture such funds shall be and remain the sole and exclusive property of Financier.

(b) Delivery shall be complete when Service Company has delivered to

CONTRACTS
FOR THE
FILM AND
TELEVISION
INDUSTRY

186

Financier in accordance with this Agreement all physical elements of the Picture, and which Financier reasonably requires to cause the Picture to be distributed throughout the world.

(c) Financier shall have the right of designation and approval in relation to all business, creative and other elements, including without limitation, cast, director, production personnel, music, locations, film laboratories, sound stages, post production facilities and all expenditures and other production matters in connection with the Picture, subject only to third party approvals and controls which are consented to by Financier and are contained in said third parties' written contract.

(d) Service Company shall perform all of its obligations hereunder to the best of its ability and in a workmanlike manner. Upon the first to occur of: (i) delivery of the Picture hereunder, (ii) Financier's exercise of takeover rights hereinafter set forth, or (iii) Financier's request following completion of the Picture, Service Company shall irrevocably and without further action assign and transfer to Financier all of Service Company's rights in and to all past, present and future "elements" of the Picture and all rights and benefits actually acquired by Service Company pursuant to any agreements with third parties in a form substantially as set forth in Exhibit "A" annexed hereto and made a part hereof. Service Company shall execute Exhibit "A" upon execution of this Agreement and hereby authorizes Financier to date it upon the occurrence of any of the foregoing events. As used herein, the term "elements" shall include, without limitation, all literary material written for the Picture, if any, acquired by Service Company, all stills, artwork and designs used in connection with the Picture, all film clips, recordings, trailers, sound tracks, and all other tangible and intangible property relating to the Picture, and all rights in and to the foregoing, exercisable throughout the universe, in perpetuity, and all subsidiary, ancillary and related rights, performing rights, publishing rights, merchandising and commercial tie-up rights, and the right to use the names, likenesses, and voices of all persons rendering services in connection with the Picture. Service Company shall include in its contracts with third parties engaged to render services on the Picture a provision that the results and proceeds of all the services rendered in connection with the Picture shall upon rendition automatically be the sole property of Service Company. Service Company's rights under any Agreement in connection with the Picture shall be freely assignable and upon Financier's request, Service Company agrees to execute, acknowledge and deliver such assignments and other documents and instruments as may be necessary or appropriate to evidence Financier's acquisition of rights hereunder. The Picture shall contain such production or presentation or release credit to Financier as Financier shall determine. Additionally, the end titles shall contain a copyright notice in the following form: "Copyright 19__ _____, Ltd. All rights reserved", or such other notice as Financier shall designate.

(e) Upon Financier's acquisition of all right, title and interest in and to the Picture as provided above, Financier shall assume, or cause the distributor of the Picture to contractually adhere to, the executory obligations of all contracts undertaken by Service Company in the normal course of business to produce the Picture.

(f) If Service Company shall fail to execute any instrument or document which Financier may reasonably require to implement any term hereof or to perfect its rights hereunder, Financier shall have the right to execute such document or instrument on Service Company's behalf, such right being an irrevocable power coupled with an interest.

2. PRODUCTION CONTRACTS: All contracts for personnel, studio hire, purchase of goods and services, laboratory work and all other licenses, contracts and obligations in connection with the production of the Picture by Service Company, shall be made and entered into by Service Company in its own name as principal and not as agent for Financier and no obligations whatsoever shall be imposed upon Financier thereunder. All such contracts or undertakings shall be consistent with the provisions of this Agreement and industry custom and practice. Such contracts and undertakings shall not be terminated, canceled, modified or rescinded in any manner which would or might prejudice the rights of Financier hereunder. All such contracts shall be assignable to Financier without restriction. Service Company shall have all responsibilities of an employer with respect to those personnel locally engaged by Service Company in the United States, including those arising under any present or future legal requirements relating to Workers' Compensation, insurance, social security, tax withholding, pension, health and welfare plans under any legal requirements or any applicable collective bargaining agreement, if any, although upon delivery of the Picture and completion of all obligations required hereunder of Service Company, Financier shall assume or cause the distributor of the Picture to assume such obligations and hold Service Company harmless therefrom. Service Company shall use due care in the selection and purchase of any items to be used in connection with the production of the Picture and shall assign Financier on demand all rights which Service Company shall obtain, by warranty and otherwise, from the supplier of such items.

3. INSURANCE: Service Company shall carry and pay for appropriate insurance, consistent with the requirements of Financier, to cover all customary risks in connection with the performance of its obligations hereunder only with respect to those persons engaged in the United States, including, without limitation, public liability, cast, and Workers' Compensation, which insurance shall specifically name Financier as an insured party (and beneficiary), and (as a condition to any payment hereunder) shall furnish Financier with certificates of insurance stating and certifying the amount and type of insurance and that Financier is an insured party thereunder and with copies of all said policies.

4. CONTRACT PRICE: Except as provided in Paragraph 15 below, on the condition that Service Company fully and completely performs all of its obligations hereunder, Financier shall pay Service Company for services rendered $____ .

5. PRODUCTION SCHEDULE: It is of the essence of this Agreement that Service Company furnish the production services respecting services and the Picture and all other elements required hereunder in accordance with the mutually approved production schedule ("Production Schedule").

6. DISTRIBUTION: The Picture shall be distributed in such manner as Financier shall determine in its sole discretion.

7. SERVICE COMPANY REPRESENTATIONS AND WARRANTIES: Service Company hereby represents, warrants and agrees as follows:

(a) Service Company is a corporation, duly organized and existing under the laws of the State of California, and has the right to grant all rights granted herein, and is free to enter into and fully perform this Agreement.

(b) No liens, encumbrances, attachments or other matters constituting or possibly constituting any impediment to the clear marketable title and unrestricted commercial exploitation or disposition of the Picture or any rights therein

CONTRACTS
FOR THE
FILM AND
TELEVISION
INDUSTRY

188

or pertaining thereto shall be permitted to occur which shall or may arise by reason of any acts, omissions or activities of Service Company in connection with the performance or enforcement of this Agreement, or attachments by Service Company in connection with any litigation in which Service Company shall be plaintiff against Financier or any other party whatsoever. Service Company will not create, make, cause or permit any lien, encumbrance, pledge (except as may be required by a film processing laboratory), hypothecation or assignment of or claim against the Picture, or any rights therein, or upon the copyrights thereof, or upon the literary material upon which the Picture is based, or the release, distribution, exploitation or exhibition rights therein, or upon any proceeds therefrom or any other rights, interests or property therein or pertaining thereto.

(c) Service Company shall at all times indemnify, defend, and hold harmless Financier, and its partners, officers, directors, employees, licensees, shareholders, subsidiaries, and agents, and their heirs, executors, administrators, successors and assigns, from and against any and all claims, damages, liabilities, actions, causes of action, costs and expenses, including reasonable attorneys' fees, judgments, penalties of any kind or nature whatsoever arising out of (i) Service Company's production and delivery of the Picture; (ii) any act or omission by Service Company or any person whose services or facilities shall be furnished by Service Company in connection with the Picture; and (iii) any breach by Service Company of any representation, warranty or agreement made by Service Company hereunder.

8. GOOD FAITH ASSURANCE: Neither party has, nor will without the other's prior written consent: (i) enter into any agreement, commitment or other arrangement, grant any rights or do any act or thing which could or might prevent or interfere with the production and completion of the Picture or prevent or impede the performance of all of the respective party's obligations hereunder; (ii) do or fail to do any act which might or could interfere with or otherwise prevent such party from fully complying with all of the terms hereof; or (iii) engage in any conduct inconsistent with this Agreement or the other party's rights hereunder. The foregoing shall not be interpreted as impairing or preventing Financier's absolute right to abandon production of the Picture at anytime and/or to refrain from or cause the termination of the distribution of the Picture, all as provided in greater detail in Paragraph 15 below.

9. DEFAULT: Service Company specifically waives all rights and remedies, if available to Service Company, of rescission, injunction, restraint and specific performance and agrees in this regard that it shall have no right to revoke, terminate or rescind any rights acquired by Financier hereunder nor to restrain production, completion or distribution of the Picture and shall have no right to compel specific performance of any of Financier's obligations hereunder. Service Company understands and agrees that its sole remedy hereunder shall be for monetary damages, if any, in the event of breach by Financier.

10. SECURITY INTEREST: As security for the delivery of the Picture hereunder, Service Company hereby mortgages, sells, assigns, pledges, hypothecates, and sets over to Financier as collateral all of Service Company's right, title and interest, if any, in and to the following:

(a) The Picture, in whatever form it may now exist or hereafter exist, including the negative, sound material and copyright thereto.

(b) The literary, dramatic and music material upon which the Picture is based or to be based including, without limitation, the Screenplay and all of Service

Company's right, title and interest in and to the copyrights to the foregoing.

(c) All of Service Company's right, title and interest in and to any properties or things of value pertaining to rights, contract rights, claims, properties and material set forth in (a) and (b) above, whether now in existence or hereafter acquired by Service Company.

(d) Any other rights Service Company may have in or relating to the Picture.

It is intended that the security granted above is and shall be a "security interest" as such term is defined in the Uniform Commercial Code and Service Company hereby agrees to execute and deliver a financing statement in form and substance which complies with the Uniform Commercial Code of any and all states which Financier may hereafter require. Service Company hereby authorizes Financier or its representative to file such financing statement(s) and to execute any continuation statements as well as to perform any and all other acts Financier may deem appropriate to perfect and continue Financier's security interest in the collateral. Service Company warrants and represents that there shall be no lien or charge or encumbrance in whole or in part upon the collateral (other than a customary laboratory lien for processing services, a lien to secure obligations under a Collective Bargaining Agreement) or proceeds derived therefrom which are equal or superior to the lien and security interest above granted and that Financier's security interest shall at all times be and remain a first and continuing lien and security interest on the collateral until Financier is repaid the entire sum herein elsewhere provided. Service Company shall at all times keep Financier advised as to the location of all collateral herein pledged.

11. TAKEOVER RIGHTS: At any time after the occurrence of any of the events hereinafter set forth, Financier shall have the right, to be exercised in its sole and exclusive discretion, to either issue directions and instructions regarding production of the Picture, or to take over production of the Picture. The events entitling Financier to exercise the aforesaid rights shall be the following:

(a) If the project cost of production in Financier's good faith judgment reasonably appears to exceed the approved budget by 5% (excluding overbudget costs that are reimbursed by insurance, or caused by force majeure or a direct consequence of a third party breach of contract that is not induced or encouraged by Service Company);

(b) An event which might permit a takeover by the company issuing the completion bond;

(c) Service Company fails to substantially carry out any instructions which Financier may issue to Service Company in keeping herewith; or

(d) Service Company breaches any of the material terms and conditions hereof.

If Financier exercises its right to issue directions and instruction in keeping with the foregoing, Service Company shall fully and faithfully abide by and follow all such instructions issued in connection with the production of the Picture and Service Company shall have no further creative approval and/or other production rights concerning production, post-production and/or distribution of the Picture. If Financier exercises its takeover rights as aforesaid, Service Company shall immediately do all that is necessary to place at Financier's disposal and under Financier's control, all persons production funds and other items of and concerning production of the Picture. For such purpose, Service Company hereby irre-

CONTRACTS
FOR THE
FILM AND
TELEVISION
INDUSTRY

190

vocably constitutes and appoints Financier as Service Company's attorney-in-fact with full power of substitution and revocation, to act in Service Company's name and stead to make withdrawals from any production account or other bank accounts relating to the Picture and to expend funds from such account and to further carry out and fully perform, at Financier's discretion, any and all agreements, or to modify, amend, compromise or terminate any such contract and to further engage or discharge personnel and to acquire, release and dispose of any equipment, real or other property relating to the Picture and to endorse, collect and deposit any checks or other instruments payable to Service Company as a result of the Picture and in general to do any and all acts which Service Company could otherwise have done had Financier not exercised its takeover rights. Service Company specifically acknowledges that if Financier takes over the Picture in keeping with the foregoing, Financier may abandon the Picture or complete production as Financier may at such time determine. Notwithstanding the foregoing to the contrary, Financier's rights concerning production of the Picture shall be subject to creative and other approvals and controls that are contained in those agreements between Service Company and third parties that were entered into with Financier's knowledge and which are not terminated by Financier.

12. FORCE MAJEURE: The date for performance of either party's obligations hereunder shall be postponed to the extent any event of force majeure delays the commencement of production or the performance of the obligations of either party hereunder.

13. STATUS OF PARTIES: The parties hereto expressly agree, each for the other, that the relationship between them hereunder is that of two principals dealing with each other as independent contractors for the sole and specific purpose that Service Company shall produce and deliver the Picture, subject to the terms and conditions of this Agreement. At no time, past, present or future, shall the relationship of the parties herein be deemed or intended to constitute a relationship with the characteristics of an agency, partnership, joint venture, or of a collaboration for the purposes of sharing any profits or ownership in common. Neither party shall have the right, power or authority at any time to act on behalf of, or represent, the other party, but each party hereto shall be separately and entirely liable for its own respective debts in all respects. This Agreement is not for the benefit of any person who is not a party signatory hereto or specifically named as a beneficiary herein. Financier may assign or license its rights hereunder in whole or in part to any person, firm or corporation. Except for assignment to Financier, Service Company may not assign or license any of its rights or obligations hereunder, or under any agreement entered into by Service Company with any third party. Subject to the foregoing, the provisions hereof shall be binding upon and inure to the benefit of the parties hereto and their respective heirs, personal representatives, administrators, executors, successors and assigns, and any past, present or future parent, subsidiary or affiliate company.

14. NOTICES: Any and all notices, communications and demands required or desired to be given hereunder by either party hereto shall be in writing and shall be validly given or made if served either personally or if deposited in the United States mail, certified or registered, postage prepaid, return receipt requested. If such notice or demand be served personally, service shall be conclusively deemed made at the time of such personal service. If such notice or demand be served by registered or certified mail in the manner herein provided, service shall be conclusively deemed made two business days after the deposit thereof in the United States mail addressed to the party to whom such notice or demand is to be given as hereinafter set forth:

Financier:

Service Company:

Any party hereto may change its address for the purpose of receiving notices or demands as herein provided by a written notice given in the manner aforesaid to the other party hereto, which notice of change of address shall not become effective, however, until the actual receipt thereof by the other party.

15. ABANDONMENT: Financier shall have no obligation to finance, release, broadcast, distribute, complete production of, not abandon or otherwise exploit the Picture, provided Financier indemnifies Service Company against any loss from contracts entered into with Financier's prior consent and knowledge.

16. MISCELLANEOUS:

(a) This Agreement shall be construed, interpreted and enforced in accordance with and shall be governed by the laws of the State of California applicable to agreements entered into and to be wholly performed therein. In the event of any conflict between any provisions hereof and any applicable laws to the contrary, the latter shall prevail, but this Agreement shall be deemed modified only to the extent necessary to remove such conflicts.

(b) Each of the parties hereto shall execute and deliver any and all additional documents, and shall do any and all acts and things reasonably required in connection with the performance of the obligations undertaken hereunder and to effectuate the extent of the parties thereto.

(c) This Agreement constitutes the entire agreement of the parties hereto and supersedes all oral and written agreements and understandings made or entered into by the parties hereto prior to the date hereof. No amendment, change or modification of this Agreement shall be valid unless it is made in writing and signed by both parties hereto, and any waiver of a failure to perform or a breach shall not operate to waive any subsequent failure to perform or breach.

(d) The captions appearing at the commencement of the paragraphs hereof are descriptive only and for convenience in reference to this Agreement and should there be any conflict between any such heading and the paragraph at the head of which it appears, the paragraph thereof and not such heading shall control and govern in the construction of this Agreement.

IN WITNESS WHEREOF, the parties hereto have executed this Agreement as of the date and year first above written.

FINANCIER:

By:_____

Print Name:

Its:_____

Service Company:

By:_____
Print Name:
Its:

CONTRACTS
FOR THE
FILM AND
TELEVISION
INDUSTRY

192

ON LOCATION

Filmmakers who shoot on location without securing a release may be subject to liability. Filmmakers don't have a First Amendment right to trespass or invade the rights of others.

Even if a landowner doesn't bring suit, a filmmaker should secure releases for every location. Without such documents it may be difficult to purchase Errors and Omissions (E&O) insurance and survive the scrutiny of a distributor's legal department. Location agreements should be sought from landowners or land possessors when shooting on private property and from the appropriate government entity when shooting on public property. Make sure that the person signing the release has authority to grant such permission.

Location agreements don't necessarily cost much. In a small community which filmmakers rarely visit, the arrival of a movie crew can generate a lot of excitement. Residents may offer the use of their property for little or no money. On the other hand, in Los Angeles, movie crews have worn out their welcome in many neighborhoods. Residents are annoyed by the traffic congestion and noise that accompanies a shoot. Homeowners may have had their property damaged by prior film crews. These homeowners are more aware of how much the studios are willing to pay for locations. They may demand top dollar which can amount to several thousand dollars per day.

LOCATION AGREEMENT

Agreement entered into this _____ day of _____, 19___, by and between_____ ("Production Company") and _____ ("Grantor").

1. IDENTITY OF FILMING LOCATION: Grantor hereby agrees to permit Production Company to use the property located at _____ _____ ("Property") in connection with the motion picture currently entitled _____ ("Picture") for rehearsing, photographing, filming and recording scenes and sounds for the Picture. Production Company and its licensees, sponsors, assigns and successors may exhibit, advertise and promote the Picture or any portion thereof, whether or not such uses contain audio and/or visual reproductions of the Property and whether or not the Property is identified, in any and all media which currently exist or which may exist in the future in all countries of the world and in perpetuity.

2. RIGHT OF ACCESS: Production Company shall have the right to bring personnel and equipment (including props and temporary sets) onto the Property and to remove same after completion of its use of the Property hereunder. Production Company shall have the right but not the obligation to photograph, film and use in the Picture the actual name, if any, connected with the Property or to use any other name for the Property. If Production Company depicts the interior(s) of any structures located on the Property, Grantor agrees that Production Company shall not be required to depict such interior(s) in any particular manner in the Picture.

3. TIME OF ACCESS: The permission granted hereunder shall be for the period commencing on or about _____ and continuing until_____. The period may be extended by Production Company if there are changes in the production schedule or delays due to weather conditions. The within permission shall also apply to future retakes and/or added scenes.

4. PAYMENT: For each day the Production Company uses the location, it shall pay Grantor the sum of $ _____ in consideration for the foregoing.

5. ALTERATIONS TO LOCATION: Production Company agrees that (with Grantor's permission) if it becomes necessary to change, alter or rearrange any equipment on the Property belonging to Grantor, Production Company shall return and restore said equipment to its original place and condition, or repair it, if necessary. Production Company agrees to indemnify and hold harmless Grantor from and against any and all liabilities, damages and claims of third parties arising from Production Company's use hereunder of the Property (unless such liabilities, damages or claims arise from breach of Grantor's warranty as set forth in the immediately following sentence) (and from any physical damage to the Property proximately caused by Production Company, or any of its representatives, employees, or agents). Grantor warrants that it has the right and authority to enter this Agreement and to grant the rights granted by it herein. Grantor agrees to indemnify and hold harmless Production Company from and against any and all claims relating to breach of its aforesaid warranty.

6. NO KICKBACKS FOR USE: Grantor affirms that neither it nor anyone acting

CONTRACTS
FOR THE
FILM AND
TELEVISION
INDUSTRY

194

for it gave or agreed to give anything of value to any member of the production staff, anyone associated with the Picture, or any representative of Production Company, or any television station or network for mentioning or displaying the name of Grantor as a shooting location on the Property (except the use of the Property, which was furnished for use solely on or in connection with the Picture.

7. BILLING CREDIT: Grantor acknowledges that any identification of the Property which Production Company may furnish shall be at Production Company's sole discretion and in no event shall said identification be beyond that which is reasonably related to the content of the Picture.

8. RELEASE: Grantor releases and discharges Production Company, its employees, agents, licensees, successors and assigns from any and all claims, demands or causes of actions that Grantor may now have or may from now on have for libel, defamation, invasion of privacy or right of publicity, infringement of copyright or violation of any other right arising out of or relating to any utilization of the rights granted herein.

The undersigned represents that he/she is empowered to execute this Agreement for Grantor.

IN WITNESSj WHEREOF, the parties have hereunto set their names and signatures:

_____
Production Company

By: _____

_____
Grantor (Name)

By:_____

CHAPTER 9

DISTRIBUTION

THEATRICAL ACQUISITION/DISTRIBUTION AGREEMENT

Some films are not produced by the studio that distributes them. These independently produced projects often use investors or pre-sale distribution deals (selling of various foreign distribution rights) to finance production. The producer enters an acquisition/distribution agreement with a distributor for release of the picture. This agreement is often referred to as a Negative Pick-up Deal.

While the terms of these deals vary, the studio/distributor typically pays for all distribution, advertising and marketing costs. The studio and producer share profits. Because the producer has taken the risk of financing production, he may obtain a better definition of net profits than if the studio financed production. Profits may be split fifty/fifty between the studio and producer without a deduction for a studio distribution fee. Of course, the independent producer takes the chance that if the film turns out poorly, no distributor will want it. In that case the producer may incur a substantial loss.

In a negative pick-up deal, the distributor will often agree to give the producer an advance on his share of profits. This money is paid after the distribution agreement is made but before distribution. The producer can use this money to repay investors. Producers want to obtain as large an advance as possible because they know they may never see anything on the back end of the deal (i.e., no profits).

The distributor wants to pay as small an advance as possible, and usually resists giving an amount greater than the cost of production. If the distributor has an advantageous definition of "net profits" or engages in creative accounting, profit participants are unlikely to see any "net profits." Consequently, a shrewd

CONTRACTS
FOR THE
FILM AND
TELEVISION
INDUSTRY

196

producer wants a large advance. He also tries to retain distribution rights to other territories and keep revenue from those territories from being cross-collateralized.[1]

Negative pick-up deals can be negotiated before, during or after production. Often distributors become interested in a film after seeing it at a film festival and observing audience reaction.

---

[1] Cross-collateralized means the monies earned from several markets are pooled. For example, let's say your picture made one million dollars in England and lost one million dollars in France. If those territories were cross-collateralized, and you were entitled to a percentage of the net revenue, you would get nothing. On the other hand, if the territories were not cross-collateralized, you would get your percentage of the English revenues and the distributor would absorb the loss incurred in France.

ACQUISITION/DISTRIBUTION AGREEMENT

THEATRICAL RELEASE

Agreement dated _____ between _____ ("Production Company")
a California corporation at _____and
_____ ("Distributor"), a California corporation
at _____.

1. PICTURE: The term "Picture" refers to the Theatrical Motion Picture set forth in Schedule "A" hereof.

2. TERRITORY AND TERM:

(a) Territory: The territory covered hereby ("Territory") is set forth in Schedule "A."

(b) Distribution Term: The term of this Agreement and the rights granted Distributor hereunder for each country or place of the Territory shall be the period of time specified in Schedule "A" ("Distribution Term"). The term of this Agreement shall commence on the date hereof and expire upon the expiration of the Distribution Term as extended unless sooner terminated as provided herein.

3. RIGHTS GRANTED:

(a) Grant: Production Company hereby grants to Distributor throughout the Territory the exercise of all rights of theatrical, television (free, pay and syndication) and home video (cassette and disc) exhibition and distribution with respect to the Picture and Trailers thereof, and excerpts and clips therefrom, in any and all languages and versions, including dubbed, subtitled and narrated versions. The rights granted herein shall include without limit the sole and exclusive right:

(i) Titles: To use the title or titles by which the Picture is or may be known or identified.

(ii) Music and Lyrics: To use and perform any and all music, lyrics and musical compositions contained in the Picture and/or recorded in the soundtrack thereof in connection with the distribution, exhibition, advertising, publicizing and exploiting of the Picture;

(iii) Versions: To make such dubbed and titled versions of the Picture, and the Trailers thereof, including, without limitation, cut-in, synchronized and superimposed versions in any and all languages for use in such parts of the Territory as Distributor may deem advisable.

(iv) Editing: To make such changes, alterations, cuts, additions, interpolations, deletions and eliminations into and from the Picture and trailer subject to prior written approval of Production Company and Director as Distributor may deem necessary or desirable, for the effective marketing, distribution, exploitation or other use of the Picture.

(v) Advertising and Publicity: To publicize, advertise and exploit the Picture throughout the Territory during the Distribution Term, including

CONTRACTS
FOR THE
FILM AND
TELEVISION
INDUSTRY

198

without limitation, the exclusive right in the Territory for the purpose of advertising, publicizing and exploiting the Picture to:

(A) Literary Material: Publish and to license and authorize others to publish in any language, and in such forms as Distributor may deem advisable, synopses, summaries, adaptations, novelizations, and stories of and excerpts from the Picture and from any literary or dramatic material included in the Picture or upon which the Picture is based in book form and in newspapers, magazines, trade periodicals, booklets, press books and any other periodicals and in all other media of advertising and publicity whatsoever not exceeding 7,500 words in length taken from the original material;

(B) Radio and Television: Broadcast by radio and television for advertising purposes and to license and authorize others to so broadcast, in any language, or any parts or portions of the Picture not exceeding five minutes in length, and any literary or dramatic material included in the Picture or upon which the Picture was based alone or in conjunction with other literary, dramatic or musical material; and

(C) Names and Likenesses: Use, license and authorize others to use the name, physical likeness and voice (and any simulation or reproduction of any thereof) of any party rendering services in connection with the Picture for the purpose of advertising, publicizing or exploiting the Picture or Distributor, including commercial tie-ins.

(vi) Use of Name and Trademarks: To use Distributor's name and trademark and/or the name and trademark of any of Distributor's licensee's on the positive prints of the Picture and in Trailers thereof, and in all advertising and publicity relating thereto, in such a manner, position, form and substance as Distributor or its licensees may elect.

(vii) Commercials: To permit commercial messages to be exhibited during and after the exhibition of the Picture.

(viii) Trailers: To cause trailers of the Picture and prints thereof and of the Picture to be manufactured, exhibited and distributed by every means, medium, process, method and device now or hereafter known.

(b) Grant of Other Rights: Production Company hereby grants to Distributor throughout the Territory the sole and exclusive right, license and privilege to exercise all literary publishing rights, live television rights, merchandising rights, music publishing rights, soundtrack recording rights, radio rights, additional motion picture rights, remake rights and sequel motion picture rights subject to the terms and conditions of the agreements pursuant to which Production Company acquired the foregoing rights with respect to the literary, dramatic and/or musical material used by Production Company in connection with the Picture. Production Company agrees that at the request of Distributor, Production Company will execute and deliver to Distributor for recordation purposes a separate document pursuant to which Production Company confirms the transfer and assignment to Distributor of said rights.

(c) Rights Free and Clear: The above-stated rights are granted by Production Company to Distributor without qualification and free and clear from any and all restrictions, claims, encumbrances or defects of any nature and Production Company agrees that it will not commit or omit to perform any act by which any of these rights, licenses, privileges and interests could or will be encumbered, diminished or impaired, and that Production Company will pay or discharge, and will hold Distributor harmless from, any and all claims that additional payments are due anyone by reason of the distribution, exhibition, telecasting, of re-running of the Picture or the receipt of its proceeds. Production Company further agrees that during the Distribution Term (as extended) with respect to each country or place, Production Company shall neither exercise itself nor grant to any third party the rights granted to Distributor pursuant to the terms hereof.

(d) Production Company's Reservation of Rights: Production Company reserves for its use non-theatrical distribution.

(e) Credits: The statements of credits required to be given pursuant to Exhibit "2" shall conform to Distributor's standard credit provisions for comparable talent, including without limitation Distributor's standard art work title provisions as set forth in Exhibit "3," attached hereto.

5. PRODUCTION COMPANY'S WARRANTIES AND REPRESENTATIONS: Production Company represents and warrants to Distributor, its successors, licensees and assigns as follows:

(a) Quality: The Picture is completely finished, fully edited and titled and fully synchronized with dialogue, sound and music and in all respects ready and of a quality, both artistic and technical, adequate for general theatrical release and commercial public exhibition.

(b) Content: The Picture consists of a continuous and connected series of scenes, telling or presenting a story, free from any obscene material and suitable for exhibition to the general public.

(c) Unrestricted Right to Grant: Production Company is the sole and absolute owner of the Picture, the copyright pertaining thereto and all rights associated with or relating to the distribution, including the absolute right to grant to and vest in Distributor all the rights, licenses and privileges granted to Distributor under this Agreement, and Production Company has not heretofore sold, assigned, licensed, granted, encumbered or utilized the Picture or any of the literary or musical properties used therein in any way that may affect or impair the rights, licenses and privileges granted to Distributor hereunder and Production Company will not sell, assign, license, grant or encumber or utilize the rights, licenses and privileges granted to Distributor hereunder.

(d) Discharge of Obligations: All the following have been fully paid or discharged or will be fully paid and discharged by Production Company or by persons other than Distributor:

(i) All claims and rights of owners of copyright in literary, dramatic and musical rights and other property or rights in or to all stories, plays, scripts, scenarios, themes, incidents, plots, characters, dialogue, music, words, and other material of any nature whatsoever appearing, used or recorded in the Picture;

(ii) All claims and rights of owners of inventions and patent rights with respect to the recording of any and all dialogue, music and other sound effects recorded in the Picture and with respect to the use of all equipment, apparatus, appliances and other materials used in the photographing, recording or otherwise in the manufacture of the Picture;

CONTRACTS
FOR THE
FILM AND
TELEVISION
INDUSTRY

200

(iii) All claims and rights with respect to the use, distribution, exhibition, performance and exploitation of the Picture and any music contained therein throughout the Territory, and

(e) No Infringement: To the best of Production Company's knowledge and belief neither the Picture nor any part thereof, nor any materials contained therein or synchronized therewith, nor the title thereof, nor the exercise of any right, license or privilege herein granted, violates or will violate or infringe or will infringe any trademark, trade name, contract, agreement, copyright (whether common law or statutory), patent, any literary, artistic, dramatic, personal, private, civil or property right or right of privacy or "moral rights of authors" or any other right whatsoever of or slanders or libels any person, firm, corporation or association whatsoever. In connection therewith, Production Company shall supply Distributor with a script clearance in a form acceptable to Distributor.

(f) No Advertising Matter: The Picture does not contain any advertising matter for which compensation, direct or indirect, has been or will be received by Production Company or to its knowledge by any other person, firm, corporation or association.

(g) No Impairment of Rights Granted: There are and will be no agreements, commitments or arrangements whatever with any person, firm, corporation or association that may in any manner or to any extent affect Distributor's rights hereunder or Distributor's share of the proceeds of the Picture. Production Company has not and will not exercise any right or take any action which might tend to derogate from, impair or compete with the rights, licenses and privileges herein granted to Distributor.

(h) Contracts: All contracts with artists and personnel, for purchases, licenses and laboratory contracts and all other obligations and undertakings of whatsoever kind connected with the production of the Picture have been made and entered into by Production Company and by no other party and no obligation shall be imposed upon Distributor thereunder and Production Company shall indemnify and hold Distributor harmless from any expense and liability thereunder. All such contracts are in the form customarily in use in the Motion Picture industry and are consistent with the provisions of this Agreement, particularly with reference to the warranties made by Production Company and the rights acquired by Distributor hereunder. Said contracts shall not, without Distributor's prior written consent, be terminated, canceled, modified or rescinded in any manner which would adversely affect Distributor's rights hereunder.

(i) All Considerations Paid: All considerations provided to be paid under each and all the agreements, licenses or other documents relating to the production of the Picture have been paid in full, or otherwise discharged in full, and there is no existing, outstanding obligation whatsoever, either present or future, under any of said contracts, agreements, assignments or other documents, unless disclosed in Schedule "A".

(j) Full Performance: All terms, covenants and conditions required to be kept or performed by Production Company under each and all of the contracts, licenses or other documents relating to the production of the Picture have been kept and performed and will hereafter be kept and performed by Production Company and there is no existing breach or other act of default by Production Company under any such agreement, license or other document, nor will there be any such breach or default during the term hereof.

(k) No Release/No Banning: Neither the Picture nor any part thereof has been released, distributed or exhibited in any media whatsoever in the Territory nor has it been banned by the censors of or refused import permits for any portion of the Territory.

(l) Valid Copyright: The copyright in the Picture and the literary, dramatic and musical material upon which it is based or which is contained in the Picture will be valid and subsisting during the Distribution Term (as extended) with respect to each country or place of the Territory, and no part of any thereof is in the public domain.

(m) Peaceful Enjoyment: Distributor will quietly and peacefully enjoy and possess each and all of the rights, licenses and privileges herein granted or purported to be granted to Distributor throughout the Distribution Term (as extended) for each country or place of the Territory without interference by any third party.

(n) Guild/Union/Performing Rights Society—Participation payments: Any payments required to be made to any performing rights society or to any body or group representing authors, composers, musicians, artists, any other participants in the production of the Picture, publishers or other persons having legal or contractual rights of any kind to participate in the receipts of the Picture or to payments of any kind as a result of the distribution or exhibition of the Picture and any taxes thereon or on the payment thereof will be made by Production Company or by the exhibitors and need not be paid by Distributor.

(o) Music Performing Rights: The performing rights to all musical compositions contained in the Picture are: (i) controlled by the American Society of Composers, Authors and Publishers (ASCAP), Broadcast Music, Inc., (BMI) or similar organizations in other countries such as the Japanese Society of Rights of Authors and Composers (JASEAC), the Performing Right Society Ltd. (PRS), the Society of European Stage Authors and Composers (SESAC), the Societe des Auteurs Compositeurs Et Editeurs de Musique (SACEM), Gesellscraft fur Misikalische Auffuhrungs und Mechanische Vervielfaltigunsrechte (GEMA) or their affiliates, or (ii) in the public domain in the Territory, or (iii) controlled by Production Company to the extent required for the purposes of this Agreement and Production Company similarly controls or has licenses for any necessary synchronization and recording rights.

(p) Television Restriction: The Picture will not be exhibited in or telecast in or cablecast in or into the Territory during the Distribution Term for each country or place of the Territory by anyone other than Distributor or its licensees.

(q) Authority Relative to this Agreement: Production Company has taken all action necessary to duly and validly authorize its signature and performance of this Agreement and the grant of the rights, licenses and privileges herein granted and agreed to be granted.

(r) Financial Condition: Production Company is not presently involved in financial difficulties as evidenced by its not having admitted its inability to pay its debts generally as they become due or otherwise not having acknowledged its insolvency or by its not having filed or consented to a petition in bankruptcy or for reorganization or for the adoption of an arrangement under Federal Bankruptcy Act (or under any similar law of the United States or any other jurisdiction, which relates to liquidation or reorganization of companies or to the modification or alteration of the rights of creditors) or by its not being involved

CONTRACTS
FOR THE
FILM AND
TELEVISION
INDUSTRY

202

in any bankruptcy, liquidation, or other similar proceeding relating to Production Company or its assets, whether pursuant to statute or general rule of law, nor does Production Company presently contemplate any such proceeding or have any reason to believe that any such proceeding will be brought against it or its assets.

(s) Litigation: To Production Company's knowledge, there is no litigation, proceeding or claim pending or threatened against Production Company which may materially adversely affect Production Company's exclusive rights in and to the Picture, the copyright pertaining thereto or the rights, licenses and privileges granted to Distributor hereunder.

6. INDEMNITY: Production Company does hereby and shall at all times indemnify and hold harmless Distributor, its subdistributors and licensees, its and their officers, directors and employees, and its and their exhibitors, licensees and assignees, of and from any and all charges, claims, damages, costs, judgments, decrees, losses, expenses (including reasonable attorneys' fees), penalties, demands, liabilities and causes of action, whether or not groundless, of any kind or nature whatsoever by reason of, based upon, relating to, or arising out of a breach or claim of breach or failure of any of the covenants, agreements, representations or warranties of Production Company hereunder or by reason of any claims, actions or proceedings asserted or instituted, relating to or arising out of any such breach or failure or conduct or activity resulting in a breach or claim of breach. All rights and remedies hereunder shall be cumulative and shall not interfere with or prevent the exercise of any other right or remedy which may be available to Distributor. Upon notice from Distributor of any such claim, demand or action being advanced or commenced, Production Company agrees to adjust, settle or defend the same at the sole cost of Production Company. If Production Company shall fail to do so, Distributor shall have the right and is hereby authorized and empowered by Production Company to appear by its attorneys in any such claim, demand or action, to adjust, settle, compromise, litigate, contest, satisfy judgments and take any other action necessary or desirable for the disposition of such claim, demand or action. In any such case, Production Company, within 20 days after demand by Distributor, shall fully reimburse Distributor for all such payments and expenses, including reasonable attorneys' fees. If Production Company shall fail so to reimburse Distributor, then, without waiving its right to otherwise enforce such reimbursement, Distributor shall have the right to deduct the said amount of such payments and expenses, or any part thereof, from any sums accruing under this Agreement or any other agreement to or for the account of Production Company. Also, in the event of any matter to which the foregoing indemnity relates, Distributor shall have the right to withhold from disbursements to or for the account of Production Company a sum which in Distributor's opinion may be reasonably necessary to satisfy any liability or settlement in connection with such matter, plus a reasonable amount to cover the expenses of contesting or defending such claim and shall have the further right to apply the amount withheld to the satisfaction of such liability or settlement and to reimbursement of such expenses.

7. COPYRIGHT:

(a) Ownership: Production Company warrants that Production Company has not heretofore transferred its ownership in and to all copyrights pertaining to the Picture throughout the world, including without limitation the rights to secure copyright registration anywhere in the world with respect to all copyrights in the Picture and to secure any renewals and extensions thereof wherever and whenever permitted. Production Company warrants that upon delivery of the Picture to Distributor, Production Company will own all copyrights in the Picture throughout the world for the full period of copyright and all extensions and renewals thereof. The negative of the Picture shall contain a copyright notice complying with all statutory requirements of the copyright laws of the United States or any country which is a party to the Berne Union or Universal Copyright Convention, such notice to appear in the main or end titles of the Picture. Production Company and Distributor shall not have the right to change the copyright notice contained in the Picture.

(b) Defense of Copyright: Distributor hereby agrees to take all reasonable steps to protect such copyrights from infringement by unauthorized parties and in particular, at the request of Production Company, to take such action and proceedings as may be reasonable to prevent any unauthorized use, reproduction, performance, exhibition or exploitation by third Parties of the Picture or any part thereof or the material on which it is based which may be in contravention of the exclusive rights granted to Distributor in respect to the Picture.

For the purpose of permitting Distributor to defend and enforce all rights and remedies granted to Distributor hereunder, and to prevent any unauthorized use, reproduction, performance, exhibition or exploitation of the Picture or any part thereof or the material on which it is based, Production Company hereby irrevocably appoints Distributor its sole and exclusive attorney-in-fact, to act in Production Company name or otherwise. Distributor agrees (consistent with commercially acceptable practices in the Motion Picture industry), in its own name or in the name of Production Company, to take all reasonable steps to enforce and protect the rights, licenses and privileges herein granted, under any law and under any and all copyrights, renewals and extensions thereof, and to prevent the infringement thereof, and to bring, prosecute, defend and appear in suits, actions and proceedings of any nature under or concerning all copyrights in the Picture and to settle claims and collect and receive all damages arising from any infringement of or interference with any and all such rights, and in the sole judgment of Distributor exercised in good faith to join Production Company as a party plaintiff or defendant in such suit, action or proceeding. Production Company hereby irrevocably appoints Distributor as its sole and exclusive attorney-in-fact, during the Term of this Agreement, with full and irrevocable power and authority to secure, register, renew and extend all copyrights in the Picture and all related properties upon each thereof becoming eligible for copyright, registration, renewal and extension.

(c) Limitation of Liability: Distributor shall not be liable, responsible or accountable in damages or otherwise to Production Company for any action or failure to act on behalf of Production Company within the scope of authority conferred on Distributor under this Clause 8, unless such action or omission was performed or omitted fraudulently or in bad faith or constituted wanton and willful misconduct or gross negligence.

8. ERRORS AND OMISSIONS INSURANCE: As provided in Exhibit 2, Distributor shall obtain and maintain or cause to be obtained and maintained throughout the Distribution Term (as extended), Motion Picture Distributor Errors and Omissions insurance in a form acceptable to Production Company, from a qualified insurance company acceptable to Production Company naming Distributor and Production Company and each and all the parties indemnified herein as additional named insureds. The amount and coverage shall be for a minimum of $1,000,000/$3,000,000 with respect to any one or more claims relating to the

CONTRACTS
FOR THE
FILM AND
TELEVISION
INDUSTRY

204

Picture or if Distributor pays an advance, the amount of the advance, whichever shall be greater. The policy shall provide for a deductible no greater than $10,000 and thirty (30) days' notice to Production Company before any modification, cancellation or termination.

9. INSTRUMENTS OF FURTHER ASSURANCE: Production Company shall execute and deliver to Distributor, promptly upon the request of Distributor therefore, any other instruments or documents considered by Distributor to be necessary or desirable to evidence, effectuate or confirm this Agreement, or any of its terms and conditions.

10. NO DISTRIBUTOR REPRESENTATIONS AND WARRANTIES: Production Company acknowledges and agrees that Distributor makes no express or implied representation, warranty, guaranty or agreement as to the gross receipts to be derived from the Picture or the distribution, exhibition or exploitation thereof, nor does Distributor guarantee the performance by any subdistributor, licensee or exhibitor of any contract for the distribution, exhibition or exploitation of the Picture, nor does Distributor make any representation, warranty, guaranty or agreement as to any minimum amount of monies to be expended for the distribution, advertising, publicizing and exploitation of the Picture. Production Company recognizes and acknowledges that the amount of gross receipts which may be realized from the distribution, exhibition and exploitation of the Picture is speculative, and agrees that the reasonable business judgment exercised in good faith of Distributor and its subdistributors and licensees regarding any matter affecting the distribution, exhibition and exploitation of the Picture shall be binding and conclusive upon Production Company.

11. DISTRIBUTION AND EXPLOITATION OF THE PICTURE: Distributor shall have the complete, exclusive and unqualified control of the distribution, exhibition, exploitation and other disposition of the Picture (directly or by any subdistributor or licensee] in the media granted to Distributor hereunder throughout the Territory during the Distribution Term with respect to each country or place, in accordance with such sales methods, plans, patterns, programs, policies, terms and conditions as Distributor in its reasonable business judgment may determine proper or expedient. The enumeration of the following rights of distribution and exploitation shall in no way limit the generality or effect of the foregoing:

(a) Terms: Distributor may determine the manner and terms upon which the Picture shall be marketed, distributed, licensed, exhibited, exploited or otherwise disposed of and all matters pertaining thereto, and the decision of Distributor on all such matters shall be final and conclusive. Production Company shall have no control whatsoever in or over (i) the manner or extent to which Distributor or its subdistributors or licensees shall exploit the Picture, (ii) the terms and provisions of any licenses granted by Distributor to third Parties or (iii) to the sufficiency or insufficiency of proceeds from the Picture.

(b) Refrain from Distribution, Exhibition or Exploitation. Distributor may refrain from the release, distribution, re-issue or exhibition of the Picture at any time, in any country, place or location of the Territory, in any media, or in any form. Production Company acknowledges that there is no obligation to exploit the soundtrack recording rights or music publishing rights or merchandising rights or literary publishing rights, it being agreed that Distributor may elect to exercise any or all of said rights as Distributor in its sole business judgment exercised in good faith may determine.

(c) "Outright Sales": Distributor may make outright sales of the Picture as Distributor in good faith may determine. Only net monies actually received and earned by Distributor with respect to outright sales of the Picture shall be included within gross film rentals.

(d) Contracts and Settlements: Distributor may distribute the Picture under existing or future franchise or license contracts, which contracts may relate to the Picture separately or to the Picture and one or more other Motion Pictures distributed by or through Distributor. Distributor may, in the exercise of its reasonable business judgment, exercised in good faith, make, alter or cancel contracts with exhibitors, subdistributors and other licensees and adjust and settle disputes, make allowances and adjustments and give credits with respect thereto.

(e) Means of Release: Distributor may exhibit or cause the Picture to be exhibited in theaters or other places owned, controlled, leased or managed by Distributor. Distributor may enter into any agreement or arrangement with any other major distributor for the distribution by such other major distributor of all or a substantial portion of Distributor's theatrical motion pictures. Distributor may also enter into any agreement or arrangement with any other major distributor or any other party for the handling of the shipping and inspection activities of Distributor's exchanges or the handling of other facilities in connection with the distribution of motion pictures.

(f) Time of Release: The initial release of the Picture in any part of the Territory shall commence on such date or dates as Distributor or its subdistributors or licensees in their respective sole judgment and discretion may determine. Such releases shall be subject to the requirements of censorship boards or other governmental authorities, the availability of playing time in key cities, the securing of the requisite number of motion picture copies, and delays caused by reason of events of force majeure or by reason of any cause beyond the control of Distributor or its subdistributors or licensees. If any claim or action is made or instituted against Distributor or any of its subdistributors or licensees as to the Picture, Distributor or such subdistributors or licensees shall have the right to postpone the release of the Picture (if it has not then been released) or to suspend further distribution thereof (if it has been released) until such time as such claim or action shall have been settled or disposed of to the satisfaction of Distributor or such subdistributors or licensees.

(g) Duration of Release: Distribution of the Picture shall be continued in the Territory or any part thereof in which it is released by Distributor or its licensees only for _____ years. Distributor shall not be obligated to reissue the Picture at any time in the Territory but shall have the right to do so from time to time as it may deem desirable.

(h) Withdrawal of the Picture: Should Distributor or its subdistributors or licensees deem it inadvisable or unprofitable to distribute, exhibit or exploit the Picture in the Territory or any part thereof, Distributor or its subdistributors or licensees shall have the right to withhold or withdraw the Picture from such Territory or any part thereof.

(i) Banning of Release: If by reason of any law, embargo, decree, regulation or other restriction of any agency or governmental body, the number or type of motion pictures that Distributor is permitted to distribute in the Territory or any part thereof is limited, then Distributor may in its absolute discretion determine which motion pictures then distributed by Distributor will be distributed in the Territory or any part thereof, and Distributor shall not be liable to Production

CONTRACTS
FOR THE
FILM AND
TELEVISION
INDUSTRY

206

Company in any manner or to any extent if the Picture is not distributed in the Territory or any part thereof by reason of any such determination.

(j) Collections: Distributor shall in good faith every six months audit, check or verify the computation of any payments and press for the collection of any monies which, if collected, would constitute gross receipts. There shall be no responsibility or liability to Production Company for failure to audit, check, or verify or to collect any monies payable.

(k) Advertising: Distributor agrees to commit a minimum of $_____ with respect to the advertising and publicity of the Picture.

(l) Expenses: Distributor may incur any expenses which Distributor, in the good faith exercise of its reasonable business judgment, deems appropriate with respect to the Picture or the exercise of any of Distributor's rights hereunder.

(m) No Preferential Treatment: Anything herein contained to the contrary notwithstanding, Production Company agrees that nothing herein shall require Distributor to prefer the Picture over any other motion picture distributed by Distributor or shall restrict or limit in any way Distributor's full right to distribute other motion pictures of any nature or description whether similar or dissimilar to the Picture.

12. IMPORT PERMITS: Distributor shall be under no duty to obtain any necessary licenses and permits for the importation and distribution of the Picture in any country or locality nor to utilize for the Picture any licenses or permits available to Distributor in limited quantity. Production Company shall on request use its best efforts to secure for Distributor any such licenses or permits. Distributor shall be entitled to the benefit of all import and/or export licenses and/ or quotas and/or similar benefits of Production Company with respect to the Picture which would entitle the Picture to be imported into any country or territory.

13. MOTION PICTURE PRINTS: Distributor shall be entitled to obtain such prints, dupe negatives and master prints of the Picture which Distributor shall deem advisable for distribution of the Picture in the Territory. All such prints shall remain the property of Distributor.

14. CENSORSHIP OR FORCE MAJEURE:

(a) Adjustment of Advance: If Distributor is required to pay or advance to Production Company any fixed or other sum before it is collected from the distribution of the Picture, and Distributor is unable to distribute the Picture in any country or area of the Territory for any reason, including, without limitation, censorship, import restriction, force majeure or failure to secure permits, the fixed payment or advance shall be reduced by the amount reasonably allocable to such country or area. The amount allocable to such country or area shall be the amount indicated in Schedule "A" or in the absence of such indication in Schedule "A," or if the country or area where distribution is prevented is one to which no allocation is made or which is a part of a country or area for which an overall allocation is made, then a reasonable allocation shall be made by Distributor for such country or area in which distribution is prevented. If the Picture is classified as unsuitable for children under 18 years of age or suitable for adults only in any country or area, the fixed payment or advance payable for such country or area shall be reduced by _____ per cent.

(b) Adjustment of Distribution Expenses: If Distributor is for any reason unable to distribute the Picture in any country or area of the Territory and Distributor has incurred any Distribution Expenses in connection with the distribution of the Picture in such country or area, Producer will on demand reimburse Distributor therefore or, at Distributor's election, Distributor shall be repaid by Production Company from any sum thereafter due from Distributor to Production Company.

15. DISTRIBUTOR'S DEFAULT: Production Company shall not be entitled to bring any action, suit or proceeding of any nature against Distributor or its subdistributors or licensees, whether at law or in equity or otherwise, based upon or arising from in whole or in part any claim that Distributor or its subdistributors or licensees has in any way violated this Agreement, unless the action is brought within one (1) year from the date of Production Company's discovery of such alleged violation. It is agreed that if Distributor breaches this Agreement and fails to begin to remedy such breach within a period of thirty (30) days after receipt by Distributor of written notice from Production Company specifying the alleged breach and fails to cure such breach within sixty days thereafter, or if after delivery of the Picture, Distributor shall fail to make any payments at the time and in the manner provided and Production Company has given Distributor ten (10) days' written notice to that effect, then in either of such events, Production Company shall have the right to proceed against Distributor for monies due to Production Company in accordance with any and all remedies available to Production Company both at law and in equity. In no event, however, shall Production Company have any right to terminate or rescind this Agreement, nor shall the rights acquired by Distributor under this Agreement be subject to revocation, termination or diminution because of any failure or breach of any kind on the part of Distributor or its subdistributors or licensees. In no event shall Production Company be entitled to an injunction to restrain any alleged breach by Distributor or its subdistributors or licensees of any provisions of this Agreement.

16. ARBITRATION: Any controversy or claim arising out of or relating to this agreement or any breach thereof shall be settled by arbitration in accordance with the Rules of the American Arbitration Association; and judgment upon the award rendered by the arbitrators may be entered in any court having jurisdiction thereof. The prevailing party shall be entitled to reimbursement for costs and reasonable attorneys' fees. The determination of the arbitrator in such proceeding shall be final, binding and non-appealable.

17. WAIVER: No waiver of any breach of any provision of this Agreement shall constitute a waiver of any other breach of the same or any other provision hereof, and no waiver shall be effective unless made in writing.

18. RELATIONSHIP OF PARTIES: Nothing herein contained shall be construed to create a joint venture or partnership between the parties hereto. Neither of the parties shall hold itself out contrary to the terms of this provision, by advertising or otherwise, nor shall Distributor or Production Company be bound or become liable because of any representations, actions or omissions of the other.

19. ASSIGNMENT: Distributor may assign this Agreement to and/or may distribute the Picture through any of its subsidiaries, parents, or affiliated corporations or any agent, instrumentality or other means determined by Distributor, provided that Distributor shall not thereby be relieved of the fulfillment of its obligations hereunder. Production Company may assign the right to receive payment hereunder to any third party; provided, however, that Production Company shall not be permitted to assign any of its obligations hereunder.

CONTRACTS
FOR THE
FILM AND
TELEVISION
INDUSTRY

208

20. NOTICES: All notices from Production Company or Distributor to the other, with respect to this Agreement, shall be given in writing by mailing or telegraphing the notice prepaid, return receipt requested, and addressed to Distributor or Production Company, as appropriate, at the address set forth in the preamble hereof. A courtesy copy of any notice to Production Company shall be sent to _____ , and a courtesy copy of any notice to Distributor shall be sent to _____ .

21. GOVERNING LAW: This Agreement shall be governed by the laws of the State of California, without giving effect to principles of conflict of laws thereof.

22. CAPTIONS: The captions of the various paragraphs and sections of the Agreement are intended to be used solely for convenience of reference and are not intended and shall not be deemed for any purpose whatsoever to modify or explain or to be used as an aid in the construction of any provisions.

23. AMENDMENTS IN WRITING: This Agreement cannot be amended, modified or changed in any way whatsoever except by a written instrument duly signed by authorized officers of Production Company and Distributor.

24. ENTIRE AGREEMENT: This Agreement, which is comprised of the general terms above ("Main Agreement") and the attached Schedule and Exhibits, represents the entire agreement between the parties with respect to the subject matter hereof and this Agreement supersedes all previous representations, understandings or agreements, oral or written, between the parties regarding the subject matter hereof.

By signing in the spaces provided below, the parties accept and agree to all the terms and conditions of this Agreement as of the date first above written.

_____
("Production Company")
By
Its

_____
("Distributor")
By
Its

Producers often license or sell film rights to distributors under terms which provide that the producer is entitled to share in the "profits" earned from the film. The profit definitions in distribution contracts are often complex and lengthy, and subject to much controversy. Some of the definitions are so skewed in favor of the distributor that profits are illusory for everyone other than the studio. On the other hand, a few stars and top directors are able to negotiate a share in a studio's gross revenues which can generate enormous revenue for them.

The term "Gross Receipts" is usually defined to include rental payments from all exhibitors and revenue derived from other markets such as television, foreign sales, cable, home video and merchandising. Profit participants with a "piece of the gross" share in gross revenue although a few deductions such as taxes are allowed. Only the top stars and directors have the clout to obtain a piece of the gross. Studios dislike gross deals because gross profit participants share in revenue from a picture even if the studio has not earned its investment back.

Suppose a studio has given a star ten percent of the gross from a film. If the film's gross revenues from all sources are $50 million, and if the film's production, marketing and distribution costs total $50 million, the distributor has broken even. However, the star is due $5 million dollars beyond his up-front fee. So the studio is losing money while the star is making a bundle. To avoid this situation, studios prefer to pay participants after the studio recoups at least some expenses such as advertising and duplication costs. This arrangement is called an ADJUSTED GROSS or MODIFIED GROSS deal.

Filmmakers and studios have devised all kinds of variations on these deals. For instance, a participant's piece of the gross might not be payable until the movie grosses two or three times its negative cost. The parties could also agree to split some markets (e.g., home video) off into separate profit pools and pay part of the gross in these markets to participants.

The least desirable deal from the profit participant's point of view, is a "NET PROFIT"[1] deal. Here so many deductions are allowed that what is left is often zero or less. Although the net profit participant may not see any money from his POINTS, or percentage of profits, the studio may make a "profit" because it receives thirty to forty percent of the gross as a distribution fee. This fee is usually far more than the actual costs the studio incurs to distribute a film. Thus the release of a picture may be very profitable to the studio although there are no "profits" for the participants.

Net profits, if there are any, are often shared fifty/fifty between the studio and the producer. While net profit participants typically receive their pieces of the profit pie from the producer's half, net profits are customarily defined in terms of the whole (one hundred percent). We say the writer is entitled to five percent of one hundred percent of the net profits. This means the writer is entitled to five percent of all the net profits, although his percentage comes from the producer's half. Parties define net profits this way to avoid ambiguity. If the contract sim-

---

[1] A "net profit" deal does not represent anyone's economic net profit but is simply a net amount determined by a contract formula.

CONTRACTS
FOR THE
FILM AND
TELEVISION
INDUSTRY

210

ply said the writer was entitled to five percent of the net profits, the question might arise, is he due five percent of the producer's half (which would amount to five percent of fifty percent) or is he entitled to five percent of the whole?

There is more room for accounting disputes when a participant is entitled to a piece of the net because the studio can deduct various expenses as well as interest, distribution and overhead fees. Any payments made to gross profit participants are also deductible before payment is due a net profit participant. Thus, even if there is no creative accounting, a net profit participant is unlikely see any profits if the studio is obligated to gross profit participants.

NET PROFITS

Each studio can define the term "net profits" as it likes. Here is one studio's definition:

NET PROFIT DEFINITION

1. DEFINITION OF PARTIES: "_____" means _____ Inc., a Delaware corporation, and its subsidiaries engaged in the business of distributing motion pictures for exhibition in theatres and for broadcasting over television stations, but shall not include any other persons, firms or corporations licensed by _____ to distribute motion pictures in any part of the world. Nor shall such term include: any person, firm or corporation distributing the Picture for purposes other than exhibition in theatres or by television stations; exhibitors or others who may actually exhibit the Picture to the public; radio or television broadcasters; cable operators; manufacturers, wholesalers or retailers of video discs, cassettes or similar devices; book or music publishers; phonograph record producers or distributors; merchandisers, etc., whether or not any of the foregoing are subsidiaries of _____. As used herein, a "subsidiary" of _____ refers to an entity in which _____ has at least a 50% interest.

"Participant" means the party under the foregoing agreement who or which is entitled to participate in the gross receipts or net profits of the Picture, and the successors and permitted assigns of such party.

2. NET PROFITS: As between _____ and Participant, the "net profits" of the Picture means an amount equal to the excess, if any, of the gross receipts (as defined in 3 hereof) of the Picture over the aggregate of the following, which shall be deducted in the order listed:

(a) _____'s distribution fees set forth in 4 hereof.

(b) _____'s expenses in connection with the distribution of the Picture, as set forth in 5 hereof.

(c) The cost of production of the Picture, plus an amount equal to interest thereon, all as provided for in 9 hereof, and plus such other costs, if any, as may have been incurred in connection with the financing of the cost of production of the Picture. Said interest and other costs shall be recouped before said cost of production.

(d) All contingent amounts consented to by _____ and not included in the cost of production of the Picture payable to Participant or any third party based upon, or computed in respect of, the gross receipts of the Picture (as defined in the relevant agreements), or any portion thereof.

Net profits shall be determined as of the close of each accounting period provided for in 10 hereof.

3. GROSS RECEIPTS: As used herein, the term "gross receipts" means the aggregate of:

(a) All film rentals actually received by _____ from parties exhibiting the Picture in theatres and on television where _____ distributes directly to such parties (hereinafter referred to as "exhibitors").

(b) Where _____ grants theatrical distribution rights to a subdistributor on a basis requiring it to account to _____ with respect to film rentals, either: (i) the film rentals received by such subdistributor from exhibitors which _____ accepts for the purpose of its accountings with such subdistributor; or (ii) _____'s share (actually received) of film rentals received by such subdistributor; whichever _____ elects from time to time as to each subdistributor.

(c) In respect of licenses of exhibition or distribution rights by means of video discs, cassettes or similar devices, an amount equal to 20% of (i) the gross wholesale rental income therefrom and (ii) the gross wholesale sales income therefrom less a reasonable allowance for returns.

(d) All amounts actually received by _____ from the following: (i) trailers (other than trailers advertising television exhibitions of the Picture); (ii) licenses of theatrical distribution rights for a flat sum; (iii) licenses of exhibition or distribution rights other than those referred to in (a), (b), (c) and (d) (ii) of this 3, specifically including licenses to cable operators; (iv) the lease of positive prints (as distinguished from the licensing thereof for a film rental); and from the sale or licensing of advertising accessories, souvenir programs and booklets; and (v) recoveries by _____ for infringement of copyrights of the Picture.

(e) All monies actually received by _____ on account of direct subsidies, aide or prizes relating specifically to the Picture, net of an amount equal to income taxes based thereon imposed by the country involved, if any. If local laws require use of such monies as a condition to the grant of such subsidy or aide, such monies shall not be included in gross receipts until actually used.

(f) See Exhibits "1," "2" and "3" attached hereto.

In no event shall rentals from the exhibition of the Picture which are contributed to charitable organizations be included in gross receipts.

4. DISTRIBUTION FEES: _____'s distribution fees shall be as follows:

(a) 30% of the gross receipts of the Picture derived by _____ from all sources in the United States and Canada.

(b) 35% of the gross receipts of the Picture derived by _____ from all sources in the United Kingdom.

(c) 40% of the gross receipts of the Picture derived by _____ from all sources other than those referred to in (a) and (b) above.

CONTRACTS
FOR THE
FILM AND
TELEVISION
INDUSTRY

212

(d) Notwithstanding the foregoing; (i) with respect to sums included in the gross receipts pursuant to 3(b)(ii) and 3(d)(ii) hereof, _____'s distribution fee shall be 15% of such sums; (ii) if _____ shall license the exhibition of the Picture on free television, the aforesaid percentages as to amounts received and collected by _____ from sources in the United States, shall be 30% if collected from a network for national network telecasts in prime time; and 35% in all other instances; and, as to amounts received and collected by _____ from sources outside the Untied States 40%; (iii) no distribution fee shall be charged on gross receipts referred to in 3(e) or 3(f) hereof.

All distribution fees shall be calculated on the full gross receipts without any deductions or payments of any kind whatsoever.

5. DISTRIBUTION EXPENSES: _____'s deductible distribution expenses in connection with the Picture shall include all costs and expenses incurred in connection with the distribution, advertising, exploitation and turning to account of the Picture of whatever kind or nature, or which are customarily treated as distribution expenses under customary accounting procedures in the motion picture industry. If _____ reasonably anticipates that additional distribution expenses will be incurred in the future, _____ may, for a reasonable time, set up appropriate reserves therefor. Without limiting the generality of the foregoing, the following particular items shall be included in distribution expenses hereunder:

(a) The cost and expense of all duped and dubbed negatives, sound tracks, prints, release prints, tapes, cassettes, duplicating material and facilities and all other material manufactured for use in connection with the Picture, including the cost of inspecting, repairing, checking and renovating film, reels, containers, cassettes, packing, storing and shipping and all other expenses connected therewith and inspecting and checking exhibitors' projection and sound equipment and facilities. _____ may manufacture or cause to be manufactured as many or as few duped negatives, positive prints and other material for use in connection with the Picture as it, in its sole discretion, may consider advisable or desirable.

(b) All direct costs and charges for advertisements, press books, artwork, advertising accessories and trailers (other than (i) prints of trailers advertising free television exhibition of the Picture, and (ii) the trailer production costs which are included in the cost of production of the Picture), advertising, publicizing and exploiting the Picture by such means and to such extent as _____ may, in its uncontrolled discretion, deem desirable, including, without limitation, pre-release advertising and publicity, so-called cooperative and/or theatre advertising, and/or other advertising engaged in with or for exhibitors, to the extent _____ pays, shares in, or is charged with all or a portion of such costs and all other exploitation costs relating to such theatre exhibition. Any re-use fees and costs of recording and manufacturing masters for phonograph records, which _____ shall advance in order to assist in the advertising and exploitation of the Picture, shall be treated as costs hereunder to the extent unrecouped by the record company. Where any _____ advertising or publicity employee (other than an executive supervisory employee) or facility is used for the Picture, the salary of such employee and the cost of such facility (while so used for the Picture) shall be direct costs hereunder. Any costs and charges referred to in this (b) (and not included in the cost of production of the Picture), expended or incurred prior to delivery of the Picture, shall be included in direct costs under this (b). There shall also be included as an item of cost a sum equal to 10% of all direct costs referred to in this (b) to cover the indirect cost of _____'s advertising and publicity departments, both domestic and foreign.

(c) All costs of preparing and delivering the Picture for distribution (regardless of whether such costs are the salaries and expenses of _____'s own employees or employees or parties not regularly employed by _____), including, without limitation, all costs incurred in connection with the production of foreign language versions of the Picture, whether dubbed, superimposed or otherwise, as well as any and all costs and expenses in connection with changing the title of the Picture, recutting, re-editing or shortening or lengthening the Picture for release in any territory or for exhibition on television or other media, or in order to conform to the requirements of censorship authorities, or in order to conform to the peculiar national or political prejudices likely to be encountered in any territory, or for any other purpose or reason. The costs referred to in this (c) shall include all studio charges for facilities, labor and material, whether or not incurred at a studio owned or controlled by _____.

(d) All sums paid or accrued on account of sales, use, receipts, income, excise, remittance and other taxes (however denominated) to any governmental authority assessed upon the negatives, duplicate negatives, prints or sound records of the Picture, or upon the use or distribution of the Picture, or upon the revenues derived therefrom, or any part thereof, or upon the remittance of such revenues, or any part thereof; any and all sums paid or accrued on account of duties, customs and imposts, costs of acquiring permits, "Kontingents," or any similar authority to secure the entry, licensing, exhibition, performance, use or televising of the Picture in any country or part thereof, regardless of whether such payments or accruals are assessed against the Picture or the proceeds thereof or against a group of motion pictures in which the Picture may be included or the proceeds thereof. In no event shall the deductible amount of any such tax (however denominated) imposed upon _____, be decreased (nor the gross receipts increased) because of the manner in which such taxes are elected to be treated by _____ in filing net income, corporate franchise, excess profits or similar tax returns. Subject to the foregoing, (i) _____'s own United States federal and state income taxes and franchise taxes based on _____'s net income; and (ii) income taxes payable to any country or territory by _____ based on the net earnings of _____ in such country or territory and which is computed and assessed solely by reason of the retention in such country or territory by _____ of any portion of the gross receipts shall not be deductible hereunder.

(e) Expenses of transmitting to the United States any funds accruing to _____ from the Picture in foreign countries, such as cable expenses, and any discounts from such funds taken to convert such funds directly or indirectly into U.S. dollars.

(f) All costs and expenses, including reasonable attorneys' fees, loss, damage or liability suffered or incurred by _____ in connection with: any action taken by _____ (whether by litigation or otherwise) in copyrighting, protecting and enforcing the copyright of, and other rights and sources of revenue to be derived from, the Picture; reducing or minimizing the matters referred to in (d) and (e) above, the collection of film rentals; and other sums due _____ from exhibitors, subdistributors and others in respect of the Picture or to recover monies due pursuant to any agreement relating to the distribution or the exhibition of the Picture; checking attendance and exhibitors' receipts; preventing and/or recovering damages for unauthorized exhibition or distribu-

CONTRACTS
FOR THE
FILM AND
TELEVISION
INDUSTRY

214

tion of the Picture, or any impairment of, encumbrance on or infringement upon, the rights of _____ in and to the Picture; prosecuting and defending actions under the antitrust laws, communications laws, and federal, state and local laws, ordinances and regulations (including censorship) affecting the exhibition and/or distribution of the Picture and/or the ability of _____ to derive revenue from the Picture and its component parts and by-products; and auditing of books and records of any exhibitor, subdistributor or licensee.

(g) Royalties payable to manufacturers of sound recording and reproducing equipment and dues and assessments of, and contributions by _____ to, AMPTP, MPAA, MPEA, the Academy of Motion Picture Arts and Sciences and other trade associations or industry groups comprised of a substantial number of motion picture producers and/or distributors, but only for purposes relating to the production, distribution, export, import, advertising, exploitation and general protection and/or promotion of motion pictures.

(h) In the event any person shall make a claim relating to the Picture against _____ or any of its licensees, which claim, in _____'s judgment, is of sufficient merit to constitute a reasonable probability of ultimate loss, cost, damage or expense, _____ may deduct either this (h) such amount as _____ may deem necessary to cover loss, cost, damage or expense which may be suffered as a result thereof. _____ shall have the right to settle and pay any such claim. After the settlement of any such claim, or after the final judicial determination thereof, the amount previously deducted hereunder shall be adjusted accordingly with the next accounting statement rendered hereunder. Nothing herein contained shall be construed as a waiver of any of Participant's warranties contained in this Agreement, or a waiver of any right or remedy at law or otherwise which may exist in favor of _____, including, but not limited to, the right to require Participant to reimburse _____ on demand for any liability, cost, damage or expense arising out of, or resulting from, any breach by Participant of any warranty, undertaking or obligation by Participant, or any right on the part of _____ to recoup or recover any such cost or expense out of Participant's share of any monies payable hereunder, rather than treating such costs or expenses as distribution expenses.

(i) All amounts paid or payable to or for the benefit of actors, writers, composers, directors and others, pursuant to applicable collective bargaining agreements and/or any law or governmental regulation or decree now or hereafter in force by reason of, and/or as a condition or consideration for, any exhibition, use, re-use, rerun, performance, sale, license and/or distribution of the Picture and/or copies of all or any part thereof, on television, supplemental markets, or otherwise (all herein called "residuals"), together with all taxes, pension fund contributions and other costs paid or payable in respect of such residuals, and in respect of participations in the gross receipts and net profits of the Picture; provided, however, that if Participant or any principal stockholder of Participant, or any heirs, executors, administrators, successors or assigns of Participant, or any such stockholder, are entitled, either directly or by way of participation in any pension fund, to any such residuals, or to compensation for services rendered beyond any guaranteed period referred to in the foregoing agreement, the amount payable on account thereof shall be treated as an advance against Participant's share of the net profits hereunder.

(j) The cost of all insurance (to the extent that the same is not included in the cost of production of the Picture) covering or relating to the Picture, including, but not limited to, errors and omissions insurance and all insurance on negatives, positive prints, sound materials or other physical property, it being understood, however, that _____ shall not be obligated to take out or maintain any such insurance.

(k) If _____ shall proceed under 3(b)(i) hereof, all items deducted by the subdistributor as distribution expenses, and which _____ accepts for the purpose of its accountings with such subdistributor, shall be treated as _____'s expenditures under the corresponding subdivision of this 5.

6. FILM RENTALS: "Film Rentals" shall be determined after all refunds, credits, discounts, allowances and adjustments granted to exhibitors, whether occasioned by condemnation by boards of censorship, settlement of disputes, or otherwise. Until earned, forfeited or applied to the Picture, neither advance payments nor security deposits shall be included in film rentals. No cost (regardless of how incurred, paid or allowed) of _____'s share of cooperative and/or theater advertising, shall be deducted in determining film rentals. Where allowances are granted and paid on account of _____'s share of cooperative theatre or joint advertising, such payments shall not be deducted in determining film rental, and where _____'s share of cooperative theater or joint advertising is deducted by the exhibitor _____'s share of cooperative theater or joint advertising shall be added back into the film rental received from such exhibitor, and all such costs, payments, discounts and allowances shall be treated as distribution expenses. Wherever _____ exhibits the Picture in a theatre or over a television station owned or controlled by _____, or licenses the Picture or rights connected therewith to theatres, television stations or other agencies in which _____ has an interest directly or indirectly, or to which _____ is obligated to pay a fixed sum for exhibiting the Picture or for the use of its premises or facilities, _____ shall include in the film rentals of the Picture such sums, determined in good faith, as may be reasonable and consistent with _____'s usual practice in such matters.

7. ALLOCATIONS: Wherever _____ (i) receives from any license either a flat sum or a percentage of the receipts, or both, for any right to a group of motion pictures (including the Picture) under any agreement (whether or not the same shall provide for the exhibition, lease or delivery of positive prints of any of said motion pictures) which does not specify what portion of the license payments apply to the respective motion pictures in the group (or to such prints or other material, if any, as may be supplied), or (ii) receives foreign currency under 8(ii) or 8(iii) hereof relating to a group of motion pictures (including the Picture), then in any and all such situations _____ shall include in, or deduct from, the gross receipts, as the case may be, such sums, determined in good faith, as may be reasonable and consistent with _____'s usual practice in such matters. All costs described in 5 hereof shall be fairly apportioned to the Picture if incurred or expended on an industry basis, or in conjunction with other motion picture producers and/or distributors, or with respect to the Picture and other motion pictures distributed by _____.

8. FOREIGN RECEIPTS: No sums received by _____ relating to the Picture shall be included in gross receipts hereunder unless and until such sums have been (i) received by _____ in U.S. dollars in the United States, or (ii) used by _____ for the production or acquisition of motion pictures or television films which can be lawfully removed from the country or territory involved, in which event they shall be included in gross receipts for the accounting period during which an amount (computed at the official or unofficial rate of exchange, as _____ may elect) equal to the amount expended for such

CONTRACTS
FOR THE
FILM AND
TELEVISION
INDUSTRY

216

production or acquisition, plus customary interest thereon, has been recouped by _____ (in excess of normal distribution fees and distribution expenses) from distribution thereof outside the country or territory involved; or (iii) used by _____ for acquisition of tangible personal property which can be and is lawfully exported from the country or territory involved, in which event the U.S. dollar equivalent of the currency utilized to acquire such property shall be included in gross receipts hereunder for the accounting period during which such property was so exported, such U.S. dollar equivalent to be computed at the official or unofficial rate of exchange, as _____ may elect, in effect on the date of export. _____ will, promptly after receipt of a written request from Participant (but not more frequently than annually) advise Participant in writing as to foreign revenues not included in gross receipts as aforesaid, and _____ shall, at the written request and expense of, Participant (subject to any and all limitations, restrictions, laws, rules and regulations affecting such transactions), deposit into a bank designated by Participant in the country involved, or pay to any other party designated by Participant in such country, such part thereof as would have been payable to Participant hereunder. Such deposits or payments to or for Participant shall constitute due remittance to Participant, and _____ shall have no further interest therein or responsibility therefor. _____ makes no warranties or representations that any part of any such foreign currencies may be converted into U.S. dollars or transferred to the account of Participant in any foreign country. In no event shall _____ be obligated to apply gross receipts of any country not actually received by _____ in U.S. dollars in the United States to the recoupment of any costs or expenses incurred with respect to the Picture in any other country.

9. COST OF PRODUCTION; INTEREST:

(a) The "cost of production" of the Picture means the total direct cost of production of the Picture, including the cost of all items listed on _____'s standard Delivery Schedule, computed and determined in all respects in the same manner as _____ then customarily determines the direct cost of other motion pictures distributed and/or financed by it, plus _____'s overhead charge. The determination of what items constitute direct charges and what items are within said overhead charge shall be made in all respects in the same manner as _____ customarily determines such matters. The full amount of all direct costs of production of the Picture (whether payable in cash, deferred or accrued) shall be included in the direct cost of the Picture at the time liability therefor is incurred or contracted, regardless of whether the same has actually been paid to the party or parties entitled thereto at the time involved. Deferments and participations in gross receipts of the Picture consented to by _____ (however defined) shall be treated as direct costs of production, whether the same shall be in a definite amount or based on a percentage of the gross receipts, and whether the same are fixed obligations or are contingent upon receipts of the Picture; provided, however, contingent participations based on a percentage of gross receipts as defined in the applicable agreement shall not be included in the direct cost of production beyond recoupment under 2(c) hereof.

(b) _____'s overhead charge shall be in an amount equal to 15% of the direct cost of production of the Picture, with the understanding that any production facilities, equipment or personnel supplied by _____ or by a studio owned or controlled by _____, or in which _____ has a substantial financial interest (and which are not furnished within the overhead charge) shall be supplied at _____'s usual rental rates charged for such items, and such charges shall be treated as direct costs of production of the Picture and shall bear said 15% overhead charge. _____'s overhead charge shall accrue and be included in the cost of production of the Picture concurrently with the incurring of the respective items of direct cost to which it applies.

(c) The amount equal to interest provided for in 2(c) hereof shall be calculated at a rate per annum equal to 125% of the prime commercial rate of First National Bank of Boston from time to time in effect. Said amount shall be calculated from the respective dates that each item is charged to the Picture until the close of the accounting period during which the cost of production is recouped under 2(c) hereof, except that interest on deferred amounts shall be calculated from the date of payment.

(d) Concurrently with delivery to Participant of the first earnings statement hereunder, _____ will (subject to revisions and correction) deliver to Participant an itemized summary of the cost of production of the Picture. Participant shall have the right to audit such statement in accordance with 11 hereof.

10. EARNINGS STATEMENTS: _____ shall render to Participant periodic statements showing, in summary form, the appropriate calculations under this Agreement. Statements shall be issued for each calendar quarter until the Picture has been in release for 4 years from and including the quarter in which the Picture was first released, and thereafter annually. Each such quarterly or annual period, as the case may be, is herein referred to as an "accounting period." No statements need be rendered for any accounting period during which no receipts are received. Statements rendered by _____ may be changed from time to time to give effect to year-end adjustments made by _____'s Accounting Department or Public Accountants, or to items overlooked, to correct errors and for similar purposes. If _____ shall extend credit to any licensee with respect to the Picture, and if such credit has been included in the gross receipts, and if, in the opinion of _____, any such indebtedness shall be uncollectible, the uncollected amount may be deducted in any subsequent earning statement. Should _____ make any overpayment to Participant hereunder for any reason, _____ shall have the right to deduct and retain for its own account an amount equal to any such overpayment from any sums that may thereafter become due or payable by _____ to Participant or for Participant's account, or may demand repayment from Participant, in which event Participant shall repay the same when such demand is made. Any U.S. dollars due and payable to Participant by _____ pursuant to any such statement shall be paid to Participant simultaneously with the rendering of such statement; provided, however, that all amounts payable to Participant hereunder shall be subject to all laws and regulations now or hereafter in existence requiring deduction or withholdings for income or other taxes payable by or assessable against Participant. _____ shall have the right to make such deductions and withholdings and the payment thereof to the governmental agency concerned in accordance with its interpretation in good faith of such laws and regulations, and shall not be liable to Participant for the making of such deductions or withholdings or the payment thereof to the governmental agency concerned. In any such event Participant shall make and prosecute any and all claims which it may have with respect to the same directly with the governmental agency having jurisdiction in the premises. The right of Participant to receive, and the obligation of _____ to account for, any share of the net profits of the Picture shall terminate if the Picture has been made available for exhibition on syndicated television in the U.S.A., and if the first earnings statement issued thereafter shows a deficit under 2 hereof which would require in excess of

CONTRACTS
FOR THE
FILM AND
TELEVISION
INDUSTRY

218

$500,000 of gross receipts before Participant would be entitled to receive any net profits hereunder. In the event a new medium of exhibition shall thereafter be developed and there shall be substantial exhibition and distribution of the Picture by such new medium which is likely to generate gross receipts of $500,000 or the amount of the deficit, whichever is larger, Participant may audit _____'s records for the purpose of determining whether the Picture has earned, or is likely to earn, any net profits, and if, as a result of such audit, it is determined by mutual agreement, or in the event of dispute appropriate legal proceedings, that the Picture has earned, or is likely to earn, net profits as herein defined, accountings hereunder and payments, if required, shall be reinstated.

11. ACCOUNTING RECORDS RE DISTRIBUTION; AUDIT RIGHTS: _____ shall keep books of account relating to the distribution of the Picture, together with vouchers, exhibition contracts and similar records supporting the same (all of which are hereinafter referred to as "records"), which shall be kept on the same basis and in the same manner and for the same periods as such records are customarily kept by _____. Participant may, at its own expense, audit the applicable records at the place where _____ maintains the same in order to verify earnings statements rendered hereunder. Any such audit shall be conducted only by a reputable public accountant during reasonable business hours in such manner as not to interfere with _____'s normal business activities. In no event shall an audit with respect to any earnings statement commence later than twenty-four (24) months from the rendition of the earnings statement involved; nor shall any audit continue for longer than thirty (30) consecutive business days; nor shall audits be made hereunder more frequently than once annually; nor shall the records supporting any earnings statement be audited more than once. All earnings statements rendered hereunder shall be binding upon Participant and not subject to objection for any reason unless such objection is made in writing, stating the basis thereof, and delivered to _____ within twenty-four (24) months from rendition of the earnings statement, or if an audit is commenced prior thereto, within thirty (30) days from the completion of the relative audit. If _____, as a courtesy to Participant, shall include cumulative figures in any earnings or other statement, the time within which Participant may commence any audit or make any objection in respect of any statement shall not be enlarged or extended thereby. Participant's right to examine _____'s records is limited to the Picture, and Participant shall have no right to examine records relating to _____'s business generally or with respect to any other motion picture for purposes of comparison or otherwise; provided, however, that where any original income or expense document with third parties relates to the Picture and to other motion pictures, Participant shall have the right to examine the entire document without deletions therefrom.

12. OWNERSHIP: Participant expressly acknowledges that Participant has and will have no right, title or interest of any kind or character whatsoever in or to the Picture, and no lien thereon or other rights in or to the gross receipts or net profits of the Picture; and that the same shall be and remain _____'s sole and exclusive property, and _____ shall not be obligated to segregate the same from its other funds, it being the intent and purpose hereof that the net profits or gross receipts after moving breakeven, as the case may be, of the Picture are referred to herein merely as a measure in determining the time and manner of payment to Participant; and that _____ shall not be deemed a trustee, pledgeholder or fiduciary. Participant shall have no right, title or interest of any kind or character whatsoever in or to the literary, dramatic or musical material upon which the Picture is based, or from which it may be adapted; and _____ shall have the sole and exclusive right to utilize, sell, license or otherwise dispose of all or any part of its rights in such material upon such terms and conditions as it may deem advisable, all without consulting or advising Participant and without accounting to Participant in any manner with respect thereto.

13. DISTRIBUTION: As between Participant and _____, _____ shall have complete authority to distribute the Picture and license the exhibition thereof throughout the world in accordance with such sales methods, policies and terms as it may, in its uncontrolled discretion, determine. _____ shall have the broadest possible latitude in the distribution of the Picture, and the exercise of its judgment in good faith in all matters pertaining thereto shall be final. _____ has not made any express or implied representation, warranty, guarantee or agreement as to the amount of proceeds which will be derived from the distribution of the Picture, nor has _____ made any express or implied representation, warranty, guarantee or agreement that there will be any sums payable to Participant hereunder, or that the Picture will be favorably received by exhibitors or by the public, or will be distributed continuously. In no event shall _____ incur any liability based upon any claim that _____ has failed to realize receipts or revenue which should or could have been realized. _____ may distribute the Picture either itself or through such distributors, subdistributors and other parties as _____ may, in its uncontrolled discretion, determine, and _____ may refrain from releasing and/ or distributing the Picture in any territory for any reason whatsoever. _____ may license the Picture or rights connected therewith to any and all theatres or other agencies in which _____ may have an interest directly or indirectly upon such terms and rentals as _____j____ may deem fair and proper under the circumstances. Nothing herein contained shall be construed as a representation or warranty by _____ that it now has or will hereafter have or control any theatres or agencies in the United States or elsewhere.

14. SALE OF PICTURE: _____ shall have the right at any time after completion of the Picture to sell, transfer or assign all or any of its rights in and to the Picture and the negative and copyright thereof. Any such sale, transfer or assignment shall be subject to Participant's rights hereunder, and upon the purchaser, transferee or assignee assuming performance of this agreement in place and stead of _____, _____ shall be released and discharged of and from any further liability or obligation hereunder. No part of any sale price or other consideration received by, or payable to, _____ shall be included in the gross receipts hereunder and Participant shall have no rights in respect of any thereof.

15. ASSIGNMENTS, ETC.: Participant shall have the right to sell, transfer or hypothecate (all herein called "assign") all or any part of Participant's right to receive the monies payable to Participant hereunder. Any such assignment shall be subject to all pertinent laws and governmental regulations and to the rights of _____ hereunder. In the event of any such assignment by Participant, a Notice of Irrevocable Authority and Distributor's Acceptance in Warner's usual form shall be executed by Participant and by the transferee and delivered to _____. If at any time more than three parties shall be entitled to receive payments, which under the terms hereof are to be paid to or for the account of Participant, _____ may, at its option, require that all such parties execute and deliver an agreement in _____'s usual form appointing a disbursing agent for all such parties.

CONTRACTS
FOR THE
FILM AND
TELEVISION
INDUSTRY

220

MUSIC PUBLISHING INCOME

There shall also be included in gross receipts of the picture:

A sum equal to 25% of the "publisher's share" of mechanical reproduction and performing fees received in U.S. currency by _____'s subsidiary or affiliated publisher with respect to music and lyrics written specifically for and synchronized in the picture as released, provided such publisher is vested with all rights therein and all of the "publisher's share" of the receipts therefrom, and provided the party entitled to share in gross receipts or net profits of the picture under the foregoing agreement is not entitled to receive composers' or lyricists' royalties in respect of such music or lyrics. The "publisher's share" of mechanical reproduction fees shall be the full amount paid by the licensee, less composers' share of such fees and less the charges of the publisher or any agent, trustee or administrator acting for the publisher for the collection of such fees, not to exceed 5% thereof. Mechanical reproduction fees do not include synchronization fees.

The "publisher's share" of performing fees shall be the net amount actually received by the publisher from any performing rights society in respect of the music and lyrics involved; or, if _____ or the publisher shall administer the collection of all or any part of performance fees, the full amount of all performance fees collected by _____ or the publisher, less the composer's share of such fees and all reasonable costs and expenses in administering the collection of such fees.

If the agreement or Exhibit to which this Exhibit is attached provides for distribution fees, no distribution fees shall be charged on amounts included in gross receipts pursuant to this Exhibit.

SOUND TRACK RECORD INCOME

In the event the party entitled to share in the gross receipts or net profits of the picture under the foregoing agreement is not entitled to receive any artists' royalties in respect of phonograph records derived from the sound track of the picture, then _____ agrees to include in the gross receipts of the picture royalties on sound track records, as herein defined, computed at the applicable royalty rate.

As used herein:

The term "sound track records" means and refers to phonograph records, tapes, or other sound recordings which contain either (i) portions of the sound track transferred directly to phonograph record masters from sound records which form a part of the sound track of the picture; or (ii) sound recordings recorded separately but utilizing substantially the same musical score, parts and instrumentation, and essentially the same artists, music and/or dialogue and/or sound effects as is contained in the sound track of the picture; or (iii) a combination of (i) and (ii). Sound track records do not, however, include any recordings produced solely for the purpose of advertising and exploiting the picture and copies of which are not distributed to the public.

The term "applicable royalty rate" means and refers to the following percentages of the prevailing retail price but in no event more than the net royalty actually received and retainable by _____ for its own account with respect to the sale of any particular copies—5% of 90% in respect of sound track records sold in the United States; 2 1/2% of 90% in respect of sound track records sold outside the United States—except that as to sound track records sold pursuant to mail order of "club" plans, the royalty rate shall be one-half of the rate otherwise applicable.

If any sound track records contain selections from other sources, the applicable royalty rate hereunder shall be prorated on the basis of the total number of minutes of selections from the sound track compared to the total number of minutes on such records.

In determining the net royalty retainable by _____, all royalties payable to artists, conductors and other third parties in respect to such sound track records shall be deducted from the aggregate royalty payable to _____ under the applicable distribution agreement.

The term "prevailing retail price" means and refers to the price generally prevailing in the country of manufacture or sale (as determined by the Record Company), less all taxes, duties and charges for containers.

There shall be deducted from amounts included in gross receipts hereunder a pro rata share of re-use fees and costs of recording and manufacturing masters advanced by _____ or the Record Company. Sales shall be determined on the basis of the number of records sold and for which the Record Company has been paid in U.S. currency, after allowing for all returns, cancellations, exchanges, applicable discounts, etc. and reasonable reserves which may be established therefor. No sums shall be included in gross receipts with respect to records given away or sold at less than the Record Company's cost or for promotional purposes, or as sales inducements or otherwise.

If the agreement or Exhibit to which this Exhibit is attached provides for distribution fees, no distribution fees shall be charged on amounts included in gross receipts pursuant to this Exhibit.

MERCHANDISING INCOME

In the event the party entitled to share in gross receipts or net profits of the picture under the foregoing agreement is not entitled to share directly in merchandising revenue, there shall be included in gross receipts of the picture:

(a) A sum equal to 50% of all license fees (in excess of all royalties and participations) received by _____ directly as a result of the exercise by _____ itself of merchandising license rights. If, however, _____ shall sublicense or sub-contract any of such merchandising license rights, _____ shall include in the gross receipts hereunder, at its election, either a sum equal to (i) 85% of the net sums (in excess of all royalties and participations) received from such sub-licensee; or (ii) 50% of such sub-licensee's license fees from the exercise of such licensing rights (from which there shall be deducted all royalties and participations), and out of the remaining 50% thereof _____ shall pay and discharge the fees of its sub-licensee.

(b) If the publication rights to the underlying literary material were owned or controlled by the party entitled to share in gross receipts or net profits of the picture under the foregoing agreement (herein called "Participant") prior to the execution of this agreement, and were acquired by _____ pursuant to or in connection with this agreement, then (i) all net sums received by _____ from nonaffiliated or nonsubsidiary publishers from the publication of such un-

CONTRACTS
FOR THE
FILM AND
TELEVISION
INDUSTRY

222

derlying literary material and of novelizations of the screenplay of the picture, and (ii) a sum equal to 5% of the net receipts of _____'s subsidiary or affiliated publishers from the publication of such material and novelizations, less, in either case, royalties paid out of (i) or (ii) to the writers of such material and novelizations.

If the agreement or Exhibit to which this Exhibit is attached provides for distribution fees, no distribution fees shall be charged on amounts included in gross receipts pursuant to this Exhibit.

The terms of gross deals vary greatly. Here is a provision that allows for participation in the gross after breakeven.

GROSS RECEIPTS AFTER BREAKEVEN

1. DEFINITION OF PARTIES: "Studio" means Studio Inc., a Delaware corporation, and its subsidiaries engaged in the business of distributing motion pictures for exhibition in theatres and for broadcasting over television stations, but shall not include any other persons, firms or corporations licensed by Studio to distribute motion pictures in any part of the world. Nor shall such term include: any person, firm or corporation distributing the Picture for purposes other than exhibition in theatres or by television stations; exhibitors or others who may actually exhibit the Picture to the public; radio or television broadcasters; cable operators; manufacturers, wholesalers or retailers of video discs, cassettes or similar devices; book or music publishers; phonograph record producers or distributors; merchandisers, etc., whether or not any of the foregoing are subsidiaries of Studio. As used herein, a "subsidiary" of Studio refers to an entity in which Studio has at least a 50% interest.

"Participant" means the party under the foregoing agreement who or which is entitled to participate in the gross receipts of the Picture in excess of breakeven, and the successors and permitted assigns of such party.

2. BREAKEVEN: As between Studio and Participant, the Picture shall be deemed to have reached "breakeven" at such time as the gross receipts (as defined in 3 hereof) of the Picture shall equal the following:

(a) Studio's distribution fees set forth in 4 hereof.

(b) Studio's expenses in connection with the distribution of the Picture, as set forth in 5 hereof.

(c) The cost of production of the Picture, plus an amount equal to interest thereon, all as provided for in 9 hereof, and plus such other costs, if any, as may have been incurred in connection with the financing of the cost of production of the Picture. Said interest and other costs shall be recouped before said cost of production.

3. "GROSS RECEIPTS" of the Picture means the aggregate of:

(a) All film rentals actually received by Studio from parties exhibiting the Picture in theatres and on television where Studio distributes directly to such parties (hereinafter referred to as "exhibitors").

(b) Where Studio grants theatrical distribution rights to a subdistributor on a basis requiring it to account to Studio with respect to film rentals, either: (i) the film rentals received by such subdistributor from exhibitors which Studio accepts for the purpose of its accountings with such subdistributor; or (ii) Studio's share (actually received) of film rentals received by such subdistributor; whichever Studio elects from time to time as to each subdistributor.

(c) In respect of licenses of exhibition or distribution rights by means of video discs, cassettes or similar devices, an amount equal to 20% of (i) the gross

CONTRACTS
FOR THE
FILM AND
TELEVISION
INDUSTRY

224

wholesale rental income therefrom and (ii) the gross wholesale sales income therefrom less a reasonable allowance for returns.

(d) All amounts actually received by Studio from the following: (i) trailers (other than trailers advertising television exhibitions of the Picture); (ii) licenses of theatrical distribution rights for a flat sum; (iii) licenses of exhibition or distribution rights other than those referred to in (a), (b), (c) and (d) (ii) of this 3, specifically including licenses to cable operators; (iv) the lease of positive prints (as distinguished from the licensing thereof for a film rental); and from the sale or licensing of advertising accessories, souvenir programs and booklets; and (v) recoveries by Studio for infringement of copyrights of the Picture.

(e) All monies actually received by Studio on account of direct subsidies, aid or prizes relating specifically to the Picture, net of an amount equal to income taxes based thereon imposed by the country involved, if any. If local laws require use of such monies as a condition to the grant of such subsidy or aide, such monies shall not be included in gross receipts until actually used.

(f) All amounts required to be included under Exhibits "1," "2" and "3" hereof.

All costs incurred in connection with any of the foregoing shall be deemed and treated as recoupable distribution expenses. In no event shall rentals from the exhibition of the Picture which are contributed to charitable organizations be included in gross receipts.

Notwithstanding anything herein contained, after the Picture shall be deemed to have reached "breakeven" as defined in 2 above, gross receipts shall be as defined and this Exhibit shall otherwise be modified as set forth in Schedule 1 attached hereto and incorporated herein by this reference.

4. DISTRIBUTION FEES: Studio's distribution fees shall be as follows:

(a) 30% of the gross receipts of the Picture derived by Studio from all sources in the United States and Canada.

(b) 35% of the gross receipts of the Picture derived by Studio from all sources in the United Kingdom.

(c) 40% of the gross receipts of the Picture derived by Studio from all sources other than those referred to in (a) and (b) above.

(d) Notwithstanding the foregoing; (i) with respect to sums included in the gross receipts pursuant to 3(b)(ii) and 3(d)(ii) hereof, Studio's distribution fee shall be 15% of such sums; (ii) if Studio shall license the exhibition of the Picture on free television, the aforesaid percentages as to amounts received and collected by Studio from sources in the United States, shall be 30% if collected from a network for national network telecasts in prime time; and 35% in all other instances; and, as to amounts received and collected by Studio from sources outside the United States 40%; (iii) no distribution fee shall be charged on gross receipts referred to in 3(e) hereof.

All distribution fees shall be calculated on the full gross receipts without any deductions or payments of any kind whatsoever, except as specifically hereinafter provided.

Notwithstanding anything herein contained, it is agreed that for the accounting period in which the Picture shall first reach breakeven, the distribution fees for the purpose of calculating breakeven shall be calculated only on that portion of the gross receipts in respect of such accounting period which is equal to the sum of the following:

(a) An amount equal to the sums specified in subparagraphs (b) and (c) of paragraph 2 of this Exhibit which are recouped or paid in respect of such accounting period; and

(b) An amount equal to the distribution fees on gross receipts equal to the sum of said deductible items, plus the distribution fees on gross receipts equal to such distribution fee.

5. DISTRIBUTION EXPENSES: Studio's deductible distribution expenses in connection with the Picture shall include all costs and expenses incurred in connection with the distribution, advertising, exploitation and turning to account of the Picture of whatever kind or nature, or which are customarily treated as distribution expenses under customary accounting procedures in the motion picture industry. If Studio reasonably anticipates that additional distribution expenses will be incurred in the future, Studio may, for a reasonable time, set up appropriate reserves therefor. Without limiting the generality of the foregoing, the following particular items shall be included in distribution expenses hereunder:

(a) The cost and expense of all duped and dubbed negatives, sound tracks, prints, release prints, tapes, cassettes, duplicating material and facilities and all other material manufactured for use in connection with the Picture, including the cost of inspecting, repairing, checking and renovating film, reels, containers, cassettes, packing, storing and shipping and all other expenses connected therewith and inspecting and checking exhibitors' projection and sound equipment and facilities. Studio may manufacture or cause to be manufactured as many or as few duped negatives, positive prints and other material for use in connection with the Picture as it, in its sole discretion, may consider advisable or desirable.

(b) All direct costs and charges for advertisements, press books, artwork, advertising accessories and trailers (other than (i) prints of trailers advertising free television exhibition of the Picture, and (ii) the trailer production costs which are included in the cost of production of the Picture), advertising, publicizing and exploiting the Picture by such means and to such extent as Studio may, in its uncontrolled discretion, deem desirable, including, without limitation, pre-release advertising and publicity, so-called cooperative and/or theatre advertising, and/or other advertising engaged in with or for exhibitors, to the extent Studio pays, shares in, or is charged with all or a portion of such costs and all other exploitation costs relating to such theatre exhibition. Any re-use fees and costs of recording and manufacturing masters for phonograph records, which Studio shall advance in order to assist in the advertising and exploitation of the Picture, shall be treated as costs hereunder to the extent unrecouped by the record company. Where any Studio advertising or publicity employee (other than an executive supervisory employee) or facility is used for the Picture, the salary of such employee and the cost of such facility (while so used for the Picture) shall be direct costs hereunder. Any costs and charges referred to in this (b) (and not included in the cost of production of the Picture), expended or incurred prior to delivery of the Picture, shall be included in direct costs under this (b). There shall also be included as an item of cost a sum equal to 10% of all direct costs referred to in this (b) to cover the indirect cost of Studio's advertising and publicity departments, both domestic and foreign.

CONTRACTS
FOR THE
FILM AND
TELEVISION
INDUSTRY

226

(c) All costs of preparing and delivering the Picture for distribution (regardless of whether such costs are the salaries and expenses of Studio's own employees or employees or parties not regularly employed by Studio), including, without limitation, all costs incurred in connection with the production of foreign language versions of the Picture, whether dubbed, superimposed or otherwise, as well as any and all costs and expenses in connection with changing the title of the Picture, recutting, re-editing or shortening or lengthening the Picture for release in any territory or for exhibition on television or other media, or in order to conform to the requirements of censorship authorities, or in order to conform to the peculiar national or political prejudices likely to be encountered in any territory, or for any other purpose or reason. The costs referred to in this (c) shall include all studio charges for facilities, labor and material, whether or not incurred at a studio owned or controlled by Studio.

(d) All sums paid or accrued on account of sales, use, receipts, income, excise, remittance and other taxes (however denominated) to any governmental authority assessed upon the negatives, duplicate negatives, prints or sound records of the Picture, or upon the use or distribution of the Picture, or upon the revenues derived therefrom, or any part thereof, or upon the remittance of such revenues, or any part thereof; any and all sums paid or accrued on account of duties, customs and imposts, costs of acquiring permits, "Kontingents," and any similar authority to secure the entry, licensing, exhibition, performance, use or televising of the Picture in any country or part thereof, regardless of whether such payments or accruals are assessed against the Picture or the proceeds thereof or against a group of motion pictures in which the Picture may be included or the proceeds thereof. In no event shall the deductible amount of any such tax (however denominated) imposed upon Studio, be decreased (nor the gross receipts increased) because of the manner in which such taxes are elected to be treated by Studio in filing net income, corporate franchise, excess profits or similar tax returns. Subject to the foregoing, (i) Studio's own United States federal and state income taxes and franchise taxes based on Studio's net income; and (ii) income taxes payable to any country or territory by Studio based on the net earnings of Studio in such country or territory and which is computed and assessed solely by reason of the retention in such country or territory by Studio of any portion of the gross receipts shall not be deductible hereunder.

(e) Expenses of transmitting to the United States any funds accruing to Studio from the Picture in foreign countries, such as cable expenses, and any discounts from such funds taken to convert such funds directly or indirectly into U.S. dollars.

(f) All costs and expenses, including reasonable attorneys' fees, loss, damage or liability suffered or incurred by Studio in connection with: any action taken by Studio (whether by litigation or otherwise) in copyrighting, protecting and enforcing the copyright of, and other rights and sources of revenue to be derived from, the Picture; reducing or minimizing the matters referred to in (d) and (e) above, the collection of film rentals, and other sums due Studio from exhibitors, subdistributors and others in respect of the Picture or to recover monies due pursuant to any agreement relating to the distribution or the exhibition of the Picture; checking attendance and exhibitors' receipts; preventing and/or recovering damages for unauthorized exhibition or distribution of the Picture, or any impairment of, encumbrance on, or infringement upon, the rights of Studio in and to the Picture; prosecuting and defending actions under the antitrust laws, communications laws, and federal, state and local laws, ordinances and regulations (including censorship) affecting the exhibition and/or distribution of the Picture and/or the ability of Studio to derive revenue from the Picture and its component parts and by-products; and auditing of books and records of any exhibitor, subdistributor or licensee.

(g) Royalties payable to manufacturers of sound recording and reproducing equipment and dues and assessments of, and contributions by Studio to, AMPTP, MPAA, MPEA, the Academy of Motion Picture Arts and Sciences and other trade associations or industry groups comprised of a substantial number of motion picture producers and/or distributors, but only for purposes relating to the production, distribution, export, import, advertising, exploitation and general protection and/or promotion of motion pictures.

(h) In the event any person shall make a claim relating to the Picture against Studio or any of its licensees, which claim, in Studio's judgment, is of sufficient merit to constitute a reasonable probability of ultimate loss, cost, damage or expense, Studio may deduct under this (h) such amount as Studio may deem necessary to cover any loss, cost, damage or expense which may be suffered as a result thereof. Studio shall have the right to settle and pay any such claim. After the settlement of any such claim, or after the final judicial determination thereof, the amount previously deducted hereunder shall be adjusted accordingly with the next accounting statement rendered hereunder. Nothing herein contained shall be construed as a waiver of any of Participant's warranties contained in this Agreement, or a waiver of any right or remedy at law or otherwise which may exist in favor of Studio, including, but not limited to, the right to require Participant to reimburse Studio on demand for any liability, cost, damage or expense arising out of, or resulting from, any breach by Participant of any warranty, undertaking or obligation by Participant, or any right on the part of Studio to recoup or recover any such cost or expense out of Participant's share of any monies payable hereunder, rather than treating such costs or expenses as distribution expenses.

(i) All amounts paid or payable to or for the benefit of actors, writers, composers, directors and others, pursuant to applicable collective bargaining agreements and/or any law or governmental regulation or decree now or hereafter in force by reason of, and/or as a condition or consideration for, any exhibition, use, re-use, rerun, performance, sale, license and/or distribution of the Picture and/or copies of all or any part thereof, on television, supplemental markets, or otherwise (all herein called "residuals"), together with all taxes, pension fund contributions and other costs paid or payable in respect of such residuals, and in respect of participations in the gross receipts and net profits of the Picture; provided, however, that if Participant or any principal stockholder of Participant, or any heirs, executors, administrators, successors or assigns of Participant, or any such stockholder, are entitled, either directly or by way of participation in any pension fund, to any such residuals, or to compensation for services rendered beyond any guaranteed period referred to in the foregoing agreement, the amount payable on account thereof shall be treated as an advance against Participant's share of the net profits hereunder.

(j) The cost of all insurance (to the extent that the same is not included in the cost of production of the Picture) covering or relating to the Picture, including, but not limited to, errors and omissions insurance and all insurance on negatives, positive prints, sound materials or other physical property, it being understood, however, that Studio shall not be obligated to take out or maintain any such insurance.

(k) If Studio shall proceed under 3(b)(i) hereof, all items deducted by the

CONTRACTS
FOR THE
FILM AND
TELEVISION
INDUSTRY

228

subdistributor as distribution expenses, and which Studio accepts for the purpose of its accountings with such subdistributor, shall be treated as Studio's expenditures under the corresponding subdivision of this 5.

6. FILM RENTALS: "Film Rentals" shall be determined after all refunds, credits, discounts, allowances and adjustments granted to exhibitors, whether occasioned by condemnation by boards of censorship, settlement of disputes or otherwise. Until earned, forfeited or applied to the Picture, neither advance payments nor security deposits shall be included in film rentals. No cost (regardless of how incurred, paid or allowed) of Studio's share of cooperative and/or theater advertising shall be deducted in determining film rentals. Where allowances are granted and paid on account of Studio's share of cooperative theatre or joint advertising, such payments shall not be deducted in determining film rental, and where Studio's share of cooperative theater or joint advertising is deducted by the exhibitor, Studio's share of cooperative theater or joint advertising shall be added back into the film rental received from such exhibitor, and all such costs, payments, discounts and allowances shall be treated as distribution expenses. Wherever Studio exhibits the Picture in a theatre or over a television station owned or controlled by Studio, or licenses the Picture or rights connected therewith to theaters, television stations or other agencies in which Studio has an interest, directly or indirectly, or to which Studio is obligated to pay a fixed sum for exhibiting the Picture or for the use of its premises or facilities, Studio shall include in the film rentals of the Picture such sums, determined in good faith, as may be reasonable and consistent with Studio's usual practice in such matters.

7. ALLOCATIONS: Wherever Studio (i) receives from any license either a flat sum or a percentage of the receipts, or both, for any right to a group of motion pictures (including the Picture) under any agreement (whether or not the same shall provide for the exhibition, lease or delivery of positive prints of any of said motion pictures) which does not specify what portion of the license payments apply to the respective motion pictures in the group (or to such prints or other material, if any, as may be supplied), or (ii) receives foreign currency under 8 hereof relating to a group of motion pictures (including the Picture), then in any and all such situations Studio shall include in, or deduct from, the gross receipts, as the case may be, such sums, determined in good faith, as may be reasonable and consistent with Studio's usual practice in such matters. All costs described in 5 hereof (and, after breakeven, all deductible items set forth in Schedule 1 hereto) shall be fairly apportioned to the Picture if incurred or expended on an industry basis, or in conjunction with other motion picture producers and/or distributors, or with respect to the Picture and other motion pictures distributed by Studio.

8. FOREIGN RECEIPTS: No sums received by Studio relating to the Picture shall be included in gross receipts hereunder unless and until such sums have been (i) received by Studio in U.S. dollars in the United States; or (ii) used by Studio for the production or acquisition of motion pictures or television films which can be lawfully removed from the country or territory involved, in which event they shall be included in gross receipts for the accounting period during which an amount (computed at the official or unofficial rate of exchange, as Studio may elect) equal to the amount expended for such production or acquisition, plus interest thereon, as herein provided, has been recouped by Studio (in excess of normal distribution fees and distribution expenses) from distribution thereof outside the country or territory involved; or (iii) used by Studio for acquisition of tangible personal property which can be and is lawfully exported from the country or territory involved, in which event the U.S. dollar equivalent of the currency utilized to acquire such property shall be included in gross receipts hereunder for the accounting period during which such property was so exported, such U.S. dollar equivalent to be computed at the official or unofficial rate of exchange, as Studio may elect, in effect on the date of export. Studio will, promptly after receipt of a written request from Participant (but not more frequently than annually) advise Participant in writing as to foreign revenues not included in gross receipts as aforesaid, and Studio shall, at the written request and expense of Participant (subject to any and all limitations, restrictions, laws, rules and regulations affecting such transactions), deposit into a bank designated by Participant in the country involved, or pay to any other party designated by Participant in such country, such part thereof as would have been payable to Participant hereunder. Such deposits or payments to or for Participant shall constitute due remittance to Participant, and Studio shall have no further interest therein or responsibility therefor. Studio makes no warranties or representations that any part of any such foreign currencies may be converted into U.S. dollars or transferred to the account of Participant in any foreign country. In no event shall Studio be obligated to apply gross receipts of any country not actually received by Studio in U.S. dollars in the United States to the recoupment of any costs or expenses incurred with respect to the Picture (or, after breakeven, of any deductible items set forth in Schedule 1 hereto) in any other country.

9. COST OF PRODUCTION; INTEREST:

(a) The "cost of production" of the Picture means the total direct cost of production of the Picture, including the cost of all items listed on Studio's Standard Delivery Schedule, computed and determined in all respects in the same manner as Studio then customarily determines the direct cost of other motion pictures distributed and/or financed by it, plus Studio's overhead charge. The determination of what items constitute direct charges and what items are within said overhead charge shall be made in all respects in the same manner as Studio customarily determines such matters. The full amount of all direct costs of production of the Picture (whether payable in cash, deferred or accrued) shall be included in the direct cost of the Picture at the time liability therefor is incurred or contracted, regardless of whether the same has actually been paid to the party or parties entitled thereto at the time involved. Deferments and participations in gross receipts of the Picture consented to by Studio (however defined) shall be treated as direct costs of production, whether the same shall be in a definite amount or based on a percentage of the gross receipts, and whether the same are fixed obligations or are contingent upon receipts of the Picture; provided, however, contingent participations based on a percentage of gross receipts as defined in the applicable agreement shall not be included in the direct cost of production beyond recoupment under 2(c) hereof.

(b) Studio's overhead charge shall be in an amount equal to 15% of the direct cost of production of the Picture, with the understanding that any production facilities, equipment or personnel supplied by Studio or by a studio owned or controlled by Studio, or in which Studio has a substantial financial interest (and which are not furnished within the overhead charge), shall be supplied at Studio's usual rental rates charged for such items, and such charges shall be treated as direct costs of production of the Picture and shall bear said 15% overhead charge. Studio's overhead charge shall accrue and be included in the cost of production of the Picture concurrently with the incurring of the respective items of direct cost to which it applies.

CONTRACTS
FOR THE
FILM AND
TELEVISION
INDUSTRY

230

(c) The amount equal to interest provided for in 2(c) hereof shall be calculated at a rate per annum equal to 125% of the rate announced from time to time by the First National Bank of Boston as its prime rate on unsecured loans to its preferred customers. Said amount shall be calculated from the respective dates that each item is charged to the Picture until the close of the accounting period during which the cost of production is recouped under 2(c) hereof, except that interest on deferred amounts shall be calculated from the date of payment.

(d) Concurrently with delivery to Participant of the first earnings statement hereunder, Studio will (subject to revisions and correction) deliver to Participant an itemized summary of the cost of production of the Picture. Participant shall have the right to audit such statement in accordance with 11 hereof.

(e) If the final cost of production shall exceed the budgeted cost by 5% or more, then for the purposes of 2(c) hereof there shall be added to the actual cost of production of the Picture an amount equal to the amount by which the final direct cost exceeds 105% of the budgeted direct cost. For the purposes of this subdivision (e), the final direct cost shall not include costs incurred solely by reason of force majeure events, union increases not reflected in the budget, and overbudget costs incurred at the request of an officer of Studio having the rank of Vice President or higher over the written objection of Participant.

10. EARNINGS STATEMENTS: Studio shall render to Participant periodic statements showing, in summary form, the appropriate calculations under this Agreement. Statements shall be issued for each calendar quarter until the Picture has been in release for 4 years from and including the quarter in which the Picture was first released, and thereafter annually. Each such quarterly or annual period, as the case may be, is herein referred to as an "accounting period." No statements need be rendered for any accounting period during which no receipts are received. Statements rendered by Studio may be changed from time to time to give effect to year-end adjustments made by Studio's Accounting Department or Public Accountants, or to items overlooked, to correct errors and for similar purposes. If Studio shall extend credit to any licensee with respect to the Picture and if such credit has been included in the gross receipts, and if, in the opinion of Studio, any such indebtedness shall be uncollectible, the uncollected amount may be deducted in any subsequent earning statement. Should Studio make any overpayment to Participant hereunder for any reason, Studio shall have the right to deduct and retain for its own account an amount equal to any such overpayment from any sums that may thereafter become due or payable by Studio to Participant or for Participant's account, or may demand repayment from Participant, in which event Participant shall repay the same when such demand is made. Any U.S. dollars due and payable to Participant by Studio pursuant to any such statement shall be paid to Participant simultaneously with the rendering of such statement; provided, however, that all amounts payable to Participant hereunder shall be subject to all laws and regulations now or hereafter in existence requiring deductions or withholdings for income or other taxes payable by or assessable against Participant. Studio shall have the right to make such deductions and withholdings and the payment thereof to the governmental agency concerned in accordance with its interpretation in good faith of such laws and regulations, and shall not be liable to Participant for the making of such deductions or withholdings or the payment thereof to the governmental agency concerned. In any such event Participant shall make and prosecute any and all claims which it may have with respect to the same directly with the governmental agency having jurisdiction in the premises. The right of Participant to receive, and the obligation of Studio to account for, any share of the gross receipts of the Picture shall terminate if the Picture has been made available for exhibition on syndicated television in the U.S.A., and if the first earnings statement issued thereafter shows a deficit under 2 hereof such that at least $500,000 of gross receipts would be required before Participant would be entitled to receive any gross receipts hereunder. In the event a new medium of exhibition shall thereafter be developed and there shall be substantial exhibition and distribution of the Picture by such new medium which is likely to generate gross receipts of $500,000 or the amount of the deficit, whichever is larger, Participant may audit Studio's records for the purpose of determining whether the Picture has earned, or is likely to earn, any gross receipts in excess of breakeven, and if, as a result of such audit, it is determined by mutual agreement, or in the event of dispute appropriate legal proceedings, that the Picture has earned, or is likely to earn, gross receipts in excess of breakeven as herein defined, accountings hereunder and payments, if required, shall be reinstated.

11. ACCOUNTING RECORDS RE DISTRIBUTION; AUDIT RIGHTS: Studio shall keep books of account relating to the distribution of the Picture, together with vouchers, exhibition contracts and similar records supporting the same (all of which are hereinafter referred to as "records"), which shall be kept on the same basis and in the same manner and for the same periods as such records are customarily kept by Studio. Participant may, at its own expense, audit the applicable records at the place where Studio maintains the same in order to verify earnings statements rendered hereunder. Any such audit shall be conducted only by a reputable public accountant during reasonable business hours in such manner as not to interfere with Studio's normal business activities. In no event shall an audit with respect to any earnings statement commence later than twenty-four (24) months from the rendition of the earnings statement involved; nor shall any audit continue for longer than thirty (30) consecutive business days; nor shall audits be made hereunder more frequently than once annually; nor shall the records supporting any earnings statement be audited more than once. All earnings statements rendered hereunder shall be binding upon Participant and not subject to objection for any reason unless such objection is made in writing, stating the basis thereof and delivered to Studio within twenty-four (24) months from rendition of the earnings statement, or if an audit is commenced prior thereto, within thirty (30) days from the completion of the relative audit. If Studio, as a courtesy to Participant, shall include cumulative figures in any earnings or other statement, the time within which Participant may commence any audit or make any objection in respect of any statement shall not be enlarged or extended thereby. Participant's right to examine Studio's records is limited to the Picture, and Participant shall have no right to examine records relating to Studio's business generally or with respect to any other motion picture for purposes of comparison or otherwise; provided, however, that where any original income or expense document with third parties relates to the Picture and to other motion pictures, Participant shall have the right to examine the entire document without deletions therefrom.

12. OWNERSHIP: Participant expressly acknowledges that Participant has and will have no right, title or interest of any kind or character whatsoever in or to the Picture, and no lien thereon or other rights in or to the gross receipts or net profits of the Picture; and that the same shall be and remain Studio's sole and exclusive property, and Studio shall not be obligated to segregate the same from its other funds, it being the intent and purpose hereof that the gross receipts in excess of breakeven of the Picture are referred to herein merely as a measure in determining the time and manner of payment to Participant; and that

CONTRACTS
FOR THE
FILM AND
TELEVISION
INDUSTRY

232

Studio shall not be deemed a trustee, pledgeholder or fiduciary. Participant shall have no right, title or interest of any kind or character whatsoever in or to the literary, dramatic or musical material upon which the Picture is based, or from which it may be adapted; and Studio shall have the sole and exclusive right to utilize, sell, license or otherwise dispose of all or any part of its rights in such material upon such terms and conditions as it may deem advisable, all without consulting or advising Participant and without accounting to Participant in any manner with respect thereto.

13. DISTRIBUTION: As between Participant and Studio, Studio shall have complete authority to distribute the Picture and to license the exhibition thereof throughout the world in accordance with such sales methods, policies and terms as it may, in its uncontrolled discretion, determine. Studio shall have the broadest possible latitude in the distribution of the Picture, and the exercise of its judgment in good faith in all matters pertaining thereto shall be final. Studio has not made any express or implied representation, warranty, guarantee or agreement as to the amount of proceeds which will be derived from the distribution of the Picture, nor has Studio made any express or implied representation, warranty, guarantee or agreement that there will be any sums payable to Participant hereunder, or that the Picture will be favorably received by exhibitors or by the public, or will be distributed continuously. In no event shall Studio incur any liability based upon any claim that Studio has failed to realize receipts or revenue which should or could have been realized. Studio may distribute the Picture either itself or through such distributors, subdistributors and other parties as Studio may, in its uncontrolled discretion, determine, and Studio may refrain from releasing and/or distributing the Picture in any territory for any reason whatsoever. Studio may license the Picture or rights connected therewith to any and all theatres or other agencies in which Studio may have an interest directly or indirectly upon such terms and rentals as Studio may deem fair and proper under the circumstances. Nothing herein contained shall be construed as a representation or warranty by Studio that it now has or will hereafter have or control any theatres or agencies in the United States or elsewhere.

14. SALE OF PICTURE: Studio shall have the right at any time after completion of the Picture to sell, transfer or assign all or any of its rights in and to the Picture and the negative and copyright thereof. Any such sale, transfer or assignment shall be subject to Participant's rights hereunder, and upon the purchaser, transferee or assignee assuming performance of this agreement in place and stead of Studio, Studio shall be released and discharged of and from any further liability or obligation hereunder. No part of any sale price or other consideration received by, or payable to, Studio shall be included in the gross receipts hereunder and Participant shall have no rights in respect of any thereof.

15. ASSIGNMENTS, ETC.: Participant shall have the right to sell, assign, transfer or hypothecate (all herein called "assign") all or any part of Participant's right to receive the monies payable to Participant hereunder. Any such assignment shall be subject to all pertinent laws and governmental regulations and to the rights of Studio hereunder. In the event of any such assignment by Participant, a Notice of Irrevocable Authority and Distributor's Acceptance in Studio's usual form shall be executed by Participant and by the transferee and delivered to Studio. If at any time more than three parties shall be entitled to receive payments, which under the terms hereof are to be paid to or for the account of Participant, Studio may, at its option, require that all such parties execute and deliver an agreement in Studio's usual form appointing a disbursing agent for all such parties.

1. "GROSS RECEIPTS" of the Picture means the aggregate of:

(a) All film rentals actually received by Studio from parties exhibiting the Picture in theatres and on television where Studio distributes directly to such parties (hereinafter referred to as "exhibitors");

(b) In respect of licenses of exhibition or distribution rights by means of video discs, cassettes or similar devices, an amount equal to 20% of (i) the gross wholesale rental income therefrom and (ii) the gross wholesale sales income therefrom less a reasonable allowance for returns;

(c) All sums actually received by Studio from grants or licenses of distribution rights in and to the Picture (in any and all gauges of film, tape and other material) from sources other than those referred to in (a) and (b) above;

(d) All net earnings of Studio from trailers of the Picture (other than trailers advertising the television exhibition of the Picture); and the lease of positive prints, tapes and other material (as distinguished from the licensing thereof for a film rental); and from the sale or licensing of advertising accessories, souvenir programs and booklets;

(e) All net sums derived by Studio from distribution of the Picture on a "road show", "reissue" and "four wall" basis, as such terms are commonly understood in the motion picture industry, whether on fixed or percentage engagements. The term "net sums" means Studio's receipts less all advertising, publicity and other distribution costs incurred directly in connection therewith;

(f) All amounts required to be included under Exhibits X, Y and Z hereof, less the aggregate of:

(i) All sums paid or accrued on account of sales, use, receipts, income, excise, remittance and other taxes (however denominated) to any governmental authority assessed upon the negatives, duplicate negatives, prints or sound records of the Picture, or upon the use or distribution of the Picture, or upon the revenues derived therefrom, or any part thereof, or upon the remittance of such revenues, or any part thereof; any and all sums paid or accrued on account of duties, customs and imposts, costs of acquiring permits, "Kontingents," and any similar authority to secure the entry, licensing, exhibition, performance, use or televising of the Picture in any country or part thereof, regardless of whether such payments or accruals are assessed against the Picture or the proceeds thereof or against a group of motion pictures in which the Picture may be included or the proceeds thereof. In no event shall the deductible amount of any such tax (however denominated) imposed upon Studio, be decreased (nor the gross receipts increased) because of the manner in which such taxes are elected to be treated by Studio in filing net income, corporate franchise, excess profits or similar tax returns. Subject to the foregoing, (i) Studio's own United States federal and state income taxes and franchise taxes based on Studio's net income; and (ii) income taxes payable to any country or territory by Studio based on the net earnings of Studio in such country or territory and which is computed and assessed solely by reason of the retention in such country or territory by Studio of any portion of the gross receipts shall not be deductible hereunder.

(ii) Expenses of transmitting to the United States any funds accruing

CONTRACTS
FOR THE
FILM AND
TELEVISION
INDUSTRY

234

to Studio from the Picture in foreign countries, such as cable expenses and any discounts from such funds taken to convert such funds directly or indirectly into U.S. dollars.

(iii) The cost of reducing or minimizing the matters referred to in (i) or (ii) above, which costs shall be fairly apportioned to the Picture if done on an industry basis or with respect to motion pictures distributed by Studio generally.

(iv) All costs of cooperative or other advertising or promotion (excluding trade and institutional advertising or promotion) incurred in connection with exhibitions of the Picture in theatres (or other places where an admission is charged) where Studio pays, shares in or is charged with all or a portion of the promotional or advertising costs relating to any such exhibitions.

(v) All amounts paid or payable to or for the benefit of actors, writers, composers, directors and others, pursuant to applicable collective bargaining agreements and/or any law or governmental regulations or decree now or hereafter in force by reason of, and/or as a condition or consideration for, any exhibition, use, re-use, rerun, performance, sale, license and/or distribution of the Picture and/or copies of all or any part thereof, on television, supplemental markets, or otherwise (all herein called "residuals"), together with all taxes, pension fund contributions and other costs paid or payable in respect of such residuals, and in respect of participations in the gross receipts and net profits of the Picture; provided, however, that if Participant or any principal stockholder of Participant, or any heirs, executors, administrators, successors or assigns of Participant, or any such stockholder, are entitled, either directly or by way of participation in any pension fund, to any such residuals, or to compensation for services rendered beyond any guaranteed period referred to in the foregoing agreement, the amount payable on account thereof shall be treated as an advance against Participant's share of the gross receipts hereunder, and conversely, any gross receipts paid to Participant hereunder shall (to the extent permissible under applicable collective bargaining agreements) constitute an advance against such residuals payable to or for the benefit of Participant or any principal stockholder of Participant, or any such heirs, executors, administrators, successors or assigns.

(vi) Dues and assessments of and contributions by Studio to AMPTP, MPAA, MPEA, the Academy of Motion Picture Arts and Sciences, and other trade associations or industry groups comprised of a substantial number of motion picture producers and/or distributors, but only for purposes relating to the production, distribution, export, import, advertising, exploitation and general protection, including actions under the antitrust laws, and/or promotion of motion pictures.

In no event shall rentals from the exhibition of the Picture which are contributed to charitable organizations be included in gross receipts. If Studio reasonably anticipates taxes, residuals, uncollectible accounts, or any matters relating to the Picture, which, if and when determined, will be deductible hereunder, Studio may, for a reasonable time, set up appropriate reserves therefor.

2. FILM RENTALS: In paragraph 6 of the foregoing Exhibit for purposes of computing gross receipts under this Schedule 1, the third and fourth sentences are deleted, and the following substituted: Where the film rental is computed on the basis of box-office receipts of the Picture, any expenses incurred in checking attendance and/or receipts of such engagements shall be deducted in determining film rentals hereunder. There shall be deducted from film rentals expenses incurred in the collection thereof.

MUSIC PUBLISHING INCOME

In the event the party entitled to share in gross receipts or net profits of the Picture under the foregoing agreement is not entitled to share directly in publishing revenues, there shall also be included in gross receipts of the picture:

A sum equal to 75% of the "publisher's share" of mechanical reproduction and performing fees received in U.S. currency by Studio's subsidiary or affiliated publisher with respect to music and lyrics written specifically for and synchronized in the picture as released, provided such publisher is vested with all rights therein and all of the "publisher's share" of the receipts therefrom, and provided the party entitled to share in gross receipts or net profits of the picture under the foregoing agreement is not entitled to receive composers' or lyricists' royalties in respect of such music or lyrics. The "publisher's share" of mechanical reproduction fees shall be the full amount paid by the licensee, less composers' or lyricist's share of such fees and less the charges of the publisher or any agent, trustee or administrator acting for the publisher for the collection of such fees, not to exceed 5% thereof. Mechanical reproduction fees do not include synchronization fees.

The "publisher's share" of performing fees shall be the net amount actually received by the publisher from any performing rights society in respect of the music and lyrics involved; or, if Studio or the publisher shall administer the collection of all or any part of performance fees, the full amount of all performance fees collected by Studio or the publisher, less the composer's or lyricist's share of such fees and all reasonable costs and expenses in administering the collection of such fees.

If the agreement or Exhibit to which this Exhibit is attached provides for distribution fees, no distribution fees shall be charged on amounts included in gross receipts pursuant to this Exhibit.

SOUND TRACK RECORD INCOME

In the event the party entitled to share in the gross receipts or net profits of the picture under the foregoing agreement is not entitled to receive any artists' royalties in respect of phonograph records derived from the sound track of the picture, then Studio agrees to include in the gross receipts of the picture royalties on sound track records, as herein defined, computed at the applicable royalty rate.

As used herein:

The term "sound track records" means and refers to phonograph records, tapes, or other sound recordings which contain either (i) portions of the sound track transferred directly to phonograph record masters from sound records which form a part of the sound track of the picture; or (ii) sound recordings recorded separately but utilizing substantially the same musical score, parts and instrumentation, and essentially the same artists, music and/or dialogue and/or sound effects as is contained in the sound track of the picture; or (iii) a combination of (i) and (ii). Sound track records do not, however, include any re-

CONTRACTS
FOR THE
FILM AND
TELEVISION
INDUSTRY

236

cordings produced solely for the purpose of advertising and exploiting the picture and copies of which are not distributed to the public.

The term "applicable royalty rate" means and refers to the following percentages of the prevailing retail price but in no event more than the net royalty actually received and retainable by Studio for its own account with respect to the sale of any particular copies: 5% of 90% in respect of sound track records sold in the United States; 2 1/2 of 90% in respect of sound track records sold outside the United States except that as to sound track records sold pursuant to mail order or "club" plans, the royalty rate shall be one-half of the rate otherwise applicable.

If any sound track records contain selections from other sources, the applicable royalty rate hereunder shall be prorated on the basis of the total number of minutes of selections from the sound track compared to the total number of minutes on such records.

In determining the net royalty retainable by Studio, all royalties payable to artists, conductors and other third parties in respect to such sound track records shall be deducted from the aggregate royalty payable to Studio under the applicable distribution agreement.

The term "prevailing retail price" means and refers to the price generally prevailing in the country of manufacture or sale (as determined by the Record Company), less all taxes, duties and charges for containers.

There shall be deducted from amounts included in gross receipts hereunder a pro rata share of re-use fees and costs of recording and manufacturing masters advanced by Studio or the Record Company. Sales shall be determined on the basis of the number of records sold and for which the Record Company has been paid in U.S. currency, after allowing for all returns, cancellations, exchanges, applicable discounts, etc. and reasonable reserves which may be established therefor. No sums shall be included in gross receipts with respect to records given away or sold at less than the Record Company's cost or for promotional purposes or as sales inducements or otherwise.

If the agreement or Exhibit to which this Exhibit is attached provides for distribution fees, no distribution fees shall be charged on amounts included in gross receipts pursuant to this Exhibit.

MERCHANDISING INCOME

In the event the party entitled to share in gross receipts or net profits of the picture under the foregoing agreement is not entitled to share directly in merchandising revenue, there shall be included in gross receipts of the picture:

(a) A sum equal to 50% of all license fees (in excess of all royalties and participations) received by Studio directly as a result of the exercise by Studio itself of merchandising license rights. If, however, Studio shall sublicense or subcontract any of such merchandising license rights, Studio shall include in the gross receipts hereunder, at its election, either a sum equal to (i) 85% of the net sums (in excess of all royalties and participations) received from such sub-licensee; or (ii) 50% of such sub-licensee's license fees from the exercise of such licensing rights (from which there shall be deducted all royalties and participations), and out of the remaining 50% thereof Studio shall pay and discharge the fees of its sublicensee.

(b) If the publication rights to the underlying literary material were owned or controlled by the party entitled to share in gross receipts or net profits of the picture under the foregoing agreement (herein called "participant") prior to the execution of this agreement, and were acquired by Studio pursuant to or in connection with this agreement, then (i) all net sums received by Studio from nonaffiliated or nonsubsidiary publishers from the publication of such underlying literary material and of novelizations of the screenplay of the picture, and (ii) a sum equal to 5% of the net receipts of Studio's subsidiary or affiliated publishers from the publication of such material and novelizations, less, in either case, royalties paid out of (i) or (ii) to the writers of such material and novelizations.

If the agreement or Exhibit to which this Exhibit is attached provides for distribution fees, no distribution fees shall be charged on amounts included in gross receipts pursuant to this Exhibit.

CONTRACTS
FOR THE
FILM AND
TELEVISION
INDUSTRY

238

TELEVISION DISTRIBUTION

Television stations and networks can attract high viewer ratings by broadcasting movies. The broadcasting networks' appetite for movies depends on several factors. The networks consider the cost of buying made-for-television movies and the kinds of ratings they can be expected to generate. Another factor to consider is how well a theatrical movie performed at the box office, and whether it has been previously distributed on pay cable television.

TELEVISION DISTRIBUTION AGREEMENT

XYZ Broadcasting Co.
444 Broadway
New York, N.Y.

Summary

Name of Licensee: _____

Address of Licensee: _____

Station: _____

No. of License: _____

Picture or Pictures: _____

Number of Runs: _____

Duration of License: _____

License Fee Per Picture: $_____

Total License Fee: $_____

Payments: (a) First payment of $_____ on or before _____; and (b) _____ monthly payments of $_____ commencing on _____ until the total license fee of $_____ has been paid.

This application for a license was executed by the Licensee on _____. Upon acceptance thereof by a duly authorized officer of the Licensor, this application shall constitute a license for the telecast of the aforesaid Picture or Series on the terms and conditions set forth above and in the Schedule hereto annexed and made a part hereof.

[Name of Licensee]

By _____
Authorized Officer

Accepted:

Date _____

[Name of Licensor]

By _____
Authorized Officer

1. LICENSE: Subject to the prompt payment of the license fees above specified and the due performance by the Licensee of all its obligations hereunder, the Licensor hereby grants to the Licensee, and the Licensee hereby accepts, a limited license to exhibit and broadcast over the facilities of the television station specified in the foregoing Summary the motion picture or the motion pictures therein specified (herein called the Pictures), and to reproduce recorded sound in connection therewith, for the period of time and the maximum number of runs therein specified, and for no other use or purpose.

2. PAYMENT OF LICENSE FEES: The Licensor shall pay the license fees specified in the Summary at the time or times therein set forth, without offset, deduction, counterclaim or credit for any claim that the Licensee may have or assert against the Licensor, regardless of whether or not the Licensee has exhibited all the Pictures available to it.

3. LICENSOR'S WARRANTIES: The Licensor represents and warrants to the Licensee that:

(a) The performing rights in all musical compositions contained in the Pictures (i) are controlled by the American Society of Composers, Authors and Publishers (ASCAP) or Broadcast Music, Inc. (BMI); or (ii) are in the public domain; or (iii) are controlled by the Licensor;

(b) With respect to music controlled by ASCAP or BMI, the Licensor has obtained the necessary licenses for the inclusion thereof in the Pictures, and the exhibition of the Pictures via television;

(c) The Pictures and the prints thereof to be furnished by the Licensor to the Licensee will be free and clear of any and all liens or encumbrances; and

(d) The Licensor has the full right to grant this license.

4. LICENSOR'S INDEMNITY: The Licensor shall indemnify the Licensee against any and all damage or expense (including reasonable attorneys' fees) that the Licensee may suffer or incur as a result of the breach of any of the Licensor's warranties, subject to the following:

(a) The Licensor's indemnity shall not apply unless it is given (i) prompt written notice of any claim; and (ii) full control of the defense thereof, through its own counsel; and (iii) the right to settle the same.

(b) The Licensee shall cooperate fully with the Licensor in the defense or settlement of any claim.

(c) The Licensor's liability on the warranty set forth in subdivision (d) of clause 3 shall be limited as provided in clause 16.

5. DELIVERY: The Licensor shall deliver to the Licensee a positive synchronized 16 mm. black and white print of each Picture scheduled for exhibition.

(a) Delivery to the Licensee's premises, or to its agent, or to a common carrier, or to the U. S. Post Office, or to any shipping agent designated by the Licensee, shall be deemed due delivery; and the Licensor shall not be liable for any loss or delay attributable to any intervening agency.

(b) The Licensee shall bear the expenses of delivery.

CONTRACTS
FOR THE
FILM AND
TELEVISION
INDUSTRY

240

(c) Unless the Licensee designates a mode of delivery, the Licensor shall have the right to select the same.

(d) The Licensor's failure to deliver any of the Pictures shall not constitute a default hereunder, but the license fee hereunder shall be reduced proportionately in the ratio that the number of runs of each undelivered Picture bears to the total number of runs for all Pictures covered by this agreement.

(e) The Licensor at its own election may substitute a product deemed by it to be equivalent to the Pictures without reduction of the license fee.

6. EXAMINATION OF PRINTS: Upon receipt of each positive print, the Licensee shall promptly examine the same to determine whether it is physically suitable for exhibition. If the print is unsuitable, the Licensee shall give immediate notice thereof to the Licensor, specifying the particular defect; and upon receipt of such notice the Licensor shall furnish a substitute print, or in lieu thereof, a print of another Picture that the Licensor deems equivalent. Unless the Licensor receives a notification in writing as to a defect at least 48 hours prior to the scheduled play date, a print received by the Licensee shall be deemed accepted as satisfactory.

7. RESTRICTIONS ON CUTTING: The Licensee shall telecast the Pictures in the form submitted by the Licensor, and shall not modify, add to or take from the same without the Licensor's written consent. Among other things, the Licensee shall telecast the screen credits and the Licensor's release credit as incorporated in the prints of the Pictures. The Licensee shall have the right to insert commercials at points selected by it, provided that, prior to redelivery, it restores each print to its original condition.

8. PLAY DATES: If no specific play dates are designated in the Summary, the Licensee shall, from time to time but at least fourteen (14) days in advance of any play date, furnish to the Licensor a list of the Pictures that the Licensee intends to telecast, together with the proposed telecast date.

(a) The Licensor shall have the right to designate a particular one of the Pictures to be shown on the proposed telecast date, except that it shall not designate a Picture that may have been previously shown by the Licensee during the term of this agreement.

(b) Not later than ten (10) days after the end of every month during the term of this agreement, the Licensee shall deliver to the Licensor a list of the Pictures that it telecast during the preceding month.

(c) If a scheduled telecast does not take place by reason of the pre-emption of the scheduled time, or for any reason beyond the Licensee's control, the Licensee shall notify the Licensor thereof within twenty-four (24) hours after the scheduled play date.

(d) If the Licensee fails to notify the Licensor as aforesaid, or if it fails to telecast any Picture on the play date for any other reason, it shall be charged with the license fee for the scheduled telecast.

9. MAXIMUM RUNS: When the Licensee reaches the maximum number of runs permitted under this license, its right to telecast the Pictures shall forthwith terminate, and the unpaid balance of the total agreed license fee for all the Pictures shall immediately become due and payable. The Licensee's failure to complete the maximum number of runs on or before the expiration date indicated in the Summary shall not extend the term of this license, nor shall it relieve the Licensee of its obligation to pay the total agreed license fee upon the expiration date.

10. LICENSEE'S COVENANTS: The Licensee covenants that:

(a) It will not telecast the Pictures except over the facilities of the station specified in the Summary. If such station suspends its operation for any reason, and the Licensee selects a substitute station, such substitute shall be subject to the Licensor's approval, which shall not be unreasonably withheld.

(b) It will not telecast the Pictures beyond any cut-off dates or in excess of the maximum number of permitted runs; and

(c) It will not permit or allow the Pictures entrusted to it to be exhibited or telecast by any other party.

11. ADVERTISING MATERIALS: The Licensor shall make available at reasonable cost to the Licensee [or to any sponsor of the television broadcasts of the Pictures, or to the advertising agencies of such sponsors], any advertising or promotional material owned by the Licensor that is available for distribution.

(a) No advertising, promotional or display material originated by the Licensee or the sponsor of the Pictures or the sponsor's advertising agency shall be used without the Licensor's prior written consent, which shall not be unreasonably withheld.

(b) Any advertising material used by the Licensee that may be copyrightable shall be registered for copyright by the Licensee in the Licensor's name.

(c) The Licensee shall not in any event use, for the purpose of a commercial tie-in or tie-up, the name or likeness of any person (producer, director, star, supporting players, and the like) appearing in or connected with the Picture.

12. ADVERTISING CREDITS: The Licensee shall comply with all the Licensor's instructions with respect to the requisite advertising credits, and shall indemnify the Licensor against any damage or expense (including reasonable attorneys' fees) that the Licensor may suffer or incur by reason of the Licensee's failure to observe such instructions.

13. ADVERTISING PRACTICES: All advertising utilized by the Licensee in connection with the exhibition of the Pictures shall be in accordance with the code requirements of the National Association of Broadcasters, as well as the applicable orders and regulations of any governmental agency.

14. RETURN OF PRINTS: Within forty-eight (48) hours after the broadcast thereof, the Licensee shall return each positive print to the Licensor or to such place or places as the Licensor may from time to time direct. Sundays and holidays shall not be included in the computation of the aforesaid period.

(a) The cost of transportation shall be borne by the Licensee.

(b) Each print shall be returned in good condition, ordinary wear and tear excepted, on the reels and in the containers in which it was received.

(c) If the Licensee fails to return a print as aforesaid, it shall be automatically charged with the laboratory cost of replacing the same, and it shall pay the charge forthwith to the Licensor.

CONTRACTS
FOR THE
FILM AND
TELEVISION
INDUSTRY

242

(d) If the Licensee claims that a print has been lost or destroyed, it shall furnish an affidavit to that effect, sworn to by one of its officers.

(e) All prints shall remain the property of the Licensor.

15. TAXES: The Licensee shall bear all taxes now or hereafter in effect that are or may be (i) imposed or based upon the Licensee's exhibition, possession or use of the prints of the Pictures, or upon the grant of this license or the exercise thereof; or (ii) measured by the license fees, however determined, paid or payable hereunder.

(a) The word "taxes" as herein used shall include, without limitation, taxes, fees, assessments, charges, imposts, levies and excises, whether designated as sales, gross income, gross receipts, personal property, storage, use, consumption, licensing, compensating, excise or privilege taxes.

(b) To the extent that such taxes are paid by the Licensor, the Licensee shall reimburse the Licensor therefor on demand; and upon its failure to do so, the Licensor shall have all the remedies herein provided for the collection of unpaid license fees, in addition to whatever other remedies it may have by law.

16. SUBSTITUTION: If the Licensor's right to grant this license with respect to any Picture is challenged by any third party, the Licensor may, at its option, either substitute a picture that it deems to be equivalent, or terminate this agreement with respect to such Picture. If the Licensor elects to terminate:

(a) The total license fee specified in the Summary shall be reduced proportionately in the ratio that the number of projected runs of the Picture involved bears to the total number of runs of all the Pictures.

(b) The Licensee shall and does waive all claims for damages that may arise from such termination, other than a claim for a refund of all prepaid exhibition fees.

17. LICENSEE'S DEFAULT: If the Licensee fails to make payment of the license fees or any part thereof when due, or if it defaults in any of its other obligations hereunder, and fails to make payment or to remedy its default within [10] days after notice from the Licensor, or if the Licensee is adjudicated a bankrupt or becomes insolvent or makes an assignment for the benefit of creditors, or if a receiver, liquidator or trustee is appointed for its assets or affairs, the Licensor shall have the right, in addition to whatever other remedies it may have by law, to terminate this license wholly or in part by written notice to the Licensee, in which event the entire unpaid balance of the total agreed license fee for all the Pictures shall immediately become due and payable.

18. FORCE MAJEURE: If the Licensor is delayed in or prevented from making delivery of the Pictures as herein provided, by reason of any act of God, labor difficulties, injunctions, judgments, adverse claims, fire, flood, transportation tie-up, public disaster or any other cause beyond its control, or if the Licensee is delayed in or prevented from telecasting the Pictures or returning the positive prints thereof as herein provided by reason of any of the aforesaid contingencies, neither party shall be liable to the other for the delay or failure so to perform; and the term of this license shall be deemed extended for a period equal to the duration of the contingency.

19. LICENSOR'S RIGHT TO ASSIGN: The Licensor shall have the right to hypothecate, pledge or assign this license to obtain loans thereon. The Licensee recognizes that lenders may be induced to advance substantial sums to the Licensor on the security of this license. Accordingly the Licensee shall pay to any assignee all moneys due to the Licensor without offset, deduction, counterclaim or credit for any claim that the Licensee may have against the Licensor.

20. NO ASSIGNMENT BY LICENSEE: This license shall not be assigned by the Licensee without the Licensor's written consent, nor shall it be assignable by operation of law insofar as the Licensee is concerned.

21. ARBITRATION: Any and all disputes arising out of or in connection with this agreement, its interpretation or performance, shall be submitted to arbitration in _____ under the then current rules and regulations of the American Arbitration Association. The decision of the arbitrators shall be binding and conclusive upon both parties.

22. GENERAL PROVISIONS: The following provisions shall apply:

(a) This license shall not be modified or waived in whole or in part except in writing.

(b) A waiver by either party of any breach or default by the other party shall not be construed as a waiver of any other breach or default.

(c) Any notices given or required to be given hereunder shall be in writing, and shall be sent by certified mail, return receipt requested, to the parties at their respective addresses shown in the Summary.

(d) This license shall be construed under the laws of the State of _____.

(e) This license is complete, and embraces the entire understanding of the parties.

CONTRACTS
FOR THE
FILM AND
TELEVISION
INDUSTRY

244

HOME VIDEO DISTRIBUTION

The so-called "ancillary" markets of home video and cable television actually generate more revenue than the "primary" theatrical market. Home video and cable distribution is also less risky and more profitable than theatrical distribution. The distributor does not have to pay for the duplication of numerous film prints, shipping to theaters and extensive newspaper advertising.

Because the right to distribute to ancillary markets is so desirable, it is difficult to interest a distributor in a theatrical release without giving it the ancillary markets in the same territory.

Some movies and programming are made for release directly to home video or cable. Exercise, children and specialty programs, for example, have successfully recouped their costs and generated significant profits without a theatrical release. The following agreement is for a series of specialty programs made for home video and cable distribution only.

HOME VIDEO LICENSING AGREEMENT

This Agreement between _____, residing at _____ (herein called "Licensor"), and _____, Inc., (herein called "Distributor"), a California corporation, is for the licensing to the domestic (United States and Canada) home video market for the program "_____," (herein "Program") a collection of four titles as set forth in Schedule "A", which is owned equally as tenants in common by the parties.

1. Licensor licenses his interest in the program to Distributor for distribution to the domestic (U.S. & Canada) home video market ("Licensed Territory") for a term of five (5) years and one month from the date this agreement is executed by both parties.

2. Licensor hereby grants Distributor the exclusive and irrevocable right, license and privilege in the Licensed territory (Domestic only) and in the Licensed Field (home video only) to manufacture Video Grams (videocassettes, videodiscs and similar devices) of the program and to sell, lease, license, rent, distribute, reproduce, perform, exploit, advertise and otherwise market such Video Grams during the term hereof. Distributor promises to use its efforts to market and distribute the program.

3. Distributor shall reproduce and incorporate the Program into Video Grams in its entirety in the form delivered by Licensor to Distributor, with no titles, credits, copyright notices, or other material changed, added to, omitted or edited without Licensor's prior written approval, which shall not be unreasonably withheld.

4. All rights not expressly granted hereunder are reserved to Licensor including the use of any Video Grams for viewing in any place of public assembly where an admission fee is charged, for broadcasting by television or cable, whether free or pay, for public exhibition in the traditional non-theatrical market, sequels and remakes, or for theatrical exhibition. Distributor shall only have the right to distribute the Program to the domestic home video market, to be used for exhibition on a television set for private home use only.

5. Licensor is not in any way obliged to license to Distributor any new programs licensor may produce in the future.

6. Distributor shall cause to be stamped or imprinted on the Video Grams or their packaging enclosures a statement substantially to the effect that: "The copyright proprietor has licensed the material contained herein for noncommercial private use only, and prohibits any other use, copying or reproduction in whole or in part."

7. For each Video Gram of the program sold, rented or otherwise vended in the Licensed Territory during the Term Distributor shall pay Licensor a royalty equal to 50% of such gross receipts as Distributor derives therefrom. "Gross receipts" shall be defined, computed, paid and accounted for in accordance with the provisions of Schedule "B" attached and incorporated by this reference. Gross receipts shall include any and all income received from the exploitation of the Program regardless of source.

8. Distributor shall bear all costs and obligations with respect to the distribution of the Program, including but not limited to all salaries, royalties, license fees, service charges, laboratory charges and the like. Licensor shall have no obligation for past, current or future salaries, royalties, residuals, deferments, license fees, service charges, laboratory charges or similar charges.

9. Distributor shall maintain complete books and records with respect to all Video Grams sold, leased, licensed or rented. Distributor will render to Licensor, on a quarterly basis, a written statement of Licensor's royalties following the conclusion of each quarterly accounting period and shall be accompanied by payment of any amount shown to be due Licensor.

10. Licensor shall have the right to examine the books and records of Distributor to the extent they pertain to the Program. Such examination shall be made during reasonable business hours, upon reasonable advance notice, at the regular place of business of Distributor where such books and records are to be maintained.

11. In any instance where revenues are earned or deductions allowed with regard to a group of films or video programs including the Program, Distributor shall make such allocations as are determined by Distributor in good faith, and gross receipts hereunder shall only include the amounts allocated to the Program.

12. All monies due or payable to Licensor shall be deemed held in trust by Distributor for Licensor. Licensor shall be deemed to have a lien or claim on the gross receipts. Distributors obligation shall include interest at 1.5% per month on any amounts due Licensor when such amounts are 30 days or more past due.

13. Distributor may assign its obligations under this agreement only to a person, corporation or other entity purchasing substantially all of the assets of the Distributor or into which Distributor shall be merged and which assumes Distributor's obligations hereunder. Licensor shall be entitled to assign its right to receive monies hereunder. No assignment shall relieve the assignor of its obligations to the other party hereunder.

14. If either party (herein called the First Party) desires to transfer his rights under this agreement to a third person, he shall give written notice by registered mail to the other party (herein called the Second Party) of his intention to do so.

CONTRACTS
FOR THE
FILM AND
TELEVISION
INDUSTRY

246

(a) In such case the Second Party shall have an option for a period of 30 days to purchase the First Party's rights at a price and upon such terms indicated in the written notice.

(b) If the Second Party fails to exercise his option in writing within the aforesaid period of 30 days, or if, having exercised it, he fails to complete the purchase upon the terms stated in the notice, the First Party may transfer his rights to the third person at the price and upon the identical terms stated in the notice; and he shall forthwith send to the Second Party a copy of the contract of sale of such rights, with a statement that the transfer has been made.

(c) If the First Party fails for any reason to make such transfer to the third person, and if he desires to make a subsequent transfer to someone else, the Second Party's option shall apply to such proposed subsequent transfer.

15. Nothing herein contained shall be construed to create a partnership or joint venture by or between the Distributor and ____ or to make either the agent of the other. Each party agrees not to hold itself out as a partner or agent of the other or to otherwise state or imply by advertising or otherwise any relationship that is contrary to the terms of this agreement. Neither party shall become liable or bound by any representation, act, omission or agreement of the other. However, all matters involving the distribution, lease, exhibition, sale, licensing and reissuing of the program, shall be exercised by the Distributor in accordance with sound business judgment and shall be subject to the prior approval of _____, such approval not to be unreasonably withheld.

16. Any controversy or claim arising out of or relating to this agreement or any breach thereof shall be settled by arbitration in accordance with the Rules of the American Arbitration Association; and judgment upon the award rendered by the arbitrators may be entered in any court having jurisdiction thereof. The prevailing party shall be entitled to reimbursement for costs and reasonable attorneys' fees.

17. This agreement shall inure to the benefit of, and shall be binding upon, the executors, administrators and assigns of the parties.

18. This agreement constitutes the entire understanding of the parties.

19. This agreement is governed by and construed in accordance with the laws of the State of _____.

20. If any provision of this Agreement or the application thereof to any Person or circumstance shall be invalid or unenforceable to any extent, the remainder of this Agreement and the application of such provisions to other persons or circumstances shall not be affected thereby and shall be enforced to the greatest extent permitted by law.

21. The parties agree to execute such further documents and instruments as they may reasonably request in order to effectuate the terms and intentions of this agreement, and in the event either party is unable to execute any such documents or instruments, each appoints the other as their irrevocable attorney-in-fact to execute any such documents and instruments, provided that said documents and instruments shall not be inconsistent with the terms and conditions of this agreement. The rights under this Clause constitute a power coupled with an interest and are irrevocable.

22. This agreement expresses the entire understanding between the parties and both agree that no oral understandings have been made with regard thereto. This agreement may be amended only by written instrument signed by both parties. Each party acknowledges that it has not been induced to enter this agreement by any representations or assurances, whether written or oral, and both parties agree that each has not received any promises or inducements other than as herein set forth.

AGREED TO AND ACCEPTED

_____   Date:

_____

By:

_____

President
_____, Inc.   Date:

IN WITNESS WHEREOF, the parties hereunto set their respective hand and seal this _____ day of _____, 19__.

_____

SCHEDULE "A"

SCHEDULE "B"

"Gross Receipts" shall be defined and all monies due hereunder shall be paid in accordance with the following terms:

(a) Definition of Gross Receipts: "Gross Receipts" means all monies (subject to the exclusions in subclause (b) below actually received by Distributor or any of its affiliates from the exploitation by Distributor of the rights granted to Distributor hereunder.

(b) Exclusions from Gross Receipts: Gross receipts shall be determined after all refunds, credits, discounts, allowances and adjustments granted to subdistributors, wholesalers, retailers and other purchasers and licensees. Additionally, gross receipts shall not include:

(i) Any monies derived by any local subdistributor, wholesaler or retailer from sale of Video Grams, whether or not such subdistributor, wholesaler, or retailer is owned, operated, managed or controlled by Distributor; provided, however, that in the event of any such owned, operated or managed subdistributor, wholesaler or retailer, Distributor agrees that the terms of sale or lease of any Video Grams to any such entity shall be substantially the same as the terms of sale or lease of Video

CONTRACTS
FOR THE
FILM AND
TELEVISION
INDUSTRY

248

Grams to unrelated entities, in accordance with industry standards. If Distributor derives any rental income hereunder from its exploitation of the Picture, Distributor agrees to negotiate in good faith with Licensor concerning any allocation of the income between the two parties.

(ii) Any sums due, but not paid Distributor; provided that Distributor agrees to use all reasonable efforts consistent with its prudent business judgment to collect such sums owed it.

(iii) The salvage value of any videotape, cassettes or other materials purchased by or manufactured by Distributor and not sold as Video Grams.

(iv) Taxes: Gross receipts shall not include any and all sums paid or accrued on account of sales, use, value added, receipts, excise, remittance and other taxes (however denominated, except income taxes) to any government authority, assessed upon the Video Grams or any other materials relating to the Program.

(v) Any sum paid or accrued on account of freight, shipping, handling and insurance in connection with the sale of Video Grams.

(vi) Royalties paid to author _____ or his assigns in accordance with the contract between _____ and the same, as set forth in "Schedule C" attached.

CHAPTER 10

MERCHANDISING

Movie merchandising can earn studios substantial revenue. Some movies have generated more gross revenues from retail sales of spin-off merchandise than from box office revenues.

Studios usually do not manufacture film-related products themselves. They license the right to sell these products to other companies (the "Licensee"). In most instances there is no risk to the studio (the "Licensor") because the licensees incur all manufacturing and distribution expenses. The studio receives an advance per product, and royalty payments, often between five and ten percent of gross revenues from retailers (i.e., the wholesale price). If the movie flops and the products don't sell, the manufacturer takes the loss.

Musicals such as *Saturday Night Fever*, *Grease*, *Flashdance*, and *Dirty Dancing*, earn substantial revenues from sales of soundtrack albums. Moreover, a hit song can effectively promote a film.

Keep in mind that few films lend themselves to extensive merchandising efforts. Movies like *Jurassic Park* that spin off toys, posters and similar items have the greatest potential. But a film like *Sleepless in Seattle*, has limited merchandising potential outside of the soundtrack album.

CONTRACTS
FOR THE
FILM AND
TELEVISION
INDUSTRY

250

MERCHANDISING AGREEMENT

AGREEMENT made _____ (date) between _____ ("Licensor") and _____ ("Licensee") with respect to certain merchandising rights in the motion picture entitled: _____ (the "Picture").

1. LICENSE:

(a) Grant of License: Licensor grants to Licensee for the term of this Agreement, subject to the terms and conditions herein contained, and Licensee hereby accepts, the exclusive right, license and privilege to utilize the names, characters, artists' portrayal of characters, likenesses and visual representations as included in Picture (collectively the "Property") solely and only in connection with the manufacture, advertising, distribution and sale of the article or articles specified in Schedule "A" attached hereto and by this reference made a part hereof (such articles being referred to herein as "Licensed Products") under the terms and conditions stated herein. Licensee agrees that it will not utilize the Property in any manner not specifically authorized by this Agreement.

(b) Limited Grant: Nothing in this Agreement shall be construed to prevent Licensor from granting any other licenses for the use of the Property in any manner whatsoever, except that Licensor agrees that, except as provided herein, it will grant no other licenses effective during the term of this Agreement, for use in the Licensed Territory of the Licensed Product(s). Licensor specifically reserves all rights not herein granted, including without limitation, premium rights. For purposes of this Agreement, premium rights shall mean use of the Property in such manner as to identify it with a particular product or service other than the Licensed Products. It is clearly understood that the Licensed Products may not be sold for use, or be used as, premiums, self-liquidators, containers, or for any secondary use without the prior written consent of the Licensor.

2. TERRITORY: The license hereby granted extends only to the territory described in Schedule "B," attached hereto and by this reference made a part hereof (hereinafter: "Licensed Territory"). Licensee agrees that it will not make, or authorize, any use, direct or indirect, of the Licensed Products or Property in any other area, and that it will not knowingly sell articles covered by this Agreement to persons who intend or are likely to resell them in any other area, to the extent the provision is permitted by law.

3. LICENSE PERIOD (THE "TERM"): The License granted hereunder shall be effective and terminate as of the dates specified in Schedule "C," attached hereto and by this reference made a part hereof unless sooner terminated in accordance with the terms and conditions hereof.

4. EXCLUSION: Anything in this Agreement to the contrary notwithstanding, Licensee's rights hereunder shall not include the right to, and Licensee hereby warrants that it will not, use the Property for any endorsement, including but not limited to the Licensed Product(s).

5. PAYMENT:

(a) Guaranteed Minimum Compensation: Licensee shall pay to Licensor, as Guaranteed Minimum Compensation under this Agreement, not less than the minimum amount specified for the respective period of time set forth in Schedule "D" (attached hereto and by this reference made a part hereof) and such

Guaranteed Minimum Compensation shall be paid in a manner and at the time specified in said Schedule "D".

(b) Percentage Compensation: Licensee agrees to pay Licensor a sum equal to the percentage specified in Schedule "E" in connection with the distribution of any units of the Licensed Products covered by this Agreement (hereinafter "Percentage Compensation") whether to third parties, to its affiliated, associated or subsidiary companies or otherwise, whether or not billed. A Percentage Compensation shall also be paid by Licensee to Licensor on all Licensed Products distributed by Licensee to any of its affiliated, associated or subsidiary companies. The amount payable to Licensor under this Sub-clause 5(b) shall be reduced by the amount of any advance paid to Licensor pursuant to Schedule "B."

6. PERIODIC STATEMENTS: Within thirty (30) days after the initial shipment of the Licensed Products covered by this Agreement, and on the tenth day of each month thereafter, Licensee shall furnish to Licensor complete and accurate statements, certified to be accurate by Licensee, showing the number, description and sales price of the Licensed Products distributed and or sold by Licensee during the preceding month, including a statement of any returns made during the preceding month. Such statements shall be furnished to Licensor whether or not any of the Licensed Products have been sold during the month for which such statements are due. Percentage Compensation as provided in Schedule "E" shall be payable by the Licensee simultaneously with the rendering of statements. Receipt or acceptance by Licensor of the statements furnished pursuant to this Agreement or of any sums paid hereunder shall not preclude Licensor from questioning the correctness thereof at any time, and if any inconsistencies or mistakes are discovered in such statements or payments, they shall immediately be rectified and the appropriate payments made by Licensee. Time is of the essence with respect to all payments hereunder.

7. BOOKS AND RECORDS: Licensee agrees to keep accurate books of account and records covering all transactions relating to the License hereby granted and Licensor and its duly authorized representatives shall have the right upon reasonable advance notice to an examination of said books of account and records and of all other documents and material, whether in the possession or under the control of Licensee or otherwise, with respect to the subject matter and the terms of this Agreement and shall have free and full access thereto for said purpose of making extracts and or copies therefrom. All books of account and records shall be kept available for at least two (2) years after the expiration or termination of this License, and Licensee agrees to permit inspection thereof by Licensor during such two (2) year period as well. The receipt or acceptance by Licensor of any of the statements furnished pursuant to this Agreement or of any Percentage Compensation paid hereunder (or the cashing of any checks paid hereunder) shall not preclude Licensor from questioning the correctness thereof at any time prior to the date two (2) years after the conclusion of the term of this Agreement, and if any inconsistencies or mistakes are discovered in such statements or payments, they shall immediately be rectified and the appropriate payments made by Licensee. Payment shall be made in United States funds. Domestic taxes payable in the Licensed Territory shall be Licensee's responsibility. If any such examination shows an under-reporting and/or payment in excess of five percent (5%) of the total amount reported and or paid for any twelve (12) month period and if that underpayment is acknowledged by Licensee or is affirmed by litigation or arbitration, then Licensee shall pay the costs of such examination and/or litigation, including, without limitation, attorneys' fees with respect thereto.

CONTRACTS
FOR THE
FILM AND
TELEVISION
INDUSTRY

252

8. COPYRIGHT AND TRADEMARK NOTICES:

(a) Copyright and Trademark Notices: Licensee shall cause to be imprinted irremovably and legibly on all Licensed Products and on at least the principal face of all packaging, enclosure materials and advertising materials for the Licensed Products the complete copyright notice: (c) (name of copyright owner date of copyright) (The year of the copyright notice shall be the year in which the latest revision of the respective Licensed Products, packaging, enclosure or advertising is first placed on sale, sold or publicly distributed by the Licensee under the authority from Licensor).

Licensee shall also cause to be imprinted irremovably and legibly on all Licensed Products and on at least the principal face of all packaging, enclosure materials and advertising materials for the Licensed Products the appropriate trademark notice, either "TM" or "R" as Licensor shall determine, and shall affix the notice as specified by Licensor.

(b) Copyright Samples, Approval and Registration:

(i) Prior to the production of any particular Licensed Product or of any packaging, enclosure, promotion and advertising therefor, Licensee shall deliver, at Licensee's expense, to Licensor the following:

(a) a complete set of art work and sketches and actual samples, if available of the applicable Licensed Product;

(b) its packaging, enclosures, promotional materials and advertising; for Licensor's written approval of the copyright and trademark form and of the manner and style of use of the Property. Once Licensor approves the trademark or copyright notice, Licensee will not deviate from the Licensor-approved notice. Licensee shall make such deliveries to Licensor each time a new Licensed Product, packaging, enclosure, promotion or advertising is to be produced. Public sale and distribution will not be made until Licensor's approval pursuant to this Subclause 8(b) is received.

(ii) Promptly after the first public sale or distribution, Licensee shall deliver, at Licensee's expense, five (5) complete of each Licensed Product, packaging, enclosure, promotion and advertising for copyright and trademark registration at Licensor's discretion and expense; however, Licensor has no obligation to obtain such registration(s). Licensee will advise Licensor in writing of the date of first public sale and distribution. Copyrights and trademarks in all such material shall be owned by Licensor.

9. LICENSOR'S APPROVAL OF LICENSED PRODUCTS, ADVERTISING, CONTAINERS, MATERIALS, ETC.:

The quality and style of the Licensed Products as well as any carton, container, packing or wrapping material shall be subject to the express written approval of Licensor prior to distribution and sale thereof by Licensee. Also, each and every tag, label, imprint or other device used in connection with any Licensed Products and all advertising, promotional or display material bearing the Property and or Licensed Products shall be submitted by Licensee to Licensor for express written approval prior to use by Licensee. Such approval may be granted or withheld as Licensor in its sole discretion may determine. Licensee shall, before selling or distributing any of the Licensed Products, furnish to Licensor free of cost, for its express written approval, three (3) prototype samples of (a) each Licensed Product, (b) each type of carton, container, packing and wrapping material used with each Licensed Product, (c) each and every tag, label, imprint or other device used in connection with any Licensed Product, and (d) all advertising, story board, script, promotional or display material bearing the Property and/or Licensed Products.

Said samples shall be sent to Licensor by means permitting certification of receipt at the mailing address stated in the notice clause herein. Failure by Licensor to approve in writing any of the samples furnished to Licensor within two weeks from the date of submission thereof shall be deemed approval thereof. After samples have been approved pursuant to this clause, Licensee shall not depart therefrom in any respect without the express prior written approval of Licensor. The prototypes shall conform to the requirements of Clause 8.

10. PROTECTION OF LICENSOR'S RIGHTS AND INTERESTS: Licensor and Licensee agree that Licensee's utilization of the Property upon or in connection with the manufacture, distribution and sale of the Licensed Products is conditioned upon Licensor's protection of its rights and obtaining the goodwill resulting from such use. Licensee agrees to protect Licensor's rights and goodwill as set forth hereinbelow and elsewhere in this Agreement.

(a) Good Will and Protection:

(i) Licensee recognizes the great value of the publicity and goodwill associated with the Property and, in such connection, acknowledges that such goodwill exclusively belongs to Licensor and that the Property has acquired a secondary meaning in the mind of the purchasing public. Licensee further acknowledges that all rights in any additional material, new versions, translations, rearrangements, or other changes in the Property which may be created by or for Licensee, shall be and will remain the exclusive property of Licensor and the same shall be and will remain a part of the Property under the terms and conditions of this Agreement.

(ii) Licensee shall assist Licensor and or Licensor's authorized agents to all reasonable extent requested by Licensor in obtaining and maintaining in Licensor's name any and all available protection of Licensor's rights in and to the Property; specifically, Licensee agrees to sign documents, give testimony, provide exhibits, provide facts and otherwise cooperate with Licensor and its agents in obtaining registrations, assignments, certificates and the like evidencing Licensor's rights in the Property. Pursuant to the foregoing, Licensee shall assign over to Licensor, at Licensor's request, formal and absolute title subject to the License granted herein, to any protectable new version, variation, revision, arrangement of compilation of the Property, ownership of which shall be absolute in Licensor.

(iii) Licensor may, if it so desires, and in its reasonable discretion, commence or prosecute any claims or suits against infringement of its right in the Property and may, if it so desires, join Licensee as a party in such suit. Licensee shall notify Licensor in writing of any activities which Licensee believes to be infringements or utilization by others of the Property or articles of the same general class as the Licensed Products, or otherwise. Licensor shall have the sole right to determine whether or not any action shall be undertaken as a result of such activity and shall have sole discretion in the accommodation or settlement of any controversies relating thereto. Licensee shall not institute any suit or take any action with respect to any such infringement or imitation without first obtaining the written consent of Licensor to do so.

CONTRACTS
FOR THE
FILM AND
TELEVISION
INDUSTRY

254

(b) Indemnification By Licensee: For purposes of this Subclause 10(b) "Indemnified Parties" refer to Licensor, and (name of copyright owner if other than Licensor), their parents, subsidiaries and affiliates, and co-producers and co-venturers of Licensor and (name of copyright owner if other than Licensor) and the performers and other personnel in or associated with the Property and Licensees of rights relating to the Property, and the person or firm whose rights are being licensed hereunder and, where applicable, sponsors of the Property and their respective advertising agencies, and officers, directors, employees and agents of each of the foregoing and all persons connected with and or employed by them and each of them.

Except for the rights licensed hereunder by Licensor to Licensee, Licensee hereby indemnifies and shall hold harmless the Indemnified Parties and each of them from and against the costs and expenses of any and all claims, demands, causes of action and judgments arising out of the unauthorized use of any patent, process, method or device or out of infringement of any copyright, trade name, patent or libel or invasion of the right of privacy, publicity, or other property right, or failure to perform, or any defect in or use of the Licensed Products, the infringement or breach of any other personal or property right of any person, firm or corporation by Licensee, its officers, employees, agents or anyone, directly or indirectly, acting by, through, on behalf of, pursuant to contractual or any other relationship with Licensee in connection with the preparation, manufacture, distribution, advertising, promotion and or sale of the Licensed Products and or any material relating thereto and or naming or referring to any performers, personnel, marks and or elements. With respect to the foregoing indemnity, Licensee shall defend and hold harmless Indemnified Parties and each of them at no cost or expense to them whatsoever, including but not limited to attorneys' fees and court costs. Licensor shall have the right but not the obligation to defend any such action or proceeding with attorneys of its own selection.

(c) Product Liability Insurance: Licensee shall obtain and maintain at its sole cost and expense throughout the term standard Product Liability Insurance, the form of which must be acceptable to Licensor, from a qualified insurance company licensed to do business in the State of _____ naming Licensor and each and all the Indemnified Parties described in Subclause 10(b) above as additional named insureds, which policy shall provide protection against any and all claims, demands and causes of action arising out of any defects or failures to perform, alleged or otherwise, in the Licensed Products or any material used in connection therewith or any use thereof. The amount of coverage shall be a minimum of One Million Dollars ($1,000,000) combined single limit for each single occurrence for bodily injury and One Hundred Thousand Dollars ($100,000) for property damage. The policy shall provide for thirty (30) days' notice to Licensee and Licensor from the insurer by Registered Mail, return receipt requested, in the event of any modification, cancellation or termination. Licensee agrees to furnish Licensor a certified copy of the policy providing such coverage within thirty (30) days after the date of this Agreement and in no event shall Licensee manufacture, distribute or sell the Licensed Products prior to receipt by Licensor of such evidence of insurance.

(d) Advertiser's Liability Insurance: Licensee shall obtain and maintain at its sole cost and expense throughout the term standard Advertiser's Liability Insurance, the form of which must be acceptable to Licensor, from a qualified insurance company licensed to do business in the State of _____ naming Licensor and each and all of the Indemnified Parties described in Subclause 10(b) above as additional named insureds. The amount and coverage shall be a minimum of Five Hundred Thousand Dollars\One Million Dollars ($500,000\$1,000,000). The policy shall provide for thirty (30) days' notice to Licensee and Licensor from the insurer by Registered Mail, return receipt requested, in the event of any modification, cancellation or termination. Licensee agrees to furnish Licensor a certified copy of the policy providing such coverage within thirty (30) days after the date of this Agreement and in no event shall Licensee manufacture, distribute or sell the Licensed Products prior to receipt by Licensor of such evidence of insurance.

(e) No Licensor Warranty: Licensor makes no warranty or representation as to the amount of gross sales or net sales or profits Licensee will derive hereunder. Licensor makes no warranty or representation concerning the quality of the Property or that production of the Property will be completed or that the Property will be released. Licensor shall not be under any obligation whatsoever to continue the distribution of the Property or to continue to use any element of the Property. If the Property is not completed, and release thereof not commenced in the United States within one (1) year after the date of this Agreement, by reason of fire, earthquake, labor dispute, lockout, strike, act of God or public enemy, any local, state, federal, national or international law, governmental order or regulation, or any other cause beyond Licensor's control, including but not limited to the death, illness or incapacity of the director or of any principal member of the cast of the Property, this Agreement shall terminate at the expiration of said one (1) year period and Licensor's only liability shall be to return to Licensee the unrecouped portion, if any, of the Guaranteed Minimum Compensation theretofore paid by Licensee to Licensor after the expiration of said one (1) year period, in which event Licensor shall make said refund within thirty (30) days after receiving said demand.

11. SPECIFIC UNDERTAKINGS OF THE PARTIES:

(a) Licensor warrants, represents and agrees that:

(i) It has certain ownership rights in and has the right to grant licenses to utilize the names (including the name of the Picture), characters, artists' portrayal of characters, likenesses and visual representations as included in the Picture and to grant the eights to the Property granted Licensee in this agreement.

(b) Licensee warrants, represents and agrees that:

(i) It will not dispute the title of Licensor in and to the Property or any copyright or trademark pertaining thereto, nor will it attack the validity of the License granted hereunder.

(ii) It will not harm, misuse or bring into dispute the Property or any part thereof;

(iii) It will manufacture, sell and distribute the Licensed Products in an ethical manner and in accordance with the terms and intent of this Agreement;

(iv) It will not create any expenses chargeable to Licensor;

(v) It will not enter into any sublicense or agency agreement for the sale or distribution of the Licensed Products;

(vi) It will not enter into any agreement relating to the Property for commercial tie-ups or promotions or otherwise, with any person or en-

CONTRACTS
FOR THE
FILM AND
TELEVISION
INDUSTRY

256

tity engaged, in whole or in part, in the production of motion pictures or television, without the prior written consent of Licensor. Licensee's advertising on television is not subject to the provisions of this subclause;

(vii) It will manufacture, sell and distribute Licensed Products of a high standard and of such quality, style and appearance as shall be reasonably adequate and suited to their exploitation to the best advantage and to the protection and enhancement of the Property and the good will pertaining thereto; that such articles will be manufactured, packaged, sold and distributed and advertised in accordance with all applicable (whether national, federal, state, provincial or local) laws: and that the policy of sale, distribution and or exploitation by Licensee shall be of high standard and at the best advantage of the Property and that the same shall in no manner reflect adversely upon the good name of Licensor, or the Property;

(viii) It will diligently and continuously solicit sales of the Licensed Products and actively offer the Licensed Products for sale, and make distribution in order to meet orders for the articles covered by this Agreement;

(ix) It will sell and distribute the articles covered by this Agreement outright at a competitive price and not for more than the price generally and customarily charged the trade by Licensee, and only to the public by direct mail order sales, to jobbers, wholesalers and distributors for sale and distribution to retail stores and merchants, and to retail stores and merchants for sale and distribution direct to the public. Licensee shall not, without prior written consent of Licensor, sell or distribute such article to jobbers, wholesalers, distributors, retail stores or merchants whose sales or distribution are or will be made for publicity or promotional tie-up purposes, premiums, giveaways or similar methods of merchandising. If any sale is made at a special price to any of Licensee's parents, affiliates or subsidiaries or to any other person, firm or corporation related in any manner to Licensee or its officers, directors or major stockholders, a Percentage Compensation shall be paid on such sale based upon the price generally charged the trade by Licensee.

Notwithstanding anything to the contrary contained herein, Licensed Products may only be sold through required distribution channels for ultimate use by the consumer and may not be sold in quantity or otherwise for any distribution method or device not contemplated by this Agreement.

(x) It will not grant exclusivity to any purchaser without the written consent of Licensor. In addition, Licensee will not require any purchaser to purchase assortments containing merchandise other than that licensed hereunder in order to obtain the articles which are the subject of this License.

(xi) It will coordinate the release, promotion, and distribution and sales activities for the Licensed Products with the release of the Property in such manner as Licensor shall request.

12. TERMINATION:

(a) If Licensee files a petition in bankruptcy or is adjudicated a bankrupt or if a petition in bankruptcy is filed against Licensor or if Licensee becomes insolvent or makes an assignment for the benefit of its creditors or an arrangement pursuant to any bankruptcy law or if Licensee discontinues its business or if a receiver is appointed for it or its business, the License granted hereunder, without notice, shall terminate automatically (upon the occurrence of any such event).

(b) If Licensee shall violate any of its obligations or conditions under the terms of this Agreement, Licensor shall have the right to terminate the License herein granted upon fourteen days notice in writing, and such notice of termination shall become effective, unless Licensee shall completely remedy the violation and satisfy Licensor that such violation has been remedied within the fourteen day period.

(c) If the License granted hereunder is terminated in accordance with the provisions of Sub clauses 12(a) or 12(b), all compensation theretofore accrued shall become due and payable immediately to Licensor, and Licensor shall not be obligated to reimburse Licensee for any payment theretofore paid by Licensee to Licensor.

13. FINAL STATEMENT UPON TERMINATION OR EXPIRATION: As soon as practical after termination or expiration of this Agreement, but in no event more than 30 days thereafter, Licensee shall deliver to Licensor a statement indicating the number and description of Licensed Products which Licensee has on hand (or in process of manufacture) as of (a) sixty (60) days prior to the end of the Term of this Agreement, or (b) fourteen days after receipt from Licensor of a notice terminating this Agreement (in the event no such notice was given, fourteen days after the occurrence of any event which terminates this Agreement) whichever shall be applicable.

14. DISPOSAL OF STOCK UPON EXPIRATION: Upon expiration of the term of this Agreement, Licensee shall have the right, pursuant to the provisions hereof, to dispose of all Licensed Products, theretofore manufactured at the time of the expiration of the License granted hereunder, for a period of ninty (90) days after the date of such expiration subject to the condition that Licensee pays to Licensor all compensation accrued to such time and delivers to Licensor a report in the form required by Clause 6 above to such time. Notwithstanding anything to the contrary contained herein, Licensee shall not sell or dispose of any Licensed Products if this Agreement was terminated for any cause set forth in Clause 12 above.

15. EFFECT OF TERMINATION OR EXPIRATION: Upon expiration of the License granted hereunder or the earlier termination thereof, all rights granted to Licensee hereunder shall forthwith revert to Licensor, and Licensee thereafter, directly or indirectly, shall not use or refer to, except as provided in Clause 14, above, the Property or any name, character, trademark or designation which in Licensor's reasonable opinion is similar to the Property, in connection with the manufacture, sale or distribution of products of the Licensee. Licensee shall upon the expiration or termination turn over to Licensor all molds and other materials which reproduce the Licensed Products, or give Licensor satisfactory evidence of their destruction.

Licensee hereby agrees that at the expiration or termination of this Agreement for any reason, Licensee will be deemed automatically to have assigned, transferred and conveyed to Licensor any and all copyrights, trademark or service mark rights, goodwill or other right, title or interest in and to the merchandising of the Property which may have been obtained by Licensee or which may have vested in Licensee in pursuance of any endeavors covered hereby. Licensee will execute, and hereby irrevocably appoints Licensor its attorney-in-fact (acknowledging that such power is coupled with an interest) to execute, if Licensee fails or refuses to do so, any instruments requested by Licensor to accomplish or confirm the foregoing. Any such assignment, transfer or conveyance shall be without consideration other than the mutual covenants and considerations of

CONTRACTS
FOR THE
FILM AND
TELEVISION
INDUSTRY

258

this Agreement. Also, upon expiration or termination of this Agreement, Licensor shall be free to license to others the right to use the Property in connection with the manufacture, sale and distribution of the Licensed Products,

16. REMEDIES OF LICENSOR:

(a) Licensee acknowledges that the failure of the Licensee to cease the manufacture, sale or distribution of Licensed Products except as herein permitted upon the expiration or earlier termination of the License granted hereunder or the failure of Licensee to fulfill its obligations specified in Clauses 4, 5, 6, 8, 9, 10, and 11, will result in immediate and irremediable damage to Licensor and to the rights of any other licensee of the Property. Licensee acknowledges that Licensor has no adequate remedy at law for any such failure referred to or referenced to in this Clause and in the event of any such failure, Licensor shall be entitled to equitable relief by way of temporary and permanent injunctions, in addition to such other further relief as any court of competent jurisdiction may deem just and proper.

(b) If Licensor uses any remedy afforded by this Clause, Licensor shall not be deemed to have elected its remedy or to have waived any other rights or remedies available to it under this Agreement, or otherwise.

17. FORCE MAJEURE: Licensee shall be released from its obligations hereunder in the event that governmental regulations or conditions arising out of a state of national emergency or war, or causes beyond the control of Licensee render performance by Licensee hereunder impossible. The release of obligations under this Clause shall be limited to a delay in time for Licensee to meet its obligations for a period not to exceed three (3) months, and if there is any failure to meet such obligations after that period, Licensor shall have the absolute right to terminate this Agreement upon fourteen days' notice in writing. Such notice of termination shall become effective if Licensor does not completely remedy the violation within the same fourteen day period and satisfy Licensor that such failure has been remedied.

18. RESERVATION OF RIGHTS: Licensor reserves all rights pertaining to the Property, except as specifically granted herein to Licensee.

19. NOTICES:

(a) All notices to be given to Licensor hereunder and all statements and payments to be sent to Licensor hereunder shall be addressed to Licensor at (address of Licensor) or at such other address as Licensor shall designate in writing from time to time. Licensee shall send a courtesy copy of each notice hereunder to Licensor's attorney, _____. All notices to be given to Licensee hereunder shall be addressed to it at _____, or at such other address as Licensee shall designate in writing from time to time. Licensor shall send a courtesy copy of each notice hereunder to Licensee's attorney, _____. All notices shall be in writing and shall either be served by Certified or Registered Mail Return Receipt Requested, or telegraph, all charges prepaid. Except as provided herein, such notices shall be deemed given when mailed or delivered to a telegraph office, all charges prepaid, except that notices of change of address shall be effective only after the actual receipt thereof.

(b) Submission: All submissions pursuant to Clauses 8 and 9 shall be forwarded by personal delivery or mail, all charges prepaid by Licensee pursuant to the provisions of Subclause 19(a) above.

20. WAIVER, MODIFICATION, ETC.: No waiver, modification or cancellation of any term or condition of this Agreement shall be effective unless executed

in writing by the party charged therewith. No written waiver shall excuse the performance of any act other than those specifically referred to therein. Licensor makes no warranties to Licensee except those specifically expressed herein.

21. NO PARTNERSHIP, ETC.: This Agreement does not constitute and shall not be construed as constituting an agency, a partnership or joint venture between Licensor and Licensee. Neither party hereto shall hold itself out contrary to the terms of this Clause, and neither Licensor nor Licensee shall become liable for any representation, act or omission of the other contrary to the provisions hereof. This contract shall not be deemed to give any right or remedy to any third party whatsoever unless said right or remedy is specifically granted by Licensor in writing to such third party.

22. NON-ASSIGNABILITY: The license granted hereunder is and shall be personal to Licensee, and shall not be assignable by any act of Licensee or by operation of law. Licensee shall not have Licensed Products manufactured for Licensee by a third party unless Licensee first obtains Licensor's approval in writing and unless the third party enters into an agreement with Licensor not to supply Licensed Products to anyone other than Licensee. Any attempt by Licensee to grant sub-licenses or to assign or part with possession or control of the License granted hereunder or any of Licensee's rights hereunder shall constitute a material breach of this Agreement. Licensor shall have the right to assign this Agreement, in which event Licensor shall be relieved of any and all obligations hereunder, provided such assignee shall assume this Agreement and all rights and obligations hereunder in writing.

23. GOVERNING LAW: This Agreement shall be deemed to have been made in, and shall be construed in accordance with the laws of the State of California, and its validity, construction, interpretation and legal effect shall be governed by the laws of the State of California applicable to contracts entered into and performed entirely therein.

24. HEADINGS: The headings used in connection with the clauses and subclauses of this Agreement are inserted only for the purpose of reference. Such headings shall not be deemed to govern, limit, modify, or in any other manner affect the scope, meaning, or intent of the provisions of this Agreement or any part thereof, nor shall such headings otherwise be given any legal effect.

25. ENTIRE AGREEMENT: This Agreement sets forth the entire understanding of the parties hereto relating to the subject matter hereof. No modification, amendment, waiver, termination or discharge of this Agreement, or of any of the terns or provisions hereof shall be binding upon either party hereto unless confirmed by a written instrument signed by Licensee and Licensor. No waiver by Licensor or Licensee of any term or provision of this contract or of any default here under shall affect the other's respective rights thereafter to enforce such term or provision or to exercise any right or remedy in the event of any other default whether or not similar.

26. SEVERABILITY: If any provision of this Agreement shall be held void, voidable, invalid, or inoperative, no other provision of this Agreement shall be affected as a result thereof, and, accordingly, the remaining provisions of this Agreement shall remain in full force and effect as though such void, voidable, invalid, or inoperative provision had not been contained herein.

27. RIGHTS AND REMEDIES CUMULATIVE: Except as otherwise provided in this contract, all rights and remedies herein or otherwise shall be cumulative and none of them shall be in limitation of any other right or remedy.

CONTRACTS
FOR THE
FILM AND
TELEVISION
INDUSTRY

260

28. EXECUTION OF AGREEMENT: This contract shall not be effective until signed by a duly authorized officer of Licensee and countersigned by a duly authorized officer of Licensor.

29. SPECIFIC ARRANGEMENT: If there is any specific arrangement between the parties, such specific situation shall be embodied in Schedule "F," attached hereto and by this reference made a part of this Agreement.

IN WITNESS WHEREOF, the parties hereto have signed this Agreements of the day and year first above written.

AGREED TO AND ACCEPTED:

LICENSOR:

By:

LICENSEE:

By:

SCHEDULES ANNEXED TO LICENSE AGREEMENT BETWEEN _____ and _____ dated _____.

Schedule "A" LICENSED PRODUCTS.

Schedule "B" LICENSED TERRITORY.

Schedule "C" LICENSE PERIOD:

Effective commencement date:

Termination date:

Schedule "D" GUARANTEED MINIMUM COMPENSATION:

The Guaranteed Minimum Compensation under this Agreement shall be _____ dollars payable upon execution of this Agreement. Such payment shall be an advance against the Percentage Compensation attributable to gross sales made by Licensee during the period for which the Guaranteed Minimum Compensation is due. The payment of Guaranteed Minimum Compensation shall be non-refundable.

Schedule "E" PERCENTAGE COMPENSATIONS:

The Percentage Compensation under this Agreement shall be seven percent (7%)) of the current wholesale price of the Licensed Products based on one hundred percent (100%) of the articles sold.

Schedule "F" SPECIAL ARRANGEMENT.

APPROVED:

By:
LICENSEE:

By:

PRODUCT PLACEMENT

Manufacturers often want to have their products shown in films in order to boost sales. The companies are happy to supply samples of their products, and sometimes money and promotions, in return for placement of a product in a film. Some manufacturers have in-house departments that arrange these placements. Other companies use product placement agents. These agents may represent products from several manufacturers.

The law does not always require that a filmmaker obtain a release to show a product in a film. Assuming you don't disparage the product, it is unlikely a manufacturer could successfully sue simply because its product was shown without consent.

If the product is momentarily on the screen and not identifiable, you need not bother to get a release.[1] No director who shoots a scene in a supermarket is going to obtain releases for every product in the background. Still, a release never hurts even if not legally required. Remember distributors and insurance carriers like to see releases for every identifiable product.

PRODUCT RELEASE

_____, 19__

Re: _____ (Picture) — PRODUCT RELEASE

Dear _____ :

When countersigned by you, on behalf of _____ ("Company"), this letter will confirm that Company has agreed to, and hereby does grant, to _____ ("Producer") the right to use its product _____ , including any related logo(s) and trademark(s) (collectively, the "Product") in the theatrical motion picture presently entitled _____ (the "Picture"). Company acknowledges that the Picture may be exhibited and exploited worldwide, in all languages and in all media now known or hereafter devised in perpetuity.

Producer agrees that the Product will not be used in a disparaging manner. Company hereby warrants and represents that it has the right and authority to grant the rights granted herein, that the consent of no other person or company is required to enable Producer to use the Product as described herein, and that such use will not violate the rights of any kind of any third parties. Company agrees to indemnify and hold harmless Producer, its officers, shareholders, assignees and licensees, and each of their successors-in-interest from and against any and all liabilities, damages and claims (including attorneys' fees and court costs) arising out of (i) any breach of Company's warranties, (ii) Producer's use of the Product, as provided herein, and/or (iii) the rights granted herein.

The sole remedy of Company for breach of any provision of this agreement shall be an action at law for damages, and in no event shall Company seek or be

---

[1] You should always have a lawyer review your script before production to determine what releases may be required.

CONTRACTS
FOR THE
FILM AND
TELEVISION
INDUSTRY

262

entitled to injunctive or other equitable relief by reason of any breach or threatened breach of this Product Release agreement, or for any other reason pertaining hereto, nor shall Company be entitled to seek to enjoin or restrain the exhibition, distribution, advertising, exploitation or marketing of the Picture.

Your countersignature below will confirm this Agreement.

Sincerely,

_____
By:
Its:

AGREED TO AND ACCEPTED:

Date: _____

"COMPANY"

_____
By:
Its:

CHAPTER 11

RETAINER AND AGENCY AGREEMENTS

ATTORNEYS

California requires lawyers to have written fee agreements with their clients whenever the client's total expenses, including fees, will likely exceed $1,000 (Business & Professions Code § 6148). A written fee agreement protects the client because it spells out how and what the lawyer charges for services.

The agreement must disclose the lawyer's hourly rate and other charges, the general nature of legal services to be provided and the responsibilities of the lawyer and client under the agreement.

As of January 1, 1993, California requires all California lawyers to disclose to their clients whether or not they have errors and omissions insurance (i.e., malpractice insurance), and the policy limits if coverage is less than $100,000 per claim, $300,000 in the aggregate.

If the lawyer fails to comply with the above requirements, the fee agreement becomes voidable at the client's option. In that case the lawyer would be entitled to a "reasonable" fee regardless of the terms of the agreement.

Lawyers are regulated and subject to discipline by their state bar.

CONTRACTS
FOR THE
FILM AND
TELEVISION
INDUSTRY

264

ATTORNEY-CLIENT FEE CONTRACT

This ATTORNEY-CLIENT FEE CONTRACT ("Contract") is entered into by and between   ("Client") and _____ ("Attorney").

1. CONDITIONS: This Contract will not take effect, and Attorney will have no obligation to provide legal services, until Client returns a signed copy of this Contract and pays the deposit called for under paragraph 3.

2. SCOPE AND DUTIES: Client hires Attorney to provide legal services in connection with entertainment counseling, negotiation and contracts. Attorney shall provide those legal services reasonably required to represent Client and shall take reasonable steps to keep Client informed of progress and to respond to Client's inquiries. Attorney's services will not include litigation of any kind, whether in court, in administrative hearings or before government agencies or judicial arbitration. Client shall be truthful with Attorney, cooperate with Attorney, keep Attorney informed of developments, abide by this Contract, pay Attorney's bills on time and keep Attorney advised of Client's address, telephone number and whereabouts.

3. DEPOSIT: Client shall deposit $_____ by _____. The sum will be deposited in a trust account, to be used to pay costs and expenses and fees for legal services. Client hereby authorizes Attorney to withdraw sums from the trust account to pay the costs and/or fees Client incurs. Any unused deposit at the conclusion of Attorney's services will be refunded.

4. LEGAL FEES: Client agrees to pay for legal services at the following rates: Attorney_____/hr; law clerks $__/hour; secretarial $__/hr. Attorney charges in minimum units of 1/4 hours. Attorney's billable time includes phone conferences with client and with third parties on client's behalf. Other arrangements:

5. COSTS AND EXPENSES: In addition to paying legal fees, Client shall reimburse Attorney for all costs and expenses incurred by Attorney, including, but not limited to fees fixed by law or assessed by public agencies, long distance telephone calls, messenger and other delivery fees, postage, photocopying at $.10 per page, parking, mileage at $.25 per mile, investigation expenses, consultants' fees and other similar items. Client authorizes Attorney to incur all reasonable costs. Attorney shall obtain Client's consent before retaining outside investigators or consultants. Attorney shall obtain Client's consent before incurring any cost in excess of $500.

6. STATEMENTS: Attorney shall send Client periodic statements for fees and costs incurred. Client shall pay Attorney's statements within ten (10) days after each statement's date. Client may request a statement at intervals of no less than thirty (30) days. Upon Client's request Attorney will provide a statement within ten (10) days. Statements unpaid for more than thirty (30) days are subject to a late charge at the legal rate of interest.

7. DISCHARGE AND WITHDRAWAL: Client may discharge Attorney at any time. Attorney may withdraw with Client's consent or for good cause. Good cause includes Client's breach of this Contract, Client's refusal to cooperate with Attorney or to follow Attorney's advice on a material matter or any other fact or circumstance that would render Attorney's continuing representation unlawful or unethical. Attorney has the right to discontinue work if client has failed to pay attorney in accordance with this agreement.

8. CONCLUSION OF SERVICES: When Attorney's services conclude, all unpaid charges shall become immediately due and payable. After Attorney's services conclude, Attorney will, upon Client's request, deliver Client's file to Client, along with any Client funds or property in Attorney's possession.

9. LIEN: Client hereby grants Attorney a lien on any and all claims or causes of action that are the subject of Attorney's representation under this Contract. Attorney's lien will be for any sums due and owing to Attorney at the conclusion of Attorney's services. The lien will attach to any recovery Client may obtain, whether by arbitration award, judgment, settlement or otherwise.

10. DISCLAIMER OF GUARANTEE/INSURANCE: Nothing in this Contract and nothing in Attorney's statements to Client will be construed as a promise or guarantee about the outcome of Client's matter. Attorney makes no such promises or guarantees. Attorney's comments about the outcome of Client's matter are expressions of opinion only. Attorney does not maintains Errors and Omissions Insurance.

11. EFFECTIVE DATE: This Contract will take effect when Client has performed the conditions stated in paragraph 1, but its effective date will be retroactive to the date Attorney first provided services. The date at the beginning of this Contract is for reference only. Even if this Contract does not take effect, Client will be obligated to pay Attorney the reasonable value of any services Attorney may have performed for Client. This contract has been entered into in the City of Santa Monica, County of Los Angeles.

_____   _____

CLIENT

Date: Date:

CONTRACTS
FOR THE
FILM AND
TELEVISION
INDUSTRY

266

AGENTS

An agent differs from an attorney in several important respects. First, the agent is a salesperson whose primary role is to find employment for his clients. An agent spends a lot of time surveying the town to determine what potential buyers (i.e., studios, producers) are seeking and then tries to fill their needs from his client list. While a lawyer might help a client find work, the lawyer's primary role is to negotiate deals and protect the legal rights of the client. Lawyers don't systematically cover the town the way agents do.

Second, agents work on a contingent fee basis. In California agents are limited to a ten percent commission. For instance, if an agent sells a client's screenplay for $50,000, the agent would receive a fee of $5,000. Lawyers, on the other hand, usually work on an hourly basis, often charging $300 or more for each hour of their time. Some law firms charge clients a percentage, often five percent, for their services. This type of deal, however, is usually offered only to clients who work on a steady basis.

From the client's point of view the advantage of a contingent fee is that the client doesn't incur any expense unless and until a deal is closed. The agent or attorney has a strong incentive to conclude the deal. On the other hand, if an attorney only spends a few hours on a deal, a contingent fee may amount to a much larger fee than if he billed on an hourly basis.

Agents may negotiate routine deals for clients without the assistance of a lawyer. More complex matters require an attorney. Clients may want both an agent and an attorney to look out for their interests. Lawyers may be more aggressive than agents. As salespeople, agents may be reluctant to push too hard because they know they need to return to the buyer next week to sell another project or client.

California and some other states license talent agents. In those states, one cannot perform the function of a talent agent without obtaining a license. An agent who engages in wrongdoing may lose his license. Personal managers, on the other hand, are not licensed. They are not supposed to solicit work for their clients, but they often do so nevertheless. In such a case, the personal manager is in a vulnerable position because the client may be able to revoke the representation agreement and not pay the manager.

Agents may enter into franchise agreements with one or more talent guilds. These franchise agreements take precedence over any agreement between the agent and a guild member. The franchise agreements require agents to provide talent with certain minimum terms. For example, talent may have the right to terminate the agency agreement if the agent is unable to secure any offers of employment within a set period.

Agents don't always enter into written representation agreements with their clients. They may work on a handshake. This may be acceptable to the client since the agent's conduct is regulated by the state and one or more guilds. Moreover, a written agreement doesn't guarantee that an agent will find the client work. From a practical point of view, if an agent is unable to secure work there is no sense in continuing the relationship for either party.

The agency agreement defines the fields in which the agent will represent the client. A client involved in multi-disciplinary activities may need several agents. For example, the client may sign a New York literary agent to represent her in publishing, a Hollywood talent agent for screenwriting, and a personal appearance agent for live performances. Some agencies cover several fields while others specialize in one. For instance, one agency may specialize in dancers, another in television commercials. While a person may have several agents, the agents will usually insist on exclusivity within their field.

CONTRACTS
FOR THE
FILM AND
TELEVISION
INDUSTRY

268

SAG MOTION PICTURE / TELEVISION AGENCY CONTRACT

THIS AGREEMENT, made and entered into at _____, by and between _____, a talent agent, hereinafter called the "Agent", and _____ , _____ (social security number) hereinafter called the "Actor".

WITNESSETH:

(1) The Actor engages the Agent as his agent for the following fields as defined in Screen Actors Guild Codified Agency. Regulations, Rule 16(g) and the Agent accepts such engagement:

[Theatrical Motion Pictures] [Television Motion Pictures]

If television motion pictures are included herein for purposes of representation and if during the term of this agency contract, the Actor enters into a series or term employment contract for services in television motion pictures, under which he agrees also to render services in program commercials or spots, this agency contract shall include representation of the Actor in connection with his employment in said commercials, and representation of the Actor in said commercials shall not be deemed included in any separate agency contract which the Actor may have entered into covering commercials.

This contract is limited to motion pictures in the above-designated field(s) and to contracts of the Actor as an actor in such motion pictures, and any reference herein to contracts or employment whereby Actor renders his services refers to contracts or employment in such motion pictures unless otherwise specifically stated.

(2) The term of this contract shall be for a period of _____, commencing _____, 199_.

(3) (a) The Actor agrees to pay to the Agent as commissions a sum equal to _____ percent of all moneys or other consideration received by the Actor, directly or indirectly, under contracts of employment (or in connection with his employment under said employment contracts) entered into during the term specified in Paragraph (2) or in existence when this agency contract is entered into except to such extent as the Actor may be obligated to pay commissions on such existing employment contract to another agent. Commissions shall be payable when and as such moneys or other consideration are received by the Actor, or by anyone else for or on the Actor's behalf. Commission payments are subject to the limitations of Rule 16(g).

(b) Commissions on compensation paid to Actors for domestic reruns, theatrical exhibition, foreign exhibition or supplementary market exhibition of television motion pictures are subject to the provisions of Rule 16(g).

(c) Commissions on commercials included herein under paragraph (1) above shall be subject to the rules governing commercials provided by Rule 16(g).

(d) No commissions shall be payable on any of the following:

(i) Separate amounts paid to Actor not as compensation but for travel or living expenses incurred by Actor;

(ii) Separate amounts paid to Actor not as compensation but as reimbursement for necessary expenditures actually incurred by Actor in connection with Actor's employment, such as for damage to or loss of wardrobe. special hairdress, etc.;

(iii) Amounts paid to Actor as penalties for violations by Producer of any of the provisions of the SAG collective bargaining contracts, such as meal period violations, rest period violations, penalties or interest on delinquent payments;

(iv) Sums payable to Actors for the release on free television or for supplemental market exhibition of theatrical motion pictures produced after January 31, 1960, under the provisions of the applicable collection bargaining agreement providing for such payment; however, if an Actor's individual theatrical motion picture employment contract provides for compensation in the event the motion picture made for theatrical exhibition is exhibited over free television or in supplemental market exhibition, in excess of the minimum compensation payable under the applicable collective bargaining agreement in effect at the time the employment contract was executed, commissions shall be payable on such compensation.

(v) Sums payable to Actors for foreign telecasting on free television of television motion pictures and commercials under the provisions of the applicable collective bargaining agreements; however, if an individual Actor's contract provides for compensation in excess of minimum under the applicable collective bargaining agreements in effect at the time of employment, commissions shall be payable on such sums.

(vi) On any employment contract which is in violation of SAG collective bargaining agreements. For example, employment contracts providing for 'free days,' 'free rehearsal,' 'free looping," "a break in consecutive employment," etc., shall not be commissionable. This paragraph is not subject to SAG waiver.

(vii) On any employment contract for television motion pictures which provide for any prepayment or buyout of domestic or foreign residuals or theatrical release, or supplemental market fees, other than those permitted by the appropriate SAG collective bargaining agreement, unless such provisions of individual employment contracts are expressly approved by SAG.

(e) Any moneys or other consideration received by the Actor, or by anyone for or on his behalf, in connection with any termination of any contract of the Actor by virtue of which the Agent would otherwise be entitled to receive commission, or in connection with the settlement of any such contract, or any litigation arising out of any such contract, shall also be moneys in connection with which the Agent is entitled to the aforesaid percentage; provided, however, that in such event the Actor shall be entitled to deduct attorneys' fees, expenses and court costs before computing the amount upon which the Agent is entitled to his percentage. The Actor shall also be entitled to deduct reasonable legal expenses in connection with the collection of moneys or other consideration due the Actor arising out of an employment contract in motion pictures before computing the amount upon which the Agent is entitled to his percentage.

(f) The aforesaid percentage shall be payable by the Actor to the Agent during the term of this contract and thereafter only where specifically provided herein and in the Regulations.

CONTRACTS
FOR THE
FILM AND
TELEVISION
INDUSTRY

270

(g) The Agent shall be entitled to the aforesaid percentage after the expiration of the term specified in Paragraph (2) for so long a period thereafter as the Actor continues to receive moneys or other consideration under or upon employment contracts entered into by the Actor during the term specified in Paragraph (2) hereof, including moneys or other consideration received by the Actor under the extended term of any such employment contract, resulting from the exercise of an option or options under such an employment contract, extending the term of such employment contact, whether such options be exercised prior to or after the expiration of the term specified in Paragraph (2), subject, however, to the applicable limitations set forth in the Regulations.

(h) If during the period the Agent is entitled to commissions a contract of employment of the Actor be terminated before the expiration of the term thereof, as said term has been extended by the exercise of options therein contained, by joint action of the Actor and employer, or by the action of either of them, other than on account of Act of God, illness. or the like, and the Actor enters into a new contract of employment with said employer within a period of sixty (60) days, such new contract shall be deemed to be in substitution of the contract terminated as aforesaid, subject, however, to the applicable limitations set forth in the Regulations. No contract entered into after said sixty (60) day period shall be deemed to be in substitution of the contract terminated as aforesaid. Contracts of substitution have the same effect as contracts for which they were substituted; provided, however, any increase or additional salary, bonus or other compensation payable to the actor thereunder over and above the amounts payable under the contract of employment which was terminated shall be deemed an adjustment and, unless the Agent shall have a valid agency contract in effect at the time of such adjustment, the Agent shall not be entitled to any commissions on any such additional or increased amounts. In no event may a contract of substitution with an employer extend the period of time during which the Agent is entitled to commission beyond the period that the Agent would have been entitled to commission had no substitution taken place. A change in form of an employer for the purpose of evading this provision or a change in the corporate form of an employer resulting from reorganization or the like shall not preclude the application of these provisions.

(i) So long as the Agent receives commissions from the Actor, the Agent shall be obliged to service the Actor and perform the obligations of this agency contract with respect to the services of the Actor on which such commissions are based, unless the Agent is relieved therefrom under express provisions of the Regulations.

(j) The Agent has no right to receive money unless the Actor receives the same, or unless the same is received for or on his behalf, and then only in the above percentage when and as received. Money paid pursuant to legal process to the Actor's creditors, or by virtue of assignment or direction of the Actor, and deductions from the Actor's compensation made pursuant to law in the nature of a collection or tax at the source, such as Social Security, Old Age Pension taxes, State Disability taxes or income taxes shall be treated as compensation received for or on the Actor's behalf.

(4) Should the Agent, during the term specified in Paragraph (2), negotiate a contract of employment for the Actor and secure for the Actor a bona fide offer of employment, which offer is communicated by the Agent to the Actor in reasonable detail and in writing or by other corroborative action. which offer the Actor declines, and if, within sixty (60) days after the date upon which the Agent gives such information to the Actor, the Actor accepts said offer of em-

ployment on substantially the same terms, then the Actor shall be required to pay commissions to the Agent upon such contract of employment. If an agent engaged under a prior agency contract is entitled to collect commissions under the foregoing circumstances, the Agent with whom this contract is executed waives his commission to the extent that the prior agent is entitled to collect the same.

(5) (a) The Agent may represent other persons who render services in motion pictures, or in other branches of the entertainment industry.

(b) Unless and until prohibited by the Actor, the Agent may make known the fact that he is the sole and exclusive representative of the Actor in the motion picture fields covered hereby. However, it is expressly understood that even though the Agent has not breached the contract the Actor may at any time with or without discharging the Agent, and regardless of whether he has legal grounds for discharge of the Agent, by written notice to the Agent prohibit him from rendering further services for the Actor or from holding himself out as the Actor's Agent, and such action shall not give Agent any rights or remedies against Actor, the Agent's rights under this paragraph continuing only as long as Actor consents thereto but this does not apply to the Agent's right to commissions. In the event of any such written notice to the Agent the 91-day period set forth in Paragraph (6) of this agency contract is suspended and extended by the period of time that the Agent is prohibited from rendering services for the Actor.

(6) (a) If this is an initial agency contract and if actor fails to be employed and receive, or be entitled to receive compensation for ten (10) days' employment in the initial 151 days of the contract, provided further that if no bona fide offer of employment is received by the Actor within any consecutive period of 120 days during the initial 151 day period, or if during any other period of 91 days immediately preceding the giving of the notice of termination hereinafter mentioned in this paragraph, the Actor fails to be employed and receive, or be entitled to receive compensation for ten (10) days' employment, whether such employment is from fields under SAG's jurisdiction or any other branch of the entertainment industry in which the Agent may be authorized by written contract to represent the Actor, then either the Actor or Agent may terminate the engagement of the Agent hereunder by written notice to the other party, subject to the qualifications hereinafter in this paragraph set forth. Each day the Actor renders services or may be required to render services in motion pictures shall count as one (1) day's employment. For the purpose of determining what is a day's employment in other fields of the entertainment industry the following rules shall govern:

(i) Each separate original radio broadcast (including rehearsal time), whether live or recorded, and each transcribed program shall be considered a day's employment.

(ii) Each separate live television broadcast shall be considered a minimum of two (2) days' employment. However, each day spent in rehearsal over the minimum of two (2) days inclusive of the day of telecast, shall be considered an additional one-half (1/2)day's employment.

(iii) A rebroadcast, whether recorded or live, or by an off the line recording, or by a prior recording, or time spent in rehearsal for any employment in the radio broadcasting or radio transcription industry shall not be considered such employment. A retelecast of a live television program and a rerun of television motion picture entertainment film or commercial shall likewise not be considered such employment.

CONTRACTS
FOR THE
FILM AND
TELEVISION
INDUSTRY

272

(iv) Each master phonograph record recorded by the Actor shall be one (1) day's employment.

(v) In all other branches of the entertainment industry, except as set forth above, each day the Actor renders services or may be required to render services for compensation shall count as one (l) day's employment.

(b) The 91 day period which is the basis of termination shall be extended by the amount of employment the Actor would have received from calls for his services in any other branch of the entertainment industry in which the Actor is a recognized performer and at or near the Actor's usual places of employment at a salary and from an employer commensurate with the Actor's prestige, which calls are actually received by the Agent and reported to the Actor in writing or by other corroborative action, when the Actor is in such a locality (away from his usual places of employment) that he cannot return in response to such a call, or when the Actor is unable to respond to such a call by reason of physical or mental incapacity or any other reason beyond his control, or by reason of another engagement in a field in which the Actor is not represented by the Agent; provided, however, that if the Actor is rendering services in another engagement in a field in which the Agent is authorized to represent the Actor, then the time spent in such engagement shall not be added to the 91 day period. Regardless of whether or not the Agent is authorized to represent the Actor on the legitimate stage, if the Actor accepts an engagement on the legitimate stage under a run of the play contract, the 91 day period which is the basis of termination shall be extended by the length of such run of the play contract including rehearsals. The 91 day period which is the basis of termination shall also be extended for any period of time during which the Actor has declared himself to be unavailable and has so notified the Agent in writing or by other corroborative action or has confirmed in writing or by other corroborative action a communication from the Agent to such effect.

(c) In the event that the Agent has given the Actor notice in writing or by other corroborative action, of a bona fide offer of employment as an actor in any branch of the entertainment industry in which the Actor is a recognized performer at or near his usual place of employment at a salary and from an employer commensurate with the Actor's prestige (and there is in fact such an offer), which notice sets forth in detail the terms of the proposed employment and the Actor refuses or fails within a reasonable time after receipt of such notice to accept such proffered employment, then the period of guaranteed employment in said offer shall be deemed as time worked by the Actor in computing time worked with reference to the right of the Actor to terminate under the provisions of this paragraph.

(d) The Actor may not exercise the right of termination if at the time he attempts to do so:

The Actor is under a contract or contracts for the rendition of his services in the entertainment industry, in any or all fields in which the Agent is authorized by written contract to represent the Actor, which contract or contracts in the aggregate guarantee the Actor:

(i) compensation for such services of Seventy. Thousand ($70,000.00) Dollars or more, or

(ii) Fifty (50) or more days' employment, during the 91 days in question plus the succeeding 273 days after said 91 day period.

(e) Saturdays, Sundays and holidays are included in counting days elapsed during the 91 and 273 day periods provided.

(f) No termination hereunder shall deprive the Agent of the right to receive commission or compensation on moneys earned or received by the Actor prior to the date of termination, or earned or received by the Actor after the date of termination of the Agent's engagement, on contracts for the Actor's services entered into by the Actor prior to the effective date of any, such termination.

(g) Periods of lay-off, leave of absence, or any periods during which the Actor is not performing and is prohibited from rendering services for others in the motion picture field under and during the term of any motion picture employment contract shall not be deemed periods of unemployment hereunder. The "term of any motion picture employment contract" as used in this subparagraph shall not include any unexercised options.

(h) Where the Actor does not actually render his services for which he has been employed but nevertheless is compensated therefor, the same shall be considered as employment hereunder. This shall not apply to employment on live television shows, which employment is computed according to the formula set forth in subparagraph (a) (ii) hereof.

(i) If, at any time during the term of the agency contract, the production of motion pictures in general (as distinguished from production at one or more studios) should be suspended, thereupon the 91-day period herein mentioned shall be extended by the period of such suspension.

(j) If the Actor is under an employment contract which provides that any part of the Actor's guaranteed compensation shall be deferred or if said compensation is spread over a period prior or subsequent to the time of the actual performance of Actor's services under said employment contract, then for the purpose of determining the Actor's right to terminate under the provisions of subparagraph (d) hereof, the guaranteed compensation shall be deemed to have been paid to the actor during the period of *the actual performance of Actor's services under said employment contract.

(k) Anything herein to the contrary notwithstanding, if the Agent submits to the Actor a bona fide offer of employment in writing or by other corrobative action, as defined in Paragraph (6) subparagraph (c), after the right of termination has accrued under Paragraph (6) but the Actor has not yet terminated the agency contract, and if the Actor thereafter terminates the agency contract pursuant to Paragraph (6) and thereafter accepts the offer within sixty (60) days of the date of submission of the offer to the Actor by the agent, the Actor shall the pay the Agent commission on the compensation received by the Actor pursuant to such offer.

(l) Other than in cases of initial agency contracts subject to the 151 day clause provided by the first paragraph of this paragraph (6), the right of termination provided by the 91 day termination provisions of this Paragraph (6), the Actor shall also have the right of termination beginning with the 82nd day of the 91 day period whenever it becomes apparent that the Agent will be unable to procure the required employment pursuant to this Paragraph (6) during such 91 day period. In considering whether it has become so apparent, the possibility that after the Actor exercises the right of termination, the Agent might preclude exercise of the right by compliance with subparagraphs (b), (c) or (d) hereof, shall be disregarded. To illustrate: If the Actor has had no employment for 82 days, Actor may terminate on the 82nd day, since only 9 days remain,

CONTRACTS
FOR THE
FILM AND
TELEVISION
INDUSTRY

274

and Agent cannot obtain 10 days' employment for the Actor in such period. If Actor received one day's employment in 83 days, Actor may terminate on the 83rd day, since only 8 days remain, and Agent cannot obtain 10 days' employment for Actor in such period.

(m) Employment at SAG minimum shall be deemed "employment" and/or "work" for purposes of this Paragraph (6).

(7) Rule 16(g) of the Screen Actors Guild, Inc. which contains regulations governing the relations of its members to talent agents is hereby referred to and by this reference hereby incorporated herein and made a part of this contract. The provisions of said Rule are herein sometimes referred to as the "Regulations" and the Screen Actors Guild, Inc. is herein sometimes referred to as "SAG."

(8) The Agent agrees that during the term of this contract the following persons only shall have the responsibility of personally supervising the Actor's business and of servicing and being available to the Actor. The name of one of the persons shall be inserted in the Actor's own handwriting.

(This italicized provision is a note from SAG to the Actor and not a part of the contract. If the Actor is executing this contract in reliance on the fact that a particular person is connected with the Agent, then the Actor should insert only such person's name in the space following. If the Actor is not executing this contract in reliance on such fact, then the Agent shall insert not more than one name, and the Actor shall insert one name.)

The Agent upon request of the Actor, shall assign either one of such persons who may be available (and at least one of them always shall be upon reasonable notice from the Actor) and whom the Actor may designate to conduct negotiations for the Actor at such city or its environs and such person shall do so; itbeing understood that sub-agents employed by the Agent who are not named herein may handle agency matters for the Actor or may aid either of the named persons in handling agency matters for the Actor. In the event both of the persons above named shall cease to be active in the affairs of the Agent by reason of death, disability, retirement or any other reason, the Actor shall have the right to terminate this contract upon written notice to the Agent. The rights of the parties in such case are governed by Sections XI and XII of the Regulations.

9) The Agent agrees to maintain telephone service and an office open during all reasonable business hours (emergencies such as sudden illness or death excepted) within the city of _____ , or its environs, throughout the term of this agreement and that some representative of the Agent will be present at such office during such business hours. This contract is void unless the blank in this paragraph is filled in with the name of a city at which the Agent does maintain an office to render services to actors.

(10) If the Actor is employed under a series or term contract the Actor shall have the right to terminate this contract during the 30day period immediately following any annual anniversary date of the series or term contract then in effect by giving the Agent 30 days' written notice of his intention to so terminate this contract. Exercise of this termination right shall not affect the Actor's commissions obligation hereunder.

(11) Any controversy under this contract, or under any contract executed in renewal or extension hereof or in substitution hereof or alleged to have been so executed, or as to the existence, execution or validity hereof or thereof, or the right of either party to void this or any such contract or alleged contract

on any grounds, or the construction, performance, nonperformance, operation, breach, continuance or termination of this or any such contract, shall be submitted to arbitration in accordance with the arbitration provisions in the Regulations regardless of whether either party has terminated or purported to terminate this or any such contract or alleged contract. Under this contract the Agent undertakes to endeavor to secure employment for the Actor. This provision is inserted in this contract pursuant to a rule of the SAG, a bona fide labor union, which Rule regulates the relations of its members to talent agents. Reasonable written notice shall be given to the Labor Commissioner of the State of California of the time and place of any arbitration hearing hereunder. The Labor Commissioner of the State of California, or his authorized representative, has the right to attend all arbitration hearings. The clauses relating to the Labor Commissioner of the State of California shall not be applicable to cases not failing under the provisions of Section 1700.45 of the Labor Code of the State of California.

(12) Both parties hereto state and agree that they are bound by the Regulations and by all of the modifications heretofore or hereafter made thereto pursuant to the Basic Contract and by all waivers granted by SAG pursuant to said Basic Contract or to the Regulations.

(13) (a) Anything herein to the contrary notwithstanding, if the Regulations should be held invalid, all references thereto in this contract shall be eliminated; all limitations of the Regulations on any of the provisions of this contract shall be released. and the portions of this contract including, but not limited to Paragraphs (8) and (11) which depend upon reference to the Regulations shall be deleted, and the provisions of this contract otherwise shall remain valid and enforceable.

(b) Likewise, if any portion of the Regulations should be held invalid, such holding shall not affect the validity of remaining portions of the Regulations or of this contract; and if the portion of the Regulations so held invalid should be a portion specifically referred to in this contract, then such referenceshall be eliminated herefrom in the same manner and with like force and effect as herein provided in the event the Regulations are held invalid; and the provisions of this contract otherwise shall remain valid and enforceable.

Whether or not the Agent is the Actor's agent at the time this contract is executed. it is understood that in executing this contact each party has independent access to the Regulations and has relied exclusively upon his own knowledge thereof.

IN WITNESS WHEREOF, the parties hereto have executed this agreement the _____ day of _____ , 19__.

_____
Actor

_____
Agent

By:

This talent agent is licensed by the Labor Commissioner of the State of California.

CONTRACTS
FOR THE
FILM AND
TELEVISION
INDUSTRY

276

This talent agent is franchised by the Screen Actors Guild, Inc.
The form of this contract has been approved by the State Labor Commissioner
of the State of California on January 11, 1991.

This form of contract has been approved by the Screen Actors Guild, Inc.

CHAPTER 12

GLOSSARY OF TERMS

Above-the-line costs Portion of the budget which covers major creative participants (writer, director, actors and producer), including script and story-development costs.

Adjusted gross participation Gross participation minus certain costs, such as cost of advertising and duplication. Also called *Rolling Gross*. If many deductions are allowed, the participant is essentially getting a "net profit" deal.

Advance Money obtained up-front in anticipation of future profits that count against monies (or royalties) that may be payable at some time in the future. A non-recoupable advance (sometimes called a *guarantee*) is a payment that is not refundable, even if future monies are never due.

Answer print The first composite (sound and picture) motion-picture print from the laboratory with editing, score and mixing completed. Usually color values will need to be corrected before a release print is made.

Art theater Shows specialized art films, generally in exclusive engagements, rather than mass-marketed studio films.

Auteur A French term, the auteur theory holds that the director is the true creator or author of a film, bringing together script, actors, cinematographer, editor and molding everything into a work of cinematic art with a cohesive vision. Anyone who has worked on a movie knows what complete nonsense this theory is. Filmmaking is a collaborative endeavor and the director is only one of the contributors.

Back end Profit participation in a film after distribution and/or production costs have be recouped.

CONTRACTS
FOR THE
FILM AND
TELEVISION
INDUSTRY

278

Below-the-line costs The technical expenses and labor including set construction, crew, camera equipment, film stock, developing and printing.

Between projects Out of work.

Blind bidding Requiring theater owners to bid on a movie without seeing it. Several states and localities require open trade screenings for each new release. Guarantees and advances may also be banned.

Blow-up Optical process of enlarging a film, usually from 16mm to 35mm.

Box-office gross Total revenues taken in at a movie-theater box offices before any expenses or percentages are deducted.

Box-office receipts What the theater owner takes in from ticket sales to customers at the box office. A portion of this revenue is remitted to the studio/distributor in the form of rental payments.

Break To open a film in several theaters simultaneously, either in and around a single city or in a group of cities, or on a national basis.

Breakout To expand bookings after an initial period of exclusive or limited engagement.

Completion bond A form of insurance which guarantees completion of a film in the event that the producer exceeds the budget and is unable to secure additional funding. Completion bonds are sometimes required by banks and investors to secure loans and investments in a production. Should a bond be invoked, the completion guarantor will assume control over the production and be in a recoupment position superior to all investors. Do you really want an insurance company finishing your film?

Cross-collateralization Practice by which distributors offset financial loses in one medium or market against profits derived from others. For example, the rentals obtained from France are combined with those from Italy, and after the expenses for both are deducted, the remainder, if any, is profit. Filmmakers don't like to have the markets for their films cross-collateralized because it may reduce the amount of money they are likely to see.

Crossover film Film that initially is targeted for a narrow specialty market but achieves acceptance in a wider market.

Day and date The simultaneous opening of two or more movie theaters in one or more cities.

Day player An actor who works a day at a time on a film. In other words, actors with bit parts.

Deferred payment   Writers, directors, actors and others may take only part of their salary up front in order to reduce the budget of the picture. The rest of their fee is paid from box-office and other revenues that may, or may not, accrue later.

Development   The process by which an initial idea is turned into a finished screenplay. Includes optioning the rights to an underlying literary property and commissioning writer(s) to create a treatment, first draft, second draft, rewrite, and polish.

Distributor   A company that markets a motion picture, placing it in theaters, advertising and promoting it. The major studios nowadays are mostly in the business of financing and distributing films, leaving production to smaller independent companies.

Direct advertising   Direct outreach to consumers such as mailing fliers. Usually targeted to a specific interest group.

Display advertising   Advertising which features artwork or title treatment specific to a given film, in newspaper and magazine advertising.

Distribution expenses   Includes taxes, guild payments, trade-association dues, conversion/transmission costs, collection costs, checking costs, advertising and publicity costs, re-editing costs, prints, foreign-version costs, transportation and shipping costs, copyright costs, copyright-infringement costs, insurance, royalties, and claims and lawsuits.

Domestic rights   Rights within U.S. and Canada only.

Double distribution fees   Where distributor uses a sub-distributor to sell to a territory. If both distributors are allowed to deduct their standard fees, the filmmaker is less likely to see any money.

Downbeat ending   A story that ends unhappily or in a depressing manner.

Exclusive opening   A type of release whereby a film is opened in a single theater in a major city, giving the distributor the option to hold the film for a long, exclusive run or move it into additional theaters based on the film's performance.

Feature film   Full-length, fictional films (not documentaries or shorts) generally for theatrical release.

Film noir   Dark, violent, urban, downbeat films, many of which were made in the '40s and '50s.

Film rental   What the theater owner pays the distributor for the right to show the movie. As a rough rule of thumb, this usually amount to about half of the box-office gross.

CONTRACTS
FOR THE
FILM AND
TELEVISION
INDUSTRY

280

Final cut   The last stage in the editing process. The right to final cut is the right to determine the ultimate artistic control over the picture. Usually the studio or the financier of a picture retains final cut.

First-dollar gross   The most favorable form of gross participation for the participant. Only a few deductions, such as checking fees, taxes and trade-association dues are deductible.

First money   From the producer's point of view, the first revenue received from the distribution of a movie. Not to be confused with profits, first monies are generally allocated to investors until recoupment, but may be allocated in part or in whole to deferred salaries owed talent or deferred fees owed the film laboratory.

First run   The first engagement of a new film.

Floors   In distributor/exhibitor agreements, the minimum percentage of box-office receipts that the distributor is entitled to, regardless of the theater's operating expenses. Generally decline week by week over the course of an engagement. Generally range from 70% to 25%.

Foreign sales   Licensing a film in various territories and media outside the U.S. and Canada. Although Canada is a foreign country, American distributors typically acquire Canadian rights when they buy U.S. domestic rights.

Four-walling   Renting a theater and its staff for a flat fee, buying your own advertising and receiving all the revenue. The exhibitor is paid his flat fee regardless of performance and receives no split of box-office receipts.

Front office   The top executives, the people who control the money.

General partners   management side of a limited partnership (the position usually occupied by the film's producers), which structures a motion-picture investment and raises money from investors who become limited partners. General partners control all business decisions regarding the partnership.

Grassroots campaign   Using fliers, posters, stickers and building word-of-mouth with special screenings for local community groups.

Gross after breakeven   The participant shares in the gross after the breakeven point has been reached. The breakeven point can be a set amount or determined by a formula.

Gross box office.   Total revenue taken in at theater box office for ticket sales.

Gross participation   A piece of gross receipts without any deductions for distribution fees or expenses or production costs. However, deductions for checking and collection costs, residuals and taxes are usually deductible. A "piece of the gross" is the most advantageous type of participation from the filmmaker's or writer's point of view. In an audit, it is the most easily verified form of participation.

Gross receipts   Studio/distributor revenues derived from all media, including film rentals, television sales, merchandising and ancillary sales.

Hot   Anyone whose last picture was a big hit, won an Academy Award or is being lionized by the media. A transitional state.

House nut   Weekly operating expenses of a movie theater.

Hyphenates   Persons who fulfill two or more major roles, such as producer-director, writer-director or actor-director.

Key art   Artwork used in posters and ads for a movie.

Limited partnership   Instrument of investment commonly used to finance movies. General partners initiate and control the partnership, limited partners are the investors and have no control of the running of the partnership business and no legal or financial liabilities beyond the amount they have invested.

Merchandising rights   Right to license, manufacture and distribute merchandise based on characters, names or events in a picture.

Mini-multiple   Type of release which falls between an exclusive engagement and a wide release, consisting of quality theaters in strategic geographic locations, generally a precludsion to a wider break.

Multi-tiered audience   An audience of different types of people who find the film attractive for different reasons, and who must be reached by different publicity, promotion or ads.

Negative cost   Actual cost of producing a film through to the manufacture of a completed negative (does not include costs of prints or advertising). It may be defined to include overhead expenses, interest and other expenses which may inflate the amount way beyond what was actually spent to make the film.

Negative pickup   A distributor guarantees to pay a specified amount for distribution rights upon delivery of a completed film negative by a specific date. If the picture is not delivered on time and in accordance with the terms of the agreement, the distributor has no obligation to distribute it. A negative pickup guarantee can be used as collateral for a bank loan to obtain production funds.

CONTRACTS
FOR THE
FILM AND
TELEVISION
INDUSTRY

282

Net profit   What is left, if anything, after all allowable deductions are taken. This usually amounts to zero. Typically expressed in terms of 100% of net profits, although payable out of the producer's share.

Off-Hollywood   American independent films made outside the studio system.

Original   A screenplay that has not been adapted from an article, book, play, old movie, etc.

On spec   Working for nothing on the hope and speculation that something will come of it.

Platforming   A method of release whereby a film is opened in a single theater or small group of theaters in a major territory and later expanding to a greater number of theaters.

Playoff   Distribution of a film after key openings.

Regional release   As opposed to a simultaneous national release, a pattern of distribution whereby a film is opened in one or more regions at a time.

Rollout   Distribution of film around the country subsequent to either key city openings or an opening in one city, usually New York.

Run   Length of time a feature plays in theaters or a territory.

Scale   The minimum salary permitted by the guilds.

Shooting script   A later version of the screenplay in which each separate shot is numbered and camera directions are indicated.

Slicks   Standardized ad mechanical, printed on glossary paper, which includes various sizes of display ads for a given film, designed for the insertion of local theater information as needed.

Sleeper   An unexpected hit. A film that audiences fall in love with and make a success.

Specialized distribution   As opposed to commercial distribution, distribution to a limited target audience, in a smaller number of theaters, with a limited advertising budget and reliance upon publicity, reviews and word-of-mouth to build an audience for the picture.

Stills   Photographs taken during production for use later in advertising and/or publicity. Stills should be in a horizontal format and should list below the photo such information as film title, producer/director and cast.

Story analyst or reader   A person employed by a studio or producer to read submitted scripts and properties, synopsize and evaluate them. Often young literature or film school graduates who don't know a great deal about story or filmmaking, but then again their bosses sometimes know even less.

Story conference   A meeting at which the writer receives suggestions as to how to improve his/her script.

Sub-distributor   In theatrical releases, distributors who handle a specific geographic territory. They are sub-contracted by the main distributor, who coordinates the distribution campaign and marketing of all sub-distributors.

Syndication   Distribution of motion pictures to independent commercial television stations on a regional basis.

Talent   The word used to describe those involved in the artistic aspects of filmmaking (i.e., writers, actors, directors) as opposed to the business people.

Target market   The defined audience segment a distributor seeks to reach with its advertising and promotion campaign, such as teens, women over thirty, yuppies, etc.

Television distribution fee   Typically 10% to 25% for U.S. network broadcast sales, 30% to 40% for domestic syndication and 45% to 50% for foreign distribution.

Test marketing   Pre-releasing a film in one or more small, representative markets before committing to an advertising campaign. The effectiveness of the marketing plan can thereby be assessed and modified as needed before the general release.

Theatrical distribution fees   Generally between 30% and 40% of gross film rentals.

Trades   The daily and weekly periodicals of the industry, such as *Daily Variety* and *The Hollywood Reporter.*

Treatment   A prose account of the storyline of a film. Usually between 20 and 50 pages. Comes after outline and before first-draft screenplay.

Wide release   The release of a film in numerous theaters (800 to 2,000).

Window   Period of time in which a film is available in a given medium. Some windows may be open-ended, such as theatrical and home video, or limited, such as pay television or syndication.

APPENDIX

SECTIONS OF THE CALIFORNIA CODE THAT ARE REFERED TO IN THIS BOOK

CIVIL CODE

§ 36 Minors; contracts not disaffirmable

(a) Contracts not disaffirmable. A contract, otherwise valid, entered into during minority, cannot be disaffirmed upon that ground either during the actual minority of the person entering into such contract, or at any time thereafter, in the following cases:

1. Necessaries. A contract to pay the reasonable value of things necessary for his support, or that of his family, entered into by him when not under the care of a parent or guardian able to provide for him or them, provided that these things have been actually furnished to him or to his family.

2. Artistic or creative services; judicial approval.

(A) A contract or agreement pursuant to which such person is employed or agrees to render artistic or creative services, or agrees to purchase, or otherwise secure, sell, lease, license, or otherwise dispose of literary, musical or dramatic properties (either tangible or intangible) or any rights therein for use in motion pictures, television, the production of phonograph records, the legitimate or living stage, or otherwise in the entertainment field, if the contract or agreement has been approved by the superior court in the county in which such minor resides or is employed or, if the minor neither resides in or is employed in this state, if any party to the contract or agreement has its principal office in this state for the transaction of business.

(B) As used in this paragraph, "artistic or creative services" shall include, but not be limited to, services as an actor, actress, dancer, musician, comedian, singer, or other performer or entertainer, or as a writer, director, producer, production executive, choreographer, composer, conductor, or designer.

3. Professional sports contracts; judicial approval. A contract or agreement pursuant to which such person is employed or agrees to render services as a participant or player in professional sports, including, but without being limited to, professional boxers, professional wrestlers, and professional jockeys, if the contract or agreement has been approved by the superior court in the county in which such minor resides or is employed or, if the minor neither resides in or is employed in this state, if any party to the contract or agreement has its principal office in this state for the transaction of business.

(b) Judicial approval; procedure; extent. The approval of the superior court referred to in paragraphs (2) and (3) of subdivision (a) may be given upon the petition of either party to the contract or agreement after such reasonable notice to the other party thereto as may be fixed by said court, with opportunity to such other party to appear and be heard; and its approval when given shall extend to the whole of the contract or agreement, and all of the terms and provisions thereof, including, but without being limited to, any optional or conditional provisions contained therein for extension, prolongation, or termination of the term thereof.

CONTRACTS
FOR THE
FILM AND
TELEVISION
INDUSTRY

286

§ 36.1 Contracts for particular services; trust or savings plan; net earnings; taxes

In any order made by the superior court approving a contract of a minor for the purposes mentioned in Section 36 of this code, the court shall have power, notwithstanding the provisions of any other statute, to require the setting aside and preservation for the benefit of the minor, either in a trust fund or in such other savings plan as the court shall approve, of such portion of the net earnings of the minor, not exceeding one-half thereof, as the court may deem just and proper, and the court may withhold approval of such contract until the parent or parents or guardian, as the case may be, shall execute and file with the court his or their written consent to the making of such order. For the purposes of this section, the net earnings of the minor shall be deemed to be the total sum received for the services of the minor pursuant to such contract less the following: All sums required by law to be paid as taxes to any government or governmental agency; reasonable sums expended for the support, care, maintenance, education and training of the minor; fees and expenses paid in connection with procuring such contract or maintaining the employment of the minor; and the fees of attorneys for services rendered in connection with the contract and other business of the minor.

§ 36.2 Continuing jurisdiction over, and termination of, minor's trust or savings plan

The superior court shall have continuing jurisdiction over any trust or other savings plan established pursuant to Section 36.1 and shall have power at any time, upon good cause shown, to order that any such trust or other savings plan shall be amended or terminated, notwithstanding the provisions of any declaration of trust or other savings plan. Such order shall be made only after such reasonable notice to the beneficiary and to the parent or parents or guardian, if any, as may be fixed by the court, with opportunity to all such parties to appear and be heard.

§ 1427 Obligation defined

OBLIGATION, WHAT. An obligation is a legal duty, by which a person is bound to do or not to do a certain thing.

§ 1428 Creation and enforcement

An obligation arises either from:

One—The contract of the parties; or,

Two—The operation of law.

An obligation arising from operation of law may be enforced in the manner provided by law, or by civil action or proceeding.

§ 1542 General release; extent

A general release does not extend to claims which the creditor does not know or suspect to exist in his favor at the time of executing the release, which if known by him must have materially affected his settlement with the debtor.

§ 1550 Essential elements

ESSENTIAL ELEMENTS OF CONTRACT. It is essential to the existence of a contract that there should be:

1. Parties capable of contracting;
2. Their consent;
3. A lawful object; and,
4. A sufficient cause or consideration.

§ 1607 Lawfulness of consideration

CONSIDERATION LAWFUL. The consideration of a contract must be lawful within the meaning of Section 1667.

§ 1620 Express contract defined

EXPRESS CONTRACT, WHAT. An express contract is one, the terms of which are stated in words.

§ 1624 Statute of frauds

The following contracts are invalid, unless they, or some note or memorandum thereof, are in writing and subscribed by the party to be charged or by the party's agent:

(a) An agreement that by its terms is not to be performed within a year from the making thereof.

(b) A special promise to answer for the debt, default, or miscarriage of another, except in the cases provided for in Section 2794.

(c) An agreement for the leasing for a longer period than one year, or for the sale of real property, or of an interest therein; such an agreement, if made by an agent of the party sought to be charged, is invalid, unless the authority of the agent is in writing, subscribed by the party sought to be charged.

(d) An agreement authorizing or employing an agent, broker, or any other person to purchase or sell real estate, or to lease real estate for a longer period than one year, or to procure, introduce, or find a purchaser or seller of real estate or a lessee or lessor of real estate where the lease is for a longer period than one year, for compensation or a commission.

(e) An agreement which by its terms is not to be performed during the lifetime of the promisor.

(f) An agreement by a purchaser of real property to pay an indebtedness secured by a mortgage or deed of trust upon the property purchased, unless assumption of the indebtedness by the purchaser is specifically provided for in the conveyance of the property.

(g) A contract, promise, undertaking, or commitment to loan money or to grant or extend credit, in an amount greater than one hundred thousand dollars ($100,000), not primarily for personal, family, or household purposes, made by a person engaged in the business of lending or arranging for the lending of money or extending credit. For purposes of this section, a contract, promise, undertaking or commitment to loan money secured solely by residential property consisting of one to four dwelling units shall be deemed to be for personal, family, or household purposes.

This section does not apply to leases subject to Division 10 (commencing with Section 10101) of the Commercial Code.

§ 1667 Unlawfulness defined

WHAT IS UNLAWFUL. That is not lawful which is:

1. Contrary to an express provision of law;
2. Contrary to the policy of express law, though not expressly prohibited; or,
3. Otherwise contrary to good morals.

CONTRACTS
FOR THE
FILM AND
TELEVISION
INDUSTRY

288

BUSINESS & PROFESSIONS CODE

§ 6148 Contracts for services in cases not coming within § 6147; bills rendered by attorney; contents; failure to comply

(a) In any case not coming within Section 6147 in which it is reasonably foreseeable that total expense to a client, including attorney fees, will exceed one thousand dollars ($1,000), the contract for services in the case shall be in writing and shall contain all of the following:

(1) The hourly rate and other standard rates, fees, and charges applicable to the case.

(2) The general nature of the legal services to be provided to the client.

(3) The respective responsibilities of the attorney and the client as to the performance of the contract.

(4) A statement disclosing whether the attorney maintains errors and omissions insurance coverage applicable to the services to be rendered and the policy limits of that coverage if less than one hundred thousand dollars ($100,000) per occurrence up to a maximum of three hundred thousand dollars ($300,000) per policy term.

(b) All bills rendered by an attorney to a client shall clearly state the basis thereof. Bills for the fee portion of the bill shall include the amount, rate, basis for calculation, or other method of determination of the attorney's fees and costs. Bills for the cost and expense portion of the bill shall clearly identify the costs and expenses incurred and the amount of the costs and expenses. Upon request by the client, the attorney shall provide a bill to the client no later than 10 days following the request unless the attorney has provided a bill to the client within 31 days prior to the request, in which case the attorney may provide a bill to the client no later than 31 days following the date the most recent bill was provided. The client is entitled to make similar requests at intervals of no less than 30 days following the initial request. In providing responses to client requests for billing information, the attorney may use billing data that is currently effective on the date of the request, or, if any fees or costs to that date cannot be accurately determined, they shall be described and estimated.

(c) Failure to comply with any provision of this section renders the agreement voidable at the option of the client, and the attorney shall, upon the agreement being voided, be entitled to collect a reasonable fee.

(d) This section shall not apply to any of the following:

(1) Services rendered in an emergency to avoid foreseeable prejudice to the rights or interests of the client or where a writing is otherwise impractical.

(2) An arrangement as to the fee implied by the fact that the attorney's services are of the same general kind as previously rendered to and paid for by the client.

(3) If the client knowingly states in writing, after full disclosure of this section, that a writing concerning fees is not required.

(4) If the client is a corporation.

(e) This section applies prospectively only to fee agreements following its operative date.

ABOUT THE AUTHOR

Mark Litwak is a veteran entertainment attorney known for aggressively representing independent filmmakers who have been cheated by distributors. He has won large awards in compensation for clients after distributors tried to defraud them through creative accounting. He also functions as a producer's representative assisting filmmakers in the marketing and distribution of their films.

Litwak is the author of numerous articles and several books: *Reel Power: The Struggle for Influence and Success in the New Hollywood, Courtroom Crusaders, Dealmaking in the Film and Television Industry,* and the upcoming *Litwak's Multimedia Producer's Guide.*

Litwak maintains his own law practice in Santa Monica, California. As a law professor he has taught entertainment and copyright law at the University of West Los Angeles, U.C.L.A., and Loyola Law School. He has lectured before many filmmakers and university audiences including presentations at the American Film Institute, Columbia University, N.Y.U., U.S.C., U.C.L.A., The New School for Social Research, the University of British Columbia, San Francisco State University, and the Royal College of Art in London.

As an authority on the movie industry, he has been interviewed on more than fifty television and radio shows, including ABC, "The Larry King Show," N.P.R's "All Things Considered," and the Cable News Network.

CONTRACTS ON COMPUTER DISK

Obtain all of the contracts included in ***Contracts for the Film and Television Industry*** on computer disk: Depiction Release (Grant with Reversion), Depiction Release (Option, Short Form), Depiction Release (Documentary, Short Form), Still Photo Release, Submission Release, Non-Disclosure Agreement, Quitclaim Release, Writer Employment Agreement (Theatrical WGA), Writer Employment Agreement (Low-Budget, Non-union), Director Employment Agreement, Actor Employment Agreement (SAG weekly Theatrical), Actor Employment Agreement (Low-Budget, Non-union Day Player), Rider to Day Player Agreement, Extra Agreement, Extra Release, Writer Collaboration Agreement, Joint Venture Agreement, Agreement to Dissolve Joint Venture, Co-production Agreement, TV Music Rights License, Composer Agreement (Low-Budget Feature), Soundtrack Recording Agreement, Finder Agreement, Prospectus, Limited Partnership Agreement, Line Producer Employment Agreement, Casting Director Employment Agreement, Crew Deal Memo, Production Services Agreement, Location Agreement, Theatrical Acquisition/Distribution Agreement, Net Profit Definition, Gross Receipts After Breakeven, Television Distribution Agreement, Home Video Licensing Agreement, Merchandising Agreement, Product Release.

Obtain all of the contracts included in ***Dealmaking in the Film and Television Industry*** on computer disk: Depiction Release, reversion, Depiction Release, option, Depiction Release, documentary short-form, Location Agreement, Option & Literary Purchase Agreement, Writer Employment Agreement, Actor Employment Agreement, SAG weekly theatrical, Actor Employment Agreement, low-budget, non-union, Extra Agreement, Extra Release, Line producer Employment Agreement, Collaboration Release, TV Music Rights License, Composer Agreement, low-budget, Acquisition/Distribution Agreement.

ORDER FORM

Qty	Title	Price @	Total
	***Contracts for the Film/TV Industry* Contracts**	$125.00	
	***Dealmaking* Contracts**	$ 99.00	

Contracts are sent on 3.5 inch high-density disks formatted for IBM and IBM compatibles. Please indicate desired format:

☐ Microsoft Word

☐ Wordstar

☐ Wordperfect

☐ ASCII

Sub-total _____

Sales Tax
(Los Angeles County residents add 8 1/4 %. Other California residents add 7 1/4 %) _____

Shipping & handling $ 3.00 _____

TOTAL _____

Ship to:

_____
(Name)

_____
(Company)

_____
(Street Address)

_____
(City/SAtate/Zip)

Send check or money order payable to **Fast Forward Production** to **P.O. Box 3226, Santa Monica, CA 90408.**

Orders are shipped via UPS (we cannot ship to P.O. boxes). Prices are subject to change without notice. All sales are final. Allow 2-4 weeks for delivery.